IMISCOE Research Series

Now accepted for Scopus! Content available on the Scopus site in spring 2021.

This series is the official book series of IMISCOE, the largest network of excellence on migration and diversity in the world. It comprises publications which present empirical and theoretical research on different aspects of international migration. The authors are all specialists, and the publications a rich source of information for researchers and others involved in international migration studies. The series is published under the editorial supervision of the IMISCOE Editorial Committee which includes leading scholars from all over Europe. The series, which contains more than eighty titles already, is internationally peer reviewed which ensures that the book published in this series continue to present excellent academic standards and scholarly quality. Most of the books are available open access.

More information about this series at http://www.springer.com/series/13502

Carmelo Danisi • Moira Dustin • Nuno Ferreira
Nina Held

Queering Asylum in Europe

Legal and Social Experiences of Seeking International Protection on grounds of Sexual Orientation and Gender Identity

Carmelo Danisi
School of Law, Politics and Sociology
University of Sussex
Brighton, UK

Department of Political and Social Sciences
University of Bologna
Bologna, Italy

Nuno Ferreira
School of Law, Politics and Sociology
University of Sussex
Brighton, UK

Moira Dustin
School of Law, Politics and Sociology
University of Sussex
Brighton, UK

Nina Held
School of Law, Politics and Sociology
University of Sussex
Brighton, UK

ISSN 2364-4087   ISSN 2364-4095   (electronic)
IMISCOE Research Series
ISBN 978-3-030-69443-2   ISBN 978-3-030-69441-8   (eBook)
https://doi.org/10.1007/978-3-030-69441-8

© The Editor(s) (if applicable) and The Author(s) 2021. This book is an open access publication.
Open Access This book is licensed under the terms of the Creative Commons Attribution 4.0 International License (http://creativecommons.org/licenses/by/4.0/), which permits use, sharing, adaptation, distribution and reproduction in any medium or format, as long as you give appropriate credit to the original author(s) and the source, provide a link to the Creative Commons license and indicate if changes were made.
The images or other third party material in this book are included in the book's Creative Commons license, unless indicated otherwise in a credit line to the material. If material is not included in the book's Creative Commons license and your intended use is not permitted by statutory regulation or exceeds the permitted use, you will need to obtain permission directly from the copyright holder.
The use of general descriptive names, registered names, trademarks, service marks, etc. in this publication does not imply, even in the absence of a specific statement, that such names are exempt from the relevant protective laws and regulations and therefore free for general use.
The publisher, the authors, and the editors are safe to assume that the advice and information in this book are believed to be true and accurate at the date of publication. Neither the publisher nor the authors or the editors give a warranty, expressed or implied, with respect to the material contained herein or for any errors or omissions that may have been made. The publisher remains neutral with regard to jurisdictional claims in published maps and institutional affiliations.

This Springer imprint is published by the registered company Springer Nature Switzerland AG
The registered company address is: Gewerbestrasse 11, 6330 Cham, Switzerland

Carmelo dedicates these volumes to Marta, Maria and Mario.
Moira dedicates these volumes to Ben.
Nuno dedicates these volumes to Giuseppe, Codie and Kayden.
Nina dedicates these volumes to all the wonderful human and non-human beings in her life.
We dedicate these volumes to all those who participated in our fieldwork, by offering their time and sharing their experiences with us, and all SOGI asylum claimants and refugees in the world – may your strength never falter.

Preface for Volume 2

This is Vol. 2 of *Queering Asylum in Europe*, which constitutes the main output of the project 'Sexual Orientation and Gender Identity Claims of Asylum: A European Human Rights Challenge – SOGICA' (www.sogica.org). This project has been funded by the European Research Council (ERC) under the European Union's Horizon 2020 research and innovation programme (grant agreement No 677693). For an extensive preface to both volumes, please refer to Vol. 1.

These volumes are constituted by 11 chapters. Vol. 1 gathered Chaps. 1, 2, 3, 4, 5 and 6 and Vol. 2 gathers Chaps. 7, 8, 9, 10 and 11. Chapter 1 offered an introduction to both volumes; Chap. 2 discussed the methodology used in the research underlying these volumes; Chap. 3 set out the theoretical underpinnings of our research; Chap. 4 explored the legal and policy framework that applies to SOGI asylum in the case study jurisdictions; Chap. 5 considered the lives of individuals before fleeing persecution, the journey and arrival in Europe; and Chap. 6 analysed SOGI asylum in the context of decision-making procedures.

Volume 2 goes on considering the legal treatment of SOGI asylum claims in the country case studies and then dissects as well the broader social experiences of SOGI asylum claimants and refugees. Chapter 7 considers how the substance of SOGI asylum claims is dealt with, Chap. 8 explores the lived experiences of SOGI asylum claimants in relation to housing and accommodation, and Chap. 9 analyses SOGI claimants' and refugees' access to healthcare services, the labour market and educational provision.

This volume is concluded with Part III, which presents our vision for a better future for SOGI asylum in Europe. Chapter 10 discusses legal and social experiences of harassment, isolation and oppression of SOGI claimants and refugees, focusing on four key themes: identities, discrimination, space and agency. Finally, Chap. 11 offers a range of policy recommendations addressed to decision-makers, policy-makers, NGOs and service providers, for improving the socio-legal framework that applies to SOGI asylum.

As forewarned in Vol. 1, this work discusses issues and contains language that – by their very nature – some readers may find offensive or disturbing. While acknowledging this, we believe that a thorough and serious analysis of our subject-matter could not circumvent such issues or avoid the language in question.

All information is correct to the best of our knowledge as of January 2020.

Brighton, UK
January 2020

Carmelo Danisi
Moira Dustin
Nuno Ferreira
Nina Held

Preface for Volume 1

These volumes are the main output of the project 'Sexual Orientation and Gender Identity Claims of Asylum: A European human rights challenge – SOGICA' (www.sogica.org). This project has been funded by the European Research Council (ERC) under the European Union's Horizon 2020 research and innovation programme (grant agreement No 677693).

Although these volumes are a collective work, each co-author has taken the lead in producing the first draft of a selection of chapters and sections, as follows: Carmelo Danisi led on Chaps. 3 (Sect. 3.2), 5 and 6; Moira Dustin led on Chaps. 3 (Sects. 3.1, 3.3 and 3.5), 9 and 10; Nuno Ferreira led on Chaps. 1, 4, 7 and 11; and Nina Held led on Chaps. 2, 3 (Sect. 3.4) and 8. All material originally in a language other than English – including primary and secondary sources – has been translated into English by the authors (sometimes with the assistance of online tools), unless otherwise indicated.

Further to these volumes, during the project's lifetime we have published a range of other outputs on the theme of sexual orientation and gender identity (SOGI) asylum. Here we provide a comparative analysis of SOGI asylum in the three countries selected (Germany, Italy, UK), while other project publications cover subjects that emerged as important in our fieldwork but that did not fit with the structure of these volumes or which we wanted to discuss in greater detail than would be possible in these volumes taking a broad, pan-European perspective.[1] These volumes should be seen as part of that broader body of work, as an overall contribution to the debate on SOGI asylum in Europe and beyond.

Throughout the life of the SOGICA project, we worked with NGOs, lawyers and policy-makers, amongst others, to facilitate improvements in SOGI asylum, in

---

[1] All other relevant publications can be found at http://www.sogica.org/en/publications/. Many of these have been presented at public events throughout the life of the SOGICA project: http://www.sogica.org/en/events/. One can also find in the project's website tables of case law regarding each one of the case studies adopted in this project, which besides the country case studies also include the European Union (EU) and Council of Europe (CoE) (http://www.sogica.org/en/case-studies/).

particular by developing a database of resources,[2] as well as creating a network of individuals working or with an interest in this field. We hope these resources will survive the formal life of our project. Many events took place after this project was conceived, such as the Brexit referendum and subsequent negotiations, and the further rise of right-wing populist movements in several European countries and beyond. Such developments have important implications for the quality and consistency of asylum standards across Europe, which we hope to continue to analyse in future publications.

Within the life of the SOGICA project, we have benefitted from the generous input of a range of people who deserve recognition and our utmost gratitude. We would like to thank in particular the members of our Advisory Board, namely Giorgio dell'Amico (Italy), Rute Caldeira (Germany), Prossy Kakooza (UK), Maggie Merhebi (Germany), Vitit Muntarbhorn (Thailand), Barry O'Leary (UK) and Anbid Zaman (Germany), for their valuable support.[3] We would also like to thank all those who became Project Friends throughout the life of the project, including individual asylum claimants and refugees, researchers involved in asylum, human rights, socio-legal studies and SOGI, as well as lawyers, NGO representatives and service providers.[4] Thanks are also due to the Department of Political and Social Sciences, University of Bologna, and Marco Balboni for co-hosting a SOGICA conference in Forlì (Italy), and to the Cornelia Goethe Centre at the Frankfurt Goethe University and Uta Ruppert for co-hosting a SOGICA conference in Frankfurt (Germany). Finally, our sincere thanks to all organisations and individuals that in one way or the other supported our fieldwork, especially by facilitating the use of certain spaces and helping us to recruit participants.

We are also very thankful for the time and dedication offered by all those who undertook placements with SOGICA, namely Ibrahim Abdella (co-founder of the online initiative 'Solidarity with Egypt LGBTQ+'), Valentina Canepa (University of Sussex), Silvia Ciacchi (University of Trento), Elif Dama (University of Istanbul), Federico Di Persio (University of Bologna), Rose Gordon-Orr (Goldsmiths, University of London), Melody Greaves (Wilfrid Laurier), Oscar Kennedy (Dorothy Stringer School), Marita Haakonsen (University of Sussex), Lisa Harrington (University of Sussex), Ssu-Chi Ho (Goldsmiths, University of London), Alessandro Pigoni (University of Sussex / University of Bologna), Marie Pritchard (University of Sussex), Isabel Soloaga (University of Sussex), and Alba Trabandt (University of Sussex / Freie Universität Berlin), as well as others who preferred to remain anonymous. Thanks are also due to: our supportive research assistants Rosa Jones, Vítor Lopes Andrade, Natalie Pearson and Anbid Zaman; Giuseppe Mascia, who created our project logo and did other design work; and Silan Anil, Ammar Cheema, Shahrzad Fouladvand, Roberto Gangemi, Ali Kassem and Khalid Khan for the

---

[2] The database contains a range of items that relate specifically to SOGI asylum (http://www.sogica.org/en/sogica-database/).

[3] http://www.sogica.org/en/the-project/the-advisory-board/.

[4] http://www.sogica.org/en/the-project/project-friends/.

support with translations into languages besides English, German and Italian. We would also like to thank all colleagues at the University of Sussex for their support for this project, in particular Eleanor Griggs, Rachael Phelps and Charlotte Shamoon, for their help in producing SOGICA resources as well as assistance in organising our final conference, Liz McDonnell, for her support on ethical guidance, and Jo Bridgeman, Bal Sokhi-Bulley and Samantha Velluti, for their feedback on earlier drafts of this work. Many thanks, equally, are owed to colleagues and reviewers at IMISCOE and Springer for their feedback and support throughout this journey. Finally, our deepest gratitude goes to all SOGICA participants – without you, this project would not have been possible. We hope that we have reflected your experiences and views adequately.

A couple of last notes: these volumes discuss issues and contain language that – by their very nature – some readers may find offensive or disturbing. While acknowledging this, we believe that a thorough and serious analysis of our subject-matter could not circumvent such issues or avoid the language in question.

All information is correct to the best of our knowledge as of January 2020.

Brighton, UK
January 2020

Carmelo Danisi
Moira Dustin
Nuno Ferreira
Nina Held

Foreword: On the Importance of Intersectionality Within Policy and Research

As the United Nations Independent Expert on sexual orientation and gender identity, I hold the protection of the rights of LGBT asylum seekers, migrants, and refugees at the core of my mandate's work. It's hard to imagine a population of persons who reunite in their body a greater simultaneous intersection of both marginalized identities and far-too-often challenged rights. The plight of LGBT asylum seekers is then further compounded by the fact that their successful (or unsuccessful) navigation of a complex, foreign, and often unfriendly bureaucratic asylum process will impact the trajectory of the rest of their life. We owe this community our deepest admiration, support, and most importantly, our strongest advocacy.

For LGBT asylum seekers, diversities of gender identity, race, ethnicity, socio-economic status, religion, disability, health, language, documentation status, and age *all* intersect and interplay with a number of rights which, unfortunately, are far too often ill-considered or outright rejected by state authorities.

From the right to have one's gender identity properly noted on state documents to the right to safe and inclusive temporary housing; from a fair and respectful interview process to the basic principle of non-refoulement, asylum agencies owe LGBT asylum seekers no "special" or "new" rights, but rather to simply extend the same basic rights afforded to them under the letter of the law with due consideration to LGBT persons unique and individual context.

As the current COVID-19 pandemic has shown, when state authorities fail to consider the underlying structural issues and barriers affecting marginalized groups like the LGBT community – even when enacting seemingly "neutral" policies – there can be dire unintended consequences. That is why, within those contexts, it is more important than ever that academe and civil society work to exhaustingly highlight and investigate all possible intersections of rights with identities, as well as always use data that is grounded directly in input from stakeholders who will be impacted by any proposed policy.

This fact makes applying the principle of intersectionality to all stages of the policy formulation process, especially during the early research and data collection stage, all the more important. Intersectionality is absolutely essential to creating asylum and migration policies that are not just inclusive, but ultimately also effective in the long run for all stakeholders involved. The colorful yet complex intersection of identities with and within the LGBT community requires civil society, academia, and state authorities to not only identify how to protect the most basic of their rights under the law, but to also take into consideration the numerous other identities that members of the LGBT community may also simultaneously hold and navigate life through with which may require additional forward-thinking in order to safeguard everyone's interests.

The sad reality is that we still live in a world where 69 countries criminalize the expression of LGBT persons' lives, love, and identities. In countless more jurisdictions, prevailing socio-cultural attitudes towards LGBT persons make their lives (whether they live openly or not) a de-facto internal prison sentence. Until the scourge of both criminalization and pervasive discrimination is ended around the world, LGBT persons must always be guaranteed the right to a safe and fair asylum process.

The work that all at SOGICA have done to study these issues from an intersectional and wide a perspective as possible is not only commendable, but also crucial to fixing what many believe is a broken asylum system in Europe. The research done so far in support of vulnerable LGBT persons around the world is of fundamental importance, and I exhort all stakeholders to continue it while bringing in as many new voices and perspectives into this discussion as possible.

We are all stronger when we fight this fight together.

Victor Madrigal-Borloz
United Nations Independent Expert on the prevention of violence and discrimination on the basis of sexual orientation and gender identity

Contents

VOLUME 2

Part II   The Legal and Social Experiences of SOGI Asylum Claimants and Refugees

7   The Asylum Claim Determination 259
    7.1   Introduction 259
    7.2   Using the Grounds for the Recognition of Refugee Status 260
        7.2.1   Choosing from the Five Refugee Convention
               Grounds 261
        7.2.2   SOGI and 'Particular Social Group' 263
    7.3   Reaching the Persecution Threshold 269
        7.3.1   The Criminalisation of Same-Sex Acts 273
        7.3.2   The 'Discretion Argument' 277
        7.3.3   The 'Internal Relocation Alternative' 283
    7.4   Proving Claims Based on SOGI 285
        7.4.1   Standard and Burden of Proof 285
        7.4.2   Types of Evidence 289
    7.5   The Assessment of Credibility 300
        7.5.1   Stereotyping 'Gayness' 303
        7.5.2   Be 'Out and Proud' – The Western Way 307
        7.5.3   A Persisting Culture of Disbelief 312
    7.6   Outcomes of the RSD Process and What Lays beyond
        SOGI – Through an Intersectional Lens 317
    7.7   Concluding Remarks: Assessing the Assessor 321
    References 324

8   Housing and Accommodation 331
    8.1   Introduction 331
    8.2   Asylum Accommodation Policies 333
    8.3   Standard of Asylum Accommodation 339

xvi Contents

8.4 Living in Shared Accommodation, Being 'in the Closet'
    and Experiencing Discrimination and Hate Crime 344
    8.4.1 Accommodation of Couples 351
    8.4.2 Intersectional Dimensions of Accommodation 352
    8.4.3 Accommodation of Non-binary, Trans and Intersex
          Claimants 356
8.5 Rural/Urban 359
8.6 Homelessness and Destitution 366
8.7 Housing After the Asylum Claim Process 368
8.8 SOGI Accommodation 372
8.9 Detention 377
8.10 Concluding Remarks 382
References. 384

9 **Health, Work and Education** 389
9.1 Introduction 389
9.2 Physical and Mental Health 391
    9.2.1 Access to Healthcare 391
    9.2.2 Access to Specialist Treatment 392
    9.2.3 Experiences of Sexual Violence and Torture 395
    9.2.4 Mental Health. 398
9.3 Work. 403
    9.3.1 The Right to Work 403
    9.3.2 Voluntary Work and Community Involvement 405
    9.3.3 Sexual Exploitation and Sex Work. 406
    9.3.4 Discrimination and Exploitation in Employment 408
9.4 Education and Training 411
9.5 Concluding Remarks 414
References. 414

Part III Forging a New Future for SOGI Asylum in Europe

10 **SOGI Asylum in Europe: Emerging Patterns** 421
10.1 Introduction 421
10.2 Identities. 422
     10.2.1 Homogenisation 422
     10.2.2 Stereotypes 423
     10.2.3 Language and Culture 426
10.3 Discrimination 429
     10.3.1 Racism. 429
     10.3.2 Homophobia, Transphobia and Cross-Cutting
            Discrimination. 431
10.4 Place. 433
     10.4.1 Receiving Country and Region 433
     10.4.2 Isolation. 436

10.5	Agency	438
	10.5.1 Losing Agency	438
	10.5.2 Taking Control	441
10.6	Concluding Remarks	443
References		444

11 Believing in Something Better: Our Recommendations 445
11.1	So What?	445
11.2	The Journey to Europe and Reception	447
11.3	The Asylum Application Process	449
	11.3.1 Institutional and Policy Framework	450
	11.3.2 Procedural Rules	454
	11.3.3 The Asylum Claim Determination	459
11.4	Detention and Accommodation	464
11.5	Life 'Beyond Papers'	466
11.6	Building Capacity and Enhancing Competences	467
11.7	Something to Look Forward To	472
References		474

Index 479

VOLUME 1

Part I Contextualising SOGI Asylum Research

1 Why Sexual Orientation and Gender Identity Asylum? 3
1.1	Seeking Asylum: Why Focus on Sexual Orientation and Gender Identity	3
1.2	The International and European Legal, Policy and Social Context	8
1.3	Framing Our Research	12
1.4	The Structure of These Volumes	15
References		17

2 Researching SOGI Asylum 23
2.1	Introduction	23
2.2	Methods	25
	2.2.1 Semi-structured Interviews	28
	2.2.2 Focus Groups	33
	2.2.3 Observations in Courts	34
	2.2.4 Online Surveys	35
	2.2.5 Documentary Analysis	39
	2.2.6 Freedom of Information Requests	40
2.3	Ethical Implications: Doing Research with SOGI Refugees	42
References		47

**3 A Theoretical Framework: A Human Rights Reading
of SOGI Asylum Based on Feminist and Queer Studies** 51
3.1 Introduction 51
3.2 A Human Rights Approach to SOGI Asylum: What Role
for Rights? 52
    3.2.1 Human Rights and SOGI: Reconsidering Personhood
Through a SOGI and Anti-stereotyping Lens 54
    3.2.2 Human Rights and the Refugee Convention:
Establishing the Right Relationship. 58
    3.2.3 Human Rights as an Independent Basis
for Protection in SOGI Asylum: From Procedural
Guarantees to Substantive Fairness 61
3.3 A Feminist Approach to SOGI Asylum 64
    3.3.1 Feminism and Multiculturalism. 67
    3.3.2 Intersectional Feminist Writing 68
    3.3.3 Anti-essentialism 70
    3.3.4 Recognising Agency 73
3.4 Queer Theoretical Approaches to SOGI Asylum. 75
    3.4.1 Queer Theoretical Understanding of Sex, Gender,
Sexuality and Identity 76
    3.4.2 Intersectional Queer Approaches 79
    3.4.3 Queer Geographies. 81
3.5 Concluding Remarks 84
References. 85

**Part II The Legal and Social Experiences of SOGI Asylum
Claimants and Refugees**

4 The Policy and Guidance 97
4.1 Introduction 97
4.2 Social and Legal Dimensions of SOGI 101
4.3 The National Asylum Systems. 104
    4.3.1 The Key Legal Instruments and Actors 104
    4.3.2 Degree of Compliance with Supranational
and International Obligations. 109
4.4 SOGI Dimensions of Domestic Asylum Systems 111
    4.4.1 Milestones in Policy and Guidance 112
    4.4.2 Vulnerability and SOGI Asylum 115
4.5 Refugee Status Determination (RSD) Outcomes
and Life After the Decision on a SOGI Asylum Claim 119
4.6 From Policy to Law, from Law to Practice 127
References. 129

Contents   xix

5 Life in the Countries of Origin, Departure and Travel Towards Europe 139
- 5.1 Introduction 139
- 5.2 Life in the Countries of Origin 141
  - 5.2.1 'Ordinary' Lives 142
  - 5.2.2 Treatment of SOGI Minorities in Countries of Origin 145
- 5.3 'It Suddenly Happened' 150
  - 5.3.1 Forced Departures 152
  - 5.3.2 Journey Experiences 155
- 5.4 The Arrival in Europe 160
  - 5.4.1 Information on SOGI Asylum 162
  - 5.4.2 Initial Screenings 166
  - 5.4.3 Initial Reception and Detention 170
- 5.5 Concluding Remarks 174
- References 176

6 The Decision-Making Procedure 179
- 6.1 Introduction 179
- 6.2 The Preparation of Asylum Claims and Legal Aid 185
  - 6.2.1 The Preparation for the Main Interview and Judicial Hearing(s) 186
  - 6.2.2 Access to, and Quality of, Legal Representation 192
  - 6.2.3 Training of Volunteers, Lawyers and Staff Working with SOGI Claimants 201
- 6.3 The Main Interview: Actors and Procedures in SOGI Asylum 204
  - 6.3.1 The Interview Setting 205
  - 6.3.2 The Selection and the Training of Caseworkers 209
  - 6.3.3 The Conduct of Interviews 213
- 6.4 The Judicial Procedure 222
  - 6.4.1 The Appeal Setting 222
  - 6.4.2 The Conduct of Hearings and the Adoption of Decisions 227
- 6.5 Country of Origin Information 234
- 6.6 Interpretation 240
- 6.7 Other Procedures 247
- 6.8 Concluding Remarks 252
- References 253

List of Acronyms and Abbreviations

AASC	Asylum Accommodation and Support Services Contracts
AIDA	Asylum Information Database
APPG	All Party Parliamentary Group
ARE	Appeal Rights Exhausted
ASGI	Associazione Studi Giuridici sull'Immigrazione
BAMF	Bundesamt für Migration und Flüchtlinge (Federal Office for Migration and Refugees)
BMI	Bundesministerium des Innern, für Bau und Heimat (Federal Ministry of the Interior, Building and Community)
CEAS	Common European Asylum System
CFR	Charter of Fundamental Rights
CJEU	Court of Justice of the European Union
CoE	Council of Europe
COI	Country of Origin Information
COMPASS	Commercial and Operational Managers Procuring Asylum Support Services
CPIN	Country Policy Information Notes
EASO	European Asylum Support Office
ECHR	European Convention on Human Rights
ECRE	European Council on Refugees and Exiles
ECtHR	European Court of Human Rights
EU	European Union
FGM	Female Genital Mutilation
FOI	Freedom of Information
FRA	European Union Agency for Fundamental Rights
GG	Grundgesetz (German Basic Law)
GIC	Gender Identity Clinic
GOT	Giudici onorari (Honorary Judges)
GP	General Practitioner
HRC	Human Rights Council
HRW	Human Rights Watch

ICIBI	Independent Chief Inspector of Borders and Immigration
ICCPR	International Covenant on Civil and Political Rights
ICESCR	International Covenant on Economic, Social and Cultural Rights
IHRL	International Human Rights Law
ILGA	International Lesbian, Gay, Bisexual, Trans and Intersex Association
IO	Immigrazioni e Omosessualità
IOM	International Organization for Migration
IRL	International Refugee Law
LeTRa	Lesbentelefon e.V.
LGBTIQ+	Lesbian, Gay, Bisexual, Trans, Intersex, Queer and Others
LISG	Lesbian Immigration Support Group
MIT	Movimento Identità Transessuale
MSM	Men Who Have Sex with Men
MSF	Médecins sans Frontières
NGO	Nongovernmental Organisation
ORAM	Organization for Refuge, Asylum and Migration
PSG	Particular Social Group
PTSD	Post-Traumatic Stress Disorder
RSD	Refugee Status Determination
SOGI	Sexual Orientation and/or Gender Identity
TGEU	Transgender Europe
UDHR	Universal Declaration of Human Rights
UK	United Kingdom
UKBA	United Kingdom Border Agency
UKLGIG	UK Lesbian and Gay Immigration Group
UKVI	United Kingdom Visas and Immigration
UN	United Nations
UNHCR	UN High Commissioner for Refugees
USA	United States of America
VCLT	Vienna Convention on the Law of the Treaties

Chapter 7
The Asylum Claim Determination

> *... they didn't believe me. I don't know why. What can I do? Get a man and... make sex close to them?*
>
> (Mahmoud, Germany)

> *... if we start thinking about these improvements [to the system], then we lose sight of the viability of the system as a whole, which is required to examine a number of cases a day, otherwise the first reception system becomes unsustainable.*
>
> (Daniele, decision-maker, Italy)

> *... each judge decides depending on how he wake[s] up from his bed. In short it's a lottery. It also depends on where your claim is heard.*
>
> (C15, UK)

7.1 Introduction

Public international law and, more specifically, international human rights law protect the right to access an asylum determination procedure and the principle of non-refoulement, as established in Chap. 3. Some would argue that asylum should not be seen by states as their own prerogative, but rather as a fundamental human right (Díaz Lafuente, 2014, pp. 206–207). How the right to access an asylum determination procedure and the principle of non-refoulement are implemented varies from country to country, including within the EU, as discussed in Chap. 4. Chapter 6 dissected the different procedures adopted to adjudicate SOGI claims of international protection in Germany, Italy and the UK. In this chapter, we focus on the decision itself by analysing the Refugee Status Determination (RSD) process in the three countries studied. In the process, we highlight similarities and differences, merits and shortcomings, and often inconsistencies with supranational and international standards.

© The Author(s) 2021
C. Danisi et al., *Queering Asylum in Europe*, IMISCOE Research Series,
https://doi.org/10.1007/978-3-030-69441-8_7

Despite the growing body of literature on SOGI asylum adjudication,[1] some areas remain under-explored and require further analysis, as we begin to do here. We start by discussing the Refugee Convention grounds used in SOGI asylum claims (Sect. 7.2.1) and the prevalent application of the notion of 'Particular Social Group' (PSG) to SOGI claims (Sect. 7.2.2). In this section, we discuss the often ignored option of SOGI minorities using Refugee Convention grounds other than PSG and highlight the difficulties that some SOGI claimants have in 'fitting' into a PSG. We then explore how the notion of 'persecution' is interpreted in SOGI claims (Sect. 7.3), in particular how adjudicators deal with the criminalisation of same-sex conduct (Sect. 7.3.1) and make use of legal tools such as the 'discretion argument' (Sect. 7.3.2) and the 'internal relocation alternative' (Sect. 7.3.3). Section 7.3 thus presents a much-needed exploration of the inconsistent ways in which the criminalisation of same-sex acts and internal relocation alternative are used in SOGI asylum adjudication, highlighting that the 'discretion argument' is still very much alive, despite conventional wisdom on this matter telling us otherwise.

Next we analyse the standard and burden of proof adopted in SOGI asylum claims (Sect. 7.4.1) and the types of evidence required and accepted (Sect. 7.4.2). Here we conclude not only that the standard of proof often applied to SOGI claims is in violation of the principle of the benefit of the doubt, but also that the way the burden of proof is applied is in violation of UNHCR guidance. This is followed by an analysis of how credibility is assessed in the context of SOGI asylum claims (Sect. 7.5), where we identify the persistence of a culture of disbelief in SOGI asylum systems. We find significant scope to improve the way SOGI claimants' credibility is assessed. The characteristics of possible and usual outcomes of the RSD process in relation to SOGI claims are then considered (Sect. 7.6), focusing on the need for an intersectional approach to ensure appropriate decision-making. A summary assessment of the substantive adjudication of SOGI asylum claims is offered at the end (Sect. 7.7), and we link our discussion to broader debates about epistemic justice in the asylum system. In this chapter, we show that many serious problems still affect SOGI asylum adjudication in Europe, often because decision-making fails to apply the theoretical and analytical frameworks adopted in these volumes.

7.2 Using the Grounds for the Recognition of Refugee Status

The international refugee regime, including the Refugee Convention, was a response to the persecution of members of religious/ethnic minorities by fascist regimes in mid-twentieth century Europe (Juss, 2018). As Oscar, a judge in Germany, pointed

---

[1] This body of literature has become so rich, that it is impossible to offer an overview of it or do it justice in this chapter. The extent and variety of this literature is patent from the 1000+ items collected in the SOGI asylum database available in http://www.sogica.org/en/sogica-database/. In this chapter, we will make reference to only a short selection of that literature.

7.2 Using the Grounds for the Recognition of Refugee Status

out, the archetypal refugee is a member of the Jewish population in Nazi Germany, which narrows down the mind-set of decision-makers until today:

> our asylum law has always almost... it brings out the image of the Jews who have tried to reach Switzerland during the Nazi regime – that's always for me the absolutely, the classic asylum seeker: persecuted because of their "race" and they knock on Switzerland['s doors] and say: "We want to have asylum here".

SOGI minorities were thus not explicitly considered during the preparation of the Refugee Convention, despite the persecution of gay and lesbian people in Nazi Germany (Grau & Shoppmann, 2013), and it took several decades to introduce and establish the idea that they could also secure protection using the Refugee Convention, namely by using the PSG ground (Chap. 1). Here we consider the range of Convention grounds available and what use SOGI claimants make of them.

7.2.1 Choosing from the Five Refugee Convention Grounds

The Refugee Convention makes express reference to five grounds on the basis of which the 'well-founded fear of persecution' can be invoked: 'race', religion, nationality, membership of a PSG and political opinion. Although there are still some – very rare – instances of decision-makers finding it difficult to connect SOGI to one of the Refugee Convention grounds,[2] it is now legal dogma that SOGI minorities fall within a PSG. Indeed, although SOGI claimants can potentially make an asylum claim on the basis of any of these grounds, it is the case that claims are almost invariably based on the PSG ground. Other reasons for persecution are mostly absent in this field, despite their potential applicability (Balboni, 2012, Chap. II; Braimah 2015b). As Cristina, a UNHCR officer, said:

> Very often there is a tendency to take for granted that SOGISC [sexual orientation, gender identity and sexual characteristics] cases fall within the particular social group, while often an evaluation of political reasons or religious reasons is not made, based on the context, so I would say that there is an insufficiently deep analytical-juridical elaboration.

Our fieldwork has confirmed the historic and current prevalence of the use of the PSG ground in SOGI asylum claims in the countries under comparison, even if we have come across a few exceptions to this rule.

One such case, referred to us by Emilia, a judge in Germany, was that of an LGBTIQ+ and Kurdish activist, who was thus potentially persecuted on grounds of membership of a PSG but also political opinion. Still in Germany, Marlen, a legal advisor, told us of an asylum claim on grounds of religion, lodged by a trans claimant who did not mention gender identity at the first claim stage but introduced that element at the appeal stage. Mariya, an NGO worker in Germany, also spoke about

---

[2] Tribunal of Palermo, decision of 31 May 2017, where the judge affirmed that the applicant – a gay man from Nigeria – could not fear persecution in relation to one of the five grounds of the Refugee Convention.

a SOGI claimant who had an ethnic minority background in the country of origin, thus exposing him to further persecution on this basis. Although the asylum claim was based on both PSG membership and 'race', the asylum authorities failed to grasp the way in which the intersection of these two grounds contributed to a stronger risk of persecution, and denied international protection. Diana spoke of her participation in theatre plays, involvement with LGBTIQ+ groups and publications in Iran, which attracted the attention of the police. This combination of activities offered her the potential to claim international protection both on grounds of membership of a PSG and political opinion. Similarly, Marhoon and Halim described their activities as LGBTIQ+ activists and human rights defenders (in the case of Marhoon, also linked to his atheist belief), and Mahmoud mentioned his political activities to BAMF, but all these three claims were eventually adjudicated exclusively on the basis of SOGI.

In Italy, we also found cases involving Refugee Convention grounds beyond PSG. One case involving a Nigerian claimant, reported to us by Valentina, a social worker, combined both sexual orientation (bisexuality) and gender identity (male-to-female), thus remaining within the PSG ground of the Refugee Convention but adding another layer of complexity to the claim. A more obvious – and successful – case of multiple grounds was described to us by Kamel, whose asylum claim was based on gender identity (PSG), activity as journalist, activist and volunteer as anaesthetist in areas of military conflict (political opinion), and atheist belief (religion). Another case, referred to us by Celeste, a social worker, was that of a claimant who was persecuted on the basis of forced marriage, SOGI and religion, thus potentially making use of two grounds of the Refugee Convention. This claim was, however, received with suspicion by the authorities, something which we will return to below (Sect. 7.5).

In the UK, as well, there were isolated instances of asylum claims combining different Refugee Convention grounds, such as the case of Miria (combining political activity and sexual orientation), Ibrahim A. (combining his sexual orientation and LGBTIQ+ activism), Ximena (combining human rights activism and gender identity), as well as Amber (combining SOGI identity, political activity and – perceived – religious identity):

> Being in a "particular social group" [LGBT], I was also involved in some political activism in Malaysia. I was one of the early members of an NGO called Pelangi. Pelangi means rainbow in English, and we are an organisation campaigning for equality and human rights. (…) we did organise events for the community, but specifically in June where we hosted a Pelangi day event consisted of a panel discussion, an iftar meal inspired by "The Big Gay Iftar" initiative by current Mayor of London, and a film screening. Little did we know, the event went viral and reached the public eye, and they deemed it as disrespectful especially towards the "Big Gay Iftar" slot, as the public is too sensitive about associating the word gay with iftar to even going as far as saying we were deliberately disrespecting the holy month of Ramadan. So, things got heated pretty quickly and many of us in Pelangi were feeling unsafe, and some of us left the group for their own safety.

Even when another Refugee Convention ground seemed more relevant than PSG, that was often sidelined:

my claim was based on my LGBT activism and on my sexual orientation, but basically they [Home Office]… she [caseworker] only focused, she asked me of course about my LGBT activism, but she only focused on my sexual orientation. (…) Not at all [interested in my political activism]. (…) What is worrying me more is my activism and the work I do. (…) Like she had it on paper and she felt like she had to mention it because I wrote it, but she didn't focus on it. Like for me the interview was mostly focused on my sexual orientation and the idea that I will not feel free to practice it if I went back to Egypt, yes (Ibrahim A.).

Such exclusive focus on the claimants' SOGI at the expense of other aspects of their lives and grounds to claim international protection reduces SOGI claimants to uni-dimensional beings who are exclusively characterised by their SOGI, but not by their political activism, religious beliefs, ethnicity, etc. Furthermore, although some decision-makers told us they fully considered all grounds for international protection available within each single claim (Maurizio, judge, Italy), with the exception of Kamel's case, decision-makers in all the cases mentioned above tended to focus on one ground and make a decision in relation to that ground, rather than considering the overall risk of persecution based on the cumulative and intersecting effect of the grounds in question. The failure to adopt an intersectional approach (Chap. 3) leads to a partial portrayal of claimants' persecutory experiences. In particular, it erases the political nature of many SOGI minorities' claims and their activism (Chap. 5).

PSG thus remains the main asylum ground for members of SOGI minorities. How to conceptualise one's membership of a PSG in terms of one's SOGI is always problematic, as we will now discuss.

7.2.2 SOGI and 'Particular Social Group'

The notion of PSG is not defined in the Refugee Convention, and it has thus been object of extensive case law and literature in different jurisdictions (Arnold, 2012; Berg & Millbank, 2013; Braimah 2015a, b; Millbank, 2009b; UNHCR, 2002a, b). In the EU context, the key source in this regard is Article 10(1)(d) of the Qualification Directive:

> a group shall be considered to form a particular social group where *in particular*:
>
> - members of that group share an innate characteristic, or a common background that cannot be changed, or share a characteristic or belief that is so fundamental to identity or conscience that a person should not be forced to renounce it, *and*
> - that group has a distinct identity in the relevant country, because it is perceived as being different by the surrounding society (our emphasis).

While SOGI are now recognised as characteristics that may lead to a finding of membership of a PSG, as we have explored elsewhere, the way these criteria have been interpreted by the CJEU is contentious (Ferreira, 2018, p. 30). The relevant criteria include two tests: the 'fundamental characteristic test' and the 'social recognition test'. UNHCR Guidelines recommend an alternative application of these tests, so it should be enough to satisfy one of them (UNHCR, 2002a, b, para. 2), but the CJEU, in *X, Y and Z*,[3] opted for a cumulative application, thus requiring that both tests be satisfied for an individual to be recognised as a member of a PSG. This reading of the norm is based on the use of the word 'and' between the tests, ignoring that the tests are introduced with the words 'in particular', implying that other defining characteristics of a PSG may exist and these criteria should not be applied in a restrictive way. Furthermore, the tangible impact for individual claimants of a cumulative two-limb test is that:

> some refugee-status decision-makers have found that, while certain applicants' claims satisfied the protected characteristics limb, they did not meet the social perception limb, either because the group of LGBTI persons are not visible within a given society or because the individuals themselves are not "out" enough to be perceived as part of that group by society (ICJ 2016, p. 201; references omitted).

In *X, Y and Z*, the CJEU more positively asserted that the existence of criminal laws targeting SOGI minorities supports the finding that those persons form or belong to a PSG. Against this background, we now look into how the three countries under comparison generally apply the notion of PSG to SOGI asylum claims.

In Germany, the 1988 seminal decision of the Federal Administrative Court applying the notion of 'political persecution' to SOGI asylum (Chap. 4) led to a long line of questionable decisions, effectively leaving some SOGI claimants without international protection.[4] For instance, in 1998 the Administrative Court of Regensburg referred to a medical report arguing that the claimant's sexuality was not 'compulsive' and 'abnormal', and that therefore he could fulfil his sexual urges by masturbating.[5] More positively, there have also been cases where asylum has been granted to SOGI claimants from countries where Sharia law applies and punishes same-sex sexual conduct, as persecution could be feared because of 'otherness', thus falling within the scope of protection of the right to political asylum and human dignity under the German Basic Law.[6] The more restrictive line of case law of the Federal Administrative Court and the administrative courts became outdated when persecution on grounds of sexual orientation came to be recognised under the PSG ground, following the definition of PSG according to the Qualification Directive (§3(1) of the Asylum Act). It now does not (or, at least, should not) matter whether the sexual orientation of the claimant is so 'inescapable' as to preclude abstinence from same-sex sexual activity.[7]

When establishing membership of a PSG, the BAMF and courts in Germany have followed the cumulative approach argued for by the CJEU (BAMF, 2017, p. 282). This means that individuals need to demonstrate *both* that they share an innate or fundamental characteristic or common background, *and* also that they are

---

[3] Joined Cases C-199/12, C-200/12 and C-201/12, *X, Y and Z v Minister voor Immigratie, Integratie en Asiel*, 7 November 2013, ECLI:EU:C:2013:720.

[4] BVerwGE, 15 March 1988, C 278.86.

[5] 4 August 1998, RN 11 K 97.31221, cited in Markard & Adamietz (2011, p. 296).

[6] Administrative Court of Gießen, 26 August 1999, 10 E 30832/98.

[7] See, for instance, Administrative Court of Frankfurt/Oder, 19 November 2015, 4 K 1099/12.A.

perceived as having a distinct identity. In internal instructions, the BAMF clarifies that at least one common group-identifying characteristic has to be identified: a shared innate characteristic, a common immutable background, or common characteristics or beliefs that are so important to the identity or conscience of the person concerned that renunciation would be unreasonable (so-called 'indispensable features'). The BAMF lists sexual orientation amongst the latter characteristics (BAMF, 2017), and, according to some of our participants, ascertaining membership of a PSG remains a key (if not *the* key) element in SOGI asylum claims in Germany (for instance, Elias, lawyer).

In order to demonstrate membership of a PSG, claimants have often needed to present a fixed and linear narrative of gay identity, according to a Western epistemic framework. In tension with the queer theoretical framework adopted in Chap. 3, decisions are often based on an understanding of sexual orientation as definitively fixed at a particular age in an individual's life;[8] we instead adopt the understanding that sexual orientation and gender identity are fluid, rather than static or siloed, categories. For example, participants in Germany pointed out that if claimants report having become conscious of their non-heterosexuality only when they reached their twenties, they would be unlikely to meet the PSG criteria because their sexuality would not be found to be 'irreversible and inescapable' (Sofia and Emma, NGO workers), in terminology reminiscent of the 1988 decision discussed above that should no longer be valid.

Furthermore, and in parallel with BAMF's culture of disbelief (Sect. 7.5), we observed a trend to deny PSG membership because of elements relating to social visibility, rather than the claimant's characteristics. For example, in letters of refusal to some of our participants, the BAMF stated that it 'is doubtful whether the social group of LGBT members for the country of origin Russian Federation can be distinguished with sufficient certainty even through the local prohibitions and/or through the nationwide propaganda ban on non-traditional sexual relations' (decisions regarding Veronica and Julia). This is inconsistent with UNHCR standards (UNHCR, 2012, para. 48) and contradicts the CJEU assertion that the existence of legislation targeting SOGI minorities supports the finding that those persons form or belong to a PSG.

Similarly, in the UK, a cumulative approach to the PSG tests is followed. Before 1999, SOGI claimants had difficulty meeting the criteria for refugee status following a High Court ruling stating that they did not constitute a PSG because their only common characteristic of sexual orientation was normally concealed.[9] SOGI claimants are now generally recognised as members of a PSG as a result of the House of Lords judgment in the case of *Shah and Islam*, where it was found that women in

---

[8] Administrative Court of Ansbach, 21 August 2008, AN 18 K 08.30201; Administrative Court of Trier, 17 January 2013, 2 K 730/12.

[9] *R v SSHD ex parte Binbasi* [1989] Imm AR 595 (QBD).

Pakistan constituted a PSG.[10] The same approach was applied to SOGI,[11] which falls in line with the EU Qualification Directive. Having to satisfy both the 'fundamental characteristic' and the 'social visibility' tests has led a practitioner to encourage clients presenting to a judge 'to bring friends from the gay community and referred to it as a "pink parade"' (Arnold 2012, p. 106).

In contrast, in Italy, decision-makers adopt an alternative approach to the 'fundamental characteristic' and the 'social visibility' tests, thus adhering to the UNHCR guidelines.[12] Consequently, for the recognition of a PSG in the Italian system, it is sufficient that its members share a common characteristic fundamental to their personality (such as sexual orientation or gender identity) *or* that they are perceived as such by the rest of society in the country of origin. In other words, when implementing the EU Qualification Directive, Italy decided that these two requirements did not need to be satisfied at the same time to identify a PSG. SOGI are expressly recognised as personal characteristics relevant to the determination of a PSG in light of the specific situation of some countries of origin. Once a claimant's SOGI is found to be credible (Sect. 7.5), establishing PSG membership is generally unproblematic, although the reasoning adopted for the finding is not always specified. Our participants rarely raised this matter, and PSG seems to be more often than not a 'given', with the RSD process tending to focus on the risk of persecution (Sect. 7.3) and credibility assessment (Sect. 7.5). This approach is also followed by territorial commissions (Celeste, social worker) and lower courts when SOGI claimants appeal against negative decisions by territorial commissions. For example, the Court of Appeal of Trieste, in a case involving a gay claimant from the Gambia, decided that it was irrelevant to ascertain whether the claimant was effectively gay or not, as what mattered was how he was perceived by Gambian society and the consequences of that perception.[13]

Across all three countries under comparison, bisexual claimants may find themselves entangled in inadequate understandings of sexual orientation, which have an impact on establishing PSG membership. This may be due to an inherent tension between, on the one hand, refugee law and related decision-making, which is about establishing facts and definitive accounts, and, on the other hand, sexual orientation, which is fluid both over time and at any one moment (Chap. 3). The reference to an 'innate characteristic' in the PSG definition in the Qualification Directive is likely to prove particularly problematic for bisexual claimants if it is prioritised over the other elements in that sentence, in particular, 'a characteristic or belief that is so fundamental to identity or conscience that a person should not be forced to renounce it'. It seems to be often assumed (even if implicitly) that bisexual claimants can choose between heterosexuality and homosexuality. Bisexuality and fluid forms of

---

[10] *Shah and Islam v Secretary of State for the Home Department*, House of Lords, 2 A.C. 629, 1999.

[11] See The Refugee or Person in Need of International Protection (Qualification) Regulations 2006, 6(e), and UKVI, 2011, p. 11.

[12] Article 8 of the Legislative decree no. 251, 19 November 2007.

[13] Judgment no. 541, 25 July 2019.

7.2 Using the Grounds for the Recognition of Refugee Status

sexuality are thus devalued and unrecognised, leading to credibility assessments based on collective heteronormative knowledge and essentialising non-heteronormative ways of life (Sect. 7.5; Hübner, 2016).

Participants in Germany told us that the BAMF tends to be dismissive of bisexual claimants, because they are perceived as needing to 'make up their minds' and able simply to 'opt for being heterosexual' (Gisela, lawyer). We were also told that it is 'harder to work' with claimants with less 'clear' and 'classic' sexual identities, such as claimants who have had opposite-sex relationships in the past and have children (Nina, legal advisor; Sofia and Emma, NGO workers). Court decisions may subsume bisexuality within homosexuality, or fail to recognise bisexuality where it is the most appropriate identifier,[14] thereby contributing to the invisibility and erasure of individuals claiming on this basis (Klesse, 2018; Monro et al., 2017). Ignoring queer theoretical approaches, decision-makers leave bisexual claimants out of the scope of protection of a PSG, as in a decision by the Administrative Court of Saarland, where the judge argued:

> Due to his predisposition, the claimant would be in a position to have a relationship with a woman in Algeria and to live out his sexuality. This assumption is supported by the fact that the claimant has already become the father of a child in Germany. In that respect, the present case differs from the cases decided by the CJEU, which dealt with the homosexual orientation of those affected. However, in case of homosexuality, the person would be, unlike the claimant in the present case, forced to completely deny their sexual orientation or to live in secret in order to escape the danger of punishment in Algeria.[15]

Even though the claimant had been in a two-year relationship with a man at the time this decision was made, the Court decided that the claimant could relocate within Algeria and carry on meeting men 'discreetly' (Sect. 7.3.2).

In Italy, bisexual claims are also problematic, indicated by the absence of such claims in our fieldwork, in other scholarship and in NGO materials. This also emerges from the fact that claimants are sometimes encouraged by legal advisors and support groups to adopt homo-narratives to be more convincing (Chap. 6, Sect. 6.2). Bisexual claimants may also face obstacles to recognition in the UK, where the leading judge in *HJ (Iran)* said that the PSG was 'defined by the immutable characteristic of its members' sexual orientation or sexuality' (para. 11). There is a perception that bisexual claimants are at a disadvantage:

> say, if the Home Office accepts someone is bisexual and if LGBT rights could be non-existent in their country, but the Home Office can always argue, and usually do that, "well, they can still have relationships, you know, they can still function in that society with sort of opposite sex partner (Amelia, NGO worker).

Similar considerations affect trans claimants, if to a lesser or different extent. The fluidity of gender identity has been explored in the context of asylum, where it has been shown that transgender people claiming asylum are not only reabsorbed

---

[14] Administrative Court of Ansbach, 21 August 2008, AN 18 K 08.30201.

[15] Administrative Court of Saarland, 18 February 2015, 5 K 534/13, pp. 11–12. See Dustin & Held (2018) for further discussion of this case.

within the gender binary system (Vogler, 2019), but may also present or be accepted as claiming on the basis of sexual orientation rather than gender identity, serving to disguise the level and nature of transgender persecution (Berg & Millbank, 2013, p. 140). This reflects a lack of understanding of the difference between sexual orientation and gender identity, and harms the chances of success of subsequent trans claims. In Germany, gender fluid claimants are seen as an 'implosion' and 'challenge' for decision-makers who wonder what is the PSG in question (Nina, legal advisor). We were also told that a trans claimant may define herself as 'gay' because she is familiar with the word 'gay', while at the same time she identifies as a woman who feels attracted to men, and is thus a 'trans woman' according to Western LGBTIQ+ terminology (Noah, NGO social worker). Decision-makers need to be receptive to variations in the use of such 'labels' and not impose a simplistic application of templates (Kadir, NGO worker). Similarly, in Italy, we were told that trans claims can constitute a challenge for decision-makers:

> In some countries, people do not call themselves trans, and in that case you cannot force a person to fall into a category that we ourselves have created, we have given to ourselves, which can be good for me, can be good for you, can be good for an Italian or American transgender person, but it may not be good for a trans person whom we perceive as trans, whom we identify as a trans from an African country or a Middle Eastern country (Cristina, UNHCR officer).

Fitting trans claims into a particular PSG is thus likely to require 'cultural translation' skills that many decision-makers lack. This is also true in the UK, where the limited information available about trans asylum claims is a challenge to decision-makers and activists alike – a challenge compounded by the absolute lack of information about intersex claims or the experiences of people claiming asylum with intersex variations (APPG on Global LGBT Rights, 2016, p. 13). To a lesser extent, trans claimants have also been underrepresented in the literature historically. An international study of transgender people's asylum claims between 1994 and 2011 found only three trans asylum decisions in the UK (Berg & Millbank, 2013). Acceptance of gender identity claims has been even slower than acceptance of claims based on sexual orientation – not helped by the UK's failure to opt into the recast Qualification Directive, which explicitly covers transgender people (Arnold, 2012, pp. 106 and 118). Gender identity issues are often omitted in research and reports on sexual minority asylum claims – the Vine Report did not cover gender identity cases (ICIBI, 2014) – or appear as an afterthought. At one time, UKLGIG stated that they received few requests for support from transgender claimants and thought claimants were often unaware that gender identity can be the basis of an asylum claim (UKLGIG, 2013, p. 7).

Significant issues thus remain for all SOGI claimants in relation to determining membership of a PSG. In line with our theoretical and analytical underpinnings (Chap. 3), decision-makers need to be more flexible in relation to SOGI identity variations (Hinger, 2010, p. 402) and aware of different cultural perceptions of certain SOGI identities that may be less familiar in the Western context, but more relevant in the case in question, such as 'men who have sex with men' (Sridharan, 2008). Only like this these identities can be tools for liberation, rather than oppression. As we heard from one of our participants, there may even be a dynamic process of self-identification throughout the asylum claim process – for example, a transition from identifying as a gay man to identifying as a trans woman – and this needs to be accommodated by decision-makers (Louis, NGO volunteer, Germany). The same claimant may present and be perceived in different ways at different times and in different contexts: one claimant who described herself as a lesbian on arrival and would have been persecuted as such in her country of origin, identified as a trans man at the time of his (successful) appeal hearing (Upper Tier Tribunal observation, London, 2018). These variations in SOGI self-identification and the different meanings accorded to the various letters in the 'LGBTIQ+' acronym in different contexts and times require far greater awareness of the fluidity of SOGI self-identification on the part of everyone involved in the asylum system (Noah, NGO social worker), something that can be improved through greater investment in training (Chap. 11).

For these reasons, there have been calls to move away from what some have described as a 'fixation' on whether claimants are 'truly' LGBTIQ+ (Jules, staff member at ILGA-Europe). Accordingly, the Italian Supreme Court has affirmed that the judge is not called to ascertain if claimants are 'truly' LGBTIQ+, but only if they may be persecuted on that ground.[16] This has also been highlighted by the CJEU in the *F* case.[17] The need to focus on the basis of persecution rather than on the individual's 'true' identity is obvious in relation to an 'imputed' SOGI, and there needs to be greater recognition in other SOGI cases that what is important is not ascertaining the claimant's identity but assessing the harm that they may suffer (Chiara, NGO worker, Italy; Silvana, judge, Italy). As also suggested by scholars (Dustin 2018), this would shift the focus from the PSG to the notion of persecution, to which we now turn.

7.3   Reaching the Persecution Threshold

Besides establishing membership of a PSG, asylum adjudicators also need to determine that there is a 'well-founded fear of persecution'. According to Article 9(1) of the Qualification Directive, for an act to constitute persecution, it needs to:

(a) be sufficiently serious by its nature or repetition as to constitute a severe violation of basic human rights, in particular the rights from which derogation cannot be made under Article 15(2) of the European Convention for the Protection of Human Rights and Fundamental Freedoms; or
(b) be an accumulation of various measures, including violations of human rights which is sufficiently severe as to affect an individual in a similar manner as mentioned in point (a).

---

[16] Supreme Court, decisions no. 2875, 6 February 2018 and no. 267, 9 January 2020.
[17] Case C-473/16, *F. v Bevándorlási és Állampolgársági Hivatal*, 25 January 2018, ECLI:EU:C:2018:36, paras. 31–32.

This definition still leaves much leeway to each country to determine who falls within their remit of protection.[18] Determining a 'well-founded fear of persecution' remains a considerable challenge in SOGI claims in some asylum systems, for example, in Germany (Gisela, lawyer).

In relation to SOGI claims, decision-makers tend to consider as relevant human rights violations such as physical or psychological violence, legal and administrative measures that are discriminatory in themselves or are applied in a discriminatory manner, and discriminatory criminal sanctions. We would however argue, in line with the framework expanded in Chap. 3, that every human rights violation can potentially lead to a well-founded fear of persecution if it leads to restricting or denying one's SOGI, especially considering that this fear is strictly individual and any person can experience it differently. The assessment of whether there is a 'severe violation of basic human rights' in the claimant's country of origin or not, is an exercise carried out with little degree of consistency across countries or even within the same country. On the contrary, it remains a subjective exercise, highly dependent on each decision-maker. In Italy, for example, there may be no consideration of specific human rights violations suffered in the country of origin. It is more important that the claimant is able to offer a coherent account of their experience (Sect. 7.5), combined with evidence that, at a general level, SOGI minorities' human rights are breached in the country of origin. This goes beyond the issue of whether or not there are laws criminalising same-sex acts (Sect. 7.3.1). For instance, the Tribunal of Milan has considered the social attitudes in the Ivory Coast against SOGI minorities to be sufficient for granting refugee status to a male claimant, despite the absence of criminalising legislation.[19] In contrast, in the UK, sometimes not even the criminalisation of same-sex conduct, police violence and social stigma is enough:

> Say someone is from Bangladesh [where same-sex acts are punished criminally] and a series of reports say police mistreated this person, a Pride march is broken up, then you've still got to pull that together. Just because someone's been beaten up, does that mean everyone will be? (Ernest, judge, UK).

As for what constitutes an 'accumulation of various measures' that may give rise to persecution, although there is no international consensus, it is clear one needs to take a holistic – and intersectional, we argue – approach to claimants' experiences:

> But I think that also when you are not in this kind of situation [risking death penalty], there can be multiple discriminations that come together, because of your sexual orientation, gender identity, but also because of other aspects that actually force you to leave the country and then look for asylum somewhere else. So I think it is very important to have this more holistic image in order to take a decision in the end (Terry, member of the European Parliament).

---

[18] For some guidance from the CJEU, see, for example, Joined Cases C-71/11 and C-99/11, Bundesrepublik Deutschland v Y and Z, 5 September 2012, ECLI:EU:C:2012:518.
[19] Tribunal of Milan, decision of 18 October 2017.

7.3 Reaching the Persecution Threshold

We can again use an Italian example, this time involving the case of a gay man from Benin. While the territorial commission denied refugee status because it found there was no risk of persecution, the Tribunal of Trieste stated that the intimidations, the loss of job, and the violence suffered by the claimant after his sexual orientation became publicly known did amount to persecution.[20] On other occasions, territorial commissions themselves deemed that the existence of a homophobic environment preventing a gay man from living openly his sexual orientation was sufficient to ascertain persecution.[21] This was also affirmed in relation to claimants from Russia, especially after the adoption of the law against 'homosexual propaganda'.[22] In Germany, however, in the case of a lesbian woman from Russia,[23] the Administrative Court of Potsdam decided that even though discrimination against SOGI minorities existed, there was no persecution of homosexuals across the country that would allow the finding that there is a 'considerable likelihood' of persecution of the claimant. Furthermore, the discrimination experienced by SOGI minorities in the host country – in this case the UK – may be used to argue that not every experience of discrimination can be the basis of international protection:

> persecution is an extreme situation. And, frankly, people are not entitled to refugee protection unless discrimination has reached that very high threshold. And, that is where, I am afraid, people have to live with discrimination. I mean, there will be parts of the United Kingdom where gay and lesbian people will suffer discrimination… (Adrian, judge).

What often also transpires in SOGI asylum decisions is the idea that SOGI claimants should be content with a smaller scope of rights and freedom than European citizens (Allan, lawyer, UK). As Butler (2004) highlights, such views on queer lives make them less liveable, if liveable at all. Even when there is legislation protecting some SOGI minorities, such as Pakistani legislation protecting the gender identity of hijras, there may be discrimination and lack of protection by public authorities (Louis, NGO volunteer, Germany), so the existence of formal statutory protection should not be interpreted as precluding persecution (UNHCR 2012, para. 37). This affects European countries themselves, with legal protection of SOGI minorities still not fully reflected in social practices and individuals still needing to escape persecution (Titti, decision-maker, Italy).

In the UK in particular, decision-makers often placed considerable importance on the degree of visibility of claimants in the host country as the basis for determining whether or not it would be safe for them to return to their home countries, sometimes using the claimant's lack of a 'public profile' to deny the risk of persecution upon return (Zena, First Tier Tribunal Appeal, London, 2018, decision paper, para. 47c). At the same time, commentators have been critical of UK Home Office decision-makers' depictions of SOGI asylum as a claim for clubbers' rights by

---

[20] Tribunal of Trieste, judgment of 8 August 2009.

[21] See, for example, the case of a gay man from Albania, reported by the Consiglio Italiano per i Rifugiati (2007).

[22] Tribunal of Salerno, decision of 18 April 2017.

[23] 6 K 435/13.A, 27 February 2014.

people from countries without a 'gay scene', rather than flight from imprisonment and violence, pointing out that this discriminates against anyone who does not fit such stereotypes (Juss 2015; Millbank 2009b, p. 19). Our fieldwork confirmed that these issues persist and we will return to this in the context of our discussion on credibility (Sect. 7.5).

It is also worrying that some decision-makers seem to require persecution to have already occurred in the country of origin, rather than focussing on the future risk of persecution. This was reported by several participants in Germany (Thomas, NGO volunteer; BAMF decision appealed in Court observations, Hesse, 2018, 2019; decision regarding participant DE34 in Held et al. 2018). The lack of past persecution, even in the case of countries with well-documented widespread homophobia like Guyana, is seen to count against claimants (Leon, NGO worker, Germany). Claimants understandably react strongly to such expectation:

> I haven't faced any violence or attack. Do I have to go back to Iraq and be beaten or killed to prove that I am in danger in my country? Would you be convinced if I was attacked in Iraq? (Court observation, Hesse, 2019).

What matters from a legal perspective is the risk of persecution upon return (UNHCR 2016, paras 24–25 and 89–92), irrespective of whether persecutory acts have already been carried out or not. Decision-makers should, therefore, always make a forward-looking assessment.

Past debates about the relevance of private actors to establishing a risk of persecution in asylum claims have been largely superseded, with asylum adjudicators in the EU now being in agreement that it is possible to grant international protection when the agents of persecution are not national authorities but private agents, under Article 6 of the Qualification Directive. What is relevant is whether the country of origin's authorities are able or not to protect an asylum claimant from private acts of persecution on one of the grounds provided by the Refugee Convention. For example, in Italy, in the case of a gay man from Ecuador who suffered violence inflicted by family members, the Court decided that 'the general situation of impunity' made the protection by Ecuadorian authorities illusory, thus warranting granting refugee status.[24] SOGI asylum claimants benefit from this understanding, as many of our participants suffered persecution at the hands of parents and carers (Ibrahim, Germany; William, Germany; Momo, Italy; Buba, Italy), partners (Rosette, Germany), cousins (Shany, Germany), extended families (Alain A., Italy), radical religious groups (Ibrahim, Germany), criminals and other members of the community (Ximena, UK), public mobs (Alphaeus, Germany) and, more generally, members of the public (Siri, Italy), as also explored in Chap. 5. Nonetheless, some of our participants were convinced that decision-makers were much less likely to grant protection when persecution was carried out by private actors, such as family members, which betrayed a troubling misunderstanding of the legal framework and the

---

[24] Giudice di pace di Genova, decision of 10 June 2010. See, also, Tribunal of Rome, decision no. 4675, 5 May 2010, in relation to a Palestinian man; and Court of Appeal of Bari, judgment no. 299, 5 March 2013.

social mechanisms of oppression in some countries of origin (Thomas, NGO volunteer, Germany).

While the role of private actors is reasonably clear, there is little consensus across, or even within, the countries studied as to what matters when assessing the 'risk of persecution'. Here, three themes emerged in our fieldwork, to which we now turn: the importance of criminalisation of same-sex acts (Sect. 7.3.1), the 'discretion argument' (Sect. 7.3.2), and the 'internal relocation alternative' (Sect. 7.3.3).

7.3.1 The Criminalisation of Same-Sex Acts

The CJEU used its judgment in *X, Y and Z* to assert that the criminalisation of same-sex acts does not in itself constitute an act of persecution. Although this decision was considered balanced and flexible enough by some of our participants (Helena, EASO staff member), it runs against UNHCR guidance stating that criminalisation should generally be sufficient to claim persecution (UNHCR 2012, para. 26 ff). The CJEU decision also ignores scholarly recommendations (Jansen and Spijkerboer 2011), and fails to place these criminal law norms within their broader societal context of discrimination and intolerance (ICJ 2014; Markard 2013). Furthermore, it ignores the realities of countries such as the Ivory Coast, where despite the lack of actual prosecutions, the legislation is used to facilitate blackmail, discrimination and harassment, including on the part of the police (Gisela, lawyer, Germany; Damiano, lawyer, Italy). Therefore, even if the criminalisation of same-sex acts is not considered persecutory in itself, we should give greater recognition to the import that it has in the asylum context:

> But the very fact that the law exists, and there is no willingness to remove it from the books… I think is a bit of a red flag. And also the very fact that they exist means that it is open to abuse. That means from today to tomorrow you can have immense problems (Jules, staff member at ILGA-Europe).

Germany, Italy and the UK have followed separate paths in this regard. In the German context, initial case law of the Federal Administrative Court focused on whether legislation criminalising same-sex acts could be justified on grounds of maintaining 'public morality'.[25] For instance, as recently as 2006, an administrative court argued that 'Islamic cultures' may restrict same-sex acts because of the country's prevailing morality without this constituting political persecution.[26] More recent case law abstains from this type of argument. BAMF instructions clarify that, in relation to the assessment of fear of SOGI-related persecution, '[a]n imminent persecution is always to be assumed if the applicant makes it credible to be threatened by a relevant imprisonment existing in the country of origin and if this is

---

[25] BVerwGE, 15 March 1988, C 278.86.

[26] Administrative Court of Düsseldorf, 14 September 2006, 11 K 81/06, cited in Hempel (2014, p. 51).

actually imposed there' (BAMF 2017, p. 289). Enforcement of criminalisation is thus taken seriously at a policy level, but the existence of 'anti-homosexuality laws' is not sufficient to prove a risk of persecution.

Refusals are often based on the reasoning that existing laws are not used, or that there is no evidence that these laws are used, or that they are used but without harsh sanctions (Barbara, lawyer; Kadir, NGO worker; Marlen, legal advisor). There seems to be an increasing number of refusals based on the idea that such cases lack 'asylum relevance'. While courts have focused more on the 'discretion argument' in the past (Sect. 7.3.2), in recent years they have more often argued that the threshold for 'asylum relevance' has not been met. For instance, in a decision by the Administrative Court of Frankfurt am Main,[27] the appeal of a bisexual man from Ghana was dismissed with the argument that, although there were homophobic tendencies in the Ghanaian society, criminal prosecution did not take place in practice and only certain homosexual practices were prosecuted, not a 'homosexual disposition' in itself. Similarly, the case of a gay man from Kenya was dismissed by the Administrative Court of Potsdam,[28] with the argument that although the Kenyan Criminal Code provides for up to fourteen years' imprisonment for homosexual acts, there is no evidence that these penalties are, in fact, imposed and executed. Other court cases, involving a gay man from Albania and a bisexual woman from Morocco,[29] offer further examples of asylum rejections on grounds of lack of 'asylum relevance', despite the existence of criminal laws against SOGI minorities in the countries of origin.

Our fieldwork also provided examples of this practice. In the BAMF refusal letter shared by one of our participants, it was argued that the 'applicant's submission of facts does not show any refugee-relevant persecution. The Federal Office has no information that homosexuality in Lebanon leads to persecution. State prosecution of homosexuals can be ruled out' (decision regarding Ibrahim). Other participants affected by this approach are lesbian women from Jamaica, who, not being explicitly targeted by Jamaican 'buggery laws', are not seen as being at risk of persecution in Jamaica, despite being victims of discrimination and hate crime as are other SOGI minorities (Angel).

There are also glaring inconsistencies in decision-making with regard to 'asylum relevance' according to country of origin. In Germany, this appeared to particularly affect claimants from Uganda and Jamaica, where courts come to different conclusions with regard to how safe these countries are for SOGI minorities. For instance, a decision by the Administrative Court of Munich on the case of a lesbian woman from Uganda dismissed the appeal, arguing that even after tightened penalties came into force in 2014, there were no convictions for homosexual charges in Uganda and government agencies did not tolerate attacks by non-state actors against

---

[27] 1 L 3416/13. F. A, 26 September 2013.

[28] 6 K 3802 / 13.A, 13 May 2014.

[29] Respectively, Administrative Court of Aachen, 16 October 2014, 1 K 1201/14.A, and Administrative Court of Cottbus, 7 November 2017, 5 K 1230/17.

7.3 Reaching the Persecution Threshold

homosexuals.[30] In the same year, however, the Administrative Court of Frankfurt am Main decided on the case of a lesbian woman from Uganda, determining that homosexuality is criminalised with up to 14 years imprisonment, homosexuals are indeed being persecuted and they do not receive state protection against attacks by private persons because of their sexuality.[31]

Inconsistencies between courts go so far as some courts considering the mere criminalisation of same-sex conduct as 'potential persecution' and granting refugee status in such cases provided credibility is established (Marlen, legal advisor). Some appeal judges are also more sophisticated in their analysis and understand the reasons behind a possible lack of prosecutions in countries where same-sex acts are criminalised:

> the fact that Pakistan is rarely acquainted with criminal cases and homosexual convictions for consensual sexual intercourse is, in essence, due to the fact that homosexuals in Pakistan hide their sexual orientation due to legal requirements and widespread reservations among the population, and, for example, lead double lives in a forced marriage. Homosexuality is tolerated in Pakistan for as long as sexual orientation remains secret or invisible (Court observation, Hesse, 2018).

Similarly, in the UK, criminalisation of same-sex acts in itself is not sufficient to find there is a risk of persecution, if the law is not enforced. This was confirmed as long ago as 2003.[32] This is reflected in Home Office guidance, for example, the 2017 Country Policy and Information Note on Kenya, which states: 'Sources suggest that the law on "unnatural offences" is rarely applied and there have only been two recent reported cases of its use, one of which was dismissed and the other still ongoing at the time of publication' (Home Office 2017, para. 2.3.5). This policy is also evident in the case law. For example, in a case regarding Sri Lanka, the Court found that 'the treatment of gay men in Sri Lanka does not reach the standard of persecution or serious harm', despite the criminalisation of same-sex acts.[33] In such cases, the claim is often refused on the grounds that the individual could safely relocate to a different part of the country of origin (Sect. 7.3.3).

As argued by UK lawyers, not accepting criminalisation of same-sex acts as persecution in itself fails to recognise that 'persecution does not begin and end with prosecutions' and that criminalisation of homosexuality, even without enforcement, is likely to be accompanied by a climate of homophobia and impunity for attacks on SOGI minorities (Briddock 2016, p. 147). For example, the articles in the Sri Lankan Penal Code relating to 'unnatural offences' and 'gross indecency' are unenforced, yet SOGI minorities are the target of extortion and violence, would not be able to rely on police protection, and 'one-third of the LBT interviewees [in an IGLHRC study] reported that they attempted suicide' (IGLHRC 2014, p. 32). The

---

[30] M 25 K 13.31348, 19 November 2014.

[31] 8 K 4089 / 14.F, 10 December 2014. See, also, Administrative Court of Regensburg, RN 1 K 17.32818, 4 September 2017.

[32] *Queen on the application of Dawkins v IAT* [2003] EWHC373 Admin, para. 49.

[33] *Sri Lanka CG* [2015] UKUT 00073 (IAC).

requirement for homophobic and transphobic law to not only exist but also be enforced effectively creates an unjustifiable two-tier system in relation to SOGI claimants, distinguishing those from countries where the law is enforced (for example, Pakistan and Cameroon) from those who come from countries where the law is not always or clearly enforced (for example, Sri Lanka and Kenya). Such distinctions have also been challenged by lawyers in court, with claimants pointing out that it may be true that criminalisation in itself does not establish fear of persecution, but that it *goes* to establishing fear of persecution (Upper Tier Tribunal observation, London, 2018).

The Italian asylum system stands as an exception amongst the three countries under comparison and most others across Europe, as it considers criminalisation of same-sex acts persecution in itself. In 2007, the Supreme Court ruled that the criminalisation of same-sex acts did not amount to persecution, as such acts were an (avoidable) expression of homosexuality, so such criminal law rules did not target an identity as such.[34] Yet, following criticism by scholars (Gasparini et al. 2011; Winkler 2011) and resistance in the lower courts,[35] in 2012 the Supreme Court affirmed that the simple circumstance of maintaining criminal sanctions of this kind hampers the individual 'fundamental right to live freely their sexual and emotional life'.[36] This makes it unnecessary to verify whether these sanctions are applied or not. It is recognised that such criminal norms constitute a serious interference with one's private life, and therefore place people in 'an objective situation of persecution'. This decision has been followed by Italian judicial and administrative decision-makers ever since, thus making Italy stand out in the field of SOGI asylum. Italian decision-makers, therefore, generally see criminalisation of same-sex acts as 'obvious indication' of persecution (Maurizio, judge). One decision-maker described this approach as follows:

> This is based on information on the countries of origin and, when the information on the countries of origin says that in that country the legislation is of a certain type, or public opinion is oriented towards a certain direction, protection is granted automatically (Daniele, decision-maker).

Decisions on SOGI claims in Italy also tend to grant international protection to claimants coming from countries where there may not be criminalisation of same-sex acts but there is social oppression against SOGI minorities, such as Russia (Cristina, UNHCR officer; Livio, lawyer).

We now consider the concept of 'discretion' where, as with criminalisation, there is little consistency in the countries under comparison.

---

[34] Supreme Court, judgment no. 16417, 25 July 2007, confirmed by the same Court in judgments no. 2907, 23 November 2007, and no. 41368, 14 October 2009.

[35] For example, Tribunal of Turin, decision no. 426, 5 November 2010, reported in *Diritto, Immigrazione, Cittadinanza*, 2011, p. 141.

[36] Supreme Court, decision no. 15981, 20 September 2012, reiterated subsequently, for example, in Supreme Court, decision no. 267, 9 January 2020.

7.3.2 The 'Discretion Argument'

The so-called 'discretion argument' or 'discretion requirement' – the idea that a SOGI claimant may be sent back to the country of origin and be 'discreet' about or 'conceal' their SOGI to avoid persecution (Dustin 2018) – has been central to the history of SOGI asylum in several countries. Although the concept was rejected by the CJEU's decision in *X, Y and Z* and has been slowly set aside across Europe and beyond (Dustin and Ferreira 2017), more subtle forms of this 'discretion argument' (or, more accurately, concealment) persist and are not necessarily held to be incompatible with the CJEU's ruling (ECRE 2017).

In the UK context, findings of credible risk of persecution have for long been tainted by this argument. In the period between 1999 and 2010, having been recognised as members of a PSG, SOGI asylum claimants were likely to be refused not only on grounds of credibility, but also (or in the first instance) because they could return to their country of origin and live 'discreetly'. This was known as the 'reasonably tolerable' requirement, according to which the question to be asked was whether the individual 'had adapted and would again adapt his behaviour so as to avoid persecution in circumstances wherein it amounted to his preferred way of dealing with the problem and a way which was reasonably tolerable to him'.[37] This thinking led to absurdities such as the 2005 case of an Algerian man, where the Secretary of State argued that 'because in Algeria there are no gay rights, there are no opportunities for displaying homosexuality with those who are of a similar mind, and it will be impossible for him not to be discreet'.[38] Painfully circular thinking such as this was also found acceptable amongst UK judiciary:

> It is the respondent's [Home Office] position that self-restraint due to fear will be persecution only if it is such that a homosexual person cannot reasonably be expected to tolerate such self-restraint. Where a person does in fact live discreetly to avoid coming to the attention of the authorities he is reasonably tolerating the position.[39]

In 2010, a pivotal moment took place: a Supreme Court ruling rejected the 'reasonable tolerable' thinking and blatant forms of the 'discretion requirement' were held unlawful.[40] In the case of *HJ (Iran)*, sexual identity was accepted as being 'a fundamental characteristic and an integral part of human freedom', and for the first time it was recognised that 'to require an applicant to engage in self-denial was to require him to live in a state of self-induced oppression'.[41] The Court, however, also found that if claimants 'chose' to conceal their sexuality for other reasons (social mores, etc.), they would not be eligible for asylum. Discretion thinking was thus

---

[37] *J v Secretary of State for the Home Department* [2006] EWCA Civ 1238; para. 13.

[38] *B v. Secretary of State for the Home Department* [2007] EWHC 2528, para. 20 (the case was remitted for redetermination).

[39] *HJ v. Secretary of State for the Home Department* [2008] UKAIT 00044, para. 10.

[40] *HJ (Iran) and HT (Cameroon) v Secretary of State for the Home Department* [2010] UKSC 31.

[41] Ibid, paras. 32 and 33.

reformulated in a new, cumbersome test.[42] This tortuous test has been widely criticised as unreasonable, discriminatory and unworkable by both scholars and the UK Equality and Human Rights Commission, and runs against UNHCR guidance (Dustin 2018; Held 2016; Khan 2016, p. 133; UNHCR 2002a, b, p. 32).[43] As the Equality and Human Rights Commission, intervening in the case, pointed out:

> Such cases [where someone can safely be returned to live "discreetly"] will be extremely rarely (if ever) encountered in the asylum system since where a claim is made on grounds of sexual orientation that will in itself require a person to "out" him or herself, at least to a limited extent and in any event a person who voluntarily wants to conceal their same-sex sexual orientation in circumstances where there was no real likelihood of it being otherwise exposed is self-evidently unlikely to claim asylum on grounds of sexual orientation.[44]

In asking decision-makers to assess the reason why an individual would behave 'discreetly', the test creates an additional hurdle for sexual orientation asylum claimants and discriminates against them relative to other people claiming asylum, none of whom are required to provide a motive for the behaviour that results in persecution (Khan 2016, p. 133). Nonetheless, such 'discretion reasoning' has been replicated in most Home Office country guidance (Chap. 6, Sect. 6.5) and enshrined in the Asylum Policy Instruction on 'Sexual orientation in asylum claims' updated in 2016 (Home Office 2010, 2016).

Several UK lawyers and advocates remained convinced that *HJ (Iran)* needed to be challenged, on the basis that it has been misinterpreted, applied too broadly (UKLGIG 2018), and had been intended to be used only in exceptional circumstances (Allan, lawyer). Indeed, as explored in Chap. 5, SOGI claimants often escape their home countries after having gone to great lengths to hide their sexuality but having been unsuccessful in those efforts, thus rendering 'discretion' a mostly theoretical debate. As Beth, a lawyer, summarises:

> *HJ* urgently needs to be revisited... if a person is LGBT in a country which persecutes those who are, then there should be no further need to explore the way in which that person would live or express themselves. There are so many fundamental flaws in the approach inquiring into how the individual will live not least that we as humans are constantly changing in our nature and behaviour. (...) the person may come to others' attention for a whole host of other reasons, even if living discreetly and privately. There is also an inherent unfairness in denying an individual protection on the basis they live privately. (...) This effectively creates a qualified protection – depending on how you live, protection is conditional – that fundamentally undermines the purpose of the Convention.

A setback for those arguing against any use of the concept of 'discretion' was the disappointing Court of Appeal in England and Wales judgment in *LC (Albania)*,[45] where the claimant argued that, to be consistent with EU law, only the first two

---

[42] Ibid, para. 82. See, also, Wessels (2012).

[43] *HJ (Iran) and HT (Cameroon) v Secretary of State for the Home Department* [2010] UKSC 31, para. 60, 37.

[44] Ibid, para. 37 and 60.

[45] *LC (Albania) v The Secretary of State for the Home Department & Anor* [2017] EWCA Civ 351; [2017] WLR(D) 318.

questions from the 2010 test should apply: '1) Is the applicant gay or likely to be perceived as gay', and '2) If so, are openly gay individuals persecuted in the individual's country of origin?' This was rejected and Justice Hinkinbottom stated that the legal analysis in the 2010 case was fully in line with EU law, and that the Supreme Court distinction between concealment for fear of persecution and concealment for other reasons is 'principled and clearly right'. The judge emphasised the clear distinction between concealment 'in response to social pressures or for cultural or religious reasons of his own choosing', stating that the distinction must be right because such social pressures exist everywhere, including the UK. The implication was that it is important to clearly distinguish persecution in 'refugee-producing countries' from discrimination in 'refugee-receiving countries', such as the UK.

It is also widely believed that, in an attempt to continue curbing recognition of SOGI claims, UK asylum adjudicators have simply shifted their focus from 'discretion' or internal relocation to credibility, tending to deny claimants' SOGI self-identification (Ashley, psychotherapist; Amelia, NGO worker; Joseph, NGO volunteer). Indeed, the risk is that the post-2010 version of 'discretion reasoning' translates into a preoccupation on the part of caseworkers with how open individuals are about their sexuality and whether they are 'out':

> The judges seem to be clear that there is a distinction between has somebody been living openly here, if they have been living openly here, then that is their life now and they could not go back and live the life that they have as an open, out, particularly when someone is a couple, person. So if somebody can show that they have been out, they have been part of the LGBT community going to Prides or they have a partner or their friends know, then often that carries a lot of weight in terms of the judge saying, "well you couldn't go back, you shouldn't be expected to have to go back into secrecy" (Debbie, NGO volunteer).

Our participants had experienced that first hand:

> they also want to know, if you are granted refugee status in the UK, that you are going to be an out gay man, you are not going to go back in the closet. So you need to provide them with, let's say, pictures and stuff that you have been out in London since you came. Which also doesn't make sense, because if you are not working and you don't have a place to sleep, the last thing you are going to think about is going out clubbing. And that was also something I found really strange (Selim).

Individuals who are not 'out' in the UK, perhaps because they want to retain the support of members of the diaspora community, may be refused on the basis that they are 'discreet' in the UK and would therefore be 'discreet' if returned to their country of origin (Khan 2016, p. 134). This is in clear tension with the human rights, feminist and queer theoretical and analytical underpinnings adopted in our analysis, to the extent that this scrutiny of how 'open' a claimant is about their sexuality relies on stereotyped, oppressive and culturally biased visions of how a 'genuine' member of a SOGI minority should act when living in the West.

During our fieldwork, we encountered evidence of the Home Office using the 'discretion requirement', stating, for example, that 'one can be anonymous in Nairobi' (Upper Tier Tribunal observation, London, 2018). Even claimants who are clearly 'out' have been expected by some judges to change their conduct and behave more 'discreetly', so that they can safely be deported, for example, by suggesting that it would be possible for a lesbian claimant to act in a 'less mannish' way (quote from First Tier tribunal decision, London 2018; this was part of the basis for the decision being overturned on appeal to the Upper Tier Tribunal, observation, London 2018). Indeed, a number of the judicial observations we carried out in the UK were dominated by discussions about whether or not the claimant would live 'discreetly' upon return and, if so, for what reason. A variation on 'discretion reasoning' is also reflected in the way decision-makers sometimes question the risks claimants have taken in their countries of origin before fleeing (Nath, lawyer). Perniciously, claimants are thrown into 'no-win' situations: 'Then there is a whole catch 22 of, if they are saying you should have been "discreet", but if you had been, then you could carry on being so you could go back and carry on being ["discreet"]' (Nath, lawyer). Decisions – including at a judicial level – even go beyond the test set out in *HJ (Iran)* and blatantly return to full-blown 'discretion reasoning': 'Yes, they are saying "oh, no, you could live a secret life, you could suppress who you are, and go back to living how you were before"' (Christina). Lesbian and bisexual claimants seem to be particularly affected by 'discretion reasoning' under *HJ (Iran)*: 'Lesbians and bisexual women are more likely to be told that they will be "discreet" for reasons supposedly not related to a [form] of persecution, such as a desire for family approval' (S4, lawyer). Jules, staff member at ILGA-Europe, shared this concern:

> if you have a person who identifies as bisexual, then you will have responses along the lines of "oh well, but if you like both the opposite sex and the same sex, you can go back home and just be with someone of the opposite sex, that simple."

To worsen this state-of-affairs, it has become apparent that this UK judgment has influenced other European decision-makers, both at domestic and international level (Amanda, NGO worker, Brussels; ECRE 2017). This seems to be the case, for example, in the Netherlands (Jansen 2019, p. 151) and with the European Court of Human Rights, as in *M.E. v Sweden*.[46] This may be interpreted as the decision in *HJ (Iran)* having a negative influence across Europe, and emboldening decision-makers in their desire to retain at least some forms of the 'discretion requirement'.

That might well be the case in Germany. Even before the judgment in *HJ (Iran)*, German decision-makers made use of the 'discretion requirement'. For instance, the Administrative Court of Düsseldorf, in a case relating to a gay man from Morocco, dismissed the appeal and suggested that 'discretion', combined with relocation, would protect the claimant from persecution.[47] The Administrative Court of Trier also dismissed the claim of a gay man from Algeria, arguing that the criminalisation of homosexual acts in Algeria was not the basis for refugee protection, because it was not about 'predisposition', but about certain sexual practices being punishable if they became public.[48] The Court argued that it was reasonable to expect the

---

[46] *M.E. v. Sweden*, Application no. 71398/12, 8 April 2015, in particular para. 36.

[47] 11 K 6778/09, 14 January 2010.

[48] 1 L 928/10.TR, 9 September 2010.

7.3 Reaching the Persecution Threshold

claimant to be 'discreet' about his 'disposition' in a large city in Algeria.[49] Although there has been some judicial dissidence, with several courts disagreeing with 'discretion reasoning' and arguing that it is unacceptable to ask a claimant to keep their sexuality secret,[50] that has not been the approach taken by the majority.

In 2010 the government formulated the 'discretion requirement' more carefully, arguing that the decision depends on the claimants' expected future behaviour, but not on the reasonableness of alternative behaviour (Hempel 2014, pp. 56–75). Following higher courts' case law, and perhaps feeling supported by the judgment in *HJ (Iran)*, the BAMF laid out that the decision on the potential risk of persecution of sexual minorities depended on the individual's 'sexual disposition', in other words, whether this 'disposition' was so strong that it would be likely that the authorities would find out about such a 'disposition'. The cornerstone element here was thus the prognosis of future conduct. If the claimant had already suffered persecution, constitutional asylum or refugee status should be granted; if the claimant had not yet been persecuted, the decision on whether to grant them refugee status should depend on what sexual behaviour was to be expected from them if returned (Kalkmann 2010, p. 7). In December 2012, in anticipation of the CJEU judgment in *X, Y and Z*, the BAMF finally confirmed that it had changed its decision-making and had abolished 'discretion reasoning' (BAMF 2012; Hempel 2014, pp. 56–75).

Nonetheless, in 2017, the BAMF again recognised that although SOGI claimants cannot be expected to avoid risky behaviour in order to evade persecution, if a claimant would be likely to choose to live their sexuality 'discreetly' on a voluntary basis, then 'it can be assumed that he or she will accept this lifestyle for themselves. Under these conditions, refugee protection can exceptionally not be established' (BAMF 2017, p. 292). The BAMF instructions also clarify that if claimants voluntarily and without impairment to their personal identity lead a life that makes it unlikely that their SOGI would become publicly known, even after their return, then a decision that the persecution threshold has not been met is reasonable. Appeal judges also ask questions about whether the claimant is visibly 'out' in Germany as the indicator of whether they would behave in the same way in their country of origin and could therefore safely be returned (Court observation, Hesse, 2018, 2019). All this is akin to 'discretion reasoning', in the same vein as *HJ (Iran)*.

Our participants confirmed that they still see 'discretion reasoning' in asylum decisions (Barbara, lawyer, Germany; Marlen, legal advisor, Germany; Sofia and Emma, NGO workers), which was also confirmed by claimants themselves

---

[49] Other examples can be found in Administrative Court of Düsseldorf, 11 K 6778/09, 14 January 2010; Administrative Court of Düsseldorf, 11 K 1003/09.A, 27 August 2009; Administrative Court of Düsseldorf, 5 K 1875/08.A, 11 March 2009; Administrative Court of Regensburg, RN 8 K 08.30020, 15 September 2008; Administrative Court of Düsseldorf, 11 K 2432/07.A, 21 February 2008; Administrative Court of Bremen, 7 K 632/05.A, 28 April 2006; and Administrative Court of Aachen, 5 K 2455/05.A, 26 February 2007.

[50] See, for instance, Administrative Court of Frankfurt/Oder, 4 K 772/10.A, 11 November 2010; Administrative Court of Chemnitz, A 2 K 304/06, 11 July 2008; Administrative Court of Neustadt/Weinstraße, 3 K 753/07.NW, 8 September 2008; Administrative Court of Munich, M 21 K 04.51404, 30 January 2007.

(Zouhair). This is seen as sending claimants 'back to the closet': 'In practical terms it means "The claimant has not lived openly as gay, so there is nothing against him continuing to live like that"' (Thomas, NGO volunteer). This is clearly used in BAMF decisions, particularly affecting claimants who had not 'come out' in their home countries (decision regarding participant DE34 in Held et al. 2018) and who were also not 'out' in Germany or did not have an active sexual life. Yet research shows that, for SOGI claimants, 'coming out' processes in host countries may take many years (Shidlo and Ahola 2013, pp. 9–10). As one of our participants pointed out, this is both a reductive and racist treatment of SOGI claimants:

> And there is still a bit the expectation of "discretion", so if it was like that until the 20th, 25th year of age, then it has to go on. That's an argument that is in several letters of refusal [of asylum]: "If the person somehow managed to carry on with their lives like that, then it is not so difficult." (...) Be quiet and it will be fine. This suggests that homosexuality implies something you just do not have to live with, in the worst case scenario, or it is enough to live it out in silence. That means that [SOGI claimants] will not have the same claim to human dignity and human rights and freedom that you have in Germany, and if you question that, if you are shocked by it, then you do not have [those rights]. That's a very racist outlook, because then if you're Arab, Persian, Afghan or whatever, or Colombian, then you cannot have the same claim [to those rights] (Kadir, NGO worker).

In Italy, in contrast, there is no evidence of 'discretion reasoning' being used in SOGI asylum adjudication. Italian decision-makers do not attach any importance to the question (Roberto, decision-maker; Daniele, decision-maker; Cristina, UNHCR officer). According to all available data, including the extensive body of case law on SOGI asylum, no SOGI asylum claims in Italy have been refused on the grounds of 'discretion'. This might be an indirect consequence of the stronger influence of the UNHCR in asylum adjudication in Italy, along with extensive use of the UNHCR 2012 SOGI guidelines (UNHCR 2012; Chaps. 4 and 6) and a human rights approach to asylum (Chap. 3).

Indeed, all forms of 'discretion reasoning' are rejected by the UNHCR in its SOGI guidelines:

> The question is not, could the applicant, by being discreet, live in that country without attracting adverse consequences. It is important to note that even if applicants may so far have managed to avoid harm through concealment, their circumstances may change over time and secrecy may not be an option for the entirety of their lifetime. The risk of discovery may also not necessarily be confined to their own conduct. There is almost always the possibility of discovery against the person's will, for example, by accident, rumours or growing suspicion (UNHCR 2012, para. 32).

We are far from seeing this guidance observed by asylum authorities across Europe. In fact, 'discretion reasoning' affects not only sexual orientation, but also gender identity-based asylum claims:

> we have heard of cases where trans people who are physically "passing" are told "well, you can go back now because you pass and so even if it is not safe for trans people, you don't look like a trans person, and so you can go back." (...) these issues disregard the fact that, ok, maybe you are passing, but that still exposes you to a higher number of risks, you could be blackmailed, you could be exposed, what is considered safe for LGBTI people is not always really safe (Jules, staff member at ILGA-Europe).

Inappropriate consideration of the 'internal relocation alternative' makes the overall picture worse.

7.3.3 The 'Internal Relocation Alternative'

The 'internal relocation alternative' refers to the possibility of asylum claimants being returned to their country of origin and moving to a different part of it where they may be able to avoid the risk of persecution. This is allowed under Article 8 of the Qualification Directive, and generally included in domestic legislation. Nonetheless, it is generally not recommended by the UNHCR in SOGI cases (UNHCR 2012, para. 51 ff). This guidance, as we will see, is largely disregarded, and once again, the differences across the asylum systems in the countries under comparison are striking.

German asylum instructions refer to 'internal relocation' of SOGI claimants in the context of claimants who have not suffered persecution previously, and establish that it is only reasonable to expect these claimants to relocate if, should their sexual orientation or gender identity be discovered, they would not need to relocate again (BAMF 2017, sec. 7.5.1). Nonetheless, when information on persecution is lacking, there is an assumption of a certain tolerance towards SOGI minorities in certain parts of the country of origin, and that internal relocation is therefore possible (Thomas, NGO volunteer; Sofia and Emma, NGO workers; Barbara, lawyer; decision regarding participant DE34 in Held et al. 2018). Yet, even if a country is large and still retains some degree of rule of law, internal relocation may not be an option. Russia is a good illustration of this:

> We lived in the city, in St Petersburg, it does not work, there are problems, then we move to a village, try to live there, and many times we try to move, yes, and again same problems, and lawyer says "the reason for judge can maybe also be that Russia is a huge country and it is possible to find a safe place, somewhere, maybe in the woods" (laughs), I do not know (Veronica).

Decision-makers, however, still proceed on the basis that internal relocation is viable in Russia (decisions regarding participants D16 and D33 in Held et al. 2018), where anti-gay propaganda laws have promoted a highly homophobic environment across the country (Ramón Mendos 2019). Smaller countries may also be mistakenly believed to be safe in some parts:

> In the decision they say I should move to northern Jamaica. Now, if you go on Google, northern Jamaica is the murder capital of Jamaica. Most murders per year, for straight people. So how would it be for a gay person, a lesbian person? If straight people aren't safe there, how am I gonna be safe there? (Angel).

Besides Jamaica and Russia, we saw internal relocation used by German decision-makers in relation to countries including Turkey, Pakistan and Uganda, with insufficient consideration of the social, economic, cultural, linguistic and personal reasons that may preclude internal relocation from being a realistic solution (Louis,

NGO volunteer; Elias, lawyer; Barbara, lawyer; Oscar, judge; focus group no. 1, Hesse; focus group no. 2, Bavaria). Internal relocation has thus become known as the latest 'trick' to deny international protection (Gisela, lawyer).

Participants also pointed out that there is an inconsistent overlap between the areas judged to be safe for internal relocation for asylum claimants, and the areas that countries' own nationals are advised *not* to visit by their own governments, for example, in Jamaica (focus group no. 1, Hesse).

The lack of consistency between different courts in this respect is noticeable (Oscar, judge). For example, in the case of a gay man from Jamaica, the Administrative Court of Giessen decided that although there was no risk of state persecution, there was a risk of persecution by private actors and therefore there was no internal relocation alternative to tourist areas in the north of the country, as the BAMF had argued.[51] Nonetheless, in the same year, the Administrative Court of Kassel suggested that another gay claimant could internally relocate (to tourist areas in the north) to avoid persecution.[52]

As in Germany, in the UK, internal relocation is a common ground for refusing SOGI claims,[53] often in connection with the idea that claimants would choose to live 'discreetly'. Home Office guidance identifies countries where relocation is an option for SOGI minorities (Home Office 2016, p. 36). Albania, for example, is on the 'safe countries' list (Chap. 6, Sect. 6.7) and Home Office guidance states that '[w]here a person has a well-founded fear of persecution from a non-state actor – including 'rogue' state agents – internal relocation is likely to be an option to escape such risk', also referring to the existence of human rights group that 'operate without government restriction' and active 'LGBTI specific NGOs' (Home Office 2019). Yet, as the International Commission of Jurists points out, '[t]his approach is legally unsustainable. The responsibility to provide effective protection and ensure access to rights without discrimination rests on the relevant State and not on NGOs or *ad hoc* group of individuals who may themselves be under threat' (ICJ 2016, pp. 245–246).

Our participants also experienced or had been told of claimants being denied international protection on grounds of – according to decision-makers – being able to relocate internally within their country of origin, such as Cameroon and Zimbabwe (Irma; Sean, lawyer). On a more positive note, and indicating some recognition of the intersections of gender and sexuality (Chap. 3), the Home Office guidance acknowledges that relocation is also likely to be more difficult for lesbians and women in general (Home Office 2016, p. 36).

Once again Italian asylum adjudicators stand out among European states in not considering internal relocation as an alternative form of protection in the country of

---

[51] 2 K 4928 17.GI.A, 2 March 2018. Similarly, Court observation, Hesse, 2019.

[52] 1 K 6981/17.KS.A, 6 June 2018.

[53] See, for example, *The Secretary of State for the Home Department and SMR* [2018] UKAITUR PA059122017; *BF (Tirana – gay men) Albania* [2019] UKUT 0093 (IAC).

origin as the basis for denying recognition of refugee status.[54] This is the direct result of the Italian legislature's earlier choice not to transpose Article 8 of the Qualification Directive. Consequently, Italian authorities have not denied international protection on the basis that in some parts of the country of origin, such as larger cities, SOGI asylum claimants may live safely (Titti, decision-maker).

Although the 2018 reform introduced the potential for using internal relocation as an alternative to protection in Italy,[55] there are as yet no public records of this happening, including in SOGI cases. However, even before this reform, some decision-makers were considering the existence of supposedly safer areas in the country of origin as a relevant factor for the purposes of deciding what kind of protection to grant – refugee status, subsidiary protection or humanitarian protection (Maurizio, judge) – a legally dubious approach made worse by the low quality of COI (Chap. 6, Sect. 6.5).

Differences between the countries under comparison are again patent, highlighting the scope for variation despite EU harmonisation efforts. This is also evident in relation to evidentiary matters.

7.4   Proving Claims Based on SOGI

Both membership of a PSG and well-founded fear of persecution need to be considered as 'proven' by asylum decision-makers. 'To what extent' (Sect. 7.4.1), 'by whom' (Sect. 7.4.1) and 'through what means' (Sect. 7.4.2) are key questions here. Adjudicators also need to be convinced of the overall 'credibility' of the claim (Sect. 7.5). Although these questions are connected, in this section we separate them for analytical reasons and explore them in the context of SOGI asylum.

7.4.1   Standard and Burden of Proof

The first question we consider is 'to what extent' SOGI asylum claims need to be proven. In other words: What is the standard of proof? The UNHCR offers some guidance in this respect, stating, in relation to persecution, that:

> In general, the applicant's fear should be considered well-founded if he can establish, to reasonable degree, that his continued stay in his country of origin has become intolerable to him for the reasons stated in the definition, or would for the same reasons be intolerable if he returned there (UNHCR 2011, para. 42).

---

[54] Supreme Court, decision no. 2294, 16 February 2012 (in relation to an asylum claim based on religious belief) and judgment no. 15781, 10 July 2014.

[55] Article 32(1)(b-ter) of the Procedure Decree, inserted by Decree Law no. 113/2018 (converted into Law no. 132, 1 December 2018), so-called 'Decreto Salvini'.

The standard of proof is therefore 'reasonable degree', also applied in the European context (EASO 2018). This is acknowledged in all three countries under comparison. In Italy, for example, we were told that the 'UNHCR manual [Handbook and Guidelines on Procedures and Criteria for Determining Refugee Status] speaks of a reasonable level of probability, even just a 5% chance of a person being killed [means that they] must be protected' (Roberto, decision-maker). In the UK, there is also – theoretically – a low standard of proof for SOGI asylum claims, as for other asylum claimants:

> The level of proof needed to establish the material facts is a relatively low one – a reasonable degree of likelihood – and must be borne in mind throughout the process. It is low because of what is potentially at stake – the individual's life or liberty – and because asylum seekers are unlikely to be able to compile and carry dossiers of evidence out of the country of persecution. "Reasonable degree of likelihood" is a long way below the criminal standard of "beyond reasonable doubt", and it is less than the civil standard of "the balance of probabilities" (i.e. "more likely than not"). Other terms may be used: "a reasonable likelihood" or, "a real possibility", or "real risk"; they all mean the same (Home Office 2015, p. 11).

In practice, decision-makers often apply a higher standard of proof, whether consciously or unconsciously:

> All those things combined mean that the Home Office and judges are forgetting the reasonable likelihood. Everything has to be proven to the Nth degree. It is not just a question of considering things. There are lots of plausibility issues. "This wouldn't have happened and you wouldn't have done this." The law on asylum more generally is pretty clear that you shouldn't really be using plausibility from your own perspective, whoever the decision-maker is. Just because something might seem implausible to you or I doesn't mean it didn't happen. I think SOGI claims are not unique with that, but they are more susceptible to that (Allan, lawyer, UK).

Even Home Office presenting officers recognise this issue: 'Judges often use – I don't know if this is because they are on autopilot – they refer to balance of probabilities, when obviously they mean low risk' (Bilal).

We also found an acute neglect of the principle of the benefit of the doubt, a central tenet of IRL. On this principle, the UNHCR Handbook states that:

> 203. After the applicant has made a genuine effort to substantiate his story there may still be a lack of evidence for some of his statements. (…) it is hardly possible for a refugee to "prove" every part of his case and, indeed, if this were a requirement the majority of refugees would not be recognized. It is therefore frequently necessary to give the applicant the benefit of the doubt (UNHCR 2011).

Instead of systematically applying the principle of the benefit of the doubt, decision-makers seem to be vulnerable to 'case-hardening' and vicarious trauma, a concern identified in relation to SOGI claims (Gray and McDowall 2013, p. 25), and also to women claiming asylum on the basis of sexual violence (Baillot et al. 2012). The intersection of a number of factors may contribute to this, including: a culture of disbelief (Sect. 7.5); a 'hostile climate' to all migrants (Chap. 4); the pressure that all public bodies are under to deliver more with less resources; and the self-protection and defensive coping mechanisms that caseworkers and judges develop to enable them to do their work. All these factors may make it harder, on an individual level, for decision-makers to connect with claimants emotionally and really *hear* their accounts of persecution on a daily basis.

Although some decision-makers made an explicit reference to the principle of the benefit of the doubt (Titti, decision-maker, Italy), at lower levels of the decision-making process we found that this principle is often disregarded, confirming a historical trend (Millbank 2009b, p. 6). As we explore in detail in Sect. 7.5, caseworkers are too often still applying the inquisitorial approach of a criminal court, where truthfulness is equated with consistency in the detail of the defendant's narrative. In asylum claims, decision-makers tend to ignore factors such as the effect that trauma and the passage of time can have on memory of painful events (Cohen 2002; Herlihy and Turner 2007, 2009; Millbank 2009b, p. 12; Shidlo and Ahola 2013). In addition, cultural differences may make it harder to provide the details required for a coherent account according to European standards, such as dates of birthdays, anniversaries and first meetings, details which may have less significance from one country and culture to another.

Yet, at the level of policy, the principle of giving claimants the benefit of the doubt was defended:

> I think we should [use more the principle of the benefit of the doubt] (…) unless you have got very, very strong sort of evidence in terms of numbers or whatever that says to you "look, this is, this is something which now is being used as sort of, I don't know, evidence of abuse [of the system]" (…) if somebody has actually been willing to leave their country of origin, particularly if they have, they are somebody who has actually made one of the long and more tortuous journeys and has been willing to put themselves through that (…) there is no really strong reason to disbelieve it, you know, you are not being told something which just seems so incredible, or which doesn't add up (…) then I think that that balance of credibility side of it should be coming in (Jean, member of the European Parliament).

Some decision-makers also endorsed a more systematic use of the principle of the benefit of the doubt:

> when the claimant's personal story is considered coherent, plausible and sufficiently detailed with reference to what he declares about his [sexual] orientation and also about the country from which he came, then normally credibility is accepted and if there is a doubt, the benefit of the doubt is conceded. So, let's say, in doubt or in difficulty of establishing credibility, there is a tendency to favour the claimant. (…) protection must be recognised, even with the risk of making mistakes, granting the benefit of the doubt (Daniele, decision-maker, Italy).

The benefit of the doubt principle should be applied where there are minor 'inconsistencies' in claimants' testimonies (Silvana, judge, Italy), when assessing whether the required standard of proof has been reached. The claimant's testimony should be accepted as the 'default truth' – or believed in principle – unless there is evidence to the contrary.

A second question one needs to address in relation to 'proving' SOGI asylum claims is who should provide proof; in other words, who has the burden of producing the evidence needed to make the claimant's case. In this regard, the UNHCR Guidelines establish that:

while the burden of proof in principle rests on the applicant, the duty to ascertain and evaluate all the relevant facts is shared between the applicant and the examiner. Indeed, in some cases, it may be for the examiner to use all the means at his disposal to produce the necessary evidence in support of the application (UNHCR 2011, para. 196).

However, because of the tendency on the part of some decision-makers to view SOGI claims with suspicion, they may (wrongly) transfer the full burden of proof to the claimant (Helena, EASO staff member).

In Germany, asylum claimants have a legal duty to cooperate in the asylum procedure. This includes giving a 'coherent' and 'complete' account of the 'events falling into his own sphere, in particular his personal experiences'.[56] Similarly, in the UK, it is the duty of the claimant to submit all material factors and the account should be 'internally consistent and coherent' (Home Office 2015). Italian asylum authorities, however, adopt a more balanced approach, with the Supreme Court recognising that the burden of proof must be shared between the claimant and relevant authorities.[57] Decision-makers are, therefore, called upon to collect all relevant proof aimed to ascertain claimants' testimonies (including their SOGI) and to verify the legislation on SOGI minorities in force in their home countries.[58] As affirmed by the Supreme Court, judges may not dismiss an asylum request solely for reasons of credibility, particularly so where decision-makers did not share the burden of proof with the claimant and play an active role in acquiring the necessary information to confirm the account of the claimant.[59] This does not mean that decision-makers need to support claimants' efforts to prove their SOGI. The Supreme Court stated in a subsequent case that the judge should collaborate in collecting information when the situation of SOGI minorities in the country of origin is not fully clear, but that the judge cannot be asked to take a proactive role in verifying the claimant's SOGI (where verification is seen to be required).[60] This approach should result in better treatment for SOGI claimants in Italy than in the other countries under comparison, but decision-makers have been critical of actual practice in Italy:

> there is a reversal of the burden of proof... as if we started from the assumption that it [the testimony] is not true, of no credibility and we ask the asylum claimant to prove their homosexuality. The approach is then permeated, in my opinion, by a fairly veiled homophobic attitude (Maria Grazia, decision-maker).

However, there have been suggestions for using the reversal of the burden of proof in asylum law in a more benign way, as is the case in discrimination law (Network of Legal Experts in the Non-Discrimination Field 2015). One of our participants argued that we should reverse the burden of proof and demonstrating lack of credibility should be the responsibility of the authorities (Philippe, European

---

[56] Federal Administrative Court, 26 October 1989, 9 B 405.89.

[57] Supreme Court, judgment no. 27310, 17 November 2008; decision no. 9946, 19 April 2017; decision no. 267, 9 January 2020.

[58] See, for example, Tribunal of Venice, decision of 24 February.

[59] Supreme Court, decision no. 26921, 28 September 2017.

[60] Supreme Court, decision no. 10549, 12 January 2018.

7.4 Proving Claims Based on SOGI

Commission staff member). This would be a bold, but certainly interesting avenue of reform, which might re-balance the power dynamics in the asylum process.

7.4.2 Types of Evidence

Having established what standard of proof and burden of proof are in question in relation to SOGI asylum claims, we need to now consider what types of evidence can be used in this context. As the individual's SOGI is central to these asylum claims, it is to be expected that evidence regarding that aspect of the claim is a crucial part of the process. How one proves one's SOGI has been a conundrum ever since international protection regimes started to recognise SOGI minorities, one that may never be satisfactorily resolved. Allan described how, in SOGI claims, 'proof' is not always available. If people are marginalised, if they are not sociable, then '[t]hey don't really have any evidence to show that they are LGBT. I think SOGI claims are more likely to suffer from that problem than other claims' (Allan, lawyer, UK).

Let us start by considering what role SOGI self-identification plays in this process. In light of the diversity across asylum claimants in terms of cultural background, national origin, ethnic group, SOGI, etc., it would arguably be more sensible and compatible with the theoretical and analytical frameworks delineated in Chap. 3 to rely, as default, on claimants' SOGI self-identification:

> in the asylum procedure, I believe, people look for templates, to create these templates and then recognise [international protection]. (...) we somehow have people not only from the countries well known through the media, but people also come from Benin and Nicaragua, from Russia, from Georgia. And if I know that cultural expressions can be so different, even identities can be so different, then I do not try to grant [international protection] to people on the basis of a few templates, but simply according to how they describe and place themselves (Mariya, NGO worker, Germany).

Some of our participants also argued for self-identification to work as the 'principle' on the basis that no-one's 'gaydar' is infallible (Frank S., legal advisor, Germany). A German judge put this idea across in quite simple, but cogent terms:

> I cannot tell [if someone is really gay or lesbian]. If they tell me that, then that's it. What, how should I ask now? You cannot query love! Yes! [laughs] That's it. If someone asks me whether I love my wife, I'd say "Yes." Whether that's true, no one knows exactly (Oscar, judge).

Yet, relying on self-identification was not seen as sufficient by all our participants:

> it presumes that the environment would be conducive to someone who would feel comfortable in self-identifying potentially. I guess by self-identifying it means proactively giving the information. (...) I think that would be welcome in the case where the person was totally cognisant of his or her sexual orientation and they felt no external pressure in which to divulge this information to an unknown person. (...) I just think that there is a stage beforehand in which the environment has to be... the individual has to be totally in the know about

their rights and about… which then also relies on the legal assistance, and legal information (…) I think self-identification works if the conditions are right, but [not] for people who might, may be extraordinarily hesitant to provide the information willingly (Amanda, NGO worker, Brussels).

A more balanced approach, some participants argued, is required:

I know there are schools of thought that say it [credibility assessment] should rely purely on self-identification, and that if a person says I am… gay, I am lesbian, I am trans, that it should be accepted as such. I can absolutely see the logic and the reasonings behind that, but I can also see where the opposition would come, in that this becomes open to abuse, because if people start saying that people are coming from a certain country, who identify themselves as being LGBTI, automatically get asylum, you open up essentially the door to anyone being able to claim this. And in the long run then that becomes harmful for people who genuinely need support, because you will at some point get backlash and you will at some point essentially create mistrust that basically anyone coming and claiming "this [claimant] is not telling the truth and is just an opportunist" (Jules, staff member at ILGA-Europe).

Whether or not self-identification should be the default starting point for SOGI asylum claims, in reality this is clearly not the approach generally adopted by asylum authorities. While it is recognised that self-perception and self-identification should be at the centre of analysis (Helena, EASO staff member), officials also argue that there has to be some kind of independent standard of proof, requiring additional questions; it is not enough for a claimant to say that they are gay and from a country where there is criminalisation of same-sex acts (Philippe, European Commission staff member).

In Germany, when decision-makers assess the overall credibility of a claim (Sect. 7.5), they also consider claimants' self-identification but have, in the past, also scrutinised the claimant on whether their sexuality is 'reversible', as in this case decided by the Administrative Court of Trier: 'In the present case, on the basis of the impression made at the hearing, the Chamber of Appeal came to the conclusion that the applicant's submission that he had been irreversibly homosexual since puberty was credible'.[61] In Italy, self-identification plays some role in the decision-making but, as already explored, decision-makers are called upon to play an active role in obtaining the necessary information to confirm the claimant's account.[62] Finally, in the UK, caseworkers and interviewers are instructed to ensure they establish all material facts and the interview should sensitively explore the claimant's self-identified SOGI (Home Office 2016, p. 26). The Gender Identity guidance also states that self-identification should be the starting point in the process, and that individuals may not have felt able to disclose their gender identity at the screening interview (Home Office 2011). SOGI self-identification remains, however, subject to scrutiny

---

[61] Administrative Court of Trier, 17 January 2013, 2 K 730/12.TR, p. 11.
[62] Supreme Court, decision no. 9946, 19 April 2017.

7.4 Proving Claims Based on SOGI

in all three countries under comparison, and self-identification is only the 'starting point', as defended by the CJEU in *A, B and C*.[63]

Consequently, asylum authorities generally expect evidence to substantiate not only the claimed SOGI, but also other aspects of the claim. The nature of the evidence submitted by SOGI asylum claimants has been much debated. The CJEU took the opportunity to introduce some clarity by precluding evidence that would undermine the dignity and privacy of asylum claimants (Ferreira and Venturi 2017, 2018). These include sexualised evidence or stereotyped assessments (including medical tests such as phallometric testing and explanation of sexual practices),[64] as well as projective personality tests.[65] However, the Court has not provided positive authoritative guidance on what types of evidence *are* appropriate, and accordingly, there is considerable variation between each country in this respect.

Detailed oral submissions provided by SOGI claimants in their substantive asylum interview remain the main form of evidence used as the basis of decision-making in Germany, Italy and the UK. In Germany, advisors generally warn against personal written statements, to avoid the risk that the BAMF find the claimant's story has been carefully fabricated ahead of the interview (Marlen, legal advisor). In Italy, the focus is generally placed on the coherence and the consistency of the personal story as reported by claimants. Detailed testimonies are also the standard expectation in the UK:

> They are asked things like "how did you first know that you were gay?"… and they are expected to give a detailed explanation of what their feelings were, at that time. So you can imagine somebody that is suddenly thrown into an interview, with a language barrier, with trauma, mental health problems, not knowing whether this person is going to be sympathetic and they may not be sympathetic. So there is all these barriers that make it difficult for them to say as much as they need to say, because they are expected to give a lot of detail (Debbie, NGO volunteer).

> if they've given you more than a few lines, OK, "can you tell me more about that?" and probe to try to get as much detail out of them as possible (…). At the end of the day, if they can provide you with that detail, you can't say them having or not having a relationship is against them, you wouldn't, it's not a tick box (Emily, decision-maker).

Many SOGI claimants strongly resented the need to provide detailed testimonies on intimate matters as evidence of their SOGI, pointing out the discriminatory nature of this expectation: 'if I was straight I wouldn't answer this question because it is feelings, it is deep down how you felt, your emotions (…) I don't think a straight person would actually answer those questions' (Ali, UK).

Other written evidence, such as relevant certificates and documents in possession of the claimant, should also be submitted. This is the case in Germany (Nina, legal

---

[63] Joined Cases C-148/13 to C-150/13, *A, B and C v Staatssecretaris van Veiligheid en Justitie*, 2 December 2014, ECLI:EU:C:2014:2406.

[64] Ibid.

[65] Case C-473/16, *F. v Bevándorlási és Állampolgársági Hivatal*, 25 January 2018, ECLI:EU:C:2018:36.

advisor), but some claimants felt that the BAMF had unreasonable expectations in relation to evidence of persecution and discrimination in the country of origin:

> [One suffers attacks] And you ask me for that evidence here? Really? It is not fair. There is no way somebody could get such evidence. No way. So it is one thing I would emphasise, BAMF should look at that the evidence that it asks for people, normally it is hard to get. Or people were not in the position of getting it. You are running for your life, you're in big trauma, you're in fear and now you're taking selfie or you're recording voices? (Alphaeus).

In Italy, claimants are also expected to bring before the territorial commissions all the information and documentation at their disposal to support their claims, even if this is not an essential requirement for the recognition of refugee status. In the UK, it was found that there was an unreasonable expectation to produce documents from the country of origin. Lubwa, for example, told us: 'So if they expect me to produce documents from back home, it is like they literally don't want me to go ahead with interview anyway' (focus group no. 1, Manchester). Milton also felt strongly about this matter:

> If someone claim[s] asylum, coming from Africa, or any part of the world, why did you expect such person to bring evidence? What kind of evidence am I going to bring when I am in danger? I remember the day I was coming, there is blood, I can show you my leg, blood here. So I cannot get evidence, which evidence they want me to bring, where I am in critical condition? (focus group no. 2, Glasgow).

This issue may be compounded by the costs of translation (Chap. 6, Sect. 6.6), with one participant explaining he did not submit emails in Arabic as evidence 'because we needed to pay for translation and they [legal representatives] couldn't afford it' (Selim).

The testimony of supporting witnesses is accepted in all countries under comparison, and partners can also be interviewed as witnesses. Nonetheless, decision-makers' attitude to supporting witnesses can be ambivalent. As Umar (legal advisor, UK) explained, judges will view the failure to call witnesses in a negative light, yet 'the point about that is that you call the witnesses, and the judges ignore the witnesses, because there is no direct evidence of the person being gay because of what the witnesses have said'.

Moreover, the expectations relating to some witnesses, particularly children, can be inappropriate to the point of inhumanity:

> I didn't even make an effort to bring my son to court, because I didn't know that him coming or not would have an impact on my case. So, in my refusal they said "oh, you didn't bring your son to court because you didn't want him to be questioned". I didn't know. I didn't know that if I come with my son to court, I personally as a parent, I was just protecting my son because I was thinking it is a sexuality case, I don't want this kind of things to be discussed in front of my teenage son. I didn't want, like, because I have a teenage son who I conceived through rape, I didn't want such kind of things to be discussed in front of people because how that will affect my son, knowing that people just know that kind of information about him. Kind of protecting him in a way (Jayne, UK).

In line with our analysis in Chap. 6 (Sect. 7.2), evidence related to NGOs also plays an important role in SOGI asylum claims, but the probative value of NGO statements may be challenged. Participants in Germany, for example, reported that

7.4 Proving Claims Based on SOGI

NGOs' supporting statements are generally disregarded, as they are seen as 'partisan'; this was judged as 'absurd' and just like ignoring 'medical evidence', especially in light of the dramatic consequences that asylum decisions possess (Sofia, NGO worker). Some NGOs are also conscious that supporting statements may be used against claimants, where they contain contradictions or information that decision-makers can use against claimants (Thomas, NGO volunteer). There is a concern that the more such statements are provided, the less probative value they are accorded (Sofia and Emma, NGO workers; Court observation, Hesse 2018). Decision-makers may also express scepticism about NGO supporting statements because they do not prove anything in relation to country of origin conditions (Oscar, judge).

In Italy, NGO supporting evidence has most often consisted of confirmation of claimants' membership of LGBTIQ+ associations. Such membership has played an overly prominent role in the recognition of refugee status or some form of international protection, sometimes practically ensuring credibility (Antonella, LGBTIQ+ group volunteer; Titti, decision-maker; Celeste, social worker; Tribunal observation, northern Italy, 2018). For example, in one case involving a gay man from Nigeria, membership of a local gay association was deemed essential to confirm his sexual orientation.[66] The need for such 'associative evidence' is such that some associations have been approached by claimants who have been told by judges that they needed to obtain evidence of involvement with LGBTIQ+ associations, regardless of the claimant's individual interests, past experience or desire to be socially or politically active in this way (Nicola and Giulio, LGBTIQ+ group volunteers). Such practices are in obvious tension with the queer theoretical approach we advocate, as they contribute to prescriptive forms of identity and 'performance', effectively limiting claimants' freedom to express their SOGI as they wish. Some decision-makers are thus critical of the simplistic way in which some territorial commissions treat evidentiary requirements, such as membership cards:

> you do not need to reach a full certainty of the claimant's sexual orientation. I don't have a gaydar to help me tell you exactly from the statements or from the demeanour [whether the claimant is LGBTIQ+]… there is no decisive proof. This is a very current debate in the Italian [territorial] commissions: "You don't have an Arcigay [national LGBTIQ+] card", "You don't have relationships here", "You don't attend groups" or the other way around… Not in this commission, but in many commissions, for sure (Roberto, decision-maker).

> We use – *in addition* – the fact that in Italy [claimants] attend associations for the protection of gay rights, which is not at all essential, it is not a necessary element. However, the same [UNHCR] guidelines say that this is an element to evaluate, the fact that he [the claimant] consciously chose to attend an association. So, the gay association membership card is irrelevant, but it can be significant that the head of the [gay] centre *voluntarily* produces a statement, makes a statement to us saying that for a year, for six months, he [claimant] attended [the gay centre] (Silvana, judge).

---

[66] Tribunal of Naples, decision 25 October 2013.

We found some NGOs only offered membership cards to claimants who were clearly involved in the activities of the organisation in question (Maria Grazia, decision-maker). Nevertheless, membership cards should not be seen as indispensable evidence in SOGI claims. As Giulia (LGBTIQ+ group volunteer) pointed out, 'one is not any less gay' for not frequenting an LGBTIQ+ organisation. We heard evidence that practice in this respect is changing:

> in relation to the membership cards, for example, they [decision-makers] have come to understand that whoever has the card, that only means that a person espouses the ideals of an associative project and not that he is a gay, lesbian, bisexual or trans person. But it took [them] some time to understand this, and this led to something. It led to that reductionism, that analogy "possession of card = possession of identity" among decision-makers (Vincenzo, LGBTIQ+ group volunteer).

In place of simply establishing membership, more elaborate statements from associations, produced on the basis of several meetings with claimants where their testimonies are explored, are now routinely submitted to territorial commissions and courts (Tribunal observation, northern Italy, 2018).[67] Such lengthier declarations are deemed increasingly important and, when no other evidence is submitted, even crucial (Daniele, decision-maker). Some decision-makers, however, remain sceptical of the probative value of any declaration from such associations:

> I value them as a statement from an employer… who can give me some sort of reference. Indeed, I would rate it in slightly lower terms. These [declarations] are indications, but they cannot establish an assessment of the reliability of the homosexual orientation (Maurizio, judge).

In the UK, NGO supporting statements are also often submitted by claimants, but may be dismissed by the Home Office, on the basis that it would be easy to 'fake' one's sexuality for the purposes of obtaining such a statement (Upper Tier Tribunal observation, London, 2018). Judges may also find NGO testimonials unconvincing, confirmed by both our participants and our past research (Held 2017):

> I wrote a letter and I said that I had seen them together and that they treated each other with affection, fondness and kindness, like lots of couples that I know. That is the wording I chose to use and that is because I didn't want to be too explicit, didn't want to talk too intimately about them. In the refusal even the judge said that my, the letter that I wrote could have been interpreted as just non-romantic friends. So it wasn't explicit enough, essentially (Chloe, NGO worker).

Evidence of a (physical or mental) medical nature may also be submitted; however, the weight given to such reports, especially when diagnosing PTSD (Chap. 9), has been a matter of debate (AIDA 2017, p. 46). In Germany, reports by psychotherapists or psychologists to assess the claimant's sexual orientation can positively contribute to the case where credibility is questioned (Zouhair; focus group no. 6, Lower Saxony, Germany). Yet, according to one participant, their probative value has diminished over time (Sabrina, NGO worker), and they can also be problematic

---

[67] See, also, Tribunal of Milan, decision of 18 October 2017; Tribunal of Venice, decision of 14 June 2016; La Migration (2018).

7.4 Proving Claims Based on SOGI

if they are used to confirm an 'irreversible homosexual disposition', especially after the CJEU's decision in the *F* case.[68]

In Italy, territorial commissions operate on the basis of generally not requesting evidence of a medical or psychiatric nature (Daniele, decision-maker). It is, however, possible to request medical exams with the consent of the claimant where it is necessary to prove the persecution previously suffered. Claimants are also free to submit psycho-social reports, often produced by professionals at reception centres, which may discuss: the process of 'coming out' for the claimant; trauma associated with their life in the country of origin, departure and journey to Europe; SOGI and related therapeutic issues; and 'vulnerabilities' and needs. These reports are particularly useful to pre-empt possible negative assessments of credibility when claimants have not offered clear, thorough or consistent testimonies (Titti, decision-maker; Chiara, NGO worker). However, it is important to avoid any inconsistency between the content of such reports and what the claimant says during the asylum interview (Giuseppe, lawyer; Mara, lawyer).[69]

In the UK, it is acknowledged that medical reports can help decision-makers, especially at appeal level, understand better elements of testimonies and demeanour that are related to PTSD or other past traumatic or violent experiences, rather than indicating lack of credibility (Ashley, psychotherapist). Yet, there are concerns that the authority of such medical reports and their authors is not sufficiently recognised by authorities (Freedom from Torture 2016).

We were told that evidence of a sexual nature (such as video recordings and pictures of sexual intercourse) was no longer submitted or expected in any of our case study countries, rightly recognising SOGI claimants' rights to dignity and privacy. Yet, while all asylum authorities may now be formally compliant with European law and guidance here, many participants reported inappropriate questioning about claimants' sexual lives. In Germany, although detailed questions about sexual practices are inadmissible (BAMF 2017), questions asked in the interview have included: 'When did you start having sex? Why did you prefer to have a man, instead of-? How many people have you slept with?' (Alphaeus), 'Are you top or bottom? What apps do you use to meet men?' (Marlen, legal advisor), 'How did you feel when you made first time sex with him?' (Prince Emrah); 'Have you ever had sex with a man? How do you feel when you're having sex with a man?' (Jolly, focus group no. 3, Bavaria); 'How lesbian sex looks like in practice' (Sofia and Emma, NGO workers); what claimants 'do with their partners', why they 'kissed in a car' (Halim), and details about a rape experience (Diana). One participant even asserted that '[s]ome people do [submit naked pictures to BAMF]. I've had people that have given them when they are having sex. Pictures. Nude pictures. And they have negatives [decisions]. Someone said that "he is not [gay]"' (Alphaeus). These reports from Germany were confirmed by our survey (C36). Similar questions were asked at

---

[68] Case C-473/16, *F. v Bevándorlási és Állampolgársági Hivatal*, 25 January 2018, ECLI:EU:C:2018:36.

[69] See, also, Tribunal of Florence, decision of 15 November 2018.

appeal level (Court observation, Hesse, 2019), even in cases where judges are empathic and supportive (Court observations, Hesse, 2018, 2019). Such lines of questioning are not only a violation of claimants' fundamental rights (Chap. 3) and illegal in the light of the CJEU's jurisprudence, they are also traumatising:

> So I was so annoyed that I even asked the lady [interviewer], I was like, "will it be okay if I asked you if you have ever slept with a man?" I know it was so negative that it maybe could have contributed to maybe 70% of my negative that I received. Because some of the questions were so annoying. (…) And I'm still traumatised. I'm still thinking of how I am supposed to align myself. I mean, yes, I will be open, I will tell you everything, but when you tell me "there are certain questions we do not ask you on your interview about [your] life", remember I lost my partner. And some of my friends are still on the run (Amis, focus group no. 2, Bavaria, Germany).

Trans claimants in Germany also reported feeling particularly disturbed by very intimate questions about the degree of gender-affirming interventions they had undergone (Bebars; Diana).

Similarly, in Italy, we heard reports of questions of a sexual nature, such as 'how was your first [same-sex sexual] experience?' (Silver, Italy), and a judge asking a claimant 'were you bottom or top?', after the claimant described a sexual encounter (Nazarena, lawyer). Giuseppe, a lawyer, also reported that:

> More than anything else, there is this insistence on purely personal aspects of one's sexual life, obviously they do not ask what you do in terms of sexual practices, but they are rather insistent on questions about what you did, where you were, how many boyfriends you had, how many boyfriends you have had sex with, have you had sexual intercourse for money, has it ever happened to you, that is, rather invasive questions.

For the most part, however, decision-makers seem to have abandoned questions of a sexual nature: 'Here is a question *not* to ask: "tell me about your first sexual relationship"; "It happened when I was twenty years old"; "So what happened exactly?"' (Titti, decision-maker). More generally:

> expecting that these people, in face of a stranger, who is sometimes even a female stranger – which, in my opinion, for a migrant who comes from Africa can constitute a further issue – can, in a free and uninhibited way, tell us about their sexual adventures, frankly, it seems quite ridiculous to me (Filippo, senior judge).

Italian decision-makers now focus more on questions related to the 'discovery' of one's sexual orientation. The questions that recurred were related to when the claimant found out they were gay and how that made them feel. Some decision-makers have highlighted the need to understand the cultural differences that affect sexual experiences and identities:

> I have met homosexual people who come from Pakistan, who live homosexuality in a very different way from how they live in the West. I don't know if they call themselves homosexuals… they spoke of having had a homosexual experience and, because of that homosexual experience, having experienced social condemnation, a form of persecution… very different from how homosexuality would be lived by a person from Western countries. And so it is also different in Africa (Maria Grazia, decision-maker).

7.4 Proving Claims Based on SOGI

Social workers also confirmed this, underlining the culturally biased nature of some questions:

> They were very Western questions (…) I remember a girl from Cameroon who was asked: "What does it mean for a young Cameroonian woman to be homosexual?" It is not an easy question. It is a very complex question, which presupposes that a person is self-aware, has accepted [their sexuality], and is not traumatised and has the logical ability to formulate a thought and say what "for me" is to be as they are (Celeste, social worker).

In the UK, evidence of sexual nature has had a particularly turbulent history. In 2013, there were reports of gay asylum claimants filming themselves having sex to prove their claim (Elgot 2013; Hall 2013). The same year, UKLGIG found that despite improvements since 2010, Home Office caseworkers were continuing to ask inappropriate questions about sexual activities (UKLGIG 2013). Highly inappropriate questions being asked in some asylum interviews were also highlighted in the media, including 'When x was penetrating you did you have an erection?' and 'What is it about the way men walk that turns you on?' (Taylor and Townsend 2014). In response to all these problematic practices, the government commissioned an independent report by the Chief Inspector of Borders and Immigration on the handling of claims based on sexual orientation (but not gender identity) (ICIBI 2014). The Vine report found that more than 10% of the questions asked in SOGI claims were 'unsatisfactory', such as '[w]hat sexual activities did you do with your girlfriends?' (ICIBI 2014, p. 24) A leading barrister in this field has also cited a case from the same year in which a Court of Appeal judge indicated that he would view a DVD with evidence of sexual behaviour (Yeo 2016). The Vine report recommendations included improved training to avoid stereotyping in interview questions, ensuring that caseworkers do not ask sexually explicit questions and equipping them to cope with sexually explicit responses. The government accepted all of the recommendations. In line with the CJEU judgment in *X, Y and Z*, sexually explicit questioning is now explicitly forbidden in Home Office guidance, which goes so far as to provide a script for caseworkers in situations where they are presented with sexually explicit material, a script beginning 'Stop please. I am not going to ask you any detailed questions about sex' (Home Office 2016, p. 29). This has been confirmed to us by a decision-maker:

> a lot of people want to tell you, I think they feel, they want you to know, sexually explicit details, and you have to say straight away "that's not an aspect you need to tell me about, that's not something I'm going to consider" (Emily, decision-maker).

Yet, like in Germany or Italy, there is no independent complaint office that SOGI claimants can approach if interviewers ask personal, intrusive questions. Furthermore, Beth, a lawyer has highlighted that:

> POs [Home Office Presenting Officers in appeal hearings] are still asking intimate, unnecessary questions which do not respect our clients' dignity and do not further the issues, there also is still a real emphasis on actual sexual experiences, which is contrary to the guidance – sometimes the questioning almost appears gratuitous or prying, which is unwarranted and a misapplication of the law.

Another demeaning and humiliating form of evidence we heard was expected, while not routinely required, was for claimants to display scars. In Germany, showing scars during the interview with the BAMF is unexceptional according to one participant (Trudy Ann), violating the claimant's right to privacy and human dignity, and potentially causing re-traumatisation. Ibrahim told us of an instance of this practice:

> The other question which he [interviewer] did – and he is not allowed to do it, because I gave him pictures of my scars, pictures from my surgery and everything – he told me "is this your scar?" I told him "yes, this is my scar". He told me "let me see it". And this is not his right, but at some point, to be honest… I knew this was not his right, but I did not realise it, because you are in a moment to prove your right to stay. So you will feel weak, to be honest. You feel weak, you do what they want you to do, just to prove that you have to stay here. So I had to take off my trousers and let him see my scar.

In Italy, too, we were told of instances where territorial commissions asked claimants to undress to show their scars: 'I have some scar on my back owing to my story, I was asked to undress to see; I undressed, they looked, they really confirmed' (Fred). This has rightly been criticised by a judge that we interviewed:

> The judge, in my view, should not even look at the scars, because that is an act against [the claimant's] human dignity. They [claimants] often want to show you their scars, but this is certainly an invasive thing that is absolutely not necessary (Silvana, judge).

More generally, claimants are routinely asked about past and current relationships, as well as questions of a 'romantic' or 'sentimental' nature, implying an expectation that claimants should be sexually active and in (or seeking to be in) an intimate relationship. This was the case across all our case study countries (Kadir, NGO worker, Germany; Leon, NGO worker, Germany; Nicola and Giulio, LGBTIQ+ group volunteers, Italy; Jayne, focus group no. 4, London, UK). In Italy, for example, Susanna, a social worker, told us of a claimant who was quickly granted international protection despite having children in his country of origin (which could have been seen to damage his credibility), mainly on account of evidence he gave of Facebook conversations and relationships with several men during the three-month period he had been in Italy. In situations where this kind of evidence is not available, territorial commissions explore other aspects of claimants' narratives:

> In fact, very recently, I'm noticing that they [territorial commissions] are asking different types of questions. No longer connected to "coming-out", of which they [some claimants] have no awareness, but linked to the way they were discovered when they were with one person rather than another, [the commissions being] aware of the zero level of schooling and lack of awareness, of the young age that makes it impossible for one to tell of a conscious experience (Silvana, judge).

This is more in line with the CJEU decision in F,[70] which emphasised the assessment of risk of persecution on account of one's – real or perceived – SOGI rather

---

[70] Case C-473/16, *F. v Bevándorlási és Állampolgársági Hivatal*, 25 January 2018, ECLI:EU:C:2018:36. For a comment, see Ferreira & Venturi (2018).

7.4 Proving Claims Based on SOGI

than ascertaining one's actual SOGI. In the UK, asylum authorities also expect evidence of relationships, which may then be disregarded:

> I put in pictures, they wanted, when I went for the interview they said they wanted pictures of me and my ex-girlfriend and I presented, they didn't want in their words anything explicit. So I took some holiday pictures and put it in there, and the judge said, they are just two women on a beach (Jayne, focus group no. 4, London).

Evidence may also include indications of the claimants' willingness to integrate, any signs of successful integration, and overall 'good character'. This is more clearly the case in Germany (Noah, NGO social worker) and in Italy, where the degree of integration in society is increasingly a factor mentioned in NGO supporting statements (Anna, LGBTIQ+ group volunteer), as it may contribute to a positive decision (Tribunal observation, northern Italy, 2018).

Decision-makers also rely on evidence from the internet, but this may not be appropriate or sensitive to different contexts. In Germany, for example, we were told that Google Maps may be relied on as a source, although the data is not always up-to-date or may include changes that occurred some years after the claimant left their country of origin (Alphaeus). In Italy, participants told us of commissions' often unrealistic expectation that relevant events will be reported by news agencies and on the internet. However, in any country (of origin or reception) there will be many incidents of violence or abuse that are not reported, especially when they take place in remote areas or areas controlled by non-governmental forces, where there is no internet connection, or where information is not made available on the internet for fear of persecution (Kennedy). Giulia, an LGBTIQ+ group volunteer, also shared with us what she had heard at an appeal hearing in this respect:

> The judge said, ah, that the guy, that it was not possible for him to have set up this LGBT anti-discrimination group because there was virtually no online record, because there is no evidence, and actually [claimant] said, "but how can I put that stuff online, if they arrested me is because I distributed flyers".

While asylum authorities expect to be given extensive evidence, they often dismiss it when they have it. For example, in Germany, SOGI claimants are asked about their involvement with LGBTIQ+ groups, but when pictures and videos of participation in Pride parades are submitted, they are often dismissed, for example, on the grounds that 'anyone can go to the Pride parade', ignoring the courage and risk involved in 'outing' oneself in this way (Gisela, lawyer; Elias, lawyer; decision regarding participant D33 in Held et al. 2018). The UK Home Office also adopts a selective approach to the way it considers evidence. For example, in the case of Lutfor, although both his statement and the report produced by the Helen Bamber Foundation stated that his father gave him money and told him to leave the country and not come back, the Home Office said: 'It is also noted that your father, brother and 4 sisters remain in Bangladesh, and there is no reason to suggest that they would not adequately support and assist you on return'. Joseph, an NGO volunteer, confirmed this selective approach to evidence by pointing out that:

often I notice with the Liverpool office, that letters from partners are ignored in the decision when it comes back. "We received this, this, this, this and this", and then no comment is made on the supportive bits and that is very common.

There is, therefore, much scope for improvement in relation to the types of evidence required, accepted and used by asylum authorities in all three countries under comparison. This has important implications for the outcome of the asylum adjudication process in contributing to the assessment of the credibility of the claim.

7.5 The Assessment of Credibility

Credibility assessment remains the single most contentious and problematic issue in the field of SOGI asylum. Despite endless debates, recommendations and reforms, consensual and good quality practices seem to be difficult to achieve (Gyulai et al. 2013; UNHCR 2013). According to UNHCR Guidance, '[c]redibility is established where the applicant has presented a claim which is coherent and plausible, not contradicting generally known facts, and therefore is, on balance, capable of being believed' (UNHCR 1998, para. 11). This includes internal credibility (consistency within the testimony) and external credibility (consistency between the testimony and publicly known information). The UNHCR adds that 'credibility should be assessed through individualized and sensitive questioning, using both open-ended and specific questions that are crafted in a non-judgemental manner' (UNHCR 2012, p. 62 ff).

This still leaves much leeway to domestic authorities as to how to use all the evidence collected to reach a decision on the credibility of SOGI claims, and decision-makers themselves are acutely aware of the risk of getting it wrong, both by refusing to grant international protection to someone who was entitled to it or by granting it to someone who was not entitled (Emilia, judge, Germany). The lack of resources prompts decision-makers to ignore the requirement for individualised credibility assessment and resort to 'staple' decisions:

there are three, four page forms, they are all copy-and-paste. That means that besides the individual rejection reasons, which are derived from the interview, one also finds copy-and-paste reasons. (…) Copy-and-paste answers that completely bypass the reality of life (Noah, NGO social worker, Germany).

Credibility is the basis of all asylum applications, but particularly difficult to ascertain in SOGI and gender-based claims, where persecution is likely to be undocumented, take place in private and often at the hands of family and other non-state actors. It is also worth pointing out that credibility is sometimes used to refer to the claim, and other times to refer to the claimant, even within the same document (UNHCR 2011). A legitimate claim is a credible claim, and a credible claimant is perceived to be a truthful claimant (Khan 2016, p. 217), but this imposes unrealistic expectations on claimants who will almost inevitably have had to use deceit of some kind to reach European soil. SOGI minorities will, by definition, have had to live

7.5 The Assessment of Credibility

covertly to some extent in their country of origin and have generally endured such traumatic experiences that they are unable to present their case to the standard required (Chap. 5).

Experiences may vary for different SOGI minority claimants. We were told that authorities:

> tend to find it easier with trans people, particularly trans people who are in some stage of medical transition, because there is a visible presentation... when it comes to sexual orientation that is extremely difficult (...) there is not necessarily any visual cue about the person's sexual orientation unless you start to rely on stereotypes. And stereotypes can never be consistent and that's where I think the bigger issue is at the moment (Jules, staff member at ILGA-Europe).

This was confirmed by our participants in different countries. In the UK, Allan, a lawyer, told us that 'generally with trans people there will be some sort of transition which will be visible so it's less likely that the decision-maker will disbelieve them on that'. Similarly, in Italy:

> for trans asylum seekers or in any case on the basis of gender identity, it is simpler than working with people who instead made the request on grounds of sexual orientation. Because, paradoxically, the medicalisation and the pathologisation of trans bodies allows us to demonstrate that we are indeed trans, with a lot of medical and psychological certificates, so when we reach the Commission, the road is open. In reality, paradoxically, trans people find no difficulty when applying for asylum. Instead, homosexual people have the difficulty that there is no scientific method to prove whether a person is homosexual or not. We must trust the story that a person presents (Valentina, social worker, Italy).

Trans claimants also acknowledge this trend:

> Fortunately, when I went to the [territorial] commission, I already had a beard, I had already started hormonal therapy a year and a half before... and how I dress, how I speak, so there is no doubt of what I said in that respect (Kamel, Italy).

Both SO and GI asylum claims, however, are subject to an assessment of credibility in all three countries under comparison, as even trans claimants only have an 'advantage' '[u]ntil a point that you are passing which, in which case it can become... something [of] a point against you' (Jules, staff member at ILGA-Europe; Sect. 7.3.2).

All three countries under comparison offer decision-makers some sort of guidance as to how to assess a claimant's credibility. In Germany, although such guidance is not publicly available, it is clear from BAMF decisions what decision-makers expect in order to consider a testimony credible: testimonies should be coherent, specific, detailed and vivid, ideally peppered with 'unnecessary, unusual and original details, which are usually hard to make up' (Decisions on case of participants DE17 and DE40 in Held 2018). Claimants' credibility is often challenged because of implausibility, inconsistency or lack of detail (BAMF decision appealed in Court observation, Hesse, 2018; Hübner 2016; Kalkmann 2010). Indeed, several of our participants in Germany saw their asylum claims refused on grounds of lack of credibility (for instance, William, Tina, Zouhair, Winifred, Veronica and Julia). The BAMF appears unable to deal with the complexity and variety of people's lives:

through the glasses of BAMF, just how drastic the narrative is, so… because not too many things must have happened… There is a woman who has, or there are now several women, but the most blatant case, one who has experienced forced prostitution in China, so from Uganda to China, then she had different [experiences], then fled to other African countries, where she was raped, and then [fled] again to Germany, where she has been almost forcibly prostituted. And… she is also lesbian, and with her partner, so to speak, and different things… escaped, and so, for the Federal Office, this is so blatant that it cannot be credible, such things. That's just too much, but it should not be too little either, so really you have to stop [at the point where] you really lose your partner, or you yourself almost got killed (Sofia and Emma, NGO workers).

Besides being expected to reach a 'perfect' degree of 'dramatic narrative' (something which may vary from decision-maker to decision-maker), the level of detail and consistency required of claimants is often also unreasonable in light of their personal circumstances: 'I can explain the suffering I went through because it happened to me. But it's the exact… these small, small things. (…) Sometimes you lose the dates. (…) Because of stress' (William).

In Italy, it has fallen to the high courts to offer some guidance. In a case related to a gay man from Nigeria, the Supreme Court established that the evaluation of an asylum request should be based on clear steps and objective criteria statutorily established. The evaluation should be made in light of the individual situation of claimants, including their social class, life experiences, sex, age, and the social context of their home country.[71] This should correspond with an intersectional approach to decision-making (Chap. 3), but whether it does is another matter. The Court also stated that contradictions related to secondary aspects of the claimant's account should not be given weight if the main event on which the claim is based is deemed credible. This should help to eliminate stereotyping and culturally-specific expectations from the Italian asylum system, but in practice that has not always happened. In relation to the notion of time, for example, commissions may have expectations based on Western conceptions that are damaging to claimants:

It is very important for an Italian, "what did you do on the fifteenth of January this year?", "What happened to you on the sixteen of January last year?" That, for an African man, is unthinkable to be able to understand, to have the same time line as a European. For them, time does not exist as we understand it. I often noticed that with the men [claimants], I give them an appointment at four, of course, for him, at four it means that day, it does not mean at four o'clock that day. So it is very complicated, it is very difficult to succeed, in the Commission, to be linear as they wish (Valentina, social worker).

Elsewhere in this section we see how Western stereotypes affect SOGI claims in other ways (Sect. 7.5.1).

In the UK too, the existence of good guidance does not necessarily lead to high-quality credibility assessment. Both the 2016 Sexual Orientation guidance (Home Office 2016) and the 2011 Gender Identity guidance (Home Office 2011) emphasise many of the issues that campaigners and advocates have raised, including in relation to credibility assessment. For example, they stress that the claimant's credibility is

---

[71] Supreme Court, decision no. 26969, 24 October 2018; Article 3(5) of the Legislative decree no. 251/2007.

not necessarily undermined by having had opposite-sex relationships or children. The Gender Identity guidance points out that where there is intolerance of non-conformity in gender behaviour, there is also likely to be intolerance of trans people (Home Office 2011, p. 15). However, these guidance instruments are not adequately applied. Credibility assessment in the UK has been found to be 'particularly poor' in relation to SOGI claimants (House of Commons Home Affairs Committee 2013, p. 27). Although after 2010 there seemed to be better protection for individuals fleeing persecution on the basis of their SOGI owing to the limitations imposed on the 'discretion requirement' (Sect. 7.3.2), in practice, claimants found credibility had become the new obstacle to recognition of their claims. 2010 has thus come to be seen as the year when the message to SOGI asylum claimants changed from 'be discreet about your sexual orientation' to 'prove that you are gay', similar to experience in Australian SOGI asylum law (Millbank 2009a). This has shifted the assessment of credibility towards elements related to membership of a PSG, rather than persecution. The Vine report found an almost complete correlation between whether a claimant was accepted as LGB and whether they were granted international protection (ICIBI 2014, p. 34). Time and again refusal letters and subsequent rejections at appeal are based on decision-makers not believing claimants' SOGI. Current practices also seem to reflect a medical and pathological notion of non-heterosexuality:

> The Home Office approach seeks answers, rather than understanding. An interrogative approach that addresses the curiosity of the questioner is framed from their perspective (and consequently, their assumptions and prejudices). By seeking factual verification, this empirical approach, in my experience, is founded on a perception of homosexuality that is deeply rooted in a medical model, and seeks evidence of it as a pathology (Fletcher 2017, p. 230).

The existence of administrative or judicial guidance is thus not a guarantee that credibility assessment is carried out to an appropriately high standard. This can be seen in the persistent use of stereotypes regarding what it means to be a member of a SOGI minority (Sect. 7.5.1), expectations about how a member of a SOGI minority should express and experience their SOGI publicly (Sect. 7.5.2), and the way that asylum authorities often deny claimants the right to provide clarification of their narrative, thus promoting a culture of disbelief (Sect. 7.5.3).

7.5.1 Stereotyping 'Gayness'

Individual prejudices and Eurocentric understandings of SOGI still plague asylum adjudication systems, polluting credibility assessments, as confirmed by Helena (EASO staff member) as well as Jules (staff member at ILGA-Europe): 'when it comes to sexual orientation, I think there is still an expectation of performance. Of performing certain stereotypes'. The use of inappropriate, culturally-biased and even offensive stereotypes in RSD has been extensively documented. As most decision-makers have a Western, heteronormative outlook on the world, claimants need to comply with certain norms in order to be perceived as credible (Gartner 2016). These stereotypes and norms include expectations of a 'coming out' narrative, identification with the opposite/another gender, involvement with LGBTIQ+ activism, attendance at LGBTIQ+ social and nightlife spaces, familiarity with LGBTIQ+ culture, being sexually active according to the self-identified SOGI, and not ever having had heterosexual partners or children (Bennett and Thomas 2013; Fernandez 2017, p. 202). Failure to meet all or most of these stereotypes may be punished with failure to recognise PSG membership or, more generally, denial of credibility. Conversely, meeting all these stereotypes too neatly may be seen as a sign of fabrication or dramatisation, which may also mean the claimant is found not credible (Batchelor 2018). For the claimant, it can feel like a no-win situation.

Our fieldwork confirmed that many of these stereotypes are still pervasive, as well as unearthing other stereotypes that affect credibility assessment. Across all our country case studies, decision-makers' personal attitudes and prejudices impact on findings of credibility (Court observations, Hesse, Germany, 2019; Nicola and Giulio, LGBTIQ+ group volunteers, Italy; Valentina, social worker, Italy; Gary and Debbie, NGO workers, UK; Oliver, NGO worker, UK). Our participants also spoke about decision-makers having various degrees of sympathy towards claimants and the impact that this has on credibility assessment (Emilia, judge, Germany). Our findings relating to the use of stereotypes by decision-makers correspond to those of a survey conducted in North Rhine-Westphalia, Germany: 22.5% of the 40 respondents who had claimed asylum on SOGI grounds met stereotypes in their interviews (Held et al. 2018).

We heard that many decision-makers are influenced by their first 'visual impression' of the claimants and their stereotypes of what an LGBTIQ+ person looks like (Frank S., legal advisor, Germany; Noah, NGO social worker, Germany; Louis, NGO volunteer, Germany). Clothes and demeanour play a critical role here, with decision-makers sometimes being more inclined to believe 'camp' male claimants and 'butch' female claimants (Thomas, NGO volunteer, Germany; Kadir, NGO worker, Germany; Sabrina, NGO worker, Germany; focus group no. 6, Lower Saxony, Germany; Gary and Debbie, NGO volunteers, UK; Oliver, NGO worker, UK). One participant reported being told by the interviewer that '[y]ou don't look so gay'. He was aware that members of an LGBTIQ+ group which he frequented had a 100% success rate where claimants attended the interview wearing make-up and female clothes; conversely, gay claimants with a 'mannish' appearance were less likely to obtain a positive decision (Zouhair, Germany). Fares (Germany) also expressed his worries about decision-makers' stereotypes:

> My best friend, he's totally gay, but at the same time his situation is really hard. He came from Iraq, and they didn't accept that he's gay. They told him "no, you are not". Just, he don't look like a gay. Should he wear make-up or something like that? This is the problem here. They didn't believe that he's gay, because he went like this, like me now. He doesn't have any make-up, just go there.

In the UK, we found that some decisions analyse at length the claimants' build, haircut, use of make-up and overall (more masculine or feminine) manner (Zena,

7.5 The Assessment of Credibility

First Tier Tribunal Appeal, London, 2018, decision paper). Such stereotypes can also be found in the judiciary:

> since then [2016] I think the bog-standard stereotypes have come back. That is more at a judicial level rather than at Home Office level. The Home Office level are a bit better at not saying the bog-standard stereotypes. I recently saw an appeal where a judge said that the client staying in contact with their children was not the actions of a genuine lesbian. They are coming back quite often in judicial (Allan, lawyer).

Such reliance on stereotypes when considering claimants' demeanour struck our participants as unfair:

> I would not consider your physical appearance and then evaluate it: "Hm, but you are not heterosexual enough. But you could let the hair grow longer and so on. And you don't have enough make-up and you can wear more earrings and skirts, please." I would never do this, so why is the opposite allowed, and say whether someone is LGBT enough or not on the basis of their physical appearance? (Kadir, NGO worker, Germany).

The intersections between sex, gender, sexuality, cultural and ethnic background possess a significant influence in this context, which is often overlooked by decision-makers despite its importance from the perspective of our feminist and queer theoretical underpinnings (Chap. 3). Lesbian claimants may struggle to convince decision-makers, as many of the most concrete SOGI stereotypes relate to gay men, while 'lesbian sexuality is either invisible or it is treated in a manner verging on the pornographic' (Lewis 2014, p. 966). An example of this was shared with us by Sean, a lawyer in the UK:

> she [claimant] was found lacking in credibility, that [according to Home Office] "she is not a lesbian and the information you provided doesn't change our mind". And we say "well, that is ridiculous, because you have got 11 witnesses who believe that she is gay, three ex-partners who know that she is gay, and all attesting to their relationships with her".

Female SOGI claimants also seem to be affected by particularly ludicrous stereotypes and crude lines of questioning:

> In court, Home Office representatives occasionally suggest that gay women cannot really have sex. They suggest or imply that female partners cannot discern each other's sexual orientation and therefore cannot give reliable evidence (S4, lawyer, UK).

Trans participants are also defined by stereotypes, with Diana (Germany) told by the interviewer: 'you don't look like a trans'. Witnesses are also expected to conform to stereotypes, with judges often expecting 'typical' LGBTIQ+ people to appear in support of claimants (Bilal, presenting officer, UK).

Unfortunately, but unsurprisingly, as SOGI claimants become aware of the power of SOGI stereotypes, they may find it expedient to adapt their behaviour to conform to those stereotypes when attending interviews and hearings, for example, wearing rainbow flag motifs when otherwise they would not do so (Tribunal observation, northern Italy, 2018; Selim, UK; Joseph, NGO volunteer, UK). In this way, SOGI asylum systems foster 'homo-cultural essentialist paradigms' (Hinger 2010, p. 389). This leads to situations such as the one described by Allan, a lawyer in the UK:

My client, I wouldn't describe him as stereotypically gay, but he had a busload of friends who all were. It was high camp at the back of court and it was all very hilarious. He had, I think, four people give evidence that he had had sex with. I'm like, what is the point in doing this case? It is completely ridiculous.

Yet, not all claimants are able, even if they wish, to conform to decision-makers' stereotypes:

Recently I have come across many cases of LGBT+ people seeking asylum had been dispersed to areas which are not diverse and there is no LGBT+ community and that has had an enormous impact on their me[n]tal health and in proving their case and Home office want to know if they had been to any LGBT+ bars or clubs since coming to UK (S145, community development worker, UK).

Stereotypes also relate to the frequent assumption by decision-makers that religious beliefs are incompatible with belonging to a SOGI minority. In Germany, for example, we observed this dialogue in an appeal hearing:

Judge: How can you be religious and gay at the same time?
Claimant: My religion was given at birth, I grew up with it. I decided to convert later. But now I don't mix my sexuality and religion together. I don't think of sex with men when I am praying to God. And I don't think of God when I am having sex with men.
Judge: So you believe in God when you are not having sex and when you have sex with men, suddenly God doesn't exist anymore. Is that what you are telling me? (judge laughs) (Court observation, Hesse, 2019).

In Italy, there were similar accounts. Antonella, LGBTIQ+ group volunteer, stated that:

A question that the Commission may ask: "but how can you, as a believer, still manage to be homosexual even if you are a believer, a Muslim" and … those are questions that are, I consider them a bit idiotic because you cannot ask someone why they are homosexual. You just are, full stop.

Giulia, an LGBTIQ+ group volunteer, also offered an example of such stereotypes:

But then he [claimant] came here [to Italy] and the first ones who spoke to him in English, who were able to communicate with him, were these Jehovah Witnesses. He goes there, spends some time with someone, has some company, has a network of contacts, that is, this somehow helps him, but he does not realise what Jehovah Witnesses say about the LGBT population, what the Witnesses' ideas are. (…) Yet, for the judge it was a cause of inconsistency [but for] the claimant this did not even go through his mind. He likes to be there [with Jehovah Witnesses], they do the meetings, and he likes to come to meetings with us because he's gay.

This problem is particularly evident in the UK. Home Office questions often require Muslim and Christian SOGI claimants to explain an assumed tension between their religious and SOGI identities (UKLGIG 2013, p. 15, 2018), assuming both that certain world religions have a single position on these issues and also that individual believers are able to reconcile different aspects of their identity in a tidy package:

Given your awareness of the treatment that lesbians receive in Pakistan, along with the fact that your own religion condemns same sex relationships, it is inconsistent to suggest that you would have felt "blessed" and thanked God when you discovered you were a lesbian (Mary, Home Office decision, 2016).

Another example can be found in a Home Office refusal letter dated July 2018: 'Given that you are a practicing Christian, your failure to raise any potential conflicts in relation to your behavior and faith raises doubts concerning your credibility'. NGOs have also confirmed this approach by the Home Office:

he [claimant] was really shocked when they confronted him about how can you be gay and Christian. He was, he said "I was completely upset and thrown by that question", because he had always been a Christian and he has always been gay and so for him it's simply how it is, the fact that it is difficult to reconcile with what people tell you, is just, it is just the way it is (Debbie, NGO volunteer).

Legal representatives are understandably concerned: 'Then there are other stereotypes about religion. That is really starting to grow. "This is not compatible with your religion." Even asking the question, "How is this compatible with your religion?" and then not accepting what the person says' (Allan, lawyer). Failure to offer an explanation that satisfies decision-makers may further undermine credibility. This approach by the Home Office is in clear tension with the anti-cultural essentialist and anti-homonationalist approach we adopt in our analysis (Chap. 3), to the extent that it reflects a reductive and stereotypical understanding of the relationship between culture, religion, ethnicity and sexuality, and presumes the decision-makers' own culture deals with such matters more convincingly. Decision-makers also display stereotypes and Western or Eurocentric values in their expectations that claimants be 'out' about their SOGI.

7.5.2 Be 'Out and Proud' – The Western Way

Across all countries under comparison, we encountered an expectation on the part of decision-makers that claimants be 'out and proud' in ways conforming to Western cultural perceptions. This expectation relates both to how claimants live their daily and personal lives and to whether they take part in community initiatives and events.

For example, having a same-sex partner was invariably beneficial for credibility assessment purposes, even if this was simply a sexual partner willing to confirm the claimant's alleged sexual orientation.[72] This expectation was most evident in the UK:

[I feel] Very scared because I don't know how to prove my sexuality. They said they don't believe me because I'm not in a relationship now and have no proof that I have been in a same sex relationship in my home country (C54).

---

[72] In Italy, for example, this was reported by Giulia, an LGBTIQ+ group volunteer, and can also be seen in case law: Tribunal of Trieste, decision of 8 August 2009 (the witness was the claimant's partner).

UK decision-makers often had precise expectations of what such relationships should be like, which they often expressed insensitively. Relationships were expected to be based on trust and full disclosure of past experiences:

> It is not conceivable that the allegation of the rape and the account of her [claimant's] experiences in Malawi would not be shared with an intimate partner and I draw the conclusion that it was not referred to because the appellant and [her ex-partner] were not in an intimate relationship at all (Jayne, First Tier Tribunal decision, Birmingham, 2017).

Relationships were expected to last for a minimum amount of time:

> People may rely on partnerships in the UK to attest to their sexuality and there are heteronormative expectations on what those partnerships should look like, therefore a person with a number of short relationships may not have someone willing to provide a witness statement because they are no longer together. There are heteronormative expectations regarding the length and longevity of relationships (S147, barrister).

Partners should share a strong emotional connection as well as a physical attraction:

> Aside from stating that [X] had a nice body and smile and was beautiful and handsome (…), you do not describe any emotions around your relationship with him. Given that you had been together for ten years prior to him passing away in a car crash (AIR Q107), it is considered that some description of your emotional connection to him would be reasonable to expect, however you purely describe your relationship as only being sexual (Vincent, Home Office decision).

Partners should be able to remember what decision-makers viewed as critical dates in a relationship:

> When asked why she was unable to remember the date, she stated that neither she nor [X] remembered this and did not pay any attention to it. I do not find it credible that the Appellant… would not be able to recall basic details about when in 2013 they met and how and when in 2014 their relationship developed into more than friendship (Mary and Zaro, appeal decision, 2016).

Legal representatives confirmed – and were critical of – such expectations:

> [Another problem] It's conflating sexuality with sex. It is saying, "You are not sexually active, therefore you are not gay." They [decision-makers] don't literally say those words, but if you go to court and you haven't got a partner, you have never had a partner, it is so much harder for them to accept your sexuality. It is, "You don't have a boyfriend now" or "You don't have a girlfriend now". Yes, but so what? That doesn't make you not gay or lesbian (Allan, lawyer, UK).

Even claimants who had endured traumatising experiences, such as slavery and trafficking, were expected to be in relationships (Zena, First Tier Tribunal appeal, London, UK, 2018). This fails to recognise how difficult it is to establish and maintain any such connections while going through the stressful and often lengthy process of claiming asylum:

> when I started asylum [in] 2015, I was in a relationship, but the process got me into so much depression, it affected [me], I lost the relationship. I just made my mind since then that I don't think I am in a right state of mind with this process to be in love with anyone, I don't

7.5 The Assessment of Credibility

think I can be able to, if I can't put up with myself, I don't think I would be able to look after somebody's emotions (Jayne, focus group no. 4, London, UK).

The expectation to have a partner is understandably perceived as unfair by claimants: 'Because it is normal for someone who is not seeking asylum to be single, but it is not normal for an LGBT asylum seeker to be single, you understand?' (Jayne, UK). Supporters see this expectation as a source of increased risk for claimants: 'the systems are institutionally bias on many levels anyway – there is much unconscious bias. People are expected to provide evidence which pressures them into unsafe relationships or situations...' (S57, NGO volunteer, UK). It is also an unacceptable interference with claimants' personal choices of when and how to develop romantic relationships (Harriet, focus group no. 2, Bavaria, Germany; Alphaeus, focus group no. 3, Bavaria, Germany). The expectation of a 'romantic' or 'emotional' narrative can also be inappropriate because it may be absent from some claimants' accounts (Roberto, decision-maker, Italy). For example, a judge in Italy told us that:

now they arrive very young – like 18 year olds – who are not homosexual at all, but were forced into prostitution and, therefore, were perceived as homosexuals by the state authorities, but who have zero awareness of their sexuality. They conceive it purely as a physical action, so they cannot express anything related to their awareness and this is often seen as a factor of non-likelihood and non-credibility. This is therefore a huge problem, of course (Silvana).

As the accounts above show, credibility assessment in Germany, Italy and the UK eventually lead to some kind of exploration of the claimants' sexual consciousness and experiences: 'that initial bit of the interview where you are talking about their realisation of their sexuality... that is the key core' (Qasim, decision-maker, UK). There is a lack of awareness that claimants' lives – like those of everyone else – are multi-dimensional and cannot be reduced to their SOGI and related experiences (Chap. 3).

In Italy, this exploration often concentrates on the claimant's journey of sexual self-realisation and the expectation that this would be 'extremely troubling' to them (Titti, decision-maker) or, at the very least, that there be a clear journey of (non-heterosexual) sexual awakening (Vincenzo, LGBTIQ+ group volunteer). To find claimants credible, asylum adjudicators seem to expect them to somehow prove the emotions and suffering they endured during this self-realisation process, by providing very specific and typically Western answers, something that happens to some extent across all asylum claims (Woolley 2017). If claimants are not able to express such feelings or suffering using notions familiar in a European context, their applications risk being rejected:

they [interviewers] said in my face, they did not feel the emotion, how sad I was. I asked myself: why do they want me to be sad? If I'm already free, why should I be sad? Why do I still have to show sadness? (...) in the Italian conception, they need, perhaps, to see the tears flow, but we are not always like that. They [decision-makers] must understand that everyone is different. There are people who will cry, there are people who will not cry. Each one is different (Cedric, focus group no. 5, southern Italy).

In contrast to some territorial commissions, Italian judges have afforded significant importance to claimants' psychological difficulties in reporting their personal story.[73] Lawyers have also showed awareness of how inappropriate such expectations of emotional display are:

> they [territorial commissions] expect a strong emotional participation, but in reality one needs to understand that a person [claimant] is speaking with some embarrassment and therefore the emotions can be externalised or not externalised, there is embarrassment, for them it is objectively very difficult to understand those that can be the real criteria (Damiano).

Some decision-makers are conscious of this issue as well, such as Maria Grazia:

> I [very often] ask [to sexual orientation claimants] "what did you feel when you kissed a man for the first time?" I mean, I try to refer to my experience, but I realise that it is *my* experience, that of a Western woman.

To avoid Western conceptions of sexuality and emotion dominating credibility assessment, appeal judges have found it credible that claimants would place more emphasis on the physical aspects of their sexuality than the emotional one, overturning decisions by territorial commissions denying international protection owing to lack of credibility.[74]

In the UK, as past research has identified (UKLGIG 2018, pp. 23–26), decision-makers expect the 'journey of sexual awakening' to be verbalised by claimants in emotional terms:

> I think the majority of LGBT applicants I felt to be, I have recommended to be a refusal because… they are not able to describe any kind of… emotional internal detail about how they came to realise that they were gay, how that has in fact impacted their life, it is, they… I tell them at the start of the interview that I don't want any kind of explicit detail, and some people tend to focus on just the sort of physical aspects on the claim. Which is a big "no, no" for us and we don't, that is not the kind of information that we are looking for. (Qasim, decision-maker).

If they want to convince officials, claimants are expected to put their emotions on full display: 'What struck me was that her account lacked any kind of emotional depth or detail of her journey towards her sexuality in a place where such relationships are criminalised and taboo' (Jayne, First Tier Tribunal decision, Birmingham, 2017). The requirement to present an 'emotional journey' is particularly unrealistic and inappropriate for claimants who may be suffering from PTSD, who experience numbing, and who wish to avoid thinking about traumatic past events in their life (Shidlo and Ahola 2013, p. 9). One survey respondent reported that this seems to 'trip up' men in particular: 'I see a number of refusals of men on the basis that they have not articulated their feelings with clarity' (S147, barrister). An example of this can be seen in the UK Home Office decision in Vincent's case:

> You state that you first began to realise your sexuality as you would have sex with your neighbour at the age of eight (AIR Q71). It is considered that your account of this claimed

---

[73] See, for example, Tribunal of Bologna, decision of 4 November 2013.

[74] Appeal Tribunal of Brescia, judgment no. 1350, 18 July 2019.

7.5 The Assessment of Credibility

experience is particularly vague, unclear and fails to actually substantiate an apparent self-realisation of your claimed sexuality based on an otherwise socially unacceptable situation with your neighbour. Therefore, concerns are raised as to this account of your realisation, due to the incoherence within it.

It is not clear why the claimant's testimony in this regard is seen as 'vague' and 'unclear'. What details was the interviewer expecting? Why did the interviewer not ask for them or seek clarification at the time? Was it deemed incoherent simply because the same standards of social acceptability are expected of everyone, regardless of culture, nationality, class and a range of other factors? Vincent's Home Office decision goes on to state:

Aside from feeling afraid and fearful of others harming you, you make no mention of your emotions of being gay in a homophobic society. It is considered that you would have some trouble coming to terms with your sexuality given the environment you were brought up in (AIR Q76) however you make no mention of this and simply state that you felt thrilled.

It is unclear how many more adjectives the decision-maker expected from Vincent describing his feelings, or what sophisticated emotional narrative would have satisfied them.

There are records of claimants having been expected to define themselves using terms familiar to the decision-maker rather than ones that are familiar and meaningful to the claimant: one claimant was reportedly disbelieved for saying the 'T' in 'LGBT' stands for 'Trans' and not 'Transgender' (Beresford 2016). 'LGBT' itself may be an unfamiliar acronym for some SOGI claimants: 'for all different social and cultural reasons, LGBT is not a commonly used term to refer to sexual identities of persons within these categories in Afghanistan' (ICIBI 2016, p. 23). Expecting SOGI self-awareness according to Western standards and terminology is unreasonable, as one survey respondent pointed out:

Applicants are also expected to have reflected on their experiences and have a degree of insight that is unrealistic where they have never had access to any kind of support and where the only message they have received about LGBTQI+ in their country of origin is that it is wrong (S4, lawyer, UK).

It is also striking that when claimants narrate their sexual experiences, transgressing social norms and engaging in risky behaviours often damages their credibility (UKLGIG 2018, p. 32): 'It is considered questionable that such overt and direct sexual behaviours were instigated in such a setting, given that being gay in Malawi is illegal and the punishment could be imprisonment' (Vincent, Home Office decision).

Decision-makers in all our country case studies also based their credibility assessment to a significant extent on whether claimants were 'out and proud' in the community or not. Claimants were frequently asked about their experiences of frequenting LGBTIQ+ venues, membership of LGBTIQ+ associations, and attending LGBTIQ+ events such as Pride. This was the case in Germany (Shany; Barbara, lawyer; Gisela, lawyer; Nina, legal advisor; Thomas, NGO volunteer; Court observation, Hesse, 2019; William, focus group no. 2, Bavaria), Italy (Giulia, LGBTIQ+ group volunteer) and the UK (Allan, lawyer). Where claimants did not have much evidence in terms of being publicly 'out' and involved with the LGBTIQ+ community, they risked receiving a negative decision. Accordingly, activist claimants with evidence of their involvement with protests and parades were more 'believable' than those claimants who had lived their SOGI 'undercover' in their countries of origin (Barbara, lawyer, Germany).

Yet, being involved with the LGBTIQ+ community should not be an expectation, in light of the lack of involvement of many 'native' LGBTIQ+ people with those structures and groups (Sofia and Emma, NGO workers, Germany). This expectation places undue pressure on claimants to reveal their SOGI in public contexts, running the risk of exposure were they to return to their country of origin. Finally, such public engagement may be difficult or impossible for some claimants, depending on their economic resources, health condition, experiences of discrimination and reception conditions (Chap. 8 and 9; Evelyne and Anne, lawyers, Germany; Jordan and Morrissey 2013, p. 14).

The impact of this sort of expectation on credibility assessment is of great concern to legal representatives:

> there is often a real "stereotypical" and wrong focus on whether the individual goes to gay clubs or particular bars or reads particular publications or is part of particular social media groups. This is treated as determinative of the individual living openly and so being at risk – which is a very narrow and restrictive approach as to how a LGBT person lives or should be required to live, and also imposes an artificial and potentially prejudiced and discriminatory expectation and projection. It is as though "one size fits all" and if you do not behave in a certain way then you should not be afforded the protection of the Geneva Convention, which cannot be right (Beth, lawyer, UK).

If claimants were given the opportunity to fully express themselves, clarify any inconsistencies in their account, and listened to with an open mind, then some of the problems highlighted above might well be resolved. However, it is clear that asylum authorities do not always give claimants the time and space they need, instead, using any inconsistencies to cast doubt on claimants' credibility, reflecting and reinforcing a 'culture of disbelief'.

7.5.3 A Persisting Culture of Disbelief

There was a clear perception amongst our participants that decision-makers use inconsistencies and contradictions to deny international protection, rather than seeking clarification from claimants through further and more sensitive questioning. In Germany, we heard that small misunderstandings are used to undermine claimants' credibility, for example, asking claimants about their participation in 'CSD' (Christopher Street Day), which is how Pride parades are known in Germany but which is an acronym that is likely to be unfamiliar to claimants, who then answer that they have not participated in such events, even when they have (Frank S., legal advisor; Nina, legal advisor). In Italy, one of our participants – Odosa – told us his asylum claim had been denied simply on account of a perceived inconsistency in his

7.5 The Assessment of Credibility

testimony (regarding how his hand had been hurt), without the interviewer taking the time to seek clarification. Other participants had similar experiences (Buba). Similarly, in the UK, both at administrative (UKLGIG 2018, p. 18) and appeal level, minor discrepancies and the failure to recall certain details or people are portrayed by the Home Office as evidence that SOGI claims are fabricated (Upper Tier Tribunal observation, London, 2018).

Yet, some decision-makers are conscious of their obligation to ask for clarification and further detail, (Oscar, judge, Germany), and some are also conscious that small inconsistencies may in fact demonstrate that events have been experienced, not simply memorised (Court observation, Hesse, Germany, 2018). Some also recognise that minor inconsistencies do not undermine a claimant's credibility where they do not relate to material points in the asylum claim (Court observation, North Rhine-Westphalia, Germany, 2019). Importantly, there is some awareness that claimants should have the opportunity to comment on elements of the testimony that the interviewer may find non-credible. In Italy, for example, Daniele, a decision-maker, told us that:

> if I have a claimant who gives me elements that from my point of view, to ascertain sexual orientation, are implausible, I don't keep them for myself. I tell him: "Look, you are telling me that you have a homosexual orientation that you have become aware of in this way, but I must point out to you that this statement of yours is very difficult to believe on the basis of how one can generally think that a sexual orientation is matured". (…) This is always done, because we know that the interview must have a cooperative character. (…) [but] Basically not everyone [amongst the commission's members] does that (laughs). I mean, if some non-plausible elements are offered, it is not the case that this non-plausibility assessment is generally shared with the claimant, but in my opinion it should be done in this way and I generally do so, ok?

In the UK, as well, Emily, another decision-maker, said that '[i]t's quite good to be able to put that [inconsistencies] to them [claimants] at the time, so that they can [clarify them], there might be a reasonable explanation, so it's good to be able to put that to them' (Emily, decision-maker). However, this awareness by some decision-makers of the need to offer claimants the opportunity to clarify any apparent contradiction or inconsistency was not evident in most interviews and appeal hearings.

Overall, we have found that there is a persistent culture of disbelief affecting all aspects of SOGI claims, resulting in negative credibility assessments for many of our participants. In Germany, for example, the BAMF sometimes doubts the claimant's ethnic origin or nationality without good cause (Ham). We also heard about the BAMF disbelieving that a claimant's landlady had an extra key of the apartment and was thus able to enter the apartment and find the claimant having sexual intercourse with a same-sex partner (decision regarding participant DE16 in Held 2018). Similarly, the BAMF was unable to believe that a claimant distributed flyers regarding SOGI matters despite the danger that entailed (Veronica and Julia). This culture of disbelief permeates German asylum adjudicators' assessment of credibility, all the way up to appeal courts:

> We have an advantage over the Federal Office: we already have a narrative, namely the narrative of the Federal Office, which has been produced relatively short after arrival [of the

claimant]. And the probability that this [narrative] is true, of course, is greater, and it is not uncommon for maybe one [claimant] or other to come up with something during their time here in Germany to increase their chances. One may hear: "Oh, here, I have been recognised with this and that story. Then try it". So, the falsest thing you can do. Then you do not believe anything anymore, but that's the right thing to do (Oscar, judge, Germany).

In Italy too, some of our participants have suggested that a culture of disbelief affects the asylum system (focus group no. 4, northern Italy; focus group no. 5, southern Italy), although seemingly to a lesser extent than in other countries. This may increase following the 2018 reform. On many occasions, judges have reversed negative decisions by territorial commissions where claimants have, according to judges, provided a coherent account that was factually in line with the information collected by the tribunal about claimants' countries of origin.[75] However, in light of the limited scope for appeals in the reformed Italian asylum system (Chaps. 4 and 6), SOGI claimants will inevitably suffer without the opportunity to establish their credibility in person before a judge (Palermo 2018). The non-verbal aspects of interviews are often lost in audio and video recordings, detracting from the authenticity of the account and negatively affecting the credibility assessment (Puumala and Ylikomi 2017).

In the UK, too, it is clear that a 'culture of disbelief' still harms SOGI claimants, as pointed out by several NGO participants:

And what they [Home Office] tend to do is start off with a great deal of scepticism, and refuse on the basis that the person hasn't provided information or details even when they don't ask for the details (...) The general things [to refuse a claim] would be the same, "we don't believe you because...", well the thing is because of anything. (...) they pick on very small parts of the interview, ignore the rest of the interview, they pick on one or two lines, or the standard one (...) is "too vague" and "too inconsistent", without defining what the vagueness or the inconsistency was (Denise and Umar, legal advisors).

Chloe, an NGO worker, also said: 'I have never worked with a gay asylum seeker who has been granted it [asylum] and had their sexuality not been disputed by the Home Office'. Yet another NGO participant believed that a 'fundamental problem is that the asylum seeker is routinely treated as a liar (...) [and there are] lengthy interviews which seem intended to catch them out' (S130, NGO volunteer). Asylum claimants made the same assessment:

They believed one thing, that I am from Bangladesh, I came here in 2009, because I came in legally with passport. Apart from this, they said I am pretending to be gay, the social media, this chatting I am doing, the copy they had, "it doesn't make any proof that he is gay, anybody can do this". Then Helen Bamber [Foundation] report[ed] the scars I had when I was in Bangladesh, [but Home Office argued that] it could [be] from a crime, maybe he did had fight with someone, this kind of, the beating is not about, could be sexuality. And, I

---

[75] See, for example, Tribunal of Bari, decision of 4 December 2014; Tribunal of Genoa, decision of 16 September 2016; Tribunal of Venice, decision of 25 May 2018. See, also, Tribunal of Genoa, decision of 13 May 2016, where the judge placed fundamental importance on the 'quality' of the information provided by the claimant when considering the difficulties experienced in reporting a traumatic personal account.

mean, they tried to make everything that I am lying. And, it really drove me, pushed me to the edge. That I almost lost hope (Lutfor).

The interview started from 11 until 6.30 in the evening. (…) Then, when the decision came, they didn't believe anything. None of the things that I said they believed. Not even one. I don't know how many questions I had, I think I had 300 and something questions, none of them [were believed], they just believed that I am from Zimbabwe. The rest, nothing (Meggs, focus group no. 1, Manchester).

Bisexual people claiming asylum are particularly likely to be disbelieved:

Bisexuals, forget it. It is so difficult for a bisexual to prove they are bisexual. I think that is the hardest category. It is not just about proving it. Say it is a bisexual male and they have had a relationship with a woman, it will be, "You are not bisexual because you had a relationship with a woman." I think that is the definition of bisexual! There is a real culture of disbelief with bisexuals generally, which manifests itself in the system (Allan, lawyer).

A case in point is that of Orashia Edwards, a bisexual Jamaican man, who spent three and a half years battling attempts of the Home Office to deport him to Jamaica and was detained a number of times, after authorities claimed he was heterosexual and had just been 'experimenting' with men (Duffy 2018). Another claimant was told by the Home Office barrister: 'You can't be a heterosexual 1 day and a lesbian the next day. Just as you can't change your race' (Dugan 2015). As a leading barrister in SOGI appeals stated: 'The Home Office has just about understood there's such a thing as a gay identity, but just doesn't understand there's a bisexual identity' (Allan Briddock, quoted in Morgan 2018). To avoid scepticism on the part of decision-makers, it is not surprising that some bisexual individuals misrepresent themselves as gay or lesbian (Khan 2016, p. 172).

The Home Office sometimes depicts claimants as plotting their asylum claim strategy years ahead of time, in a way that appears far-fetched under any circumstance: Diamond saw his asylum claim refused by the Home Office, which discredited his claim to be HIV positive as a ploy to claim asylum on sexual orientation grounds at a later date.

At the end of the day, some are left feeling at an impasse:

it is very much down to "damned if you do, damned if you don't". "Why didn't you have a girlfriend, why did you, how could you now have a girlfriend when it is so dangerous" (…) which then damages the credibility of the whole of the case (Amelia, NGO worker).

The problems with credibility assessment in SOGI claims are pervasive across all countries under comparison. This is also the conclusion reached by European-level NGO workers and policy-makers. The anger and frustration of not being believed, especially in relation to an aspect of someone's identity that is likely to be so important to SOGI claimants, is enormous:

No [they didn't believe me], then how can I? Should I go and put my ass, they fuck my ass to prove that I am gay? That's the question they said, "No, you have to prove us that you are gay". Can I get my boyfriend and go and have sex in front of the court for them to know that I am gay? If they want that, then I will do it (Amis, focus group no. 2, Bavaria, Germany).

you're asking me deep, deep question, which you expect me to answer. And you are asking me irrelevant dates. I told you I'm running from my country, and you're asking me dates. So you expect me running, I'm sick on the way, I spent, in fact I witness here, you are expecting me to answer the questions I ought to forget. And then you determine which that if I'm right or I'm qualified to get your visa or not, your documents, that is bullshit, it's wrong. Forgive me for using that word, it's very, very wrong, it's not good. You cannot assess a man or a woman just by looking at the person and asking the person a question based on a piece of paper (Nice Guy, focus group no. 1, northern Italy).

Expectations regarding the narrative required from SOGI claimants thus need to change: bearing in mind how differently SOGI is legally regulated and socially experienced throughout the world, European decision-makers need to stop neglecting the specificities of countries of origin, go beyond a Euro-centric lens of what 'homosexuality' means and be open to different narratives. As Dina Nayeri (2019, p. 233) puts it, at the end of the day:

> [e]very true story has strangeness, things that can only happen to *those* people at that time – the unbiased listen for it, trying to imagine an unknown world. But the biased look only for *familiar* oddities, the ones that match and validate their own story.

Nor should one overlook the discriminatory and often demeaning nature of this intensive probing of individuals' SOGI, a probing that is unimaginable in relation to heterosexual and cis-gendered asylum claimants, and which would be seen as highly offensive and inappropriate outside the asylum context:

> I do not go to a judge and say, "Well, I do not think you're heterosexual. Prove it to me!". "Yes, I have two children and built a house and have a German shepherd dog." "Oh, well, that's not the standard now." "What do you expect, then?" It could be like that (Noah, NGO social worker, Germany).

Until a social and cultural revolution of sorts takes place in asylum adjudicators' minds, it will very often be the case that:

> [t]he law may have adapted, but the nuances of coming out haven't sunk in for the individual asylum officers. Until they do, you can't be a quiet, bookish lesbian. Forget about being questioning, bi, celibate, heartbroken and not in the mood for new love, culturally beaten down or too afraid to act. Every gay person has to be a flamboyant scene-kid, out at clubs and fashion shows and on Grindr texting strangers at a nightclub (Nayeri 2019, p. 252).

The lack of belief in stories that do not fit asylum adjudicators' conceptions of what an LGBTIQ+ person is, reflects the homonormativity that permeates the European legal and political institutions, in general, and asylum systems in particular (Duggan 2002). In the process, we inflict violence on SOGI asylum claimants, and the principle of the benefit of the doubt and the fairness of the European asylum system are shredded to pieces.

7.6 Outcomes of the RSD Process and What Lays beyond SOGI – Through an Intersectional Lens

In light of the experiences of claimants described in Chap. 5 and the analysis above, refugee status or, at least, some form of international protection would seem the only legally appropriate and humane decision in many SOGI asylum applications. Yet, SOGI claimants receive international protection in a relatively small number of cases and, even then, are often not given full refugee status, depriving them of the degree of permanency needed to move on with their lives. According to our survey with SOGI claimants, claimants see their claims rejected because the decision-maker does not believe they were persecuted or at risk of persecution in their country of origin (40%), the decision-maker does not believe in the claimants' stated SOGI (32%), there is allegedly an 'internal relocation alternative' (14%) and claimants can return and be safe by living 'discreetely' (9%).

In Germany, refugee status is often granted to SOGI claimants when claims are found to be credible. Yet, there are cases, such as Ibrahim's, where although the claimant presents a credible claim, the authorities only grant subsidiary protection. Moreover, in the case of Syrian claimants, authorities generally only grant subsidiary protection if they only claim to be escaping conflict (ECRE, AIDA & Asyl und Migration 2019, p. 65). Syrian nationals who are members of SOGI minorities may not mention their SOGI during the asylum process to secure the speedy recognition of some form of international protection and avoid disclosing their SOGI, as in the case of Fares. That has as a consequence only being granted subsidiary protection instead of refugee status, despite the SOGI of those claimants putting them at risk of individual persecution.

In Italy, as well, some judicial decision-makers tend to either confirm administrative decisions denying SOGI claimants asylum,[76] or grant a lesser form of international protection than refugee status, such as subsidiary protection or humanitarian protection.[77] This has led one decision-maker to talk of some members of territorial commissions seeing international protection as a sort of 'reward', which should be given only rarely, resulting in more decisions of humanitarian protection than subsidiary protection or refugee status (Maria Grazia, decision-maker). A lawyer also explained that decision-makers sometimes see humanitarian protection as a compromise in cases of doubt about the claimant's credibility (Mara). This trend seems to depend both on the (disputable) understanding of the different forms of international protection (for example, from assertions we heard from a participant judge), but also on the human right at stake. In the case of a Ukrainian citizen who could not enjoy family life with her partner because of social attitudes, the Tribunal of Brescia only granted her humanitarian protection. The reason was based on the fact that the

---

[76]Tribunal of Ancona, decisions of 26 September 2018, 3 October 2018, 24 October 2018, 21 November 2018, 28 November 2018, 19 December 2018 and 30 January 2019 (unpublished).

[77]Tribunal of Ancona, decisions of 17 October 2018, 24 October 2018, 28 November 2018, and 19 December 2018 (unpublished).

claimant was deprived of the enjoyment of the right to respect for family life, which is not a non-derogable right for the purpose of granting refugee status, and the right to family life could be secured through the issuance of a humanitarian permit.[78] When it comes to gender identity, although international protection is generally granted, the recognition of refugee status can also constitute a challenge. For example, in a 2011 case related to gender identity, the claimant was granted humanitarian protection, although a careful reading of the case could have led to the recognition of the status of refugee.[79]

In the UK, the number of refused SOGI asylum claims is also high and there are regularly internet and social media campaigns – some of which appear to be successful – to prevent deportation of SOGI asylum claimants on charter flights, such as Jimmy Kyesswa, whose deportation to Uganda was postponed in December 2016 following an online petition (Butterworth 2016). It has been suggested that gender identity applications tend to be more successful than sexual orientation applications (Berg and Millbank 2013). This likely higher acceptance rate is attributed to the fact that 'trans applicants were accepted as credible when their bodies conformed to a visual typology *and* their narratives to accepted western tropes of gender dysphoria' – that is to say, when decision-makers could identify the classic transsexual 'wrong body' narrative (Berg and Millbank 2013, pp. 128–129).

The intersectional and feminist approaches informing our analysis make it clear, however, that decisions on SOGI claims are about much more than the claimants' SOGI. Our survey with people who work with or support SOGI claimants confirmed that, besides their SOGI, SOGI claimants' country of origin (62%), cultural background (53%), demeanour (clothes and mannerisms) (49%), educational background (46%), religion (45%), and gender (44%) are key factors in decision-making. These, along other factors such as socio-economic status, age and disability, are overlooked or subsumed by a focus on SOGI. Many decisions refusing international protection to SOGI claimants reflect a poor understanding of the intersectional nature of the harm suffered and feared by these claimants. This problem can be seen, for instance, in the failure to recognise how sexual orientation and gender come together for women claiming international protection. In the UK, for example, in the case of a 19-year-old Belarusian lesbian woman, gang raped along with her girlfriend, the Tribunal judge in the case said that '[t]he appellant appears to have been targeted only because of her sex and vulnerability rather than her sexuality' (reported in UKLGIG 2013, p. 26). Gender also affects the kinds of harm experienced, with research suggesting that lesbian and bisexual female asylum claimants experience the most severe psychological harm and UK Home Office guidance not adequately recognising that (Khan 2016, p. 127). Several women claimants we interviewed in the UK had experienced gender-based violence, such as rape and

---

[78] Tribunal of Brescia, decision of 29 May 2018 (unpublished), discussed by Danisi (2019, p. 372) in the context of the relationship between IRL and IHRL (Chap. 3).

[79] Tribunal of Rome, decision of 18 November 2011.

7.6 Outcomes of the RSD Process and What Lays beyond SOGI ...

forced marriage, and it was not clear that these intersections were adequately recognised by decision-makers. In the German context, as well, we were told that:

> she [lesbian claimant] has to be outed first as a woman, to understand her rights as a woman, to be first [able] to speak about her sexuality. (…) They have these issues of not being taken seriously, or the fear of speaking about their sexuality (Ibrahim).

Socio-economic status is another significant factor that SOGI asylum adjudication needs to consider, particularly in the way harm is risked and one's SOGI identity is experienced:

> [In Pakistan] Some people say that they have relatives in the police and politics and the government and they are particularly worried because not only will they be known by everybody, but their family has got this extra kind of concern about honour and one person said to me "my parents wouldn't have any fear about killing somebody, getting rid of somebody and no one would know, because of their status" (Debbie, NGO volunteer, UK).

Socio-economic status is often intertwined with one's educational level:

> Class and cultural and educational background all affect how able an applicant is to provide the kind of self-reflective narrative the Home Office is looking for. They also play a part in stereotypes. People from more conservative nations and ethnicities appear to face more scepticism from the authorities, and people from poorer nations and ethnicities are more likely to be labelled "economic migrants" (S4, lawyer, UK).

Some decision-makers willingly recognise that claimants' educational background has an impact on the quality and cogency of their testimony – for example, in relation to claimants' ability to speak about their journey of sexual awakening – thus influencing their credibility:

> the tools, the culture, the capacity, even the school background is fundamental [to be able to establish one's credibility]. A person who has never studied, who has always been a shepherd since he was ten, will have difficulty talking about himself because he has never done it before (Titti, decision-maker, Italy).

This consciousness, however, seems to be insufficiently reflected across all SOGI asylum decisions. That is also clear at appeal level, with 'middle class', articulate claimants being able to present their cases much more cogently and confidently than claimants from more disadvantaged socio-economic backgrounds with lower literacy (Court observation, North Rhine-Westphalia, 2019; Court observation, Hesse, 2019). Elias, a lawyer in Germany, also asserted that 'we often deal with people who have little education. That means they do not know how to spontaneously respond to criticism'. One judge in the UK also suggested that appeals may be more successful when claimants have a better educational background:

> I think in general, the sort of people we would tend to have… before us will by and large have some level of education and sophistication and so normally will perhaps with a little bit of help… be able to open up and just explain what it is (Adrian, judge, UK).

Less cognitively able gay men may find it more difficult to articulate their case in terms that resonate with European decision-makers than other SOGI claimants. An example of this is a gay claimant in the UK who was denied asylum because the

Home Office did not believe that someone with learning difficulties could be gay, finding that 'you have failed to show that you are a homosexual man' (Strudwick 2018).

Educational achievement is often intertwined with social class, religious, national and cultural backgrounds in inextricable ways, as legal representatives are aware:

> You cannot clarify being LGBTI as a ground for persecution without mentioning racism and class issues. Yes? So, if a gay man, White, academic, comes and could talk concretely about what happened to him, then he gets a handshake after that and two days later he has his positive decision. If a Cameroonian who has been to school for four years comes from somewhere, you do not believe him. Since he cannot talk about it at all, because he cannot express it at all. He has experienced an environment that is (…) he has a very different kind of repression, that is, a very different inner [life] and outer community. No one is able to understand that. He talks in a quite different manner. And he does not even know how to say "how I realised that", yes? (Barbara, lawyer, Germany).

> If one has done nothing but two years of Koranic school in a poor country, he only answers the questions that are asked and says things that seem miserable… This is, however, something that I have noticed over the years: wealth and oral ability count for a lot, those who are able to speak and those who are not (Livio, lawyer, Italy).

Educational attainment is also, however, sometimes used perniciously to undermine credibility:

> all they could say to me was "well, you seem like an educated person", but what does my education have to do with knowing legal things? I have never been in a situation where I needed a lawyer even back home, so all of this is new, I am sure even somebody who had a PhD in that situation, you can't think straight, you are confused, you don't even know what is going to happen to you (Stephina, UK).

Similarly, educational attainment can be used to deny risk of persecution: 'And after he [interviewer] told me "you seem educated. An educated woman in Africa can survive anywhere"' (Julian, focus group no. 5, Bavaria, Germany).

Strong individual and community religious beliefs also often play a role in the nature and virulence of persecution and lack of protection by public authorities, in particular if the claimant's family holds a position of responsibility in the religious community (Siri, Italy). More generally, socio-economic factors such as education, class and caste may intersect with religion and SOGI to render places more or less safe. Religion and ethnicity also intersect with gender, relevant to understanding why some women of a certain religion may find it difficult to talk about their SOGI if the interpreter or legal representative is also of the same religion (Jivraj et al. 2003, para. 8.8; Chap. 6).

Although generally neglected, age may also play a role in SOGI claims, with older claimants potentially being more experienced and self-confident in their dealings with asylum adjudicators, or being more resilient and resourceful during the asylum process. Thomas, an NGO volunteer in Germany, told us, for example, of a 20-year old claimant who felt intimidated and was 'systematically challenged' during an appeal hearing that lasted for three and a half hours, to the point of speaking lower and lower and having to be told to speak louder during the cross-examination. Conversely, older age may also decrease a claimant's credibility, with a survey respondent stating that the 'Home Office [is] less likely to believe someone is gay if older for some reason' (S155, solicitor, UK). This was confirmed by another partici-pant, who stated:

> when I was in court, I was about 35 thereabout or so, "oh, you can go back to Jamaica because you are getting old now, you are up in age, and you are single, so you won't need a partner" (SGW, focus group no. 4, London, UK).

'Older' claimants – especially women – are thus expected to return to their home countries and live alone because no-one will question their lack of children (as they could have grown up) or a partner (as the claimant could be widowed or separated). Youth may also benefit claimants in other ways, albeit by relying on equally inappropriate stereotypes. For example, in a case involving a Nigerian gay claimant in Italy, the territorial commission made a negative assessment of credibility on the basis that the claimant, amongst other things, had offered a 'generic' testimony and focused on the physical aspects of his relationships. The judicial instance of appeal rejected the commission's stereotypical assumption that relationships are about emotional engagement. Instead, the Tribunal used the stereotype that younger people are 'understandably' more focused on sex than emotions, as if young people value sexual activities more than older people.[80]

Yet another often neglected factor in this field is disability. A claimant's disability may be misunderstood to the point of hurting their credibility and, consequently, the RSD process outcome:

> They think that we people who are moving with crutches, who are disabled, we cannot move. They do not understand how I came to Europe from Africa, they think that we disabled people do not move, but there are people who have empathy and who help. (…) I can move, and somebody helped me to get my ticket to get here, I did not come by foot (Betty, Germany).

An understanding of the diversity *within* SOGI claims, but also of the intersectional nature of identity, is critical to the development of an asylum system that is responsive to claimants' experiences, rather than one that imposes a single model of SOGI identity based on Western stereotypes. Gender differences must be recognised to understand the different experiences of male-to-female and female-to-male transgender claimants, and a variety of religious, ethnic, social, educational and cultural differences need to become ingrained in the minds of asylum adjudicators if we are to move towards a more socio-culturally sensitive, appropriate and fair system.

7.7 Concluding Remarks: Assessing the Assessor

Much has been written about SOGI asylum legal adjudication. Yet, some crucial issues have been the object of only limited research or, despite having been discussed widely, remain under-theorised or inadequately explored. In this chapter, we

---

[80] Appeal Tribunal of Brescia, judgment no. 1350, 18 July 2019.

have scrutinised matters relating to: the failure to consider Refugee Convention grounds other than PSG for SOGI minorities, despite the difficulty some SOGI claimants face in 'fitting' into a PSG; inconsistencies in the consideration of criminalisation of same-sex acts and the internal relocation alternative; the persistence of the 'discretion argument' in more subtle forms than previously; the standard of proof applied in violation of the principle of the benefit of the doubt; the failure to apply the burden of proof according to UNHCR guidance; the continuing culture of disbelief; and the ongoing inadequacy of credibility assessment. Trust in the SOGI asylum decision-making systems across Europe has been repeatedly questioned in this research. Our fieldwork brought to light good reasons to doubt the quality and fitness of current systems. Some of our participants in Germany went so far as describing the system as 'horrible' (Fares, Germany), 'unfair', a 'betting game' and a 'lottery' (focus group no. 1, Hesse, Germany). Others call it 'absurd':

> So there are such things as "It is well known that in Uganda gay men are being persecuted and threatened with jail, but that, it does not contradict that the refugee [claimant] settles in another part of the country." Although there is police threat, so in his case and although his family is after him and Uganda is not USA or something, Uganda is Uganda. So completely absurd (Thomas, NGO volunteer, Germany).

Moreover, political pressures and limited resources mean that decision-makers often lack the capacity to make decisions sufficiently in light of claimants' individual circumstances. For decision-makers, it is also a daunting task to deal with the amount and nature of claims lodged. Emilia, a judge in Germany, described deciding on SOGI asylum claims as 'poking in the fog'. As lawyers told us: 'there is also a lot of copy and paste. (…) we had thousands of grotesquely poorly written, template-decisions in recent years. (…) [false positives are] a joke compared to the whole false negatives [issue]' (Elias, lawyer, Germany). This was confirmed by claimants themselves: 'Even the grounds they gave us on why you're rejected are the same for 15 people' (Julian, focus group no. 5, Bavaria, Germany).

Ostensibly, the Italian system appears to be the most 'friendly' towards SOGI asylum claimants, compared to Germany and the UK, based on the facts that the 'alternative approach' is adopted in relation to the notion of PSG, criminalisation of same-sex conduct is considered persecution in itself, and internal relocation is not considered in asylum claims. The overall picture is, however, much more complex. From a legal perspective, the latest Italian reforms (Chaps. 4 and 6) have introduced elements that are likely to be highly detrimental for SOGI asylum claimants, in particular the removal of a second degree of appeal and the replacement of a hearing in person with a video-recorded administrative interview. Furthermore, the broader SOGI legal framework and social environment in Italy is arguably far less welcoming than in most other EU countries.

Nonetheless, whichever country is dealing with a SOGI claim, there are risks for claimants. Often there is also the sense that 'in becoming an asylum officer, you relinquish all imagination and wonder' (Nayeri 2019, p. 158). Even worse, there is a fear that decision-makers can – if they so wish – distort the evidence submitted in order to deny international protection:

7.7 Concluding Remarks: Assessing the Assessor 323

that is the crux of the matter, because people who come from Georgia are rarely doubted about being queer. For people who come from Cameroon, however, it is much more often doubted that they are queer. And of course, the impression I have is that, in Georgia, there is no persecution, no prosecution, even if there is massive social [discrimination]. So one can calmly say, "the person is homosexual, but there is no persecution." On the other hand, in Cameroon, the people have to explain their sexuality very... yes... credibly, so to speak (Sabrina, NGO worker, Germany).

Elias, a lawyer in Germany, confirmed this by saying that '[i]f a judge really wants to discredit a client, then they succeed'. This happens both at administrative and judicial levels, as reported to us in Germany: 'The whole [judicial] hearing was about looking for reasons to reject' (Thomas, NGO volunteer).

Although we found no evidence of this, the high levels of refusals make some NGOs and claimants believe decision-makers are given quotas for acceptance and refusal rates (Sofia and Emma, NGO workers, Germany; S130, NGO volunteer, UK). Even if that may not be the case, it seems that decision-makers search for the weakest element of the claim (PSG, persecution, credibility, etc.) and reject the claim on that basis. As explained by Kadir, an NGO worker in Germany, the question decision-makers ask themselves is not whether they should grant international protection, but whether there is any grounds *not* to grant international protection. For this purpose, we present a hypothetical 'charter of denial'. A cynical view of the system – collecting all the flawed aspects of decision-making explored in this chapter and applied in different ways to each country – might characterise the worst kind of decision-making mind-set in the following way:

(a) You are not who you say you are [gay/lesbian/bisexual/trans/queer/etc.] and/or your testimony is not credible, because [not enough evidence, claim submitted a long time after arrival, evidence submitted is staged/self-serving, etc.];

(b) [If a religion applies] You cannot be LGBTIQ+ because your religion frowns upon such identities/behaviours;

(c) Even if you are who you say you are, you can go back to your country because there is no law affecting you;

(d) Even if there is a law criminalising same-sex acts (or LGBTIQ+ identities / behaviours), it is not enforced or not enforced systematically;

(e) Even if the law is enforced, you would be 'naturally discreet' or 'discreet' through your own 'choice', so you would not run any risk upon return;

(f) Even if you were to run a risk, you can always relocate to another part of the country to avoid it;

(g) Even if the country may be dangerous for SOGI minorities, you lied about x or were inconsistent about y, so we cannot believe you in general;

(h) Etc.

In short, when there is the will to discredit a claim, there is a way. As Fernandez puts it, 'even when the credibility of both identity and persecution is reasonably established, immigration officials are often inconsistent in their interpretation of case law and can be surprisingly inventive in their contorted counter-explanations justifying the denial of eligibility for asylum' (Fernandez 2017, p. 205).

SOGI asylum thus becomes a striking illustration of the broader issue of the epistemic injustice produced by asylum systems: asylum systems are designed and operationalised in a way that privileges adjudicators' epistemic resources over claimants' resources, in order to legitimise the prerogative decision-makers have to 'arbitrarily and ambiguously misinterpret asylum applicants' experiences, cultures, and countries' – the so-called 'institutional comfort' enjoyed by decision-makers (Sertler 2018, p. 3). This is particularly evident in testimonial injustice (which includes denying claimants' experiences, ignoring available information, and deciding which information/criteria to use) and contributory injustice (which consists in knowingly and voluntarily employing prejudiced hermeneutical resources to undermine the epistemic agency of the claimants) (Sertler 2018, pp. 2 and 16). All these phenomena apply to SOGI asylum, as seen in this chapter, and the result is an excessive and inappropriate use of autonomy in decision-making by asylum adjudicators.

It may be beyond the power of asylum law and practice to completely overcome such testimonial and contributory injustices in SOGI claims. The task may simply be too complex and insurmountable in size and nature. The economic, resource and logistic pressures on current asylum systems are recognisably very significant. And they are not likely to diminish to any significant extent, so asylum adjudicators need to be supported in developing the necessary skills and competences that will allow them to offer decisions of better – even if not perfect – quality, more aligned with our theoretical and analytical underpinnings (Chap. 3), avoiding to a great extent the pitfalls discussed in this chapter. Recommendations to this effect will be explored in Chap. 11.

More generally, a claimant's life is not reduced to 'obtaining papers', no matter how important those 'papers' may be. In fact, for many LGBTIQ+ people we met during our fieldwork, their accommodation (Chap. 8), health, education and employment (Chap. 9) were greater priorities. We now turn to those areas of concern.

References

AIDA – Asylum Information Database. (2017). *Country report: Germany*. AIDA – Asylum Information Database. http://www.asylumineurope.org/sites/default/files/report-download/aida_de_2017update.pdf

APPG on Global LGBT Rights. (2016). *The UK's stance on international breaches of LGBT rights*. APPG. https://www.appglgbt.org/lgbt-report-2016

Arnold, S. K. (2012). Nexus with a Convention ground: The particular social group and sexual minority refugees in Ireland and the United Kingdom. *Irish Law Journal, 1*, 93–119.

Baillot, H., Cowan, S., & Munro, V. E. (2012). 'Hearing the right gaps': Enabling and responding to disclosures of sexual violence within the UK asylum process. *Social & Legal Studies, 21*(3), 269–296. https://doi.org/10.1177/0964663912444945.

Balboni, M. (2012). *La protezione internazionale in ragione del genere, dell'orientamento sessuale e dell'identità di genere*. Giappichelli.

BAMF – Bundesamt für Migration und Flüchtlinge. (2012). *Letter to member of parliament Volker Beck*. http://www.lsvd.de/fileadmin/pics/Dokumente/Recht/BAMF-121227.pdf

References

BAMF – Bundesamt für Migration und Flüchtlinge. (2017). *Dienstanweisung Asylverfahren – Verfolgung wegen Zugehörigkeit zu einer bestimmten sozialen Gruppe, DA-Asyl Stand.* https://www.proasyl.de/wp-content/uploads/2015/12/DA-Asyl-April-2017.pdf

Batchelor, T. (2018). *Gay man denied asylum in Austria because he was 'too girlish'.* The Independent. https://www.independent.co.uk/news/world/europe/austria-gay-man-asylum-application-denied-girlish-lgbt-iraq-a8506091.html

Bennett, C., & Thomas, F. (2013). Seeking asylum in the UK: Lesbian perspectives. *Forced Migration Review, 42,* 25.

Beresford, M. (2016). *The Home Office quizzed a bisexual asylum seeker on LGBT terminology during his interview process.* PinkNews. https://www.pinknews.co.uk/2016/11/12/the-home-office-quizzed-a-bisexual-asylum-seeker-on-lgbt-terminology-during-his-interview-process/

Berg, L., & Millbank, J. (2013). Developing a jurisprudence of transgender particular social group. In T. Spijkerboer (Ed.), *Fleeing Homophobia* (pp. 121–153). Routledge.

Braimah, T. S. (2015a). Defining a particular social group based on the meaning of non-discrimination in international human rights law: Utilizing the definition in deciding refugee claims based on sexual orientation. *Global Journal of Human Social Science: C Sociology & Culture,* 15(2), 23–31.

Braimah, T. S. (2015b). Divorcing sexual orientation from religion and politics: Utilizing the Convention grounds of religion and political opinion in same-sex oriented asylum claims. *International Journal of Refugee Law,* 27(3), 481–497. https://doi.org/10.1093/ijrl/eev033.

Briddock, A. (2016). The recognition of refugees based on sexual orientation and gender identity in the UK: An overview of law and procedure. *Birkbeck Law Review,* 4(1), 123–157.

Butler, J. (2004). *Undoing gender.* Routledge. https://www.routledge.com/Undoing-Gender-1st-Edition/Butler/p/book/9780415969239

Butterworth, B. (2016, December 5). *Just in: Gay man's deportation to homophobic Uganda postponed.* PinkNews. https://www.pinknews.co.uk/2016/12/05/friends-terrified-for-safety-of-gay-man-set-to-be-deported-to-uganda/

Cohen, J. (2002). Questions of credibility: Omissions, discrepancies and errors of recall in the testimony of asylum seekers. *International Journal of Refugee Law,* 13(3), 293–309.

Consiglio Italiano per i Rifugiati. (2007). Cir Notizie. 9 September 2007.

Danisi, C. (2019). Crossing borders between international refugee law and international human rights law in the European context: Can human rights enhance protection against persecution based on sexual orientation (and beyond)? *Netherlands Quarterly of Human Rights,* 37(4).

Díaz Lafuente, J. (2014). *Refugio y asilo por motivos de orientación sexual y/o identidad de género en el ordenamiento constitucional español.* Universitat de Valencia.

Duffy, N. (2018). *Bisexual Jamaican man wins right to stay in the UK after deportation battle.* PinkNews. https://www.pinknews.co.uk/2016/01/18/bisexual-jamaican-man-wins-right-to-stay-in-the-uk-after-deportation-battle/

Dugan, E. (2015). *Home Office says Nigerian asylum-seeker can't be a lesbian as she's got children.* The Independent. http://www.independent.co.uk/news/uk/home-news/home-office-says-nigerian-asylum-seeker-can-t-be-a-lesbian-as-she-s-got-children-10083385.html

Duggan, L. (2002). The new homonormativity: The sexual politics of neoliberalism. In D. Nelson & R. Castronovo (Eds.), *Materializing democracy: Toward a revitalized cultural politics.* Duke University Press.

Dustin, M. (2018). Many rivers to cross: The recognition of LGBTQI asylum in the UK. *International Journal of Refugee Law,* 30(1), 104–127. https://doi.org/10.1093/ijrl/eey018.

Dustin, M., & Ferreira, N. (2017). Canada's Guideline 9: Improving SOGIE claims assessment? *Forced Migration Review,* 56(October), 80–83.

Dustin, M., & Held, N. (2018). In or out? A queer intersectional approach to 'particular social group' membership and credibility in SOGI asylum claims in Germany and the UK. *GenIUS – Rivista di studi giuridici sull'orientamento sessuale e l'identità di genere (Special Issue on SOGI Asylum),* 5(2), 74–87.

EASO – European Asylum Support Office. (2018). *Compilation of jurisprudence: Evidence and credibility assessment in the context of the common European asylum system.* Publications Office of the European Union. https://www.easo.europa.eu/sites/default/files/eca-ceas-cj_en.pdf

ECRE – European Council on Refugees and Exiles. (2017). *Preliminary deference? The impact of judgments of the Court of Justice of the EU in cases X.Y.Z., A.B.C. and Cimade and Gisti on national law and the use of the EU Charter of Fundamental Rights.* http://s3.amazonaws.com/ecre/wp-content/uploads/2017/03/14102648/CJEU-study-Feb-2017-NEW.pdf

ECRE – European Council on Refugees and Exiles, AIDA – Asylum Information Database, & Asyl und Migration. (2019). *National country report: Germany, 2018 update.* ECRE – European Council on Refugees and Exiles. https://www.asylumineurope.org/sites/default/files/report-download/aida_de_2018update.pdf

Elgot, J. (2013). *Gay and Lesbian asylum seekers 'feel forced to show sex films to prove sexuality to UK border agency'.* HuffPost UK. https://www.huffingtonpost.co.uk/2013/02/04/gay-and-lesbian-asylum-seekers-sex-films-prove-_n_2615428.html

Fernandez, B. (2017). Queer border crossers: Pragmatic complicities, indiscretions and subversions. In D. Otto (Ed.), *Queering international law: Possibilities, alliances, complicities, risks* (pp. 193–212). Routledge. https://www.routledge.com/Queering-International-Law-Possibilities-Alliances-Complicities-Risks/Otto/p/book/9781138289918.

Ferreira, N. (2018). Reforming the common European asylum system: Enough rainbow for queer asylum seekers? *GenIUS – Rivista di studi giuridici sull'orientamento sessuale e l'identità di genere (Special Issue on SOGI Asylum),* 5(2), 25–42.

Ferreira, N., & Venturi, D. (2017, November 24). Tell me what you see and I'll tell you if you're gay: Analysing the Advocate General's Opinion in Case C-473/16, F v Bevándorlási és Állampolgársági Hivatal. EU Immigration and Asylum Law and Policy. http://eumigrationlaw-blog.eu/tell-me-what-you-see-and-ill-tell-you-if-youre-gay-analysing-the-advocate-generals-opinion-in-case-c-47316-f-v-bevandorlasi-es-allampolgarsagi-hivatal/

Ferreira, N., & Venturi, D. (2018). Testing the untestable: The CJEU's decision in case C-473/16, F v Bevándorlási és Állampolgársági Hivatal. European Database of Asylum Law. https://www.asylumlawdatabase.eu/en/journal/testing-untestable-cjeu%E2%80%99s-decision-case-c-47316-f-v-bev%C3%A1ndorl%C3%A1si-%C3%A9s-%C3%A1llampolg%C3%A1rs%C3%A1gi-hivatal

Fletcher, A. (2017). Queering the pitch: Sexuality, torture and recovery. In J. Boyles (Ed.), *Pschological therapies for survivors of torture. A human-rights approach with people seeking asylum* (pp. 223–245). PCCS Books.

Freedom from Torture. (2016). *Proving torture: Demanding the impossible—Home Office mistreatment of expert medical evidence.* http://www.refworld.org/docid/58495c5f4.html.

Gartner, J. L. (2016). *(In)credibly queer: Sexuality-based asylum in the European Union.* https://www.humanityinaction.org/knowledge_detail/incredibly-queer-sexuality-based-asylum-in-the-european-union/

Gasparini, A., La Torre, C., Gorini, S., & Russo, M. (2011). Homophobia in the Italian legal system: File not found. In L. Trappolin, A. Gasparini, & R. Wintemute (Eds.), *Confronting Homophobia in Europe. Social and legal perspective* (pp. 139–170). Oxford: Hart.

Grau, G., & Shoppmann, C. (Eds.). (2013). *The hidden Holocaust?: Gay and lesbian persecution in Germany 1933-45.* Routledge. https://doi.org/10.4324/9781315073880.

Gray, A., & McDowall, A. (2013). LGBT refugee protection in the UK: From discretion to belief? *Forced Migration Review,* 42, 22–25.

Gyulai, G., Kagan, M., Herlihy, J., Turner, S., Hárdi, L., & Udvarhelyi, É. T. (2013). *Credibility assessment in asylum procedures—A multidisciplinary training manual—Volume 1.* Hungarian Helsinki Committee. https://www.refworld.org/docid/5253bd9a4.html

Hall, J. (2013). *'Inhuman and degrading': Gay asylum seekers feel they must go to extreme lengths to prove their sexuality, including filming themselves having sex.* The Independent. https://

References 327

www.independent.co.uk/news/uk/home-news/inhuman-and-degrading-gay-asylum-seekers-feel-they-must-go-to-extreme-lengths-to-prove-their-8480470.html

Held, N. (2016). What does a 'genuine lesbian' look like? Intersections of sexuality and 'race' in Manchester's Gay Village and in the UK asylum system. In F. Stella, Y. Taylor, T. Reynolds, & A. Rogers (Eds.), *Sexuality, citizenship and belonging: Trans-national and intersectional perspectives* (pp. 131–148). Routledge.

Held, N. (2017). *What does a genuine lesbian/gay relationship look like in the eyes of asylum decision makers?* Discover Society. https://discoversociety.org/2017/05/02/what-does-a-genuine-lesbiangay-relationship-look-like-in-the-eyes-of-asylum-decision-makers/

Held, N., Rainbow Refugees Cologne-Support Group e.V., Aidshilfe Düsseldorf e.V., You're Welcome – Mashallah Düsseldorf, Kölner Flüchtlingsrat, Projekt Geflüchtete Queere Jugendliche, & Fachstelle Queere Jugend NRW / Schwules Netzwerk NRW e.V. (2018). *Projektbericht: Erfahrungen mit der Anhörung von LSBTIQ* Geflüchteten.* https://schwules--netzwerk.de/wp-content/uploads/2018/10/Projektbericht-zur-Anh%C3%B6rung-von-LSBTIQ-Gefl%C3%BCchteten.pdf

Hempel, J. J. (2014). *Sexuelle Orientierung als Asylgrund: Entwicklungen der europäischen Asylrechtspraxis am Beispiel Deutschlands* [Diplomarbeit]. Universitaet Wien.

Herlihy, J., & Turner, S. W. (2007). Asylum claims and memory of trauma: Sharing our knowledge. *The British Journal of Psychiatry, 191*(1), 3–4. https://doi.org/10.1192/bjp.bp.106.034439.

Herlihy, J., & Turner, S. W. (2009). The psychology of seeking protection. *International Journal of Refugee Law, 21*(2), 171–192. https://doi.org/10.1093/ijrl/eep004.

Hinger, S. (2010). Finding the fundamental: Shaping identity in gender and sexual orientation based asylum claims. *Columbia Journal of Gender and Law, 19*(2), 367–408.

Home Office. (2010). *Sexuality judgement welcomed.* GOV.UK. https://www.gov.uk/government/news/sexuality-judgement-welcomed

Home Office. (2011). *Gender identity issues in the asylum claim: Transgender.* GOV.UK. https://www.gov.uk/government/publications/dealing-with-gender-identity-issues-in-the-asylum-claim-process

Home Office. (2015). *Asylum policy instruction. Assessing credibility and refuge status.* Home Office.

Home Office. (2016). *Asylum policy instruction. Sexual orientation in asylum claims. Version 6.0.* GOV.UK. https://assets.publishing.service.gov.uk/government/uploads/system/uploads/attachment_data/file/543882/Sexual-orientation-in-asylum-claims-v6.pdf

Home Office. (2017). *Country policy and information note. Kenya: Sexual orientation and gender identity. Version 2.0e.* GOV.UK. https://assets.publishing.service.gov.uk/government/uploads/system/uploads/attachment_data/file/602447/Kenya_-_SOGI_-_CPIN_-_v2__March_2017_.pdf

Home Office. (2019). *Country policy and information note. Albania: Sexual orientation and gender identity. Version 6.0.* GOV.UK. https://assets.publishing.service.gov.uk/government/uploads/system/uploads/attachment_data/file/849856/Albania_-_SOGIE_-_CPIN_-_v6.0__December_2019_.pdf

House of Commons Home Affairs Committee. (2013). *Asylum. Seventh report of session 2013–14.* Volume I. House of Commons.

Hübner, K. (2016). Fluchtgrund sexuelle Orientierung und Geschlechtsidentität: Auswirkungen von heteronormativem Wissen auf die Asylverfahren LGBTI-Geflüchteter. *Feministische Studien, 34*(2). https://doi.org/10.1515/fs-2016-0005.

ICIBI – Independent Chief Inspector of Borders and Immigration. (2014). *An investigation into the Home Office's handling of asylum claims made on the grounds of sexual orientation March-June 2014.* GOV.UK. https://assets.publishing.service.gov.uk/government/uploads/system/uploads/attachment_data/file/547330/Investigation-into-the-Handling-of-Asylum-Claims_Oct_2014.pdf

ICIBI – Independent Chief Inspector of Borders and Immigration. (2016). *Inspection of country of origin information November 2016 report*. GOV.UK. http://icinspector.independent.gov.uk/wp--content/uploads/2017/02/Inspection-of-Country-of-Origin-Information_November-2016.pdf

ICJ – International Commission of Jurists. (2014). *X, Y and Z: A glass half full for "rainbow refugees"? The International Commission of Jurists' observations on the judgment of the Court of Justice of the European Union in X, Y and Z v. Minister voor Immigratie en Asiel.* ICJ – International Commission of Jurists.

ICJ – International Commission of Jurists. (2016). *Refugee status claims based on sexual orientation and gender identity: A practitioners' guide (Practitioners' Guide No. 11).* http://www.refworld.org/docid/56cabb7d4.html

IGLHRC – The International Gay and Lesbian Human Rights Commission. (2014). *Violence: Through the lens of lesbians, bisexual women and trans people in Asia.* https://www.outrightinternational.org/sites/default/files/LBT_ForUpload0614.pdf

Jansen, S. (2019). *Pride or shame? Assessing LGBTI asylum applications in the Netherlands following the XYZ and ABC judgments.* COC Netherlands. https://www.coc.nl/wp-content/uploads/2019/01/Pride-or-Shame-LGBTI-asylum-in-the-Netherlands.pdf

Jansen, S., & Spijkerboer, T. (2011). *Fleeing homophobia: Asylum claims related to sexual orientation and gender identity in Europe.* Vrije Universiteit Amsterdam. https://www.refworld.org/docid/4ebba7852.html

Jivraj, S., Tauqir, T., & de Jong, A. (2003). *Safra project initial findings. Identifying the difficulties experienced by Muslim lesbian, bisexual and transgender women in accessing social and legal services.* Safra Project.

Jordan, S., & Morrissey, C. (2013). 'On what grounds?' LGBT asylum claims in Canada. *Forced Migration Review, 42,* 13–15.

Juss, S. (2015). Sexual orientation and the sexualisation of refugee law. *International Journal on Minority and Group Rights, 22*(1), 128–153. https://doi.org/10.1163/15718115-02201005.

Juss, S. (2018). Recognising transnational refugee law. *TLI Think!*, Paper 14/2018. https://papers.ssrn.com/abstract=3259930

Kalkmann, M. (2010). German report. *Fleeing Homophobia, Seeking Safety in Europe: Best practices on the (legal) position of LGBT Asylum Seekers in the EU Members States.* https://www.yumpu.com/en/document/view/21133881/draft-questionnaire

Khan, T. (2016). *Investigating the British Asylum system for lesbian, gay and bisexual Asylum-seekers: Theoretical and empirical perspectives on Fairness* [PhD thesis]. University of Liverpool.

Klesse, C. (2018). On the government of bisexual bodies: Asylum case law and the biopolitics of bisexual erasure. In H. Richter (Ed.), *Biopolitical Governance: Race, Gender and Economy* (pp. 163–190). Rowman & Littlefield International.

La Migration. (2018). *Manuale per operatori.* La Migration. https://arcigaypalermo.wordpress.com/2018/10/15/la-migration-il-manuale-per-operatori/

Lewis, R. A. (2014). 'Gay? Prove it': The politics of queer anti-deportation activism. *Sexualities, 17*(8), 958–975.

Markard, N. (2013). EuGH zur sexuellen Orientierung als Fluchtgrund: Zur Entscheidung 'X, Y und Z gegen Minister vor Immigratie en Asiel' vom 7.11. 2013. *Asylmagazin, 12,* 402–408.

Markard, N., & Adamietz, L. (2011). Keep it in the Closet? Flüchtlingsanerkennung wegen Homosexualität auf dem Prüfstand. *Kritische Justiz, 44*(3), 294–302.

Millbank, J. (2009a). From discretion to disbelief: Recent trends in refugee determinations on the basis of sexual orientation in Australia and the United Kingdom. *The International Journal of Human Rights, 13*(2–3), 391–414. https://doi.org/10.1080/13642980902758218.

Millbank, J. (2009b). The ring of truth: A case study of credibility assessment in particular social group refugee determinations. *International Journal of Refugee Law, 21*(1), 1–33.

Monro, S., Hines, S., & Osborne, A. (2017). Is bisexuality invisible? A review of sexualities scholarship 1970–2015. *The Sociological Review, 65*(4), 663–681.

References

Morgan, J. (2018). *Bisexual asylum seeker says UK system is driving him to suicide.* Gay Star News. https://www.gaystarnews.com/article/bisexual-asylum-seeker-suicide/

Nayeri, D. (2019). *The ungrateful refugee.* Canongate Books.

Network of Legal Experts in the Non-Discrimination Field. (2015). *Reversing the burden of proof: Practical dilemmas at the European and national level.* Publications Office of the European Union. https://publications.europa.eu/en/publication-detail/-/publication/a763ee82-b93c-4df9-ab8c-626a660c9da8/language-en

Palermo, P. (2018). Orientamento sessuale e identità di genere nel sistema dell'asilo in Italia anche alla luce della riforma Minniti. *GenIUS – Rivista di studi giuridici sull'orientamento sessuale e l'identità di genere (Special Issue on SOGI Asylum),* 5(2), 43–58.

Puumala, E., & Ylikomi, R. (2017). *The dynamics of asylum determination interviews: An analysis of interaction, vulnerability and the politics of protection.* Nordic Asylum Law Seminar, University of Iceland, Reykjavík.

Ramón Mendos, L. (2019). *State-sponsored homophobia 2019: Global legislation overview update.* ILGA. https://ilga.org/downloads/ILGA_World_State_Sponsored_Homophobia_report_global_legislation_overview_update_December_2019.pdf

Sertler, E. (2018). The institution of gender-based asylum and epistemic injustice: A structural limit. *Feminist Philosophy Quarterly,* 4(3), 2.

Shidlo, A., & Ahola, J. (2013). Mental health challenges of LGBT forced migrants. *Forced Migration Review,* 42, 9–11.

Sridharan, S. (2008). *The difficulties of U.S. Asylum claims based on sexual orientation.* Migration Policy Institute. https://www.migrationpolicy.org/article/difficulties-us-asylum-claims-based-sexual-orientation

Strudwick, P. (2018). *The government threatened to deport this man with learning disabilities because they didn't believe he could be gay.* BuzzFeed. https://www.buzzfeed.com/patrickstrudwick/the-government-refused-to-believe-this-asylum-seeker-was

Taylor, D., & Townsend, M. (2014). Gay asylum seekers face 'humiliation'. *The Observer.* https://www.theguardian.com/uk-news/2014/feb/08/gay-asylum-seekers-humiliation-home-office

UKLGIG – UK Lesbian and Gay Immigration Group. (2013). *Missing the mark. Decision making on lesbian, gay (bisexual, trans and intersex) asylum claims.* UKLGIG – UK Lesbian and Gay Immigration Group.

UKLGIG – UK Lesbian and Gay Immigration Group. (2018). *Still falling short. The standard of Home Office decision-making in asylum claims based on sexual orientation and gender identity.* https://uklgig.org.uk/wp-content/uploads/2018/07/Still-Falling-Short.pdf

UKVI – UK Visas and Immigration. (2011). *Transgender identity issues in asylum claims.* UK Visas and Immigration. https://www.gov.uk/government/publications/dealing-with-gender-identity-issues-in-the-asylum-claim-process

UNHCR – UN High Commissioner for Refugees. (1998). *Note on burden and standard of proof in refugee claims.* UNHCR – UN High Commissioner for Refugees. https://www.refworld.org/docid/3ae6b3338.html

UNHCR – UN High Commissioner for Refugees. (2002a). *Guidelines on International Protection No. 1: Gender-Related Persecution within the context of Article 1A(2) of the 1951 Convention and/or its 1967 protocol relating to the status of refugees (HCR/GIP/02/01).* UNHCR – UN High Commissioner for Refugees. http://www.unhcr.org/publications/legal/3d58ddef4/guidelines-international-protection-1-gender-related-persecution-context.html

UNHCR – UN High Commissioner for Refugees. (2002b). *Guidelines on International Protection No. 2: 'Membership of a Particular Social Group' Within the Context of Article 1A(2) of the 1951 Convention and/or its 1967 Protocol Relating to the Status of Refugees.* UNHCR – UN High Commissioner for Refugees. http://www.unhcr.org/uk/publications/legal/3d58de2da/guidelines-international-protection-2-membership-particular-social-group.html

UNHCR – UN High Commissioner for Refugees. (2011). *Handbook on procedures and criteria for determining refugee status under the 1951 convention and the 1967 protocol relating to the status of refugees.* UNHCR – UN High Commissioner for Refugees. http://www.unhcr.org/

uk/publications/legal/3d58e13b4/handbook-procedures-criteria-determining-refugee-status-under-1951-convention.html

UNHCR – UN High Commissioner for Refugees. (2012). *Guidelines on International Protection No. 9: Claims to Refugee Status based on Sexual Orientation and/or Gender Identity within the context of Article 1A(2) of the 1951 Convention and/or its 1967 protocol relating to the status of refugees (HCR/GIP/12/09)*. UNHCR – UN High Commissioner for Refugees. http://www.unhcr.org/509136ca9.pdf

UNHCR – UN High Commissioner for Refugees. (2013). *Beyond proof, credibility assessment in EU asylum systems: Full report*. UNHCR – UN High Commissioner for Refugees. https://www.refworld.org/docid/519b1fb54.html

Vogler, S. (2019). Determining transgender: Adjudicating gender identity in U.S. Asylum law. *Gender & Society,* 33(3), 439–462.

Wessels, J. (2012). HJ (Iran) and HT (Cameroon) – Reflections on a new test for sexuality-based asylum claims in Britain. *International Journal of Refugee Law,* 24(4), 815–839. https://doi.org/10.1093/ijrl/ees057

Winkler, M. (2011). 'A silent right is not a right': Orientamento sessuale, diritti fondamentali e 'coming out' a margine di una sentenza inglese in tema di rifugiati. *Il Corriere Giuridico,* 10, 1375–1383.

Woolley, A. (2017). Narrating the 'asylum story': Between literary and legal storytelling. *International Journal of Postcolonial Studies,* 19(3), 376–394.

Yeo, C. (2016, August 8). *New Home Office API on gay asylum claims: Not fit for purpose*. Free Movement. https://www.freemovement.org.uk/new-home-office-api-on-gay-asylum-claims-not-fit-for-purpose/

Open Access This chapter is licensed under the terms of the Creative Commons Attribution 4.0 International License (http://creativecommons.org/licenses/by/4.0/), which permits use, sharing, adaptation, distribution and reproduction in any medium or format, as long as you give appropriate credit to the original author(s) and the source, provide a link to the Creative Commons license and indicate if changes were made.

The images or other third party material in this chapter are included in the chapter's Creative Commons license, unless indicated otherwise in a credit line to the material. If material is not included in the chapter's Creative Commons license and your intended use is not permitted by statutory regulation or exceeds the permitted use, you will need to obtain permission directly from the copyright holder.

Chapter 8
Housing and Accommodation

> *Lesbians shouldn't be taken to villages where they are not wanted. They should stay here in the town where they are wanted. (...) They can't express themselves in villages.*
>
> (Winifred, Germany)

> *We are here for freedom, but in this case almost two years I am in the camp, there is nothing like freedom still. Because I am caged like a chain, could not go out, could not go sleep out, could not go to a club, that is out of me.*
>
> (Mamaka, Italy)

> *The first night I had to go up and down with the night bus because I didn't know where I would sleep. So I would rather get this bus, from [location A] to [location B], drop off, wait for another one so that the driver would not see me.*
>
> (Meggs, UK)

8.1 Introduction

The SOGI claimants we interviewed were often more or as concerned about their living conditions in the host country than they were with the asylum process. This was especially the case in the interviews in Germany and Italy, where issues around housing and accommodation often dominated the discussion, both in interviews with SOGI claimants and with professionals. For instance, Elias, a lawyer in Germany, told us that his clients were often less concerned about the legal procedure and more about 'the problems around it. Less legally, less tangibly in relation to the procedure, but rather: "What about the accommodation situation?"; "How can I rebuild a life appropriate to my sexual orientation?"'.

In our European-wide online survey, most respondents (59%) were accommodated in reception or accommodation centres provided by the government or local authority, followed by privately rented accommodation (19%), and a small percentage of respondents (7%) were staying with friends and family. Forty-four per cent

© The Author(s) 2021

C. Danisi et al., *Queering Asylum in Europe*, IMISCOE Research Series,

https://doi.org/10.1007/978-3-030-69441-8_8

of the respondents said they felt safe in their accommodation, while a staggering 41% did not feel safe (15% were not sure).

While there has been an increase in research on SOGI asylum claims in Europe and beyond – as the previous chapters have demonstrated – there has been less of a focus on the social experiences of LGBTIQ+ claimants and refugees. Some research on the experiences of SOGI asylum touches upon housing issues (Bennett and Thomas 2013; Dyck 2019; Jansen and Spijkerboer 2011), and other research has looked specifically at SOGI claimants' physical and mental health needs (Alessi et al. 2018; Allsopp et al. 2014; Namer and Razum 2018). In this chapter we aim to address this gap by offering an in-depth analysis of LGBTIQ+ asylum claimants' experiences with housing and accommodation in Germany, Italy and the UK.

As we explored in Chap. 5, arrival and reception are often not easy for SOGI claimants, who do not receive the support they need to deal with their trauma and feel safe. As we outlined, none of the three countries has specific policies in place with regard to the initial reception of SOGI claimants. This is not untypical for EU member states, as the EU Reception Directive also fails to refer to SOGI (Ferreira 2018). Reception conditions for SOGI claimants has now been recognised as an important issue by EU policy-makers. As Alfred, a European Parliament staff member, told us, members of the European Parliament are trying to bring in a reference to LGBTI asylum claimants so that their specific needs are taken into account, and 'there can be measures during the reception conditions provision, such as specific housing or perhaps protective measures'. If successful, this will be the first time such a provision has been mentioned in a legal instrument. As Terry, a member of the European Parliament, explained, 'just letting it go [homophobic and transphobic attacks in reception centres] is not the answer, so you have to have a proactive, preventive stance on how can you protect LGBTI people in such situations'.

Beyond EU law, all three countries are bound by human rights treaties that, directly or indirectly, protect a right to adequate housing. Besides what emerges from the ECtHR's jurisprudence in relation to reception of asylum claimants belonging to sexual minorities (Sect. 5.4.3, Chap. 5), universal human rights bodies have specified the scope of this right as well as how to implement it effectively. For instance, the 'Guidelines for the Implementation of the Right to Adequate Housing' by the UN Special Rapporteur on adequate housing specify that:

> [T]he right to adequate housing should not be interpreted narrowly, as a right to mere physical shelter or to housing conceived as a commodity. Rather, the right to housing must be understood in relation to the inherent dignity of the human person (Human Rights Council 2019, p. 4).

This includes the right to be treated equally with regard to housing and not to be discriminated against on grounds of gender, 'race', sexual orientation, gender identity, disability, age, 'refugeeness', religion and/or intersectional discrimination (Human Rights Council 2019, pp. 10–12).

This chapter explores SOGI claimants' and refugees' experiences with housing by first outlining the asylum accommodation policies in Germany, Italy and the UK (Sect. 8.2) and discussing general issues that SOGI claimants have with housing

(Sect. 8.3), before looking at specific SOGI-related issues such as sharing accommodation, being in the closet and experiencing discrimination and hate crime (Sect. 8.4), rural vs. urban accommodation (Sect. 8.5), homelessness and destitution (Sect. 8.6), accommodation after the asylum process (Sect. 8.7), SOGI-specific accommodation (Sect. 8.8), and detention (Sect. 8.9).

8.2 Asylum Accommodation Policies

Different housing policies exist in Germany, Italy and the UK. In Germany, claimants are placed in one of the three main types of accommodation: initial reception centres, collective accommodation centres and decentralised accommodation. The federal states are required to establish and maintain the initial reception centres and there is at least one centre in every state. The branch offices of the BAMF are usually located in these centres, and some of these offices deal with particular nationalities.[1]

In all of the interviews with professionals the 'EASY-roulette' (Frank S., legal advisor) was a major topic of conversation. Germany operates a distribution system called 'EASY' ('Erstverteilung der Asylsuchenden – Initial Distribution of Asylum Seekers'), which allocates asylum claimants to reception centres in a certain federal state and then accommodation within certain municipalities within that state, according to the capacity of the reception facilities, nationality of the claimant and the 'Königstein Key' ('Koenigsteiner Schluessel'), which determines the reception capacity of the 16 federal states.[2] Consequently, it is a 'roulette' where a claimant ends up. According to a 2019 parliamentary request (BMI 2019, p. 5), when claimants are distributed according to the EASY process, no criteria exist for considering sexual orientation or gender identity.

While the 'allocation of the asylum seeker to a particular area is not a formal decision that can be legally challenged by the individual' (ECRE, AIDA & Asyl und Migration 2018, p. 72), it is possible to request relocation on the basis of specific needs, but it has become increasingly difficult to have such requests approved (Kadir, NGO worker; Marlen, legal advisor; Matthias, social worker). When relocation requests to the federal state administration are made, the authorities often argue that it is the responsibility of the municipality to make sure that people feel safe, but as Matthias (social worker) explained, the situation puts an enormous strain on SOGI claimants' mental health (Chap. 9). Some participants were positive about the regulations in Saxony, which was seen as a relatively good example of a federal state, where SOGI claimants are usually housed in one of the three big cities (Chemnitz, Dresden and Leipzig) after leaving the reception centre (Matthias, social worker). Here, NGOs work together to inform the authorities about vulnerable

---

[1] For instance, the BAMF office in Munich deals with claimants from Uganda and Nigeria.

[2] Their capacity depends on the size and economic strength of the federal State in question.

persons, and then the Federal Directorate of Saxony ('Landesdirektion Sachsen') decides to which city the person is allocated. Local civil servants in Leipzig then also check with NGOs which claimants they can put together, and they offer flats specifically for SOGI claimants. Yet, this was not always effective and there had been cases where people were allocated to rural areas even though the authorities knew about their vulnerabilities. Two reasons why accommodation provision appears to work better in Saxony than in other federal states are that one of the Ministers of state ('Staatsministerin') is very supportive of SOGI refugees and that the housing market in general in cities such as Leipzig, is still not as stretched as in other urban areas (Sabrina, NGO worker).

Kadir (NGO worker), for instance, campaigns for smaller LGBTIQ+ decentralised accommodation in all of the cities in each federal state, not just the biggest. This would also make the whole process easier as claimants would not have to make a relocation request in the first place, if there is LGBTIQ+ accommodation in their municipality. For this to work, however, local authorities need to be supportive of such projects and have an understanding of why SOGI refugees may be vulnerable and in need of specific accommodation in urban areas. In Leon's (NGO worker) view, the Frankfurt am Main City Council, for instance, is supportive, while other city councils would argue that 'homosexuality is completely normal in our society, that's why we treat people totally normal'.

Once someone is allocated to a different municipality, it is difficult to relocate, not only during the asylum claim but also after (Sabrina, NGO worker). After receiving status, and if they rely on state benefits, claimants have to stay for 3 years in the federal state where their claim was processed, and in some federal states even within the municipality to which they were assigned, under the residence obligation legislation.[3] On 13 May 2019, the German Parliament (Bundestag) decided to render this residence obligation ('Wohnsitzauflage') an indefinite policy (it was initially introduced in July 2016 for a period of 3 years). During the debate in the German parliament, it was argued that this policy has proven to be successful for integration (Deutscher Bundestag 2019). However, with this regulation the federal government is reducing the choices of refugees and further increasing their social isolation.

In general, policies vary considerably between the federal states, and there is no common standard for reception centres. The 'Federal Initiative for the Protection of Refugee People in Refugee Accommodation', founded jointly under the auspices of the Federal Ministry for Family Affairs, Senior Citizens, Women and Youth and the United Nations Children's Fund (UNICEF), has developed guidelines with minimum standards for the protection of refugees in refugee accommodation, including an annex on the implementation of minimum standards for SOGI refugees (BMFSFJ 2018). This includes the development of an internal protection concept and the sensitisation of all persons working in accommodation facilities to the needs of SOGI

---

[3] These specific regulations were introduced on 1 April 2018 in Bavaria, Baden-Wuerttemberg, North Rhine-Westphalia, Hesse, Saarland and Saxony (ECRE, AIDA & Asyl und Migration 2018, p. 102).

8.2 Asylum Accommodation Policies

refugees. However, there is no monitoring of the extent to which these non-binding guidelines are applied. The government has confirmed it has no plans to establish an independent complaints office, which SOGI refugees could contact in case of accommodation problems (BMI 2019, pp. 6–7).

The distribution policies and new reforms that allow claimants to be kept in reception centres for up to 24 months (rather than 6 months, as before, Chap. 4) can exacerbate social isolation, as claimants often end up in 'the middle of nowhere' (Angel, Ibrahim, Trudy Ann). This is in particular difficult for SOGI claimants, as we explain in Sect. 8.6. For instance, Tina was only supposed to stay in the camp for 6 months, but then the law changed:

> they said they made another law that said you have to stay two years in the camp before you leave. No school, no working, just stay (...) For somebody to be in this situation, you're just in one place, one position, your life is on hold, you're not allowed to do anything, school, work... in that aspect it's frustrating, in that way.

In addition, there is a 'residence obligation' ('Residenzpflicht') in place that restricts the movement of claimants outside the area of the reception centre for a period of (usually) 3 months (ECRE, AIDA & Asyl und Migration 2019, p. 71). In most federal states, claimants need special permission to travel to other parts of the state or to other parts of Germany during that time.[4]

Similarly to Germany, Italy is bound by the EU recast Procedures and Reception Directives. Here, the Directive was implemented through the introduction of new legislation on reception conditions and procedures in 2015, which identifies SOGI claimants as vulnerable if they are victims of torture, rape or serious violence. This means that SOGI asylum claimants may now benefit more easily, always as individuals rather than as a group, from services addressing their specific needs.[5] However, whether or not a person is considered in need of specific protection always depends on whether they receive a careful individual evaluation of their case on arrival, as SOGI claimants are not comprehensively identified and treated as a 'vulnerable' group (Chap. 5).

Italy has two distinct forms of reception, which are very different in terms of services provided to people claiming asylum. On the one hand, the CAS ('centri di accoglienza straordinaria' – extraordinary reception centres) are basic and temporary reception centres, set to deal with the growing number of arrivals. CAS are established by agreements between the government and private bodies (through local authorities, the 'prefettura'), which can manage these centres with a considerable degree of liberty. Their size and services provided vary considerably, depending on the professionalism of the management. On the other hand, a more structured form of reception is provided through the SPRAR system ('Sistema di Protezione per i Rifugiati e i Richiedenti Asilo' – System of Protection for Refugees and Asylum Claimants), which brings central authorities together with local entities and

---

[4] One SOGI claimant who lived in Bavaria and wanted to come to the SOGICA conference in Frankfurt in July 2019 was not able to come, as she did not obtain the permission in time.

[5] See Legislative Decree no. 142, 18 August 2015.

associations working in the field to provide asylum claimants with more than the basic material conditions provided in the CAS.[6] The SPRAR aims to provide people in need of international protection with a wider range of social and life support services.[7] Those hosted in such reception centres are indeed involved in a variety of activities associated with social inclusion and integration, for example, acquiring better language skills, and more easily accessing basic services, including health assistance. In parallel, they also provide assistance during the RSD process through the preparation for personal interviews before the territorial commissions (Chap. 6). However, because of the SPRAR's overall capacity, it should be noted that a very limited number of people are included in this kind of reception system (Anci et al. 2016, p. 71).

While SOGI minorities in the process of claiming asylum were potentially entitled to access these reception centres where they fell into one of the vulnerable groups mentioned above, the 2018 reform reserved SPRAR centres only for those already granted international protection, leaving asylum claimants with few options (Chap. 4).[8] Even more worrying, the new system privileges large centres instead of the small-scale facilities that had previously existed. The implications of the new policy for people claiming asylum, including those who flee homophobia and transphobia, appear to be extremely negative (Ziniti 2018). As Vincenzo (LGBTIQ+ group volunteer) described:

> So, these two last reforms, the one that has eliminated a degree of appeal and the one that has completely revised access for example to the SPRAR, all unfortunately have an important impact on people seeking international protection on grounds of sexual orientation and gender identity. Because the SOGI factor in relation to the time factor is not considered in any way, as it is an aspect that is not self-evident, not easy to narrate, not easy to recognise, not easy to legitimise, can emerge belatedly, (…) can be hindered by the presence of an interpreter or translator, it can be distorted because the person was afraid to tell something else in a certain way compared to what was said previously.

As Daniele (decision-maker) explained, the reception system in Italy needs improving, but authorities are trying to deal with a large number of arrivals and it was positive that the government tried to avoid large-scale accommodation facilities by generally distributing only 12–15 refugees to each accommodation centre, thus it is easier to have close relationships with claimants and respond to their needs. One issue that was highlighted was that the people who run the receptions centres were often not interested in the well-being of refugees or in supporting their integration, rather 'there are many who open a reception centre to make money' (Antonella, LGBTIQ+ group volunteer). Owing to this profit-based approach, managers of centres would also try to save money on psychologists, lawyers, etc.:

---

[6] See www.sprar.it.

[7] Decree of the Minister of Internal Affairs, 10 August 2016, which contains guidelines for the functioning of SPRAR: www.gazzettaufficiale.it/eli/id/2016/08/27/16A06366/sg.

[8] Article 12 of Decree Law no. 113/2018 (converted into Law no. 132, 1 December 2018), so-called 'Decreto Salvini'.

8.2 Asylum Accommodation Policies

All the reception system that was also given to private individuals, to people who were not in the social sector and who saw each other from day to day to do a social job that must be enormously prepared and instead they do it for profit, so they look to save on the psychologist, the mediator, the lawyer and therefore they are managing people who have a whole complexity of problems that are sometimes, because many structures are completely isolated from society, so how can we involve migrants, integrate them if in a year they are lost in the mountains (Susanna, social worker).

Moving to another area is also difficult in Italy: 'relocation is difficult; if you are under the prefecture of Vicenza, I cannot send the person to Emilia-Romagna where perhaps there is a centre for LGBT claimants' (Giulio, LGBTIQ+ group volunteer). Here, the support given by lawyers and NGOs is invaluable. For instance, Ken needed the intervention of his lawyer to be able to move out of the reception centre, where he faced discrimination by other residents (Chap. 6).

In the UK, 'accommodation is a huge issue' (Nath, lawyer) too and SOGI claimants can face abuse and harassment in their shared housing (David, official). Accommodation and subsistence support, known as 'section 95 support', is provided to claimants pending a first decision on their application (Home Affairs Committee 2018). In 1999, the UK government introduced the policy of 'dispersal', with the intention of relocating people seeking asylum who tended to go to London and the South East to areas of the country where accommodation was cheaper (House of Commons Home Affairs Committee 2017, p. 16). However, claimants with support networks in particular places may choose to stay with friends rather than taking the accommodation provided by the Home Office (Olivia, government official). Since 2012, under COMPASS (Commercial and Operational Managers Procuring Asylum Support Services), asylum accommodation has been contracted out to private companies, including Serco, which also runs detention centres such as Yarl's Wood (House of Commons Home Affairs Committee 2017). In response to dissatisfaction with the operation of COMPASS on the basis of efficiency and quality of service, the system was replaced with new asylum contracts awarded in 2019 and renamed AASC (Asylum Accommodation and Support Services Contracts).[9] There is – theoretically – a 'cluster limit' of no more than one asylum claimant per 200 residents in an area (House of Commons Home Affairs Committee 2017, p. 16). However, distribution of claimants is unequal, with less than a third of local authorities 'actively supporting dispersal' (Home Affairs Committee 2018, p. 23).

The Scottish Refugee Council reported that, in 2018, there were 2859 asylum claimants in 'dispersed accommodation' in Scotland (Scottish Refugee Council 2019). Until 2001, relatively low numbers of asylum claimants and refugees settled in Wales compared to some parts of the UK. This changed in 2001, when Cardiff, Newport, Swansea and Wrexham became official dispersal areas and, by 2016, it was estimated that Wales had provided sanctuary to 397 Syrian refugees and nearly 3000 asylum claimants from other countries (Equality, Local Government and Communities Committee 2017, p. 12). There are no official yearly figures for the number of people claiming asylum in Northern Ireland, but in the period of April to

---

[9] https://www.gov.uk/government/news/new-asylum-accommodation-contracts-awarded.

June 2015 there were 497 people living in asylum support accommodation, while in the same time period the figures were 24,791 for England and 2649 for Scotland (Fergus 2015).

SOGI-related issues are not taken into account when people are dispersed and accommodation is chosen for them, as:

> essentially the Home Office policy is that when deciding on the dispersal of individuals to asylum accommodation who have declared as homosexual or whatever, it makes no difference to where to house them and so they will put someone who has declared, into a house with another male from perhaps a country where culturally this is going to be a really difficult thing. And then rely on the LGBTI individual to raise an issue about it, to say this isn't going to work. Which does seem to me to be rather risky and remarkably unnecessary. (…) I am not sure that there is, there is a recognition of issues around LGBTI (David, official).[10]

A Home Office Guide to Living in Asylum Accommodation was published in July 2019 in English and ten other languages.[11] It specifies that residents need to treat housemates with respect regardless of characteristics including sex, gender and gender identity, but does not mention sexual orientation (Home Office 2019, p. 19). There are specific concerns for SOGI minorities relating to failings in accommodation provision, as a report on asylum accommodation by the Independent Chief Inspector in 2018 demonstrated. It identified SOGI minorities as 'particularly vulnerable' and on that basis recommended that the government kept data on them and reviewed the appropriateness of providing no-choice accommodation and forced bedroom-sharing (ICIBI 2018, p. 14). The inspection team heard of LGBTIQ+ people being harassed and abused by other accommodation receivers (ICIBI 2018, p. 60). The Home Office was not able to provide the inspection team with figures for the number of LGBTIQ+ asylum claimants provided with accommodation on a 'no choice' basis.[12] In its response, the Home Office accepted all the ICIBI's recommendations (Home Office 2018, p. 6).

While policies on asylum accommodation differ between and within the three countries, so do the standards of accommodation, as we now explore.

---

[10] However, as David described, one of the three main housing providers came up with an initiative to house SOGI claimants together in a 'Rainbow' house.

[11] https://www.gov.uk/government/publications/living-in-asylum-accommodation.

[12] '[A] Home Office senior manager explained that the Home Office's current position with regard to the allocation of asylum accommodation was that LGBTQI+ asylum seekers should be "mainstreamed" (routed in the normal way), and if problems arose the individual should inform the Provider. This appeared to ignore the fact that the individual may not feel able to complain, and that the strong message from the Home Office was that asylum accommodation was provided on a "no choice basis"' (ICIBI 2018, pp. 60–61).

8.3 Standard of Asylum Accommodation

Many of the SOGI claimants we interviewed talked about general issues with regard to housing that affect all claimants, such as the quality of housing, hygiene and the food offered. Nonetheless, SOGI claimants experience these general issues together with more specific issues that relate to their SOGI. We briefly discuss the former as the basis for then exploring SOGI-specific experiences.

In Germany, as housing policies vary between the federal states, there is no common standard for reception centres. Generally, the initial reception centres have at least several hundred places, while some facilities can host large numbers of persons (one AnkER centre in Bavaria has a capacity of 3400 and has accommodated 1500 people at a time: ECRE, AIDA & Asyl und Migration 2018, p. 79). William, for instance, told us that he stayed in a reception centre that housed around 1100 people.

These centres are often (re-furbished) former army barracks, reported as sometimes being cockroach infested (Scott 2014). According to Komaromi (2016), security at reception centres is sub-contracted to private companies, usually on the basis of the cheapest bid, in all federal states other than Bavaria. This is highly problematic, as staff generally lack training in reception centres (Chap. 6). These companies can also attract neo-Nazi employees, and cases of racist abuse and violence against asylum claimants by these security guards are known, but not always taken seriously by the state and rarely penalised (Komaromi 2016). While the policies in place usually include housing single women and families in separate buildings or wings of buildings, this is not always the case. A shower can be shared by 10–12 people (sometimes more), and there is rarely shared kitchen space available (food is provided and served in canteens). Asylum claimants often have to report to security personnel when leaving and re-entering. In 2015 and 2016, Germany was overwhelmed and unprepared for the high number of asylum claimants, and people were often put in emergency shelters such as gyms, schools, containers, office buildings, warehouses and tents. This situation has changed considerably owing to the decreasing number of claimants reaching Germany and many reception centres have closed or have vacant places (ECRE, AIDA & Asyl und Migration 2018).

After the initial period in reception centres (which may now be up to 24 months), asylum claimants are sent to local accommodation centres, known as 'collective accommodation' ('Gemeinschaftsunterkuenfte'), usually in the same federal state, where they stay for the rest of their claim (including appeal procedures, but this is handled differently in different municipalities). These accommodation centres are also often former barracks or (formerly empty) apartment blocks and are either managed by the responsible authorities themselves or by NGOs or private facility management companies. As AIDA reports: 'Because different policies are pursued on regional and local level, it is impossible to make general statements on the standards of living in the follow-up accommodation facilities' (ECRE, AIDA & Asyl und Migration 2018, p. 80). The living conditions in these accommodation centres differ significantly between regions and even between towns. These centres, especially the larger ones, are often referred to as 'camps' by asylum claimants and refugees. Although conditions in these centres are often far from ideal, some claimants have to stay in them for several years (including asylum claimants who have 'tolerated stay'/'Duldung'). As Mariya (NGO worker) described, 'from the initial reception facility to the accommodation centres, the conditions of refugee accommodation are still terrible'. Asylum claimants and refugees have actively campaigned against these conditions, especially in Berlin (Bhimji 2016).

In our interviews, most participants did not give positive reports of their accommodation. Angel's experiences in different types of asylum accommodation led her to conclude that: 'How I feel personally is like we refugees, and I'm not just saying Jamaicans or Black people, we refugees on a whole, we are treated less than human, to me. Based on my observation'. At the time of the interview, Angel had been living with her teenage daughter in asylum accommodation, a remote army barracks in the woods in deep Hessen (Sect. 8.6). She asked to be moved and a social worker from an LGBTIQ+ organisation, who visited her regularly, helped her with the application for transfer ('Umverteilungsantrag'). However, it seemed unlikely that the application would be approved, as they had already offered her accommodation once in a nearby town that she had refused to take. Angel had gone there with a friend, who helped her and her daughter with the move. Angel described to us how she felt when she arrived in the accommodation centre:

> As soon as I saw the room, I called the social worker and I was like, "no", I burst into tears, I couldn't control my emotions, I was like, "no". I know I'm a refugee and I know I'm seeking protection from Germany, but I wouldn't let my dog live in that room.

Instead, she took all her belongings and went back to her accommodation in the army camp, paying for the taxi herself. At the time of the interview she was still desperate to move out. She was told by the local authorities that she could rent private accommodation, but she struggled to find any owing to her refused asylum claim and limited residence permit. Her accommodation choices were also restricted because she needed to stay within the specific district ('Landkreis') which had only one or two reasonably large towns.

Trudy Ann described the reception centre where she and her partner had to stay for 10 days as '[t]hat place is like a prison there'. She said that the camp was smelly and dirty, and that women and men were mixed: 'I hated it there (…) that place is not for human beings. It's dirty. Very filthy. The people there are nasty, very nasty'. Trudy Ann described the beds in the reception and accommodation centre as 'prison beds'. She found her living conditions distressing: 'Sometimes I'm at school and my mind is not there. I'm like saying, I left my own country to come here, went through so much. Sleep here, sleep there, eat this, eat that'. At the time of the interview, she and her partner were sharing a room in an accommodation centre in Hessen, where they could cook for themselves, however, under rather unhygienic conditions. Also other participants talked about inadequate and unhygienic conditions. Rosette told us that the toilets in the reception centre were always blocked, so 'you can stay for a week without visiting a toilet' or go to the nearby McDonalds to use the toilet there. And yet, claimants are expected to take what they are offered

8.3 Standard of Asylum Accommodation

without complaining. As William described, when he went to the regional office for foreigners' affairs (Landesamt fuer Auslaenderangelegenheiten) to ask for a transfer, he was told: 'You came [here] thinking that Germany is heaven. Now you want a big house'.

As people do not have privacy in the reception and accommodation centres, there is also the risk of their belongings being stolen. This happened to Marhoon and Prince Emrah. Prince Emrah had their mobile phone and other items, including shoes, stolen. In the accommodation centre, Marhoon's roommate had a friend visiting; when he woke up in the morning, they were both gone and had stolen his rucksack, which he always kept under the bed, and new boots that he had just bought:

> What else can I handle...you know? I was disowned by my family, I was threatened, I can't go back to my country, and all of this and now this. Treated like shit in the camp, nobody cares, and this arsehole who had been preaching about [religion] (...) and then eventually steal from me and runs away.

As Marhoon's account demonstrates, some of the negative experiences SOGI claimants have in reception and accommodation centres (like their belongings being stolen) might affect all claimants, and are not related to claimants' SOGI. Yet, for SOGI claimants, such experiences can be particularly difficult, as they often cannot fall back on family support, and because of their SOGI they are often isolated in the accommodation centres.

Another issue is that specific SOGI-support is often not available, especially when claimants are accommodated in rural areas (Sect. 8.6). The women who participated in the focus groups no. 3 and no. 4 (both in Bavaria), and who lived in the South of Bavaria, felt that the system gave the owners of their hotels, which now functioned as asylum accommodation centres, too much power which could be abused. In their view, '[t]he housemasters are the problem' (Lynn, focus group no. 4). Jolly described the roles of their 'housemaster': 'At one point he was our security guard, he was the office messenger, he was the administrator, he was every[thing], the social, everything in one person'. There were no groups or NGOs, like Caritas, present in the hotel, such as was the case in other accommodation centres (for example, Hilda, focus group no. 4). Because there was no Caritas or social workers coming to the hotel, there was no one to go to, when the housemaster mistreated them, or for additional help (for example, in getting health insurance to see a doctor, as we heard from Winifred). One of the hotel owners harassed the residents by checking what they had bought, and forcing people to carry out cleaning when they were ill or had back problems (Jolly, focus group no. 3; Lynn, focus group no. 4). This harassment was possible due to the hotel owners' power to have residents' asylum support cut; they just had to tell the authorities that the residents were not fulfilling their house tasks or not respecting the house rules. Chidera talked about the relief she felt when she finally left the hotel and the housemaster she was afraid of. After what she had experienced in the hotel, she was overwhelmed by how welcome she felt in her new place: 'Like I've never felt such acceptance in my life before. I was given a separate room, self-contained, everything inside the room. They were treating me like a princess, like seriously. I was like "God..."'.

Women were particularly vulnerable to sexual exploitation by the housemasters. Mayi (focus group no. 4) told us that the housemaster had made sexual advances towards her, which she rejected: 'This man has slept with all the women on the compound'. Women expressed their sense of powerlessness (Lynn, Hilda, focus group no. 4) as they felt unable to take any kind of action. We were told that, were they to call the police, they would not be able to communicate with them, and the housemaster would start talking to the police in German.

Others recounted positive experiences with their housemasters, and said of the ones who were more supportive, 'those ones are not racist' (Nana, focus group no. 3). The feeling of members of focus group no. 4 was also that the bad housemasters were racist (Ayeta), while other people were really caring and supportive (Ayeta, Mayi, Violet).

Also in Italy, asylum claimants are dispersed throughout the country, without being able to choose where to live (and they cannot appeal against the decision of being placed in a certain centre as this is not done through a formal decision). Claimants are dispersed depending on the availability of places, and according to the criteria to house 2.5 claimants per thousand inhabitants in each region (ECRE, AIDA & ASGI 2019, p. 90). Most asylum claimants are hosted in governmental initial reception centres and CAS accommodation, including SOGI claimants, in light of the lack of dedicated reception centres for people asking asylum on these grounds. As AIDA reports: 'In practice, reception conditions vary considerably among different reception centres and also between the same type of centres. While the services provided are the same, the quality can differ depending on the management bodies running the centres.' (ECRE, AIDA & ASGI 2019, p. 96). In the absence of widespread monitoring and consistency standards, life in these centres may vary considerably for SOGI claimants, who reported both highly positive experiences thank to the presence of trained staff (Odosa), and extremely negative episodes of racism and a total lack of services (Mamaka).

As Daniele (decision-maker) described:

[T]here is a certain difference between those who go through the SPRAR and those who do not. Because those who go through the SPRAR, which has a reduced number of places, compared to this there is a more developed subsequent system made up of agreements with local authorities. (...) For others, it depends on the ability of the local authority to organise itself, say, on a large scale.

As only a small number of claimants overall are given SPRAR accommodation, it is no coincidence that only a few of our participants were hosted in these reception centres (Alain A., Nelo, Kamel, Silver, Kennedy).

Participants in Italy, as well as in Germany, struggled with not being able to cook for themselves in the reception centres. This was also difficult because of cultural differences: 'they serve you what they want, Italian and African food is very different' (Nelo, Italy; also Odosa and Buba). In Germany, participants mentioned that they were offered a lot of bread: 'in the morning it is bread, in the afternoon it is bread, in the evening it is bread' (Tina, focus group no. 4, Bavaria; also Trudy Ann

8.3 Standard of Asylum Accommodation

and Rosette). For Dev (Italy), not being able to decide what food he ate was one of the things that restricted his freedom:

> Because already perhaps, you are not free, because already the food is essential, already for the fact that we are not fed as we want, consequently we do not eat food like meat, we are forced to eat cookies, pizzas, and it's not food, the body needs fats and all that, and we do not find them in cookies, so that's the first factor, and the second is the fact of feeling imprisoned, because we are in prison, we are adults we are not minors, a father of 36 years like me.

Nonetheless, the food schedule in reception centres can at least give some structure to the endless days where you just 'eat and sleep and wait for Monday, Saturday, this is how we live (…) anytime we wait for food, you wait for dinner, you wait for lunch, you know this is under control, you know' (Franco, Italy).

In the UK, a parliamentary committee report in 2017 found accommodation for asylum claimants was often sub-standard and unfit, with reports of vermin, asbestos risks, overcrowded conditions and insufficient food: 'Some of this accommodation is a disgrace and it is shameful that some very vulnerable people have been placed in such conditions' (House of Commons Home Affairs Committee 2017, p. 49). And yet, 2 years later, in August 2019 the Guardian still reported the inhumane conditions of asylum accommodation in London, where claimants lived in overcrowded housing that was infested with cockroaches, mice and rats (Taylor 2019). The Labour party has called for 'the return of responsibility for asylum accommodation, and the billions that come with it, to local authorities' (House of Commons 2018).

Claimants are expected to accept what is provided without complaint. Jayne's example is illustrative of that. When she was moved to Birmingham with her son (who was 14 at the time), a people carrier car was provided to transport them:

> so we thought we are taken to somewhere where at least would be liveable. So, we go to an address in [town] and the driver said, "it is here, we have arrived", and this car was parked in the front garden (…) and flats that looked dilapidated, and my son started like shaking, refusing to get out of the car, he said "maybe you should take us back where you took us from, it is ok, I am not getting out of the car if this is where you are taking us". So, we went upstairs to the flat with the G4S man, and it was very, very bad. It looked like maybe the place was used by homeless people, with… smears on the walls, with what looked like, maybe to me, it looked like even bullet holes in the walls, it was quite scary.

Jayne told the G4S driver she was unhappy with the accommodation, so he called the area manager who then came and said it was 'OK' and asked her what was wrong with it.

> So I remember I asked him, I said "can you live here yourself", he said "yes". At that point then he said, "you know, if you continue to refuse to stay here, I am going to call Home Office for you and you don't want that". I said, "you know what, if it was just me on my own, I really wouldn't have minded staying here, but as a parent I am not going to put up with my son in a place like this.

She insisted on obtaining another opinion:

> So, he rang the Home Office guy, who came, very tall, well-built man, came and like stood in my face like this and said, "what do you expect?" At that time I just broke down, I just

started crying and I didn't know what to say, because I was thinking maybe this is the person coming to rescue me, so when I broke down crying (...) I couldn't get any word out of my mouth.

Eventually, Jayne and her son were taken to a hostel where they stayed for two nights and then went back to the flat, which was now in a more liveable condition. Even though it was not ideal, they did not mind as the hostel where they had had to stay 'was also worse': they had to use the toilet facilities at a nearby branch of McDonalds.

Not only the conditions of asylum accommodation but also the practice of forced bedroom-sharing in dispersal accommodation has been a concern for parliamentarians (House of Commons 2018). The House of Commons Home Affairs Committee report on asylum accommodation recommended that particularly vulnerable claimants (including expectant mothers, those living with mental health needs and victims of trafficking, rape and torture) should not have to share a room, and that room sharing in general should be phased out (House of Commons Home Affairs Committee 2017). The government responded that:

> Room sharing allows the Providers to use their portfolio to meet the demands of asylum intake and ensure that destitute asylum seekers are housed safely and securely. There are strict criteria set out in the Statement of Requirements around when room sharing can take place and who can share a room (House of Commons Home Affairs Committee 2017, p. 14).

Some city councils have banned forced room sharing but accommodation providers do not necessarily comply with the ban (Bulman 2018). However, in the UK, forced bedroom sharing is not as problematic as in Germany and Italy, as we explore in the next Section.

8.4 Living in Shared Accommodation, Being 'in the Closet' and Experiencing Discrimination and Hate Crime

In all three countries, asylum claimants are mainly accommodated in shared housing, and often also have to share bedrooms. This is particularly true in Germany, where claimants usually need to share rooms with strangers over extended periods of time, which can be even more difficult for SOGI claimants. As Mariya (NGO worker, Germany) explained:

> Generally I find the concept that people who have just gone through terrible things in their country of origin come here and somehow just want to have a rest and want a stable, somehow, new life, that they have to share a room for several months and sometimes years with unknown people and unfortunately this is not just the exception for queer people. And yes, because that's just such a sensitive topic, "how do I deal with my sexuality", and often they are super tight spaces – sometimes it's six-square-metre, eight-square-metre, where it is also a bit difficult to hide things from each other, what you look at on the laptop or on the phone, with whom you chat, and such spaces or situations force you to get in touch with each other and people ask each other: "Why are you here?" "What happened to you?" And if people do not want to come out, it's psychologically very difficult.

8.4 Living in Shared Accommodation, Being 'in the Closet' and Experiencing...

SOGI claimants' difficult experiences with asylum accommodation have been highlighted by NGOs and others (Awadalla and Rajanayagam 2016), and 'there are hundreds of newspaper articles about violent incidents' (Marlen, legal advisor). SOGI claimants may experience discrimination, verbal and physical violence, not only at the hands of other claimants, but also of security personnel, administrative staff and interpreters (Emanvel 2016). All the participants who supported LGBTIQ+ claimants provided examples of claimants facing difficulties in reception and accommodation centres, and many of the LGBTIQ+ claimant participants told us of such difficult experiences from a general fear to 'be out' in their shared accommodation to experiencing verbal and/or physical abuse. This fear of being out is often due to the heteronormative environments of the accommodation centres as well as their surroundings, as these two survey respondents described:

> At my place of residence, I [live] with straight people and my roommates and the people around always talk evil things about gay people, and because of this reason I don't feel free to open up. But I always feel free when I am at [NGO] during our meetings. (C55, Germany)

> It's not easy to open up about my sexual orientation because of the surrounding and the stigma. (C39, Germany)

When Emroy (focus group no. 1, Hesse) arrived in Germany, he first had to stay at Frankfurt airport's detention centre. There, he felt protected, as the staff looked out for him. Despite being in a detention centre, he felt safe, a feeling which changed in subsequent accommodation. When he was moved to the reception centre in Giessen, he feared homophobic fellow claimants:

> And I feel threatened. And I am scared for my life because I am coming from a country where I've been through a lot (…) In Jamaica you have to hide, and I'm sick and I'm tired of hiding my sexuality (…) Germany is a good place, but it's not safe for gay people because you're mixing us up with people who are not gay, even people from Jamaica. They might not be the ones who attack us before, but as soon as they find out that we're gay, they're going to attack. Even if they don't attack, they will say things, and they will try to tell their friends that "oh, so you are gay", so that whenever they see you, they will try to attack you.

As William (Germany) explained: 'That is why when we're in the reception centres we try to hide. You live "in the closet". Because you don't know who is your neighbour'. Stephen (focus group no. 2, Bavaria, Germany) described how an incident in his accommodation centre made him fearful of 'coming out'. He was glad that other gay men lived in the accommodation centre and were, like him, part of the LGBTIQ+ support organisation Rainbow Refugees Munich. Together they put up some posters about the organisation, thinking there might be others in the accommodation centre who would like to join the group, but the next morning the posters were gone: 'so that gave me a lot of fear if that, if I'd come out' (Juliane, a public official, told us of a similar incident in a reception centre in Hannover).

Alphaeus talked about being threatened in his reception centre: 'They start discriminating against you, they start treating you like you're not a human being'. Gisela, a lawyer, thought that if you 'out' yourself or are 'outed', then 'life there is hell'. She had a gay client from Sierra Leone who experienced such a high degree of harassment from the people he lived with – including being spat at and prevented from using the shared facilities – that he attempted suicide and was eventually sent to a psychiatric institution. An official of the Bavarian government suggested that it had been his own fault for being 'out'. According to Gisela, the government tends to move the trouble-makers but not the victims, instead of providing accommodation for vulnerable people. Another one of Gisela's clients was in a reception centre when the mass shooting in the gay club in Orlando happened in 2106 and found himself surrounded by people cheering and celebrating the event. When Gisela's client spoke up and effectively 'outed' himself, he had to be transferred for his own protection. One survey respondent was particularly affected by an incident with her roommate: 'My roommate told me face to face that he wished all gay people would be denied asylum and that he wished the worse for all of us, a statement that can never go off my mind' (C38, Germany).

Even where SOGI claimants had managed to secure a place in an LGBTIQ+ accommodation centre, following experiences of bullying, violence, homo- and transphobia, and even death threats in 'mainstream' accommodation centres, their relocation claims were often rejected. They might even be dispersed to another district, disrupting any mental health (for instance, therapy sessions) or other kinds of support they were receiving. In the LGBTIQ+ accommodation centre in Berlin, for instance, some claimants were only able to stay a few days before dispersal to a rural area in another federal state (Frank S., legal advisor). The Bavarian government, in turn, does not even provide LGBTIQ+ accommodation and does not consider these individuals to be members of a vulnerable group. In this context, Thomas (NGO volunteer) was concerned that it would take a violent death in asylum accommodation to prompt authorities to act appropriately. Thomas told us of one member of his organisation who was violently assaulted in their accommodation and was removed by the authorities in the middle of the night. NGOs tried to raise awareness among accommodation staff by distributing posters, talking to them and offering them training (Thomas, NGO volunteer; Knud, NGO worker; Juliane, public official). Yet, as Thomas (NGO volunteer) said, this is likely to take a long time, particularly given that SOGI minorities are still not fully accepted in wider German society.

Participants told us that when they experienced harassment, they did not feel they received adequate support in reception and accommodation centres. For instance, Mahmoud experienced verbal and physical abuse by people in his accommodation centre, but when he told social workers about it, they said they could not do anything. Here, incidents escalated to the point of Mahmoud asking the police to intervene. Eventually an organisation helped him to move out. Similarly, Veronica and Julia (Germany), who lived in an eight square meter room with only two beds in their reception centre, which they shared with their children, experienced verbal abuse from other residents. When they reported it to a member of security staff and a social worker, both individuals merely advised them to be careful and not to disclose their sexual orientation to anyone. The security staff worker added that they should be glad that it was 'just' verbal abuse and that in other centres people experience sexual violence. The social worker, who was also from Russia, told them: 'What do you want? In Germany 80% of people are against it as well. No one is

8.4 Living in Shared Accommodation, Being 'in the Closet' and Experiencing... 347

going to help you, so you better not say that you are lesbians'. The social worker suggested that they pretend to be sisters. Veronica and Julia were shocked by these responses:

> It was really hard to hear, because you were trying to save yourself, to lead another, normal life. You are in another country and there people say almost the same as in Russia. "Everyone is against it"; "Be glad that there is no sexual violence". Where are we, Julia? (Veronica)

Because of the re-traumatising effects of the abuse she experienced in the accommodation centre, Julia saw a psychologist, who also told her that it would be better if she was not 'out' in the centre.

As we explore in Chap. 9, such experiences of housing put a strain on SOGI claimants' mental health and prevent them from thinking about their future, as William (Germany) explained: 'And when life is safe you can have a future to think about. We sit down and think about what next'. He argued that the large accommodation centres are counter-productive to fostering acceptance, as refugees are segregated from wider society and cannot familiarise themselves with German ways of life: they 'cannot accept it when you are still together like this'.

In Italy too, we heard of examples of verbal and physical violence experienced by SOGI claimants in reception and accommodation centres, and also of NGOs trying to raise awareness of these issues (Giulia, LGBTIQ+ group volunteer, Italy). Here once again the major issue was the failure to consider the identities of individuals allocated shared housing. Some participants, for instance, found it problematic that people were housed in reception centres according to nationality (Silvana, judge). Similar to Germany, claimants have to share rooms, often with many people. Mamaka, for instance, told us she was housed in a room of four, where previously six claimants were, and that there were also rooms of eight in the accommodation centre. She found it very difficult to live there; the women in her room would be drinking and smoking and there were 'lots of fighting'. At the time of our interview, she had been waiting for 5 months for an answer to a transferral request. Gbona shared a room with six other men, he said it was 'not easy, but it's OK'. He had lived there for a year. Silver lived in a house in Florence for 7 months that accommodated 15 young men and spoke of the troubles he faced once they found out that he was gay. They normally cooked for each other and when it was his turn, they told him that they did not want to eat his food and that everything in the kitchen needed to be separated: 'they said it was an abomination for our culture and: "You can't cook for me to eat, but we have to separate everything. You take your pot, your glass, your spoon, your plate and you don't have to touch this." You don't have to cross this part or else they kill you'. He told a centre staff member, but she did not believe him and thought he was exaggerating. One day, when one of the other residents started a fight with him in the kitchen, the social worker intervened and finally agreed to move Silver to another accommodation facility. Although he went back 'into the closet' in the new accommodation, he again suffered discrimination from other asylum claimants when they found out he was gay, however here he felt supported by accommodation managers. Nicola and Giulio (LGBTIQ+ group volunteers) talked about one of their clients being discriminated against in his housing and suffering harassment. He then was transferred to SPRAR as a vulnerable person. Also Susanna (social worker) had a client who was beaten up in the reception centre and had to be transferred.

Some LGBTIQ+ claimants told us that 'hiding' their SOGI was their only copying strategy. For instance, Ken (Italy) had experienced problems in the first camp where he stayed, where other men harassed him verbally and physically started fights with him. Therefore, in his second accommodation he stayed 'in the closet' and the situation was better because he was:

> pretending to be a "normal" young man. (...) because I have to live a fake life, I have to hide, I have to behave like a "normal" young man, I have to behave like others, so it is ok for now (...) It is difficult to live a life you are not, just because you don't want people to start talking and I am coping, I am trying.

Also Alain A. (Italy) told us of his experience of being in the closet in the reception centre, where he had to stay for almost a year, and was afraid that the other African people in the camp would find out about his sexuality:

> So I lived a quiet life there. I think… my identity was not exposed, nobody knew like I was gay so I was, I still lived like I was in Africa, still trying to hide a lot of things (…) I have a lot of my friends they don't feel free in their camps, because the people maltreat them because they found out that they are LGBT.

Other claimant and refugee participants had similar experiences, and, in fact, did not discuss their SOGI in their reception and accommodation centres. For instance, Moses was living in a flat that accommodated six claimants, all from Nigeria, and he was sharing a room with another person. Nobody knew about his sexuality and he was careful that they should not find out: 'It is not really easy, it is, it is not really easy'. Diarra lived in small camp of only four people in the countryside and was very careful that the other three men did not find out about his sexual orientation. For Fred, it would take time to find people with whom he could be open and tell his story: 'that's my own story, my story I've never told anyone, since I have not found a good person to listen to me yet. In any camp I went through, I did not find someone so open that I could tell him my story; so I always have my story in my heart'.

Participants struggled with their situation: they fled their country of origin because of facing SOGI-related discrimination and violence. Having had to live most of their lives 'in the closet', they then are often put in an environment similar to the one in the country of origin.

As Nice Guy (focus group no.1, northern Italy) explained:

> LGBT life for we asylum seekers here in Italy is somewhat terrible, very, very, to an instance (...) because we left our country for the sole purpose of discrimination and persecution, and that is exactly what we find here, but in the camps that we are and even outside too. No, no, no, not from white people, from, but from the same, our fellow blacks, because we are everywhere. You see? It's not easy for somebody, the country you are comfortable in, living your life, and one day you have one or two big problems and you leave, or you think that's OK, after going through hell, you are going to somewhere you will be comfortable. Only getting there. There is no, there is no separation, we are still in the midst of the same people that criticise and crucify you. It's impossible for you to release, OK, here I am in Europe, I'm free, no, you are not free. (...) So for me, I'm not finding it fun…

However, other participants acknowledged that the situation was still better than in their country of origin. For instance, Siri, who shared a room with one person and was not 'out' in the camp, but at the same time was not hiding as he was not afraid nor ashamed, told us that in Italy he knew he was free. Dev (focus group no. 5) told us that in the camp, he 'was stigmatized verbally because maybe they had an idea about my sexual orientation, they stigmatized me verbally but they did, it's not physically, verbally'. However, he said that in contrast to living in Africa, he knew he had rights and that such behaviour was not acceptable in Italy. At the same time, he cautioned that Italy was also not very progressive with regard to LGBTIQ+ issues: 'Homosexuality in Italy, I think it's still a taboo subject – even Italians are not 'out' [in town x]. It means that Italy is similar to Africa ... just on the paper legalised, so go *bene* [well], but at the mental level Africa and Italy *uguale* [the same]'. Also other participants thought that living in Italy as an LGBTIQ+ person was generally not easy. Kennedy told us that he also had Italian gay friends who did not come out and were afraid of him visiting their house, as they were afraid that their parents would find out about their sexuality, so they would also be hiding. One of the survey respondents explained that he was open about his sexual orientation, but that 'it's difficult here like it is in everywhere in the world to be a gay person' (C63, Italy).

Not everyone felt the need to be open about their SOGI in the accommodation centres. For instance, Gbona and Fido did not see any reason why they should be 'out' as 'everyone has his story' (Gbona, Italy). Others said that for them it was easy to be open about their sexuality (Cyrus and Patrick, focus group no.2, northern Italy). Cyrus felt confident about telling people in the reception centre that he was gay when they asked him, seeing that he went to gay Pride events: 'I'm proud to be gay'. In that respect, the importance of meeting other gay men for not feeling ashamed to be out (Fido, focus group no. 4, northern Italy) and connecting with NGOs to feel safer in accommodation centres and be able to talk about sexuality (Bakary, focus group no. 2, northern Italy) was also mentioned.

We also heard some positive examples of SOGI claimants living with non-SOGI claimants, indicating that 'people should always have the choice' about their accommodation (Jonathan, LGBTIQ+ group volunteer, Italy). For instance, Junio (Italy), who arrived in Europe as a child, felt 'very looked after' by social services and shared 'very good accommodation' with another girl. Similarly, Momo lived in a hotel, along with two other gay friends; other residents knew they were gay, but '[t]here are no problems there. There everyone respects'.

In the UK, not only the report on asylum accommodation by the Independent Chief Inspector referred to LGBTIQ+ claimants being harassed and abused by other accommodation receivers (ICIBI 2018, p. 60; Sect. 8.2), but research conducted by Citizens Advice Liverpool also found that 9 of the 17 LGBTIQ+ claimants interviewed reported being abused, bullied or discriminated against in shared housing. The study found that especially initial accommodation was unsuitable for LGBTIQ+ claimants (Citizens Advice Liverpool 2018, p. 17). In the many years working with SOGI claimants, Melisa (NGO worker) witnessed how 'they were facing bullying, they were being beaten up, they were facing extreme homophobia'. When we asked

Amadin whether he felt safe and comfortable in his asylum accommodation, he responded: 'I do not really feel safe because I live with people who are not LGBT so I am scared to tell them what was my case and who I am, so I was scared and hide my life here.' At the time of his interview with us, Lutfor had problems with one of the men living in his house, and he had been physically assaulted by him, to the point of calling the police. However, the solution of SERCO, the accommodation provider, was to move Lutfor, rather than his persecutor and despite Lutfor's wish to stay because of his good relationship with the other residents.

Some of the participants did not experience verbal or physical abuse directly but were fearful because of what other people had told them. For instance, Selim (UK) was afraid to accept Home Office accommodation, as he had heard other asylum claimants talking about their experiences of being abused and raped by people from their own country with whom they had to share rooms in asylum accommodation:

> Can you imagine putting, let's say, an Iraqi guy here because he is gay, escaping from straight people in Iraq, in the same room with another Iraqi who is here escaping the war? And he is straight. So there was a lot of abuse, there was a lot of stories about abuse and rape and threatening and all these things, so the last thing I wanted to do is to be in this accommodation with those asylum seekers, because I don't know what reason they are claiming asylum upon.

The housing providers might think that they are doing something positive when they put together people from the same country/community, but this can be problematic for SOGI claimants (Joseph, NGO volunteer, UK; Mariya, NGO worker, Germany).

Some participants talked about the consequences of 'coming out' or having their SOGI found out. When Meggs (UK) started to feel more comfortable about her sexuality after a few months living in the UK and 'outed' herself to the two women with whom she shared a house:

> they also started to exclude themselves from me, like they were really, really against my sexuality I would say. Though they would not like say, when I say it they were kind of shocked like "wow, really, we have not seen any boyfriend coming here" (…) So we used to like, as girls we were just, if it is hot we would just go bra top naked and things like that, but everything started to change and you know when people look at you like you raped them or something, like that, yes. So, I started to feel like excluded as well, but I didn't know I had a right to complain about it with SERCO.

Yet, being 'out' or being 'in the closet' might not only be a problem in asylum accommodation. Sometimes, SOGI claimants stay with relatives or friends and they might have to move out once their SOGI is found out. For instance, Rosa (NGO, UK) said that during the transition period, during which claimants granted international protection only have 28 days to find accommodation, people might be 'forced back into the closet', if they are dependent on someone else for accommodation.

As shared bedrooms are less common in the UK, in contrast to Germany and Italy, SOGI claimants here may have better accommodation experiences. Participants in the North West of England we spoke to were positive about the support structures in place, especially from self-organised groups, and the social life that existed for SOGI refugees (Amelia, NGO worker; Meggs, focus group no. 1, Manchester). In some instances, we heard that bisexual and lesbian women had been (purposefully?) put together by the accommodation providers and that despite the problems with housing that many people faced, there were some SERCO staff 'who are trying really hard, and who are on the side of, and who want these refugees to have a decent quality house and a safe house and kind of demonstrate kindness' (Chloe, NGO worker).

These accounts illustrate that most LGBTIQ+ asylum claimants experience their current 'home' as a heteronormative space, where they do not represent the 'sexual norm', and therefore any reference to their sexual identity will be experienced as a 'coming out'. We now look in a bit more detail at the intersectional dimension of accommodation and how these spaces are experienced by trans and non-binary claimants as well as couples.

8.4.1 Accommodation of Couples

Hiding SOGI is particularly difficult when having a partner. As Vincenzo (LGBTIQ+ group volunteer, Italy) explained, one of the main issues here is that asylum claimants are:

> de-sexualized in some way, or if sexuality emerges, it does so in forms considered more "problematic", such as pregnancy, like the person who has a sexually transmitted disease. In those cases it may emerge and there is an emergency taking charge, but the right to sexuality, the right to pleasure and affection and intimacy, no. So these things are problematic.

Fred and his boyfriend Dev (Italy) were living in the same accommodation centre but were not allowed to share a room with each other. Even though people had to share rooms, the manager of the camp argued that the accommodation was only for single people and not for couples. Luckily, Dev's roommates were understanding, and one of them knew they were a gay couple and was accepting, so they could spend time together in Dev's room.

We also heard from other LGBTIQ+ claimants who had difficulties being housed with partners (Damiano, lawyer, Italy; Stephen, focus group no. 2, Bavaria, Germany). Giulio (LGBTIQ+ group volunteer, Italy) told us that individuals would need to prove that they were part of a couple, and even show a marriage certificate. As Jonathan (LGBTIQ+ group volunteer, Italy) argued, being housed together might be difficult for an unmarried heterosexual couple too. However, one difference is that gay couples will not have had the chance to marry in their country of origin. Some of the couples we interviewed described feeling as if they were still back in their country of origin, as they were not able to openly show affection towards each other (Dev and Fred, Italy; Veronica and Julia, Germany): 'we still feel like in Africa' (Dev).

Because claimants have to share accommodation, couples lack privacy and being with a partner is extremely difficult, especially when that partner also lives in shared asylum accommodation (Tina, Germany). In addition, when they have met during their asylum process, it is difficult for one person to be relocated so the couple can be together, as Liz (focus group no. 5, Bavaria, Germany) and her partner experienced. Each lived in remote areas far away from each other, and neither had the financial means to pay for costly public transport tickets. They asked to be relocated closer to one another, but this request was rejected: 'We have tried everything and there is no way out' (Liz, focus group no. 5, Bavaria, Germany).

It was also problematic for claimants to have partners outside their accommodation centres. Buba (Italy) talked about his difficulties in talking to his boyfriend in the Gambia, as no one in the camp (a hotel) knew about his sexuality and he shared a room with four people. Kennedy (Italy) also described being very careful so that the other men in his room would not find out about his sexuality; he was not able to talk to his boyfriend freely, and always had to watch out in case someone came into the bedroom. He was also afraid that someone would see messages from his boyfriend on his phone. As he described it: 'It makes me feel bad, it makes me feel very, very bad, because sometimes I don't have the, the freedom to chat with my loved one'.

Whether in an intimate relationship or not, SOGI claimants' experiences in accommodation are shaped by the intersections of different social categories such as gender, sexuality, disability and religion, as we demonstrate in the following section.

8.4.2   *Intersectional Dimensions of Accommodation*

Owing to their intersecting experiences of exclusion and discrimination, SOGI claimants may feel unsafe for different reasons. For some participants, it was the intersection of gender and sexuality that shaped their experience. Tina (Germany) lived in a large camp where only around ten women were single like her (without a partner or children). Most of the people there were in families with children, pregnant women, or mothers with babies. She had to share a room with four heterosexual women and a baby, and had lots of problems with her roommates and faced discrimination: 'I don't feel comfortable at all'. She tried to stay out of the room until it was time to go to bed, because 'there are times you want to relax, [but] you can't, it's really terrible'. As her asylum claim was refused, she was likely to stay in that camp for a long time, and although there seemed to be places available in a safe women's house, she struggled to be accommodated there, as it was in a different district.

The heteronormative environment of reception and accommodation centres is difficult for non-heterosexual (cis-)women, who get 'advances' from men, and are often also pressured by the other women with whom they live to have a relationship with a man (Tina and Hilda, focus group no. 4, Bavaria, Germany). As Tina (focus group no. 4, Bavaria, Germany) described her situation:

And yeah, [laughs] I would stay [with] four people in the room and wherever I had... very many people had their boyfriends that they move on with, but for me I had no-one. So they

8.4 Living in Shared Accommodation, Being 'in the Closet' and Experiencing... 353

could force me, saying "why not have a man?" This kind of things. My roommate would be on me.

The often mixed-gendered accommodation centres can bring women into unsafe situations, as Julian's (focus group no. 5, Bavaria, Germany) example demonstrates. She was living 'in the closet' in the accommodation centre as she was told in her first interview to keep her sexuality as a secret, but men harassed her and were irritated when she did not respond to them, leading them to assume that she was a lesbian. For a few nights she was alone in her room as the woman with whom she shared her room and who was pregnant had gone to the hospital. One night she woke up to find in her room a man who lived in the room next door: 'We are not allowed to lock ourselves in. So I was sleeping. I woke up from a dream and the man was sitting in the room. So I felt "I am dreaming"'. When she told the staff in the office the next day, they did not take it seriously, did not want to give her a bedroom key and told her that if something were to happen, she should scream and then security would come:

> The next time, I woke up, there were now two [men]. So I had to scream. So that security this time finds evidence for themselves. When security came, they said "but they are just seated, they are not touching you, they are not forcing you." I told them "yes, they are not touching me, but it's funny, if we are not friends, ask them do they know my name? They don't know my name, so how can you say we are friends? I just met them because in the camp we eat together. Please tell them not to come back here." So those security people never took it seriously (...) for them, they didn't think of me maybe in that angle, that I'm a lesbian. I have grounds why I'm scared.

Feeling desperate, Julian packed her belongings and went to speak with the woman in charge of the camp to tell her that:

> "if I am to stay here give me a key to lock myself up when I'm sleeping, or else they could rape me, and the next time they will rape me, you will say the same thing, I'm being dramatic, I'm being chaotic, I'm being scared." (...) she refused [the request for a bedroom key]. So they called the police. Because now I was being dramatic. And when the police came, I told the police officer "I don't want to talk to a man, I'm kindly requesting if a policewoman [can talk to me]".

The policewoman helped Julian contact an organisation that hosted her for a week, before she was transferred to another place. Julian's account demonstrates how vulnerable women can be in mixed-gender camps. Julian was very outspoken and she felt for the women who were not: 'But imagine I had not insisted on fighting'.

Accommodation centres are not only heteronormative spaces but they are also spaces where the 'somatic norm' (Puwar 2004) is able-bodied, as Betty's (focus group no. 3, Bavaria, Germany) experiences demonstrate. At the time of the interview, she had been living in the asylum accommodation centre (a hotel) in a small village for 2 years and 3 months and felt 'like a prisoner' because of not being able to walk for long distances. In addition, it was difficult for her to walk with all her pots to the kitchen, which was far away from her room, and she had to use a crutch. When she asked to be relocated, they wanted to offer her a place in another village, where she would not have to cook, not understanding that her problem was not having to cook but being expected to carry her kitchen utensils all the way to the kitchen. With the people living in the hotel, she experienced another layer of discrimination:

> The problem is really how they put us with other people, people discriminate us. People, they do not want to stay with me, they think I am a curse and that they will have to help me every time, people think I am useless, they do not want to associate with us, most of the time. They just see that I move differently from them. And when you talk, they do not let you talk, as they think you have to be oppressed, that you be under that person. I think that Europeans and natives, they are different, they are happy to help you. And I do not get any support. If I tell the housemaster, he says that I need to share a room with somebody. He does not know what I am going through, he does not know what is happening inside the room, and he doesn't want to hear.

As a Black, disabled, lesbian refugee, she felt out of place everywhere: in the hotel, in the village, and even at the lesbian refugee organisation she attended, where she also felt like the other women did not treat her as equal but assumed that she belonged to 'another category of people'. Betty's account reminds us of how important it is to look at the intersectional experiences of SOGI refugees, not to treat them as a homogenous group, but like any other group based on identity, where membership is shaped by inclusions and exclusions (Butler 1991).

For some participants, it was the combination of their sexual and religious or non-religious identity that shaped their experience. When Marhoon (Germany) was moved from the reception centre to an accommodation centre, he told the Red Cross that he was gay and an atheist and asked whether he could share a room with like-minded people. Two days later, a room became vacant and they gave it to him. But then later two more people were put in the room: 'And then came a third roommate, from Iraq, and I was surprised they put us together because I'm atheist, the guy from Iran is Shia and then the guy from Iraq is Sunni. And as you know the Sunni and the Shia don't get on very well. So I was really confused, why have they put them in the same room?' Although there had been some tension between his two roommates because of their different religious backgrounds, they were both all right with him being gay and an atheist:

> I told them because I wanted to see their reaction. If it was negative, I'd kick them out or force the camp to send someone else. Because the camp also told me not to talk about it. (…) They told me not to tell people that I'm gay or atheist, which apparently is illegal, or they don't have the right to tell me to say that. So I told them both, no problem whatsoever. I was impressed, ok, there is hope. So both had no issues with it.

Yet, Marhoon did have problems because of his atheist beliefs when another resident felt offended by a picture that Marhoon had painted in an art project. He perceived it to be an insult to God and Islam and came into Marhoon's bedroom and threatened him, leaving Marhoon shaking: 'It was terrible, but from that moment everyone in the building distanced themselves from me. "Oh, you are one of these atheists, because now you're an atheist you think now you can offend Islam"'.

When looking at the intersectional dimensions of accommodation, it is important to look not only at LGBTIQ+ claimants' experiences *within* accommodation centres but also *outside* of them. As Halim's (Germany) experience demonstrates, SOGI claimants might feel unsafe in both situations, with different aspects of their identity, or a particular combination of identities making them targets of violence and abuse in different spaces (Chap. 3). Being housed in a refugee camp in an area in East Berlin known for increasing numbers of neo-Nazis, Halim felt unsafe in the accommodation because of his queer identity, while outside the accommodation centre he felt visible and threatened as a refugee. He talked about having split identities: 'it's all part of me but depending on where I am, I feel uncomfortable or unsafe because of certain things'. Halim did not 'out' himself in the camp: 'I had the privilege that maybe I can hide somehow, I'm not so visibly queer in that sense'. Yet, he struggled because of the hostile surroundings, and was 'always scared of going in and out'. As he had to share a room, he did not have any private sanctuary to which he could retreat: 'it was very bad for my mental health, I was very depressed at the time'. He was then moved to another refugee camp even further East, in Marzahn, an area which 'has since the 1990s had an image as a no-go area for foreigners' (Young 2017). There, an old school had been turned into refugee accommodation, and there had been anti-refugee protests against it (Spiegel online 2013). Halim described seeing German flags displayed on the balconies of local tower blocks. He was there for two and a half months, and had to share a room with five other people. Some of them were from the same country as him and this made it even more difficult as 'it felt even harder for me to hide who I am because they can read me better'.

Lesbian women who participated in focus groups no. 3 and no. 4 in Germany, who lived in rural areas in southern Bavaria (Sect. 8.5), told us of experiences with high levels of racism in the surroundings of the accommodation camps. People in the area would not even look at them when they greeted them and that '[s]uddenly, they keep their space. They don't want to come near you' (Hilda, focus group no.4, Bavaria, Germany). Sometimes, on public transport, people would not sit next to them, or they would move away once you sit next to them and we were told of occasions when fellow passengers pulled their nose to indicate that our participants smelled bad (focus group no. 4, Bavaria, Germany). In shops, our participants' bags would be checked to make sure they had not stolen anything (Hilda and Liz, focus group no. 4 Bavaria, Germany). Ayeta (focus group no. 4, Bavaria, Germany) described walking around in the town where she stayed and 'there was a lady coming towards me. When she saw (...) I was Black she held her nose, then she turned and spit. I just turned to her and told her "God bless you"'. In these focus groups there was a sense that Black refugees are treated differently to other refugees, and that there was what Haritaworn has called a specific 'anti-Black racism in Germany' (Haritaworn 2015, p. 14).

At times, they experienced a combination of homophobia and racism, as Jolly's, Betty's and Winifred's (focus group no. 3, Bavaria) account demonstrate. They were accommodated in a hotel in a small town in south Bavaria, more than 2 h away from Munich, surrounded by mountains. It had been a tourist area before the hotel closed down and reopened to accommodate asylum claimants. They described the town as mainly White and populated by older people: 'We are few Blacks there. And most of them are the natives around there, yeah. They are the natives, and actually not really young natives. Elderly only. Then maybe their children come once in a while' (Jolly). They told us that within, as well as outside their accommodation, people would assume that the few single Black women housed there were all lesbians. As Jolly described:

> Different reasons bring people to Europe, or in Germany. And whenever they get any suspicion about you that you're a lesbian, they tend to backbite, to push you away. There's a way they look at you, as someone who's... as if you're not a person, you get it, right. So discrimination is too high, yeah. And maybe not only from the Blacks, even from the Whites, yeah. Still even in the area where we are putting up right now, it's not easy. People around there, they think that we are contaminating their children, contaminating the area around where we are.

They felt a combination of racism and homophobia in their everyday lives. The women were upset by their experiences. As Winifred explained, they were already suffering from mental health problems, so:

> When I find this person and he doesn't want to associate with me, or I'm seated somewhere, you don't want to sit with me, it hurts me. It's like I'm still in my country where I'm neglected for my status.

In shared accommodation, the intersectional dimension of experiences is problematic in particular because claimants do not have the choice of where to live and with whom. This is especially difficult when social identifiers are very visible, which increases the risk of experiencing harassment and violence, as is often the case for non-binary, trans and intersex claimants.

8.4.3 Accommodation of Non-binary, Trans and Intersex Claimants

While some LGBQ people might be able to hide their SOGI, for non-binary, trans and intersex people this may be considerably harder. Trans claimants are often allocated accommodation according to the sex indicated in their legal documents, so they become very visible and vulnerable to physical, sexual and verbal abuse (Jules, staff member at ILGA-Europe; Kadir, NGO worker, Germany; TGEU 2016, p. 5). From Maryia's (NGO worker) experience, in Germany sometimes trans claimants' self-identification is accepted, but this is not always the case. However, Kadir (NGO worker, Germany) also cautioned that placing trans women in cis-women accommodation, for instance, might not always be the best solution, as it can be difficult for the cis-women (depending on their past experiences). Considering the small number of trans refugees and their vulnerability, Kadir advocated for decentralised housing for them, and reception centres in Lower Saxony, where he works, have increasingly dealt with these cases in more flexible ways, leading to trans claimants obtaining individual accommodation or being offered small flat shares (see also Matthias, social worker; Juliane, public official). At least trans refugees' need for a single room should thus be respected, as well as their wish to be in urban areas,

8.4 Living in Shared Accommodation, Being 'in the Closet' and Experiencing...

where support structures and health services for trans claimants are available, and where 'people do not hear for the first time of hormone treatment' (Louis, NGO volunteer, Germany).

As TGEU highlights: 'Using the toilets, showers or common areas can pose a daily risk' to trans claimants' (TGEU 2016, p. 5). As bathrooms are usually binary-gendered (in asylum accommodation as well as in public spaces in general, see Spade 2015, Chap. 3), if people are non-binary or in transition, this can become a topic for conversation and conflict, and claimants' gender may be questioned by staff and other residents (Mariya, NGO worker, Germany). This was the experience of Trudy Ann's partner, who was often challenged when she wanted to use the female bathroom for 'looking like a man'. Both Trudy Ann and her partner usually went to the bathroom together, as they did not feel safe otherwise, also because there were men around (as families were housed in the accommodation centre). Such experiences might be re-traumatising for people who have fled their country of origin because of abuse on grounds of their gender identity. Staff in the camps might also 'out' trans claimants, for instance, when they call out the wrong name/sex (Ibrahim, Germany; Jules, staff member at ILGA-Europe).

In Germany, the trans claimants we interviewed all had negative experiences with asylum accommodation because of being placed in the wrong gendered accommodation and/or because of being housed rurally (also Sect. 8.6). Diana was placed together with three men in accommodation, as her passport revealed her male birth sex. She later received her own room but had to share a kitchen and bathroom. She was so scared of transphobic violence that she went to a friend's house when she wished to have a shower. At night she would receive knocks at her door and people would threaten her. Similarly worrying, Bebars was put in a mixed-gender accommodation centre. He tried to explain with the help of an interpreter that he was not accepted by anyone in the accommodation centre. He also reported this to the welfare office, but was not taken seriously. He felt that the main problem in the accommodation centre was that there was 'no contact person for us [SOGI claimants]'. He tried to explain to staff why it was difficult for him to undress and change clothes in front of the (heterosexual) married couple, who were also from Syria, and with whom he had to share a room. This was especially difficult for him because he wore a bandage around his breasts, 'but they did not care'. He was then moved to a second accommodation facility that was completely for women. Despite putting pressure on the social services every few days to move to another accommodation, nothing happened for 4 months: 'they did not want to do it, I got on their nerves'. When he was finally moved, he was placed in accommodation in a small village, where he was incredibly isolated (Sect. 8.6). Trans claimant Rolla (focus group no. 6, Lower Saxony, Germany) was also accommodated in a small village for some time. The security there felt sorry for her as they saw how people treated her, so they gave her a cat to look after, which she loved. She was glad when she was moved to a big city but here then she experienced a very hurtful transphobic incident, when someone abused her verbally and spat at her on the street.

Also in Italy, shared accommodation is extremely difficult for trans claimants. Kamel lived in small apartment together with five (cis-)men and had to share a room with one of them. He was scared of his roommate, had a panic attack and couldn't sleep. He told us: 'I spent a year and a half like a wolf. I slept with one eye open and the other one closed. Always with that feeling of risk'. He wore a bandage to tighten his breasts, which should only be used for a maximum of 6 h, but because he did not have any privacy and could not even lock the bathroom, he wore the bandage 24 h a day. He told the housing managers that '[i]n fact, you put me more at risk', as they did not allow locks on the bathroom. Because of wearing the bandage all day, he had developed serious health problems, including not being able to breathe well and feeling hot all the time (Bebars, in Germany, had similar problems). He also witnessed a fight where one of the residents was holding a knife to another resident saying "you're gay, that sucks!". He tried to call the housing manager, but no one answered. Like Bebars (Germany), Kamel did not receive any support in the accommodation centre but rather felt that the managers were 'too ignorant, they don't know what trans means', and were also unable to provide contacts to relevant organisations that could offer specialised support and advice to Kamel. While he did not feel safe inside the accommodation centre, he was also worried about his safety outside the accommodation centre, and feared racist attacks, especially after the general elections on 4 March 2018, which were won by a centre-right coalition led by Matteo Salvini's right-wing League:

> That is on the 4th March, I felt sick. I felt again what I felt before in Libya, because I am afraid of going out into the street at night, alone, that someone is beating me. I'm afraid of those people. I mean, if anyone happens to wear a black shirt, I'm scared.

He told us that he also experienced racism at the Pride in Bologna in 2016, where he was on stage with a LGBTIQ+ migrant organisation (MigraBo) and heard two women shouting '"first the Italians, go back to your home!" Someone shouted "Vive Salvini!", I felt bad.'

In the UK, the lack of choice was also patent. Christina, for example, was never asked what kind of accommodation they preferred. For almost 3 years they had to share a house with three men, which was 'very, very uncomfortable'. Christina thinks that mixed accommodation centres are not safe for SOGI claimants and that trans claimants should be placed in private accommodation:

> It is not safe. I think if you identify as homosexual, you should be living with homosexuals. If you identify as lesbian, you should be living with lesbians. If you identify as trans, you should get your own space. Because you need to feel safe, and comfortable.

Similarly, Janelle was also not consulted about her accommodation preferences. She would have preferred trans or LGBTIQ+ accommodation, but was put in male accommodation because of the male name on her passport. She was housed with three men, 'they tried to like attack me within the house and they were like calling me names'. She reported it to the housing provider G4S, but they did not do anything about these incidents. As she did not feel safe in the house, she stayed mainly in her room.

Not neatly fitting the expected gender performances in cis-gendered accommodation can also be problematic for intersex clients. One of Melisa's (NGO worker, UK) intersex clients, whose passport stated male as their birth sex but presented as a woman, was put in accommodation facilities with men on more than one occasion, and in each facility faced bullying and sexual harassment:

> at some point they [client] had to leave the house in the night and take a walk in the night or try and find a friend who was available where they could stay on their sofa. In some instances they were forced to just stay in the kitchen, you know, to just sit there and wait until the other person slept, so it was a continual harassment and... they tried complaining to different departments within the housing provider, the COMPASS providers, and they were not supported or they didn't get the help that they needed.

Only when Melisa's organisation stepped in, did the Home Office act promptly, and the client was then moved to the organisation's safe accommodation: 'the first thing they said when I went to pick them up, they cried, so much'.

As this section has shown, shared accommodation can be extremely difficult for SOGI claimants, who often try to hide their SOGI because of fear of homophobic and transphobic verbal and physical violence. Hiding becomes more difficult when claimants have partners or when their gender expression does visibly not confirm to strict gender norms. We now want to look at experiences of discrimination and hate crime, not only within reception and accommodation centres, but also in the surrounding areas. It is important to explore these experiences to highlight the intersections of experienced sexism, homophobia, transphobia and racism.

As shown above, in Germany, Italy and the UK, many SOGI participants had difficult experiences of asylum accommodation. In Germany, for some participants these experiences were even more difficult where they were accommodated in extremely rural areas, as we now explain.

8.5 Rural/Urban

When we visited Angel (Germany), it was snowing heavily and we had to walk along a main road to get from the small village where the bus left us to the accommodation centre (the bus that stopped at the centre came only three times per day). Angel shared a flat there with a heterosexual couple and a baby, and with another gay man from Jamaica. Her room was small, containing a bunk bed, a wardrobe and a small table. When Angel's teenage daughter came back from school, she would do her homework and then go to bed as she had nothing else to do. Outside the barracks, there was a path that led into the woods with a sign 'trespassing forbidden, army shooting territory' (Figs. 10 and 11).

Angel told us that they regularly heard shooting, even at three in the morning. Both Angel and her daughter seemed to us to be depressed, and Angel said she felt hopeless. Her claim had been refused and she was waiting for her court hearing. Living so remotely, she could not attend any LGBTIQ+ group gatherings and events. Any visit to a bigger city involved a long and expensive journey with public transport but with no way to get back to the accommodation centre, as the bus only ran until early evening. To go shopping, Angel had to take the bus to the next town and then wait several hours for the bus to return:

Fig. 10 Signs outside accommodation

Fig. 11 'Trespassing forbidden, army shooting territory'

8.5 Rural/Urban

361

> When [I arrived to this accommodation], to be honest... I was terrified before I reached here, because I noticed the more I drive, the more landscape I see and the less civilisation I see, you understand? And it's not something that I'm used to. I was born in the city, I was grown in the city, I don't know no other life than city life. (...) Even though I was isolated in Jamaica, it was by choice because I wanted to protect myself and my child. Here, I have no choice. (...) I am from a minority group that go through a lot of negativity, and I am not able to participate in any form of social groups because of my location.

Angel described her surroundings as somewhere even German people find too isolated:

> The middle of nowhere. A wilderness, you know? It's like... I don't even know what to say [laughs], because, it's like, I don't even see animals here, you understand? So it's just like basically in the middle of – even Germans, when I give them my address they're like, "Oh you live in the middle of nowhere", you understand? And they are born Germans.

As Marlen (legal advisor, Germany) put it, it is hard for German LGBTIQ+ people to live in a small village where they do not fit with the heteronormative lifestyles. Consequently, many LGBTIQ+ people who grow up in villages move to bigger cities: 'and they can easily do that, there are no restrictions; you cannot say that about the refugees, they are very bound and cannot decide freely where they want to live' (Matthias, social worker). Angel was not even housed in a village, but some miles distant from the closest village. She was the first person we interviewed in Germany who was accommodated so remotely, but during the course of our research we became aware that her situation was, in fact, quite common.

Germany consists of 16 federal states, of which three are city states. When people are allocated to one of the three city states, living remotely is not a significant issue (Kadir, NGO worker; Maryia, NGO worker; Barbara, lawyer), but when they are allocated to one of the 13 non-city states ('Flaechenlaender'), they can end up in 'the middle of nowhere' (Angel). Submitting an application for a transfer ('Umverteilungsantrag') was one of the main support needs, as all NGO workers and some of the lawyers confirmed, however the success rate of such applications was variable. Elias (lawyer in Hessen), for instance, said that when he worked on a claim, if he demonstrated the claimant's family connections and particular vulnerabilities, then it would often be successful. In North Rhine-Westphalia, it was estimated that in about two thirds of the cases a request to be allocated to a bigger city was accepted (Joachim, NGO worker). In contrast, Leon (NGO worker), who worked in the same federal state, had only two claims accepted in 4 years, out of approximately 15–20 submitted. In Lower Saxony, it had also become increasingly difficult to get such requests accepted, and requests seem to take longer than in other federal states (Kadir, NGO worker; Matthias, social worker). One reason for refusals to such requests is likely to be that bigger municipalities are reluctant to take asylum claimants from smaller municipalities, yet at the same time, LGBTIQ+ people usually want to move to the bigger cities (Kadir, NGO worker). Claims for relocation in Bavaria also seemed to have an extremely low likelihood of success. Amis (focus group 2, Bavaria, Germany), for instance, had been offered a place for vocational training ('Ausbildung') in a care home in Munich (an area of work where people are very much needed), but was not allowed to move out of 'the forest' in southern Bavaria. As he explained: 'We people staying in Oberbayern [southern Bavaria], we are not allowed to do Ausbildung [training] in Munich. We have to do it there, but it's a village. Where to do it from? So it's a torture, a psychological torture'. Amis was housed in a small container (Fig. 12) together with only a few other asylum claimants. There were only fields around the containers (Fig. 13) and he had to walk for 40 minutes through the forest to get to a bus stop and felt extremely isolated: 'you can't even stay there for a week'. In addition, he felt extremely unsafe, as he had received death threats from one of the residents. Although Amis had lived there for one and a half years, he sometimes chose to sleep on the streets in Munich, as he felt safer there.

While NGOs have put pressure on the government and municipalities and some positive changes have been made in some federal states, in many cases, even if the person is experiencing abuse and harassment in rural accommodation, the Regional Administrative Council ('Regierungspraesidium') argues that the municipality needs to offer adequate support. So, the Council staff refuse to relocate the individual to a town or city where LGBTIQ+ support is available, on the basis that if they do, then everyone will make such claims (Noah, NGO social worker). As Leon (NGO worker) argued, the situation for SOGI claimants is very different from other

© Amis

Fig. 12 Accommodation in Bavaria – containers

8.5 Rural/Urban

© Amis

Fig. 13 Accommodation in Bavaria – field

refugees, as they usually do not have a connection to their ethnic community, and often even try to avoid members of their ethnic community:

> Because of the break with the community of origin, what gays have been doing for centuries, or the queer community, LGBTIQ community for centuries, we've sort of built our structures. This is our family. And one must not separate people from this lifeline. Because the inner peace, the identity, the self-realisation, which one needs in order to provide the integration performance that is expected, depends on that. When I find myself in my environment, when I can be at peace with myself by being able to reflect myself in my environment, then I have a self-confident sexuality, then I protect myself, then I have access to information, then I am enlightened, then I exercise my rights, then I have the mind free to integrate, because the pressure from the outside is manageable. And that offers, so to speak, the connection to the community. And that's what people need to understand in social care. Social care must take this into account. It is not a privilege to enable an LGBTIQ refugee to access his community, but I don't, so to speak, cut the lifeblood.

How that 'lifeblood' was cut became obvious in many of our participants' accounts, who also described how the social isolation they experienced from living in rural areas impacted on their mental health. For instance, after the initial reception centre, Zouhair (focus group no. 6, Lower Saxony, Germany) was housed alone in a two-bedroom flat in a small village in Lower Saxony, about 16 km away from the next bigger town. Only 50–70 people lived there, and half of the houses were empty: 'Well, they are all empty. Houses are empty. Who wants to live there?

Nobody!' His social isolation was striking: 'And I just went crazy, because I did not have any contact with anyone. I had to sit at home all day'. Public transport was expensive but there was not even a supermarket in the village, so Zouhair had to take a bus or walk for 30–40 min to the next village. He stayed there for 11 months, without an internet connection or any way of learning German. He explained that LGBTIQ+ refugees' social isolation is exacerbated by not fitting in:

> because for Germans, we are refugees, we are refugees like the others or asylum seekers like the others, but for the others [refugees] we are ... we are [laughing] gays and lesbians and inter and trans, so we do not belong to the German society (…) for other refugees we are, we are not refugees. We also do not belong to this parallel society. So we are totally isolated. (…) As queer refugees, I think we are out of category, so we do not belong to one, or the other, it's just, it's difficult.

Zouhair's expression of queer refugees being 'out of category' reminds us of Crenshaw's (1989) description of Black women falling through the gaps. In her seminal 1989 article, where she coined the term intersectionality, she talked about anti-discrimination law not suiting Black women because they experience discrimination on grounds of being women *and* being Black (Chap. 3). We can see from Zouhair's account that queer refugees' experiences are shaped by being queer *and* being refugees, meaning they belong neither to the refugee community nor to the host community, and this is particularly evident in rural locations. For Zouhair, 'we are victims in our countries, and we are victims here as well'. At the time of the interview, Zouhair was working for a queer refugee group and estimated that 70–80% of those who come for support bring up issues related to accommodation in isolated locations: 'People are always isolated and far away from everything, they have no contact. They are alone'. He witnessed how people become depressed and unhappy without any support. One group member travelled for 4 h to attend group meetings simply to have some contact with people he could relate to: 'And if you are in a small village and everyone knows that you are gay or lesbian or intersex or trans, that is, that's really terrible, believe me'.

Living rurally, opportunities to learn German, work, or volunteer for an organisation and socialise with Germans were limited: 'So it's literally being dead there as you wait. Yeah. You can't do anything' (Lynn, focus group no. 4, Bavaria, Germany). More crucially, claimants who were refused needed to find legal representation for their appeal; it is far harder to find a lawyer with expertise in SOGI claims in rural areas. It is also difficult to find romantic or sexual partners. Trans claimant Rolla (focus group no. 6, Lower Saxony, Germany) was lucky to find a partner in her rural accommodation, but because of limited mobility, most SOGI claimants housed in rural areas find it impossible. Yet, during the asylum process they are often asked whether they have sexual relationships (Chap. 7). As Nana (focus group 3, Bavaria, Germany) described: 'We can't go to parties because like me, in the interview they say I have to look for a girlfriend. Every time I go to look for a girlfriend when I'm in the village, how am I going to do that?'

As Gisela (lawyer) and many other participants argued, when allocating people to accommodation centres, the importance of a protected environment and access to LGBTIQ+ support groups, etc., needs to be taken into consideration. As Ibrahim

8.5 Rural/Urban

explained, SOGI claimants have 'already faced isolation because of their sexuality (...) they came here to have at least a social life'. Where people are housed also makes a difference if they experience difficulties *within* the accommodation centre. In a city, people can then, at least, be out all day and keep themselves busy, but in a small place:

> you have to stay with those people, you have to always hear what they say, or their comments (…) It is easier for you, when you are connected in the city, you can escape the reality of the camp. You can go out, you can go to organisations, to groups. You can go anywhere. Just walk around. But if you are in the middle of nowhere, there is nothing to do (Ibrahim).

Veronica and Julia faced homophobic comments in the reception and accommodation centres where they were housed in a rural area, but when they were accommodated in Cologne they received support within the gay area: 'you do not feel alone' (Veronica and Julia). Similarly, Milad explained that, for the first one and a half years of his time in Germany, while he lived in a rural location, he did not see, let alone visit, a gay club:

> I did not even know something like that exists in Berlin. After that, uuuuahh! For example, [name of club]. There is a disco, cafe only for gay and lesbian people… Oh, awesome – I have something like that – so it was amazing for me. But after a while, I see half Berlin is gay-friendly or LGBT-friendly. You can see the flyer on the REWE [supermarket] entrance or the Lidl [supermarket] entrance. You feel better: "Oh, that's nice, I'm happy about that" and so.

For SOGI claimants, being accommodated in rural areas is especially difficult due to their intersectional experiences of homophobia, racism and transphobia (Marlen, legal advisor; Mariya, NGO worker). However, being located in a town or city was no guarantee that claimants felt safe (Sect. 8.4). For instance, Lutfor (UK) experienced homophobia and racism in Manchester, hearing things like 'go back to your country' and 'look at the ugly fags'. Janelle (UK) talked about her experiences of transphobia on the streets of Sheffield, which might not be separate from other forms of hate crime, as TGEU highlights:

> While xenophobia, racism and Islamophobia are on the rise [in Europe], trans asylum seekers and refugees are even more vulnerable to discrimination or violence. (...) Trans asylum seekers and refugees often face intersectional discrimination on the basis of their gender identity and expression, gender, race or ethnicity, religious background, migrant status and perhaps other factors as well. (TGEU 2016, p. 8).

With regard to being accommodated in rural areas, we have focused on examples from Germany, as in Italy and the UK not many participants discussed this issue. In Italy, some NGO workers and lawyers mentioned the issue of SOGI claimants being accommodated in rural areas, like Anna (LGBTIQ+ group volunteer) who said that SOGI claimants 'are scattered, lost in places that are not accessible by public transport'. Being housed rurally was seen as problematic especially because of the difficulties of accessing LGBTIQ+ support and attending events (Anna, Antonella, and Jonathan, all LGBTIQ+ group volunteers; Livio, lawyer). It was generally seen as counter-productive for integration to accommodate claimants in rural areas: '[B]ecause many structures are completely isolated from society, so how can we involve migrants, integrate them if in a year they are dispersed in the mountains' (Susanna, social worker). A number of SOGI claimants told us that they were accommodated in small towns or villages (Diarra, Gbona, Ken, Kennedy, Odosa), and they briefly talked about issues such as not being able to access LGBTIQ+ events (Odosa, Italy) or organisations (Ken), and having poor mobile phone connections (Kennedy). However, they did not talk in depth about these experiences and some, like Diarra liked living in a small town.

In the UK, some claimants had been dispersed to smaller towns, but these generally had good transport links and therefore mobility and accessing LGBTIQ+ support and groups was not a significant issue. However, here we heard many accounts of homeless and destitution, to which we turn now.

8.6   Homelessness and Destitution

When we analysed our fieldwork data, it was shocking to see how many of our participants had experienced homelessness during or after their asylum claims in the UK, where destitution can happen at four points for claimants:

> on arrival, before making a claim; when they claim asylum and there are administrative errors and S95 [section 95 subsistence support] doesn't come through; during the application, when problems arise including trying to live on a very small S95 sum; and after the decision – even if it's positive, when support ends, but especially for people who are Appeal Rights Exhausted, the majority of whom become destitute (Gareth, consultant, UK).

For those who are classified as Appeal Rights Exhausted (ARE) but remain in the UK, the risk of becoming destitute is high following the removal of section 4 support under the Immigration Act 2016. Research by the Refugee Council showed that a high number of those using their destitution services came from five countries: Sudan/South Sudan, the Democratic Republic of Congo (DRC), Eritrea, Somalia and Zimbabwe. With the exception of DRC, homosexuality is illegal in all these countries (Ramón Mendos 2019; Refugee Council 2012). While issues of homelessness and exploitation are likely to be common to all asylum claimants, they take a specific form for SOGI claimants. SOGI claimants who do find themselves ARE but stay in the UK are more likely than others to find it difficult to seek support from families and community organisations, where they may experience discrimination. They may also be more vulnerable to sexual exploitation when they become destitute (Meggs, focus group no. 1, Manchester, UK; Melisa, NGO worker).

The participants who told us about their experiences with homelessness, stayed in different places over night. Selim slept a couple of nights in a cemetery; Mary and Zaro were homeless for 1 month and slept in a park in London; Meggs spent a night on a night bus, when she was evacuated from her accommodation. Lutfor was evicted from his house, after his claim was refused and before he submitted a fresh claim. He was homeless and slept in different parks; in 4 days he lost everything, including his papers. He talked about being out of place as an Asian person:

8.6 Homelessness and Destitution

oh, I mean, it is a real experience when I was living in the street. I saw people around me who are homeless, nobody is Indian or Asian, and you know in homeless people they have a like, community like this, but I was outcast from this, so I was travelling on my own.

When he submitted his papers, he was allowed back into his old accommodation: 'Same house. When I was homeless my room was empty, but I don't know why they made me homeless. When I went to court appeal to London, they send me to the same home'.

Research on housing and homelessness experiences of LGBT people seeking asylum in 2009 found that SOGI asylum claimants were at a particular disadvantage, as 'most interviewees lived with people who would take them into their own accommodation on a rent-free basis, knowing their sexuality and often expecting sexual favours in return' (Bell and Hansen 2009, p. 16). Bell and Hansen's report (2009) demonstrates the importance of collecting data on homelessness from an intersectional perspective; however, there is no more recent research on LGBTIQ asylum claimants' and refugees' experiences of homelessness. A survey commissioned by The Guardian in 2017 found general high levels of destitution and homelessness among newly-recognised refugees, but did not discuss any SOGI-related experience (Refugee Council 2017). A report commissioned by the Metropolitan Community Church of North London (Dyck 2019, pp. 12, 48) touches upon housing issues, and especially SOGI claimants' fear of being 'outed' when staying with family or people who are not LGBTIQ+-affirming and potentially losing their accommodation.

As Melisa (NGO worker) explained, when SOGI claimants experience violence and harassment in asylum accommodation, they often prefer to leave their accommodation and be homeless, as they are afraid to report the abuse suffered and risk having to continue to live in the same accommodation if no action is taken to address the issues. People may also be afraid to report to the police because of their experiences in their country of origin (also Sabrina, NGO worker, Germany). Many of our participants were vulnerable to exploitation and abuse in order to keep a roof over their head:

not only are they homeless, but they also face sexual exploitation… you know, just for a roof over their head. In terms of women, we have seen a lot of domestic servitude, where LGBT women are looking after children, doing domestic chores, and just for a roof over their head. Sometimes they are given a little bit of money but sometimes they are not (Melisa, NGO worker).

SOGI claimants may be afraid to access general housing charities, where they would have to disclose their sexuality or be worried that they would have to share accommodation with people who are homophobic (Debbie, NGO worker). Trans claimant Amber was homeless for two-and-a-half months after falling out with their ex-boyfriend. They slept at friends, strangers, moved around, and sometimes did not even have a blanket: 'I did get involved with sex work and asked strangers for money to help me get by, it was one of the darkest time in my life if I'm honest'. Kamel (Italy) also risked being homeless because, as a trans claimant, accommodation centres based on a binary ratio were not able to fit them in.

Irma (UK) had to leave NASS accommodation and became homeless because her benefits had been cut and she received a letter ordering her to move out: 'I was crying. Nowhere to go. It was hard. And it is a journey'. Before becoming homeless, Lutfor lived in a houseshare without paying rent, and cooked and cleaned for his housemates in exchange for board and lodging, explaining that 'sometimes we can even offer our services for free, just so that we can get accommodation' (focus group 6, Manchester). Sadia (UK) lived in someone's garden house and did housework for them and looked after their children. Selim (UK) had to move around a lot, was homeless, stayed in hostels and people's houses and then met a 'gay guy' who 'was quite crazy but of course I had to swallow the [pride], you know, I had to, I needed a place to stay, so even if he is crazy I had nothing else to do'.

Meggs (focus group no. 1, Manchester, UK) talked to other young bisexual and lesbian women in preparation for a conference presentation she was giving on the topic and was shocked to hear about their experiences of destitution:

> And in those cases, on the refusals the judge will have clearly said, "I believe she has been raped", "I believe she is HIV+", it is sensitive issues that they believe on, but still they kick that kind of a person out of the accommodation.

Women would often end up in abusive relationships 'because you have got nowhere to go, you just have to put your head down and just go along with everything they do' (Meggs, focus group no. 1, Manchester; see also Chap. 9). Many other participants in the UK would have ended up homeless, and in potentially exploitative situations, if they had not received help from friends and LGBTIQ+ or LGBTIQ+ friendly organisations (Diamond, Ibrahim A., Edith, Miria, Martin, Jayne, Ximena, Stephina).

One of the key triggers for destitution is the transition period, after people are granted international protection: 'So, on the Monday you get your letter from the Home Office saying you have been granted leave to remain. On the Tuesday you have a party, a month later you are homeless' (Oliver, NGO worker). In fact, for many of our participants, issues with accommodation and homelessness were not resolved once they received refugee status, but in some cases, were made worse, as we now discuss.

8.7 Housing After the Asylum Claim Process

Most research on SOGI asylum focuses on the time during the asylum process, but it is also important to look at what happens when SOGI claimants are finished with their asylum claims. In all three countries life is not necessarily becoming easier after the asylum claim.

In Germany, the social isolation that SOGI claimants face during the asylum process often continues after their claims have been successful due to the residence obligation legislation (Sect. 8.2). The requirement to stay in the same municipality where the claim was processed (as it is the case in some federal states) is especially

8.7 Housing After the Asylum Claim Process

difficult for SOGI refugees (Marlen, legal advisor). As Noah (NGO social worker) described: 'I do not want to live in [town x] as a gay man. I would perish there. There is nothing there'. Again, under special circumstances, people can request permission to move to a different area. For instance, at the time of the interview, Bebars, a trans claimant with refugee status, had been waiting for 4 months to receive a response to his relocation request. He regularly had to travel almost 3 h to see his doctor (for hormone treatment, etc.), who was based in the city where he would like to move to. He had also signed up for a German language class where he lived, but had been waiting for almost a year and still had not been given a place.

The downside of living in larger cities however is that it is generally difficult for anyone to find affordable and acceptable housing, but SOGI refugees face multiple layers of discrimination in the housing market (Frank S., legal advisor; Diana, Ibrahim, Milad, Zouhair). They may have to stay in asylum accommodation for years (Ibrahim), if they do not find alternative accommodation, and there is often no social housing available (Finn, representative of a German municipality). In addition, council housing is tied to the legally established rental levels ('Mietspiegel'), but property owners often request more for their flats (Juliane, public official).

While all refugees are likely to face discrimination, for SOGI refugees there are often additional issues, for instance if they are visibly trans (Frank S., legal advisor), or when 'there is a mismatch' between their gender expression and their ID document, thus trans refugees face more challenges than other refugees, or other trans people, when trying to find housing because of the intersection of their gender, their legal status, their race, ethnicity or religion (TGEU 2016, p. 10).

Diana was looking for a flat in Berlin for about 7 months after being granted international protection. She said that there were always around 40 people at the flat viewings and 'obviously Germans were in front'. When she finally found a flat, she told us it was because she had an advantage, as the estate agent was a lesbian. In larger and more expensive German cities, the situation is particularly difficult, as 'the housing market looks very bad anyway and obviously refugees have no chance at all' (Thomas, NGO volunteer). As William described it:

> we the people who are Black, it's very hard to get a house to stay. To the extent that when you get a house, an apartment up there, and the Markler [estate agent] tells the property owner that "you know what, the person who is coming to this house is a Black man, or a Black woman or a Black family", they say "eh, eh, eh, I don't have a house.

Mayi (focus group no. 4, Bavaria) also thought that once you have been granted international protection, 'you look for a room. They never give you [one] if you are Black, they say you are dirty, they don't want you dirtying their house. Then you can never get a house'. As Diana described, the situation is rendered more difficult because refugees have a blue (rather than red) passport and only 3-year residence permit, and property owners are ignorant and fearful of this type of documentation.

There is a dearth of organisations specifically tasked with helping (SOGI) refugees to find housing (Diana, Alphaeus, William), but the LGBTIQ+ community can sometimes help in this regard. Rainbow Refugees Munich have managed to get some of their members into housing through private contacts (Thomas, NGO volunteer). Marhoon had to spend 8 months in the accommodation centre, then LSVD helped him to find a flat through a property owner who was an 'ally'. Marhoon was lucky that when he received refugee status and collected his papers, the public authorities asked him where he wanted to live in the federal state, and he chose the biggest city in the state: 'I think maybe they know in the document that I'm gay and atheist, so they will not send me to a village'.

Houseshares are very common in Germany (called 'Wohngemeinschaft'). Halim, Alphaeus, Fares, Zouhair, Ahmed and Rolla (focus group no. 6, Lower Saxony) all lived in this type of accommodation. Yet, when people are severely traumatised, it is more difficult for them to find a flat or a room in a houseshare, and they then need to stay in asylum accommodation, where they have to share rooms, for a long period, despite the likely negative impact on their mental health and recovery (Frank S., legal advisor).

In Italy, life after being granted international protection may be difficult too. Limited support is provided to refugees unless they are accommodated through SPRAR. Some kind of support is sometimes granted in CAS accommodation, but this depends on the specific CAS. Even when people are supported by SPRAR accommodation, it is not guaranteed that they will be able to find housing. For instance, Alain A. was moved to SPRAR after he was granted refugee status, but he was worried about finding a place where to live: 'And I have seen so many people in the project and they leave, they don't have a place to stay and they stay on the street. And now, I am thinking like, when I leave, where will I go to'. He explained that SPRAR would cover the costs for initial accommodation, but people need to obtain a housing contract. He was worried that because he was so young, he would not be able to obtain one.

Those not moving into SPRAR accommodation on receiving status risk eviction from the reception centre irrespective of the availability of alternative accommodation. Usually claimants have 6 months from being granted international protection to look for alternative accommodation, but we also heard of occasions where claimants had to leave earlier. For instance, Just Me (focus group no. 3, northern Italy) had to leave the reception centre very suddenly:

> I wasn't even told I am going to leave, it was just early in the morning, they came with the letter from the Questura [police local headquarters] say that I have to leave today, now. I have to take my bag and things. So strange. Yes, I wasn't informed maybe in three days' time you are going to leave, or I should know what to do. It was so sudden. (…) to say you have to leave the camp, you are going to the city, into the community, without no work, without no place to stay, with nothing, without not even money to even get support yourself or your wellbeing. It is like they are telling you they are exposing you to crime.

In addition, nobody informed Just Me that he could apply for a place at SPRAR. He added that he was 'strong enough not to force myself into doing something, into committing crime or going against the law. But it is not easy'. Once homeless, he tried to survive with the help of friends and his supporting group, and then lived on a farm, where he worked (focus group no. 3, northern Italy). During the focus group, his dire situation and the pain that he felt recounting this experience

8.7 Housing After the Asylum Claim Process

was evident. His eyes were empty and every word he pronounced was followed by silence. Everyone in the group was emotionally affected by his account.

Many claimants also thought that because of racism, it was more difficult for refugees to find housing. Silver said that he would like to find a job and a room in a houseshare, but thought that this would be difficult as a Black gay refugee:

> I mean, if I were an Italian, when I see Blacks, maybe like they do things that are bad, maybe then I have to be afraid. I do the same. Whites think that Blacks are all the same, but it is not. There are Blacks who are better than others, but Italians think they are all the same.

Indeed, Giulia (LGBTIQ+ group volunteer) said that their organisation has witnessed 'many young people who have obtained the documents to whom nobody rents, even if they have a job, because they are Black'. Kamel also described how some private property owners said 'we rent to Italians' and 'only to Italians'. Cyrus (focus group no. 2, northern Italy) described accompanying a friend to rent housing, but the man who showed them the accommodation said to them 'the owner of the house told me not to give the house to foreigners, to Blacks, not to give the house to Blacks', which Cyrus promptly qualified as discriminatory and abnormal.

In the UK, housing problems are not necessarily resolved when SOGI claimants are granted international protection. The transition period can be especially difficult for claimants in the UK, who, as mentioned above, have only 28 days to leave their asylum accommodation. Debbie and Gary (NGO workers) explained that sometimes official documentation does not come through in time for the person to move to the general benefits system. There are other obstacles too, for instance, delays in issuing the UK identity card without which individuals cannot access housing and benefits. Refugees are likely to find it difficult to rent accommodation in the private sector following the extension of immigration responsibilities to private landlords (Home Office 2016). A survey by the Residential Landlords Association in 2018 found that 'half of landlords are now less likely to consider renting to someone without a British passport because of the government's Right to Rent policy' (Smith 2017). In March 2019, the UK High Court ruled that this legislation was incompatible with Article 14 read with Article 8 of the ECHR.[13]

When their asylum support stops many claimants become homeless and have to turn to friends and family – something which may be harder for SOGI minorities, leaving them more dependent on food banks and charities (Basedow and Doyle 2016, p. 43). Research with 50 lesbian and gay refugees in London and Manchester found the majority living below the poverty line (Micro Rainbow International 2013). Most reported feeling discriminated against on the basis of their sexual orientation both in their country of origin and the UK. The isolation resulting from being member of a sexual minority can lead to low self-esteem, depression or other mental health problems (Micro Rainbow International 2013). For many individuals:

---

[13] *R (Joint Council for the Welfare of Immigrants) Claimant and Secretary of State for the Home Department* [2019] EWHC 452 (Admin). Appeal against this decision was allowed in *The Secretary of State for the Home Department v R (on the application of) Joint Council for The Welfare of Immigrants* [2020] EWCA Civ 542 (21 April 2020).

the land of opportunity merely represents a downward social mobility ladder. It emerged from the study that often the material circumstances and conditions to live a "dignified life" in the new country were far worse than those the refugee had in their country of origin (Micro Rainbow International 2013, p. 28).

The dispersal policy is also problematic here. SOGI claimants might have established social support networks and are then dispersed and moved away from that source of support: 'So you could end up being quite isolated in a small town somewhere just because of the vagaries of the system' (Gary, NGO worker). In addition, when applying for council housing in a particular area, people need to demonstrate ties to the community, but if they have only lived for 2 years in that area, they will not be eligible for council housing and will then need to find private accommodation (Melisa, NGO worker).

Thus, life does not necessarily become easier once SOGI claimants are granted international protection. Short timeframes to leave asylum accommodation makes life hard especially in Italy and the UK, while in all three countries they may face transphobia and racism on the housing market. Separate SOGI accommodation may help to make life a little easier for SOGI claimants, especially during, but also after the asylum process.

8.8 SOGI Accommodation

Because of the discrimination SOGI claimants experience in shared accommodation, most participants thought that '[t]o open centres for only LGBT community, it is one of the best ideas. Yes, it is one of the best ideas, because it is an environment where they will feel safe' (Alain A., Italy). In our European-wide survey for people who support SOGI claimants, 65% of the respondents considered the provision of separate accommodation for LGBTIQ+ people seeking asylum or who have been granted asylum to be a good idea (8% did not think so, and 27% were not sure). All three of our case countries have some LGBTIQ+ accommodation established, however limited, and some of our participants had experience of living in such type of accommodation (Michael, UK; Amber, UK; Mahmoud, Germany; Prince Emrah, Germany).

In Germany, since 2015 NGOs have put pressure on the federal governments to fund specific LGBTIQ+ accommodation projects and in many cities such projects have been established. The largest of these is an LGBTIQ+ accommodation centre in Berlin, run by the NGO Schwulenberatung ('Gay Counsellling'), which accommodates 122 SOGI claimants (Nina, legal advisor). Other significant LGBTIQ+ accommodation centres are located in Dresden and Leipzig, which each accommodate approximately 100 SOGI claimants, and in Chemnitz, which accommodates approximately 80 SOGI claimants (Thomas, NGO volunteer). In other cities, such as Frankfurt am Main, Cologne and Hannover, there are either 'official' accommodation centres or beds in flats for SOGI asylum claimants, and in some other cities there are unofficial arrangements to the same effect (Awadalla and Rajanayagam

2016; Benirschke 2016; Queer.de 2017; The Local 2016). In Cologne, SOGI claimants are seen as a vulnerable group and specific flats are offered, accommodating 20–25 people in total (Ibrahim). Hannover accommodates nine SOGI claimants in smaller flats (Kadir, NGO worker; Matthias, social worker; Juliane, public official), and Frankfurt am Main has an accommodation centre for SOGI claimants that accommodates 21 SOGI claimants and with social workers based there (one full-time equivalent, according to Knud, NGO worker). In some of these accommodation centres people need to share rooms (Berlin, Frankfurt am Main), and as participants argued, the aim should then be to move people on as quickly as possible into private accommodation, as shared accommodation, whoever one's room-mate, is 'just an extreme burden for all people and therefore also for LGBTI and maybe even in particular for LGBTI, having to share a room with people over such a long period of time' (Nina, legal advisor).

Specific LGBTIQ+ accommodation was not supported in all federal states. For instance, the Bavarian government did not provide it. In Nuremberg, there was only a small amount of LGBTIQ+ accommodation (20 places), and the city of Munich had agreed to create 19 places for LGBTIQ+ claimants (in smaller flats), but had only made eight available at the time of our fieldwork. This was a very small allocation in comparison to other federal states (Thomas, NGO volunteer).

However, claimants who had lived in SOGI accommodation facilities did not always have positive experiences. For instance, Prince Emrah (Germany) experienced physical violence in the SOGI accommodation centre in Berlin, and had their nose broken by another resident. They were critical of the LGBTIQ+ accommodation centre and said that while they had faced discrimination in the general accommodation centre, in the LGBTIQ+ centre it had been worse. Mahmoud had also lived in LGBTIQ+ accommodation for 18 months. He told us that he felt that not everyone there was a member of a SOGI minority, and that he had lots of problems with other residents (Awadalla and Rajanayagam 2016; Benirschke 2016; Queer.de 2017; The Local 2016).

Some participants favoured smaller LGBTIQ+-specific accommodation, for example, flats or houseshares (Frank S., legal advisor; Kadir, NGO worker). This was the approach taken in Hannover and Cologne, where the 'idea was to have separate flats in the city, so they [residents] feel integrated, they feel they are in a home place, but they have social workers who always check up on them' (Ibrahim). And although in Germany we learned of many more SOGI asylum accommodation projects than in Italy and the UK, participants still felt that the LGBTIQ+ accommodation that existed was insufficient.

In Italy, two reception projects specifically for SOGI minorities have been developed by the two main Italian LGBTIQ+ NGOs. A proposal by the transgender organisation MIT – Movimento Identità Transessuale ('Transexual Identity Movement') has led to the opening of the first facility for transgender asylum claimants and refugees in Italy (QMagazine 2017). The project 'Raise the Difference – Accogli la differenza' was funded by local and central authorities, including the national anti-discrimination office (UNAR). MIT is in charge of the management of the centre and assists, together with the social cooperative Camelot, in hosting asylum claimants during and after the RSD procedure. While it is the first European reception centre dedicated to people claiming asylum on grounds of their gender identity and is part of the SPRAR reception system, it does not seem to be permanent (its contract being regularly renewed on a temporary basis). Moreover, it can only host a few claimants and by no means meets the needs of trans claimants in the whole of Italy.[14] The second SOGI accommodation project in Italy aims to open a reception facility based on collaboration between local authorities and the NGO Arcigay (national umbrella LGBTIQ+ rights platform). Apart from these two initiatives, there is a centre already open in the northern Italy, run by the social cooperative Kaleidoscop, but it caters only for gay men and is not reserved for those claiming international protection (it also hosts Italian gay men disowned by their families, for instance).[15] Moreover, this centre too has limited capacity.

In the UK, in 2017 the NGO Micro Rainbow International opened its first safe house for SOGI claimants and refugees in London, with a second safe house subsequently established in the West Midlands.[16] The demand for this accommodation exceeds availability, and there is a waiting list. After being homeless for 2 months, Amber was offered a space at one of the Micro Rainbow accommodation facilities, 'where it's all safe and for the first time in months I could inhale the air with a clear head, because it is with other LGBT asylum seekers and refugees and I don't have to worry about my safety anymore'. Melisa (NGO worker) talked about the importance of their accommodation for their clients. For instance, one of the clients who moved in told them that they 'can't believe I am in a space where I can finally be free to be myself'. They also said that 'I couldn't sleep when I was there [previous accommodation], because the other person had the bed opposite and they kept wondering if they are going to wake up and attack them'. Melisa (NGO worker) explained that the organisation first aimed for a larger accommodation facility, but smaller flats had the advantage that they were less visible.

In general, many of the asylum claimant and refugee participants were in favour of LGBTIQ+ specific accommodation to feel safe and not have to hide their SOGI (Ham and Stephen, focus group no. 2, Bavaria, Germany; Ken, Kennedy, Odosa, Gbona, Buba, Moses, Mamaka, all in Italy; Nice guy, focus group no. 1, Italy), and many of the NGO workers were supportive of such projects (Antonella, Diego, Riccardo and Giulia, all LGBTIQ+ group volunteers, Italy; Mara, lawyer, Italy). As one survey respondent argued:

> LGBTQI asylum seekers need to have a place where they can feel safe and supported; this is often not the case where they are placed in NASS housing, with potentially homophobic housemates, a situation which contributes to further stress and sometimes mental health problems (S130, LGBTIQ+ organisation member, UK).

---

[14] No official information is, however, available, due to the choice of the MIT – the association that manages this centre – to ensure the privacy of the guests (especially in light of the new political context).

[15] This information has been collected during a conversation with Giorgio Dell'Amico, SOGICA Advisory Board member, who has been directly involved in these projects.

[16] https://microrainbow.org/housing/.

8.8 SOGI Accommodation

Some participants argued that accommodation specifically for trans claimants was also important (Celeste, social worker, Italy; Kamel, Italy). Kamel (Italy) felt that because of their heightened visibility, trans claimants are in particular need of separate accommodation:

It's something I often say – we trans people need a special structure for us. Not a male structure, not a feminine structure. I will not accept to fit into a feminine structure, but neither will I be in a male structure.

There was also some caution expressed that the visibility of larger LGBTIQ+ centres might increase the risk of violence, if homophobic or right-wing groups find out about their location (Maryia, NGO worker, Germany). In the focus group discussions we held, there were different opinions on LGBTIQ+ housing. While in some groups, participants cheered enthusiastically and applauded the idea (focus groups no. 3 and 4, Bavaria, Germany), or generally liked the idea (focus groups no. 2, 3 and 4, northern Italy), in others there was less consensus. For instance, in focus group no. 1 in Hesse, Germany, Emroy said that after having lived with three heterosexual men who would make homophobic comments, and worrying whether he would wake up the next day, he would be happy to live in LGBTIQ+ accommodation. For Sandy, in contrast, LGBTIQ+ housing was not so important; it was more important to be housed near LGBTIQ+ organisations, groups and people. In other focus groups, it was also argued that the visibility of LGBTIQ+ accommodation centres may make them unsafe (focus group no. 4, northern Italy; Nelo, Italy), and that it should not be mandatory for SOGI claimants to be separately housed (focus group no. 2, northern Italy).

As well as those who were undecided, there were also some voices against the creation of separate accommodation centres for SOGI claimants. For instance, for Siri (Italy) the need was not obvious, as in Italy, the same rules and regulations about how to behave apply to everyone. Giulio (LGBTIQ+ group volunteer, Italy) also argued that when there are problems in a reception centre, more work needs to be done in that centre. In his view, segregating SOGI claimants would also give a wrong impression: 'an LGBT person does not relate all his life with LGBT people'. He agreed that there needed to be accommodation for particular vulnerable claimants, but that this should focus on an 'all-round vulnerability... not only linked to being [a member of a] SOGI [minority]'. Silvana (judge, Italy) was also against the idea as 'it would ghettoise them'. Instead, there should be 'cultural mediators' in the centres, who 'are indispensable to try to mediate the differences that are still huge', not only in terms of SOGI but also in terms of religion, politics and other differences that occur between any individuals forced to share living space. Others saw the main problem as simply that of shared asylum accommodation: 'I think people whenever possible should get out of camps as soon as possible, because it's not good for people, it's a solution but it's a temporary solution, and it doesn't help people feel like their safety and individuality' (Halim, Germany).

SOGI refugee housing is created on the basis of residents sharing a common SOGI, thus being a purposefully constructed sexualised space (Chap. 3). Yet, these spaces are not only sexualised but also gendered, racialised, classed, and so on, and organisations providing SOGI housing often do not pay sufficient attention to the intersecting identities of the people living in these facilities. As Juliane (public official) described:

> And then we realised that these are all gay men, but that's the only thing that connects them! These are also different people. Since we did not think about it in the beginning, that these are also different people from different countries of origin, what just connects them is that they are just gay, and they also handled it quite differently.

Some of the NGO workers we interviewed stressed the point that SOGI asylum claimants and refugees are not a homogenous group and that there are differences related to language, education, etc. Even having eight people living in a flat (like in Hannover) can be challenging, similarly to a student houseshare (Kadir, NGO worker). In other SOGI accommodation centres, it was also reported that people sometimes did not get on with each other. Louis (NGO volunteer) described potential tensions within the community of SOGI refugees – between gay men and trans people for instance, owing to preconceptions about gender roles. So, from an intersectional perspective, such differences between SOGI claimants need to be born in mind and duly considered. As in general, it '[d]epends on the situation; some feel safe[r] in separate housing some don't; it should be offered and then be up to the person' (S141, LGBTIQ+ organisation member, Germany).

Rather than establishing SOGI accommodation projects as akin to 'ghettos' (Chiara, NGO worker, Italy), some participants suggested establishing LGTIQ+-friendly, rather than LGBTIQ+ accommodation (Nicola, LGBTIQ+ group volunteer, Italy). Some participants preferred mixed accommodation to help SOGI claimants integrate with wider society (Celeste, social worker, Italy; Marhoon, Germany; Nicola, LGBTIQ+ group volunteer, Italy; William, Germany), or suggested LGBTIQ+ accommodation as only a short-term or temporary measure (Alphaeus, Germany; Halim, Germany; Mariya, NGO worker, Germany). In fact, the LGBTIQ+ accommodation centre in Berlin was intended as just such a temporary solution for claimants in the asylum process, but became a longer-term solution for individuals unable to find move-on accommodation or needing continuing social and psychological support (Nina, legal advisor, Germany).

Focus group no. 5 in southern Italy began with members agreeing with the idea of LGBTIQ+ accommodation centres, but concerns developed, with some even arguing that such provision would constitute discrimination:

> Alain B.: Well, for me, the idea is that it's a good idea, to design a reception centre for gays, but if we design a reception centre only for gays, it wants to say that the population does not agree that they accept you as you are, so it is not quite easy. For me it's not good.
>
> Dev: Indeed! It means that the population is still homophobic! We cannot accept everything, we cannot force others to live together.
>
> Alain B: It's not good.
>
> Dev: It's discrimination.

Although not everyone was in favour of specific LGBTIQ+ accommodation, the majority of our participants felt that the current provisions that exist were not sufficient. Like any other LGBTIQ+ space, the construction of these spaces is on the basis of a shared sexual identity and can foster certain forms of homonormativity. We now look at very different kinds of spaces, namely spaces of incarceration, and how these were experienced by our participants.

8.9 Detention

As we have addressed in Chaps. 4 and 5, questions of vulnerability are paramount when looking at issues of detention. In our survey, 23% of SOGI claimants were detained; 15% for less than a month and 8% for more than 6 months. There were stark differences with regard to the experiences of detention in the three case countries. This is no surprise as Germany and Italy are both bound by the current Reception directive, which restricts the use of detention, while the UK is bound by the original Reception directive, which does not refer to detention (Chap. 4).

As discussed in Chap. 4, detention is not a significant issue in Italy except for the situation of 'irregular migrants' in centres of identification and expulsion. Similarly, in Germany, detention is not a widespread practice, only affecting a very limited number of asylum claimants. Amongst our participants in Germany, only a few people had had experiences of detention (Emroy, Junior and Sandy, focus group no. 1, Hesse; Angel; Shany; Trudy Ann), and in most cases they were detained only briefly at the time of their arrival. One of these participants was from Morocco, and the others were from Jamaica. The maximum time someone had spent in detention was 2 weeks. While most participants did not have positive experiences of accommodation overall, those participants who had been detained were positive about the conditions and the staff in detention centres. For instance, Angel was detained for a week at Frankfurt airport after she arrived, and astonishingly she described this experience as the best she had with regard to living conditions:

> Since I've been here the best living condition was Frankfurt, even though that was the detention centre. And yet, still, that was the cleanest, the most, under the circumstances, the most comfortable, the most liveable, everything. Even though you couldn't go out on the road and see people.

This was confirmed by other participants who had had similar experiences (focus group no. 1, Hesse). Junior – who stayed in the detention centre in Frankfurt airport for about 2 weeks (sharing a room with other gay men) – said that whereas he felt safe and 'there were people there who protected me and everything', this changed once he arrived at the reception centre, where 'it was like, no-one cares about me'. The difference was that in the detention centre there was a church group, security officers and workers 'that treat us or treat me how I'm suppose... as a human, how I feel I'm supposed to be treated. So yes, I felt like I was safe'. Junior also felt that staff in the detention centres 'looked out' for gay people and protected them.

Participants in the focus group agreed that they were well looked after in the detention centre, something that was not the case in subsequent accommodation facilities. Emroy told us he thought that if the security or police officials from his detention centre had made the decision on his claim, he would have been granted international protection. Sandy had wanted to take the interpreter she had in the detention centre with her to the main interview, because the interpreter spoke:

> perfect English, she explained everything to me and let me understand that, you know, "this is what we're going to do, this is what we want to know, you don't have to go into details, leave that for your big interview, just tell us your main reason why...". She was really nice.

Trudy Ann was in the same detention centre with her girlfriend for a week after they arrived: 'It was kind of okay, but worrying. Feel like a prisoner. But then we have to go through that process anyway'. Some of the other people in the centre 'would make up them faces' when they saw them, but a security person told her not to 'pay them any mind because [in] Germany [being LGBTIQ+] is not taboo'.

In the UK, detention is far more widespread than in Germany or Italy. Moreover, the treatment of immigration detainees in general has long been a concern, also gaining media attention.[17] For instance, an undercover documentary in 2015 by Channel 4 News highlighted the mistreatment of women detainees at Yarl's Wood and staff referring to them as 'animals', 'beasties' and 'b**ches' (Channel 4 News 2015). The UN special rapporteur on violence against women was refused entry to Yarl's Wood in 2014.[18] In 2018, a BBC Panorama programme revealed malpractice and abuse by staff at Brook House, a centre run by G4S (Shaw 2018). Crucially, in 2018, the High Court found that some conditions at Brook House did not comply with the Equality Act 2010 or the ECHR.[19] The account of one of our survey respondents illustrates this mistreatment:

> This was my worst nightmare. At first I was in [an] open dormitory with about 50 people. Just like beds in [a] hall. Then taken to another detention. To be honest I really don't want to talk about it. I was told to take off my clothes to be checked. I remained totally naked (C59, UK).

There have been concerns about 'vulnerable' detainees in particular. In 2008, the Independent Asylum Commission expressed concern that 'LGBT detainees are not adequately protected in detention' (Independent Asylum Commission 2008, p. 84). The Shaw report on the welfare of vulnerable people in detention was commissioned by the then Home Secretary Theresa May and published in 2016. Replies to Freedom of Information requests in 2016 showed that a minimum of 76 SOGI asylum claimants were detained throughout the UK between 1 January and 18

---

[17] In 2008, the Independent Asylum Commission expressed concern that 'LGBT detainees are not adequately protected in detention' (2008, p. 84).

[18] See Parliamentary Question on 6 May 2014 by Lord Ramsbotham asking 'why the United Nations special rapporteur on violence against women was refused access to Yarl's Wood immigration detention centre while on an official visit to the United Kingdom.' The Government's answer was that the visit 'was never agreed as part of this fact-finding mission' (House of Lords 2014).

[19] *Hussein v Secretary of State for the Home Department & Anor* [2018] EWHC 213.

November 2016 (UK Parliament 2017). Lesbian women and transgender people appear particularly vulnerable to mistreatment in detention. It has been estimated that 340 lesbian women are detained each year (House of Commons et al. 2015). Yet, while the Shaw report highlighted instances of bullying and harassment of LGBT detainees, it recommended only that 'transsexual people should be presumed unsuitable for detention' (Shaw 2016, p. 194). Moreover, as discussed in Chap. 4, there are acknowledged inconsistencies in the way the term vulnerability is understood and used.

Research by UKLGIG and Stonewall also found that 'LGBT asylum seekers face discrimination and harassment in detention centres' and that '[t]rans asylum seekers face particular threats of violence in detention' (Stonewall and UKLGIG 2016, p. 8). This is the case in particular when they are placed in detention centres that do not relate to their gender identity but the sex on their passport. As Zadeh (2019) argues: 'Detention centres are possibly the most dangerous places in the country for LGBT+ people'.

Allan, a lawyer, pointed out that SOGI claimants do not only face homophobic abuse in detention, but their vulnerability also makes it more difficult to work on their claim, for instance if they 'are worried about a fax from UKLGIG coming in'. Preparation for their cases is also more difficult: phone and internet access is limited, many websites are blocked in detention centres, and the remote location of the centres means that detainees often cannot get support to retrieve the evidence that they may need (Singer 2019, p. 11; Stonewall and UKLGIG 2016, p. 25).

Often the lawyers assigned to SOGI claimants in detention (if they do not already have one) may not have experience with SOGI cases or have limited time available to prepare often complex cases (Stephina). While SGW (focus group no. 4, London) was in detention, her solicitor dropped her case. She said he told her that 'he can't do anything else'. She told us:

> All that was going in my head was deportation, that was what I was thinking, because I think a few weeks after I got there, there was a charter flight and I just saw how many women were taken out and deported and I just thought that would be me. So, it was, it was, it was hard, it was very painful, and I had now realised that I was getting more depressed the way I got in, but what else can you do.

She was not able to find another solicitor, so she 'ended up having to be in the detention centre sitting before a judge, with my little paperwork, you know'. She felt that this situation 'has progressively gotten worse now with the strains with the legal aid. So that is a big problem'.

Nine of our asylum claimant and refugee participants in the UK spoke of their direct experiences with detention (Irma, Lubwa, Luc, Lutfor, Miria, Patti, SGW, Stephina, Wabz), and there may have been others who did not talk about it in our interviews with them. Several NGO participants also talked about their examples of clients being detained (Chloe; Amelia; Ashley; Oliver). We heard that people were detained for variable but often considerable periods, ranging from 1 week (Miria) to a shocking 32 months (Luc). The duration of detention is not surprising, as the UK is the only country in the EU that does not have a time limit on detention (Chap. 4).

Yet, as NGO worker Oliver told us, it is not always clear what the reasons are for detaining someone. He always assumed that the decision to detain somebody was based on the potential risk of absconding, but then witnessed examples of 'inappropriate use of detention', for instance, when one woman seemed to have been detained purely for the purpose of collecting proof of her nationality and issuing her with a travel document (even though she was released afterwards): 'I don't know what that was about'.

Lutfor thought that LGBTIQ+ people should not be detained, as they have faced 'too much violence for their sexuality'. Because of the fears they have around their sexual orientation, and the difficulties of talking about it, they should instead be offered counselling. When Lutfor applied for asylum, he found that he 'was not welcome at all', but instead treated 'like a criminal' and put into detention. His lawyer made an application for bail on the basis that he was vulnerable and 'fortunately they accepted the bail and they released me on like the next day'.

Hearing participants' accounts of detention raises questions about the kinds of 'abuse of the system' and 'risks to the public' invoked by the Home Office to justify indefinite detention (Chap. 4). All nine UK participants who were detained were subsequently released with no explanation and proceeded with their asylum claims. Nor did the NGO workers we interviewed have any SOGI (or other) claimants who had been detained before being removed from the UK, though there were situations that came close: 'I have on a couple of occasions been on the phone to someone as they are boarding, being boarded on a plane, before the next injunction to get them off has come through' (Ashley, psychotherapist). Amelia (NGO worker) also had a similar experience:

> I mean, certainly it has come very close sometimes, yes, there was quite a few members detained and a couple of members, you know, were very close to the plane... sort of booked on a flight and it has been right down to the wire a couple of times.

It is noticeable that most of the SOGI claimants we interviewed were supported by NGOs and, therefore, perhaps had a higher chance of being released from detention. Meggs told us that three women at the Lesbian Immigration Support Group (LISG) had been detained when they signed in with the authorities, as requested to do regularly and got support immediately:

> So, unless the organisations that are out there know you are in there, then they will start to, to do the petition for you to fight for you, so that you can be released while you are waiting on your claim, then it helps a lot. But if no one knows anything about you, definitely you are gone.

Amelia (NGO worker) explained that many members of LISG had experiences of detention and that the impact on the women detained was 'devastating', having a huge impact on women's mental health. Usually women were detained when they went to report at the Home Office centre Dallas Court in Greater Manchester, which some were required to do every fortnight or every month and 'then the next time they go to Dallas Court to sign on and it is just, it just keeps that fear, all wrapped up'. This fear was described by Edith, who had not been detained, but said that she was 'afraid of being detained and because I have suffered even being in jail in Kenya, I don't like even going to Home Office itself, it makes me sick'.

It is clear that the absence of a time limit for detention 'adds to the already traumatising experience of the government taking away your liberty' (Zadeh 2019). Even after their release, the experience of incarceration often continues to have a detrimental effect on claimants' physical and mental wellbeing (Zadeh 2019). Miria, who was detained in Yarl's Wood when she claimed asylum, does not remember much from her time in detention, only that she mostly stayed in her room and was comforted by a young woman who she met there. Even though she was detained for 'only' a week:

> by that time when I got out of that detention, I was just touching the walls to walk, I couldn't manage to stand on my own, I was very weak, very sick, because I was not eating. I was not sleeping, so it wasn't, it was really, really bad time. It was really, really hard time for me.

As Meggs (focus group no. 1, Manchester), who had not been detained herself but had seen the effects on friends, explained:

> So, they will be going through NHS counselling, maybe for the whole year or for two years and taking antidepressants, and all things like that, because of the tortures that they experienced back home. So, and then it becomes a process you slowly get to trust people (…). On First Wednesday [social support group in Manchester] sometimes, something about 80 or 60 of us were going to counselling. And then when you are up there, when you are trying to find your feet for your own health and benefit, then you get detained. You drop, you drop, you go back to zero. You know, and then when you come out there, you are even worse. (…) you are starting to have flashbacks, it becomes even worse. So that particular person has to start again, with the counselling, if she will ever recover, suicidal thoughts and all that.

Meggs also spoke about the irony of the government supporting SOGI claimants with their mental health by providing them free NHS counselling, while then destroying that mental health recovery work and worsening the trauma by detaining asylum claimants. As Lubwa (focus group no. 1, Manchester), who was detained for 2 months, explained:

> I remember when I was in detention, like, I felt like I am being targeted for no reason and (…) my emotional state was so bad, like, and I wanted to like, you know, commit suicide and I said I wanted, I don't want to live anymore, I just want to like kill myself, and get away from it.

Lubwa did not understand why he had to be detained. He told us that his solicitor was convinced that Lubwa did not need to be in detention, and wrote to the Home Office to say her client was vulnerable. Lubwa met all bail conditions (including a financial guarantor and accommodation), but officials argued that he was likely to abscond, and it was only when a judge intervened that he was freed from detention:

> At the end they have to give me bail, so all I wonder is why would you waste my two months inside, why? Because now I still go for counselling, because it is, it wasn't something good for me and, you know, you have got nightmares, you have got like, you know, it was bad experience over there and I feel like I was the one who faced torture and everything I faced, I faced like I was the victim of like torture back home as well, so as here, and why would you put me in prison. I wasn't a criminal, I have not done any crime, I was the one who was at risk.

Lutfor said he felt lucky because he was detained for only 26 days (as other people in detention had told him that people usually stay for 3 or 4 months before they even obtain legal advice) and he thought that the 'staff there who was working there, they were really nice (…) the detention, I don't know, it affected me somehow'. However, he told us that he had '[t]raumatic distress, I didn't want to go out, I don't want to talk to anyone. Then, after therapy, I went for therapy, counselling, then I found LGBT Foundation, I start to come here, talk to them, then I start to do voluntary works'. Recovering from a period in detention is clearly a long and arduous journey, which is added to a usually already difficult set of mental and physical issues. This will be further explored in the next chapter.

8.10 Concluding Remarks

If we define the 'right to adequate housing' as including respecting the dignity of the person and ensuring equality and non-discrimination (UNHCR 2013, sec. 1), then we can say that this right is not respected or implemented in all its dimensions when it comes to asylum accommodation for SOGI claimants in Germany, Italy and the UK. There are often poor material conditions in reception and accommodation centres and SOGI claimants have to live in accommodation and in areas where they experience homophobia, transphobia, racism and disablism, and at times intersecting discrimination.

There are no specific policies relating to the accommodation of SOGI claimants in Germany, Italy or the UK. Yet all three countries have seen the establishment of LGBTIQ+ accommodation projects, however limited and whether managed by the state or NGOs or by a partnership of the two. Campaigns for LGBTIQ+ accommodation can be delicate and contentious, potentially reinforcing stereotypes that other (non-SOGI) asylum claimants are sexist and homophobic, feeding a homonationalist depiction of an LGBTIQ+-welcoming Europe (in contrast to homophobic countries of origin). This discourse risks homogenising both SOGI and non-SOGI claimants. Our theoretical and analytical frameworks, explored in Chap. 3, debunk such simplistic binaries, and many participants helped us gain a more sophisticated understanding of such complex realities.

While it is important to demonstrate the specific needs of SOGI claimants in accommodation centres, and perhaps campaign for SOGI housing, from an intersectional perspective these needs should be assessed on an individual basis. It is important to avoid homonationalist discourses that depict (White) Western nations and people as liberated and gay-friendly and (non-White) non-Western nations and people as homophobic and transphobic. There is a danger that the struggles of LGBTIQ+ refugees are instrumentalised for racist discourses (Awadalla and Rajanayagam 2016). As Maryia (NGO worker, Germany) pointed out, simplistic distinctions between LGBTIQ+ refugees on the one hand, and homo and transphobic refugees on the other, do not correspond to reality:

8.10 Concluding Remarks

> Because I think it's a lot more complex and there are a lot of differences within very different social groups and other things like "race", class, education, health, all sorts of things play a role too, so for sure it is very important to talk about what kind of discrimination people experience among each other in the accommodation, but it is more important to look at how the society receives them, how it treats them, and what opportunities there are, so to speak, to start a new life.

We therefore rather want to consider asylum accommodation centres to be like many other spaces, namely heteronormatively structured. As geographers of sexualities have shown, everyday spaces (such as the street, the home, the workplace) are constituted as heterosexual through repetitive heterosexual performances (Bell and Valentine 1995; Johnston and Longhurst 2009; Valentine 1996; Chap. 3).

SOGI claimants may also have specific needs because of other dimensions of their identity, such as religion (as in Marhoon's case, Germany) or disability (Betty, Germany). One claimant referred to 'being out of category' being LGBTIQ+ and also being a refugee (Zouhair, Germany). While SOGI claimants often experienced difficulties in their accommodation, they were also often lucky to have effective support structures in place (at least in urban areas). Many participants were helped by LGBTIQ+ organisations, for example, when they were homeless, or when they were harassed or victimised in their accommodation. Such practical and emotional support was indispensable to SOGI claimants' well-being. As has been highlighted, community support is invaluable to decrease isolation (TGEU 2016).

From our interviews, it also became clear that authorities (and housing providers) need greater awareness of and sensitivity to the housing needs of SOGI claimants, in particular the issues of where (and with whom) individuals are housed. Particularly in Germany, many of our participants experienced extreme social isolation, often accommodated in rural areas, where they encountered homophobia, transphobia and racism. The UNHCR 'Resettlement Assessment Tool' for LGBTI refugees describes that: 'In most cases, LGBTI refugees will gravitate towards major urban centers as they offer greater opportunities for social support networks, and more specific resources. However, LGBTI refugees can be successfully resettled to more rural communities' (UNHCR 2013, p. 12). Our research shows that this is often difficult, and all the LGBTIQ+ claimants and refugees we talked to, who were living in rural areas, were quite isolated and preferred to live in more urban areas. However, also cities can do more to 'foster cultures of diversity and inclusion', for instance through cultural festivals and neighbourhood gatherings (Ruckstuhl 2016, p. 5).

While NGOs campaign for LGBTIQ+ accommodation centres and generally smaller accommodation centres, some participants were concerned that the far right trends in Germany and Italy will not make things better, and reforms introduced in the meantime have indicated that such concerns are warranted. In Germany, as of January 2020, claimants have to stay for up to 24 months in 'arrival centres' in Bavaria, and this might become the case in other federal states. In Italy, support offered in accommodation during the asylum process is also likely to diminish with recent reforms only offering SPRAR accommodation to people who have been recognised refugee status. In the UK, we will have to see what impact Brexit will generally have on asylum policies.

We now turn to an analysis of the range of physical and mental health issues SOGI claimants face, as well as challenges they deal with in relation to work and education.

References

Alessi, E. J., Kahn, S., Greenfield, B., Woolner, L., & Manning, D. (2018). A qualitative exploration of the integration experiences of LGBTQ refugees who fled from the Middle East, North Africa, and Central and South Asia to Austria and the Netherlands. *Sexuality Research and Social Policy*. https://doi.org/10.1007/s13178-018-0364-7.

Allsopp, J., Sigona, N., & Phillimore, J. (2014). *Poverty among refugees and asylum seekers in the UK* (IRiS Working Paper Series 1/2014). https://www.birmingham.ac.uk/Documents/college-social-sciences/social-policy/iris/2014/working-paper-series/IRiS-WP-1-2014.pdf

Anci, Caritas, Cittalia, Fondazione Caritas Migrantes, & UNHCR. (2016). *Rapporto sulla protezione internazionale in Italia*. www.anci.it/Contenuti/Allegati/Rapporto%20protezione%20 internazionale%202016.pdf

Awadalla, A., & Rajanayagam, I. (2016). *LGBT*I*Q refugees in Germany*. Lernen Aus Der Geschichte. http://lernen-aus-der-geschichte.de/International/content/12840

Basedow, J., & Doyle, L. (2016). *England's forgotten refugees: Out of the fire and into the frying pan*. London: Refugee Council.

Bell, D., & Valentine, G. (Eds.). (1995). *Mapping desire: Geographies of sexualities*. Psychology Press.

Bell, M., & Hansen, C. (2009). *Over not Out. The housing and homelessness issues specific to lesbian, gay, bisexual and transgender asylum seekers*. London: Metropolitan Support Trust.

Benirschke, M. (2016). *Unterbringung: Hamburg bietet Wohnungen für schwule Flüchtlinge an*. Welt. https://www.welt.de/regionales/hamburg/article157496751/Hamburg-bietet-Wohnungen-fuer-schwule-Fluechtlinge-an.html

Bennett, C., & Thomas, F. (2013). Seeking asylum in the UK: Lesbian perspectives. *Forced Migration Review, 42*, 25.

Bhimji, F. (2016). Visibilities and the politics of space: Refugee activism in Berlin. *Journal of Immigrant & Refugee Studies, 14*(4), 432–450. https://doi.org/10.1080/15562948.201 6.1145777.

BMFSFJ. (2018). *Mindeststandards zum Schutz von geflüchteten Menschen in Flüchtlingsunterkünften*. https://www.bmfsfj.de/bmfsfj/service/publikationen/ mindeststandards-zum-schutz-von-gefluechteten-menschen-in-fluechtlingsunterkuenf ten/117474

BMI – Bundesministerium des Innern, für Bau und Heimat. (2019). *Kleine Anfrage der Abgeordneten Ulla Jelpke u.a. Und der Fraktion DIE LINKE: Situation von LSBTI-Geflüchteten (BT-Drucksache19/10308)*. https://www.ulla-jelpke.de/wp-content/ uploads/2019/06/19_10308-LSBTI-Gefl%C3%BCchtete.pdf

Bulman, M. (2018). Home Office subcontractors force asylum seekers to share bedrooms in breach of council policy. *Independent*. https://www.independent.co.uk/news/uk/home-news/home-office-asylum-seekers-share-bedrooms-policy-breach-a8269131.html

Butler, J. (1991). Imitation and gender insubordination. In D. Fuss (Ed.), *Inside/out: Lesbian theories, gay theories* (pp. 13–31). New York: Routledge.

Channel 4 News. (2015). Yarl's Wood: Undercover in the secretive immigration centre. *Channel 4 News*. https://www.channel4.com/news/ yarls-wood-immigration-removal-detention-centre-investigation

References

Citizens Advice Liverpool. (2018). *'You feel like a nobody': An investigation into the support and advice needs of LGBT+ asylum seekers in Merseyside*. https://www.citizensadviceliverpool.org.uk/lgbt-research-project

Deutscher Bundestag. (2019). *Zustimmung zur Entfristung der Wohnsitzauflage für Asylberechtigte*. Deutscher Bundestag. https://www.bundestag.de/dokumente/textarchiv/2019/kw20-pa-inneres-wohnsitz-641764

Dyck, J. (2019). *LGBT African asylum Seeker Research Project Report*. Metropolitan Community Church of North London. http://mccnorthlondon.org.uk/wp-content/uploads/2019/09/LGBT-African-Asylum-Seeker-Research-Project-Report.pdf

ECRE – European Council on Refugees and Exiles, AIDA – Asylum Information Database, & ASGI. (2019). *National Country Report: Italy, 2018 update*. ECRE – European Council on Refugees and Exiles. http://www.asylumineurope.org/sites/default/files/report-download/aida_it_2018update.pdf

ECRE – European Council on Refugees and Exiles, AIDA – Asylum Information Database, & Asyl und Migration. (2018). *National Country Report: Germany, 2017 update*. ECRE – European Council on Refugees and Exiles. http://www.asylumineurope.org/sites/default/files/report-download/aida_de_2017update.pdf

ECRE – European Council on Refugees and Exiles, AIDA – Asylum Information Database, & Asyl und Migration. (2019). *National Country Report: Germany, 2018 update*. ECRE – European Council on Refugees and Exiles. https://www.asylumineurope.org/sites/default/files/report-download/aida_de_2018update.pdf

Emanvel, B. (2016). The difficulties of being an LGBT refugee in Germany. *Women Across Frontiers Magazine*. http://wafmag.org/2016/06/difficulties-lgbt-refugee-germany/

Equality, Local Government and Communities Committee. (2017). *"I used to be someone": Refugees and asylum seekers in Wales*. London: National Assembly for Wales.

Fergus, L. (2015). New figures reveal 500 people seeking asylum in Northern Ireland. *The Detail*. https://www.thedetail.tv/articles/500-seeking-aslyum-in-northern-ireland

Ferreira, N. (2018). Reforming the Common European Asylum System: Enough rainbow for queer asylum seekers? *GenIUS – Rivista di studi giuridici sull'orientamento sessuale e l'identità di genere (Special Issue on SOGI Asylum)*, 5(2), 25–42.

Haritaworn, J. (2015). *Queer lovers and hateful others: Regenerating violent times and places*. London: Pluto Press.

Home Affairs Committee. (2018). *Asylum accommodation: Replacing COMPASS*. House of Commons. https://publications.parliament.uk/pa/cm201719/cmselect/cmhaff/1758/175807.htm#_idTextAnchor059

Home Office. (2016). *Right to rent document checks: A user guide*. https://assets.publishing.service.gov.uk/government/uploads/system/uploads/attachment_data/file/573057/6_1193_HO_NH_Right-to-Rent-Guidance.pdf

Home Office. (2019). *A Home Office guide to living in asylum accommodation – In English*. GOV. UK. https://assets.publishing.service.gov.uk/government/uploads/system/uploads/attachment_data/file/821324/Pack_A_-_English_-_Web.pdf

House of Commons. (2018). *Westminster Hall debate on the asylum accommodation contracts*. https://hansard.parliament.uk/commons/2018-10-10/debates/18101068000002/AsylumAccommodationContracts

House of Commons, APPG on Refugees & the APPG on Migration. (2015). *The report of the inquiry into the use of immigration detention in the United Kingdom*. APPG on Refugees and the APPG on Migration. https://detentioninquiry.com/report/

House of Commons Home Affairs Committee. (2017). *Asylum accommodation. Twelfth report of session 2016–17*. House of Commons. https://www.publications.parliament.uk/pa/cm201617/cmselect/cmhaff/637/63702.htm

House of Lords. (2014). *Yarl's Wood Immigration Removal Centre*. https://hansard.parliament.uk/Lords/2014-05-06/debates/14050619000592/Yarl%E2%80%99SWoodImmigrationRemovalCentre

Human Rights Council. (2019). *Guidelines for the Implementation of the Right to Adequate Housing: Report of the Special Rapporteur on adequate housing as a component of the right to an adequate standard of living, and on the right to non-discrimination in this context (A/ HRC/43/43)*. https://undocs.org/en/A/HRC/43/43

ICIBI – Independent Chief Inspector of Borders and Immigration. (2018). *An inspection of the Home Office's management of asylum accommodation provision*. GOV.UK. https://assets. publishing.service.gov.uk/government/uploads/system/uploads/attachment_data/file/757285/ ICIBI_An_inspection_of_the_HO_management_of_asylum_accommodation.pdf

Independent Asylum Commission. (2008). *Fit for purpose yet? The Independent Asylum Commission's interim findings. A nationwide review of the UK asylum system in association with the Citizen Organising Foundation*. http://www.independentasylumcommission.org.uk/

Jansen, S., & Spijkerboer, T. (2011). *Fleeing homophobia: Asylum claims related to sexual orientation and gender identity in Europe*. Vrije Universiteit Amsterdam. https://www.refworld.org/ docid/4ebba7852.html

Johnston, L., & Longhurst, R. (2009). *Space, place, and sex: Geographies of sexualities*. Lanham: Rowman & Littlefield.

Komaromi, P. (2016). Germany: Neo-Nazis and the market in asylum reception. *Race & Class, 58*(2), 79–86.

Micro Rainbow International. (2013). *Poverty, sexual orientation and refugees in the UK*. London: Micro Rainbow International.

Namer, Y., & Razum, O. (2018). Access to primary care and preventive health services of LGBTQ+ migrants, refugees, and asylum seekers. *SpringerBriefs in Public Health, 9783319736297*, 43–55. Scopus. https://doi.org/10.1007/978-3-319-73630-3_5

Puwar, N. (2004). *Space invaders: Race, gender and bodies out of place*. Oxford: Berg.

QMagazine. (2017). Bologna, apre il primo centro di accoglienza per rifugiati LGBT. *QMagazine*. https://quiikymagazine.com/bologna-apre-il-primo-centro-accoglienza-rifugiati-lgbt/

Queer.de. (2017). *München schafft Schutzräume für LGBTI-Flüchtlinge*. queer.de. https://www. queer.de/detail.php?article_id=28030

Ramón Mendos, L. (2019). *State-sponsored homophobia 2019: Global legislation overview update*. ILGA. https://ilga.org/downloads/ILGA_World_State_Sponsored_Homophobia_ report_global_legislation_overview_update_December_2019.pdf

Refugee Council. (2012). *Between a rock and a hard Place: The dilemma facing refused asylum seekers*. https://www.refugeecouncil.org.uk/information/resources/ between-a-rock-and-a-hard-place/

Refugee Council. (2017). Newly recognised refugees face homelessness and destitution. *Refugee Council*. https://www.refugeecouncil.org.uk/latest/news/5017_newly_recognised_refugees_ face_homelessness_and_destitution/

Ruckstuhl, A. (2016). *Protecting LGBTI refugees: The role of cities*. UNU-GCM. https://i.unu.edu/ media/gcm.unu.edu/publication/3405/LGBTIcitiesAustinRuckstuhl.pdf

Scott, P. (2014). Black African asylum seekers' experiences of health care access in an eastern German state. *International Journal of Migration, Health and Social Care, 10*(3), 134–147. https://doi.org/10.1108/IJMHSC-11-2013-0043.

Scottish Refugee Council. (2019). *Facts and figures about asylum seekers and refugees*. Scottish Refugee Council. http://www.scottishrefugeecouncil.org.uk/media/facts_and_figures

Shaw, S. (2016). *Review into the welfare in detention of vulnerable persons*. Home Office.

Shaw, S. (2018). *Assessment of government progress in implementing the report on the welfare in detention of vulnerable persons: A follow-up report to the Home Office by Stephen Shaw*. https://assets.publishing.service.gov.uk/government/uploads/system/uploads/attachment_data/ file/728376/Shaw_report_2018_Final_web_accessible.pdf

Singer, S. (2019). 'Desert Island' detention: Detainees' understandings of 'Law' in the UK's immigration detention system. *Refugee Survey Quarterly, 38*(1), 1–29. https://doi.org/10.1093/ rsq/hdy020.

References

Smith, D. (2017). *Landlords 'playing it safe' on right to rent*. RLA Campaigns and News Centre. https://news.rla.org.uk/right-to-rent/

Spade, D. (2015). *Normal life: Administrative violence, critical trans politics, and the limits of law*. Durham: Duke University Press.

Spiegel. (2013). *Far-right protests new refugee shelter S*. https://www.spiegel.de/international/germany/right-wing-protests-over-asylum-shelter-in-berlin-a-917832.html

Stonewall, & UKLGIG – UK Lesbian and Gay Immigration Group. (2016). *No safe refuge. Experiences of LGBT asylum seekers in detention*. http://www.stonewall.org.uk/resources/no-safe-refuge-2016

Taylor, D. (2019). Asylum seekers crammed into rat-infested rooms. *The Guardian*. https://www.theguardian.com/world/2019/aug/20/asylum-seekers-crammed-into-cockroach-infested-accommodation-home-office

TGEU – Transgender Europe. (2016). *Welcome to stay*. http://tgeu.org/wp-content/uploads/2016/10/TGEU_TransAsylumBrochure_WEB.pdf

The Local. (2016). Berlin opens Germany's first major gay refugee centre. *The Local*. https://www.thelocal.de/20160223/berlin-opens-germanys-first-gay-refugee-centre

UK Parliament. (2017). *Asylum: LGBT People: Written question – HL6078*. UK Parliament. https://www.parliament.uk/business/publications/written-questions-answers-statements/written-question/Lords/2017-03-14/HL6078/

UNHCR – UN High Commissioner for Refugees. (2013). *Resettlement assessment tool: Lesbian, gay, bisexual, transgender and intersex refugees*. UNHCR – UN High Commissioner for Refugees. https://www.refworld.org/pdfid/5163f3ee4.pdf

Valentine, G. (1996). (Re)negotiating the 'heterosexual street. In N. Duncan (Ed.), *BodySpace: Destabilizing geographies of gender and sexuality* (pp. 146–155). London: Routledge.

Young, H. (2017). Beautiful to unbearable: What life is like for refugees in Berlin's 'Nazi' neighbourhood. *The Local*. https://www.thelocal.de/20171020/beautiful-to-unbearable-what-is-life-like-for-refugees-in-berlins-nazi-neighbourhood

Zadeh, L. (2019, September 13). Opinion: Detention is one of the most dangerous places for LGBT+ refugees. The government must enforce a time limit. *The Independent*. https://www.independent.co.uk/voices/lgbt-refugees-detention-government-refusal-time-limit-28-days-hostile-environment-a9103726.html

Ziniti, A. (2018). *Decreto sicurezza, Arci: 'Futuro Sprar incerto, centinaia di migranti già in mezzo a una strada'*. Repubblica.it. https://www.repubblica.it/cronaca/2018/11/28/news/arci_su_decreto_salvini_sicurezza-212851162/

Open Access This chapter is licensed under the terms of the Creative Commons Attribution 4.0 International License (http://creativecommons.org/licenses/by/4.0/), which permits use, sharing, adaptation, distribution and reproduction in any medium or format, as long as you give appropriate credit to the original author(s) and the source, provide a link to the Creative Commons license and indicate if changes were made.

The images or other third party material in this chapter are included in the chapter's Creative Commons license, unless indicated otherwise in a credit line to the material. If material is not included in the chapter's Creative Commons license and your intended use is not permitted by statutory regulation or exceeds the permitted use, you will need to obtain permission directly from the copyright holder.

Chapter 9
Health, Work and Education

You think I don't value what I lost, to come and start from zero?
I went to school for fifteen years and I come here to
kindergarten here in Deutschland?

(William, Germany)

[s]ome people go to bed for money, you know those kind of
people, they want to eat and they need house, you understand.
(Edoardo, focus group no. 3, northern Italy)

I know that self-medicating is not illegal but there are risks to it,
but as long as you know what you're taking and confident
enough which I am, go for it. I have some complications with it
in the past, but I need to keep going as it's good for my mental
health and it alleviates my gender dysphoria massively.

(Amber, UK)

9.1 Introduction

In this chapter, we look at the experiences of SOGI minorities who are claiming asylum or who have reached the end of the asylum process in relation to health, work and education. We define these three spheres broadly, including, for example, volunteering and impacts from having experienced sexual violence torture, as well as sex work. Ostensibly, LGBTIQ+ asylum claimants experience the same difficulties in applying for work and accessing health and education as most other asylum claimants. In reality, this is not always the case. Here, referring back to our theoretical underpinnings, including intersectionality, highlights some particular areas of need, in many cases relating to the discrimination they encounter on the basis of SOGI in addition to other characteristics. As with the previous chapter, we again show that SOGI minorities encounter particular problems outside the legal asylum process as well as within it.

To provide some context, we first briefly outline the international legal framework relating to the needs and entitlements discussed in this chapter, developing the contours of international protection that were identified in Chap. 4. While the 1951

© The Author(s) 2021
C. Danisi et al., *Queering Asylum in Europe*, IMISCOE Research Series,
https://doi.org/10.1007/978-3-030-69441-8_9

Refugee Convention defines employment and educational entitlements for refugees (Articles 17–19 and 22), it does not address the rights of individuals while their claim is being assessed. Here, the main reference is the recast 2011 Reception Directive and in the case of the UK, the 2003 Reception Directive, underpinned by the ECHR and the CFR, as well as other international human rights treaties and domestic laws, all of which may complement or exist in tension or conflict with one another (Chap. 4).

During the period that individuals are claiming asylum, the recast Reception Directive requires member states to: provide education to children in line with that of nationals (Article 14); grant access to employment within nine months from the date of application for protection with some qualifications, including that member states may prioritise citizens and nationals (Article 15); and offer emergency health-care and treatment for 'serious mental disorders' (Article 19). General provisions also require member states to consider the specific needs of vulnerable persons, including those 'who have been subjected to torture, rape or other serious forms of psychological, physical or sexual violence…' (Article 21), and to assess whether claimants have such 'special reception needs' (Article 22) (Chap. 5).

While all three of our case study countries have some version of a welfare state system (Ferrera et al. 2013; Kennett and Lendvai-Bainton 2017), they also all have legislation and regulations in place controlling access to healthcare, employment and further education based on immigration status (European Commission 2020). Full discussion of these is beyond the scope of this chapter, although some details will be mentioned below. However, it is important to keep sight of the fundamental rights relating to health, employment and education under the ECHR and wider IHRL that all individuals are entitled to on a non-discriminatory basis (UNHCR 2020). We emphasise this universality precisely because of the failure to apply 'every day' human rights instruments to asylum claimants and refugees. Indeed, there are many international instruments that do not distinguish between citizens, nationals, asylum claimants and refugees and, when considering access to health, work and education, these need to be better recognised and vindicated.

In Sect. 9.2, we discuss health, beginning with access to healthcare and continuing to consider access to specialist treatment, where the needs of transgender people were clearly a particular concern, as well as those with HIV support requirements. The following Section addresses sexual violence and torture, and their impact on SOGI minorities. We then identify some of the specific mental health issues that we heard about from our participants. Section 9.3 discusses work and defines it broadly to include voluntary work and community involvement (Section 9.3.2) as well as sex work and the sexual exploitation some of our participants experienced (Section 9.3.3). We also look at other kinds of exploitation that our participants encountered. The chapter concludes with a short discussion about education and training where there were relatively few SOGI-specific concerns compared to other areas.

9.2 Physical and Mental Health

9.2.1 Access to Healthcare

We begin by considering the access to basic health care by SOGI minorities claiming asylum which, of course, is the same as that of any claimant. Health entitlements for asylum claimants and refugees vary between and within the countries under comparison.

In Germany, asylum claimants have only restricted access to healthcare, defined as 'necessary medical and dental treatment' for 'acute illnesses and pain conditions'.[1] As the law is not clearly defined, health professionals and local authorities have some leeway; however, the main obstacle is the need for asylum claimants in many municipalities, but not all, to secure a health insurance voucher – 'Krankenschein' – from social welfare offices, something that is difficult for people accommodated in rural areas. Those without a voucher are likely to encounter delays in health provision, and may even be refused treatment (ECRE, AIDA & Asyl und Migration 2019, pp. 85–86). In Italy, asylum claimants and beneficiaries of international protection must register with the National Health Service and should then enjoy the same treatment as Italian citizens. On registration, asylum claimants receive a European Health Insurance Card, but delays and obstacles to issuing this have been aggravated by the 2018 asylum reform (ECRE, AIDA & ASGI 2019, p. 104). In the UK, asylum claimants are entitled to register with a medical General Practitioner (GP) and receive free hospital treatment; however, individuals often experience difficulty in accessing these healthcare entitlements (ECRE, AIDA & Refugee Council 2019, pp. 74–75; EHRC 2019).

Reception service-providers may be charged with responsibility for informing asylum claimants about their health entitlements and putting them in contact with doctors and other health services. This form of support also took place in the CAS and SPRAR centres in Italy, prior to the reforms restricting access to healthcare beneficiaries of international protection (ECRE, AIDA & ASGI 2019, p. 80). In the UK, the companies contracted to provide accommodation for asylum claimants (Serco, Mears Group and Clearsprings) are also responsible for supporting individuals through the asylum system, including explaining how to register with a local doctor and access other National Health Service (NHS) treatment (ECRE, AIDA & Refugee Council 2019, p. 58).

Nonetheless, in all three countries under comparison, access to healthcare is reported as inconsistent from one location to another. In Germany, there is a health insurance card scheme but it has only been implemented in some municipalities (ECRE, AIDA & Asyl und Migration 2019, p. 85). In Italy, practices vary throughout the country and from one reception centre to another; for example, exemptions from medical charges are reportedly not applied in Lazio, Veneto and Tuscany in the same way as in Piedmont and Lombardy (ECRE, AIDA & ASGI 2019, p. 105). In

---

[1] §4 of Asylbewerberleistungsgesetz (AsylbLG, Asylum Seekers Benefits Act).

the UK, charges for those without leave to remain were introduced in April 2015 (ECRE, AIDA & Refugee Council 2019, pp. 75–76). Not only does the UK government's policy of dispersal of asylum claimants disrupt continuity in healthcare (EHRC 2019, p. 7), but there are also national differences: in Scotland, all asylum claimants, including those whose claims have been refused, are entitled to full free healthcare, while in England, free hospital treatment is theoretically not available to asylum claimants who are not receiving benefits (Piwowarczyk et al. 2017).

In all countries under comparison, regional differences, language barriers, repeated changes in entitlements and lack of awareness by both providers and receivers of healthcare are reasons why many refugees and asylum claimants are unable to access the healthcare they need, particularly given that asylum claimants often experience poverty to a degree that damages their health (EHRC 2018). Yet, SOGI minority individuals face some particular obstacles. There is not as much understanding of these obstacles as is needed – research on the physical and mental health of SOGI minorities rarely addresses asylum, while research on the health of migrants and refugees rarely covers SOGI issues (Ohonba 2017, p. 1; Piwowarczyk et al. 2017, p. 724).

In a rare piece of research concentrating on the health of SOGI asylum claimants, the UNHCR identified '(p)rejudicial health care and lack of access to HIV prevention and treatment' as particular concerns, and also pointed out that '(t)ransgender individuals often do not have access to the treatment they need, including transition-related care' (UNHCR 2013, p. 4). The particular problems in the area of health for SOGI claimants that arose in our research related to: trans people's healthcare needs (Sect. 9.2.2); torture diagnosis and treatment (Sect. 9.2.3); and mental health (Sect. 9.2.4). While torture, sexual violence and mental health problems are not unique to people from SOGI minorities seeking asylum, they were experienced in a particular way by our participants. HIV status was also a factor highlighted by participants, though not necessarily in the context of lack of provision in the host country.

9.2.2   Access to Specialist Treatment

Problems of access to appropriate healthcare were most evident for transgender participants in our research, corresponding to reports by NGOs (Action for Trans Health 2015). Delays in obtaining the documents necessary to access treatment are a particular problem for transgender people who may have started or wish to start regular hormone treatment. Furthermore, '[w]orryingly the immigration detention centre protocols do not explicitly mandate access to hormones and other transition related healthcare' (Action for Trans Health 2015). Transgender Europe also points out that:

> Many trans refugees are likely to have already started HRT [hormone replacement therapy] before arriving in Europe, either under medical supervision or by self-medicating using hormones purchased through the black market. (…) Interrupting hormone intake can have serious consequences and is by definition a decision to be taken by the individual concerned,

9.2 Physical and Mental Health

on medical advice. (…) The continuation of HRT and all necessary monitoring is therefore essential to ensure the health and wellbeing of trans asylum seekers and mitigate against the risks of self-medication (TGEU 2018).

In addition, and in particular for trans people who are detained in Immigration Removal Centres in the UK, there are often deficiencies in access and provision:

The protocol allows trans people in detention centres to wear wigs, packers, binders, and breast-forms. Unlike the protocol for UK prisoners, these do not have to be provided by the institution, so it is likely that many trans detainees will be forced to make do with makeshift equipment/prosthetics (Action for Trans Health 2015).

Participants in all countries highlighted difficulties in access to and continuity of hormone treatment. In Germany, there are daunting complexities for trans people claiming asylum and trying to access treatment that is designed for German citizens. The provision of only basic healthcare is a 'bitter' problem for people who have had hormone treatment in their country of origin or transit and are unable to continue with it in Germany (Noah, NGO social worker). Furthermore, medical practitioners and NGO workers struggle to provide support in specialist areas, especially when there are also language and cultural barriers (Leon, NGO worker).

Even when individuals are granted refugee status, 'it remains a common struggle to wrest these funds from the health insurance funds and find doctors who follow this path' (Noah, NGO social worker). One individual, Bebars, was told by his doctor that health insurance would not continue to cover his hormone treatment, because he had not received sufficient psychotherapeutic care; he needed to see a psychotherapist for three months, otherwise he would need to pay for treatment himself. Surgery for gender reassignment is covered through health insurance only after completion of a year and a half of psychotherapy (Nina, legal advisor). People who had come to Germany via Turkey are often particularly affected:

They come here, they stop their hormone process. It is easy for them to have it in Turkey, you just directly go to the pharmacy. You can directly have your hormones. It's not like here, where it's a procedure. As a result of this and other reasons, we heard of people choosing to go back to Turkey (Ibrahim, Germany).

In Italy, access and cost were also concerns, as were regional variations. Whereas in Emilia Romagna treatment was free:

in Sicily, in Calabria, Naples, in Milan, they pay. Not only the ticket to visit and do the analysis, but also the hormones. And hormones are expensive! For example, if we talk about Nibido, which is a drug for testosterone, hormones that trans FtM take every three months, with the safety of the endocrinologist, I mean, it even reaches 150–200 euros! (Kamel, Italy).

As a result, Kamel, a transgender claimant, was no longer receiving the medical supervision he needed for hormone treatment, had heart problems and his weight had reached almost 100 kg. He pointed out that '[a] refugee who escaped from war or from any other country is stressed and suffers… he's not a prince charming who comes with a bag full of money'.

Amber had started transitioning before she came to the UK:

> and then for the whole two months when I was homeless, I couldn't get any bridging hormones because my pills has run out. I didn't bring enough, because I didn't have time to get that from Malaysia before I fly. So the whole two months, I was really struggling on how to, what do I do, because I had no pills and my body is going backwards now. Because I made the decision to transition because it was either transitioning or, or I would kill myself.

GPs are advised to collaborate with a Gender Identity Clinic (GIC) to provide 'effective and timely' treatment for trans patients. They may provide bridging prescriptions, which are 'intended to mitigate a risk of self-harm or suicide' (General Medical Council 2020). However, in 2019 it was reported that 'GPs are facing increasing difficulties addressing patient requests for "bridging" prescriptions, particularly for those patients who have self-started medication, including medication which they have procured over the internet'(General Medical Council 2020, p. 6). Trans asylum claimants are likely to feel the impact of this acutely, perhaps compounded by language and communication problems, disruptions in hormone treatment received in countries of passage, and dispersal to areas within the UK particularly lacking in expertise.

Amber's experience exemplifies the difficulties caused by frequent relocation in conjunction with inconsistencies in GP support. As she explained: 'You just have to hop [between] GPs if they aren't helpful, because it's up to them to prescribe this kind of hormones'. She had registered with a GP in Canterbury who had referred her to a Gender Identity Clinic (GIC), but she had not been prescribed any medication. Amber then moved to Croydon temporarily before moving on again to Essex, where she registered with another doctor. During this period, she had difficulty obtaining a prescription for bridging hormones and felt 'really stressed out and frustrated about how I was treated'.

Because accessing NHS treatment had been difficult, Amber had been self-medicating with supplies from friends:

> I know that self-medicating is not illegal but there are risks to it, but as long as you know what you're taking and confident enough, which I am, go for it. I have some complications with it in the past, but I need to keep going as it's good for my mental health and it alleviates my gender dysphoria massively.

Amber ended up resorting to private healthcare and explained she had been lucky enough to have friends willing to cover some of her medical costs. Registering with a private doctor cost Amber an initial set-up fee of GBP50, a monthly registration of GBP25, plus there were costs for prescribed medication. She was unable to afford initial counselling and, as she was already self-medicating, she knew what she wanted. Looking ahead, she was on the waiting list for treatment and intended to request removal of her Adam's apple and full body laser hair removal. Breast augmentation would need to be done privately.

The common experience for trans people was of inconsistences in access and provision within and between countries, meaning that individuals were dependent on luck in finding individual doctors who would support them. Others resorted to non-regulated private sources and, for some, the lack of access to continuous hormone treatment caused them to leave the EU (as we heard from Ibrahim, UK; Ximena, UK; Jules, staff member at ILGA-Europe).

While a greater number of our participants shared with us problems relating to hormone treatment, we also talked to several individuals with an HIV diagnosis, for whom access to medical treatment was also a priority and a cause of anxiety. As Susan (focus group no. 3, Bavaria, Germany) explained:

> I don't have medicine, I don't have anything. They told me I have to go to some doctor. I went to that doctor. Doctor wants insurance. I have to come back to the same doctor. That doctor told me I have to wait. HIV, I have to take medicine every day. Every day! I don't have medicine, they told me I have to go. I walk, I walk, I walk… Whenever I go to the hospital they give me insurance for three months, so on 10th it's going to be the last insurance, if the government does not put meds on me.

HIV status was also a factor in some individuals' asylum claim. Diamond was studying hotel management in the UK and near completion of his course when he was diagnosed with HIV and found himself unable to cope with his studies:

> But when I realised I am HIV [positive], I was scared because (…) I know now you need every six month or yearly to get a check-up what is your CD4 count viral and some point you need a medication even so what, definitely the doctors and the people will come to know [if I returned to my country of origin], so that is why I decided to claim asylum in UK, so at least I can get a right here and I can continue with my studies and even medication I can get it, without any problems. Back home that is a really very big problem.

However, this was not enough to eliminate his fears about his future: he told us that when he returned home from the group he would have daydreams about people killing or beating him and was unable to sleep at night. The impact of trauma on people's mental health, including their ability to sleep, is something we look at again below.

9.2.3 Experiences of Sexual Violence and Torture

While statistics are not available, many asylum claimants experience sexual violence and torture as part of the experiences that lead to their flight. One study suggests that more than a quarter of 'forced migrants' in high-income countries are torture survivors (Sigvardsdotter et al. 2016, p. 47).[2] There is also evidence of higher rates of sexual trauma among SOGI asylum claimants (Alessi et al. 2016; Hopkinson et al. 2017; Reading and Rubin 2011). Similarly, one small-scale study found that of 'the 61 LGBT asylum seekers identified, 66% had experienced sexual violence as part of their persecution history' and there was a significantly higher incidence of suicidality among this group (Hopkinson et al. 2017, p. 1658). If torture is defined as broadly as it should be under Article 3 ECHR jurisprudence, then we would argue

---

[2] The target population for this review – forced migrants – was taken to include refugees, quota refugees, internally displaced persons (IDPs), persons under temporary protection, asylum claimants and people whose asylum claims were refused (Sigvardsdotter et al., 2016, p. 43).

that many more individuals from SOGI minorities claiming asylum should be recognised as having experienced torture or the threat of torture in the form of rape and other forms of sexual violence, beatings or in other ways than is the present case.

Our findings confirm this body of literature. One survey respondent in Germany reported that '[m]y front teeth and right arm were broken and they hurt time to time' (C55). We heard about individuals surviving mock executions (Frank S., legal advisor, Germany). In Italy, NGO workers and volunteers have worked with children who had been raped (Chiara, NGO worker). In the UK, one participant told us he 'thanked God' that he had marks on his body from torture, as they had been the basis for a doctor providing verification of his trauma (focus group no. 1, Manchester, UK). The degrading expectation that asylum claimants display their scars to show credibility has already been discussed (Chap. 7).

While many asylum claimants experience torture, it came up repeatedly as part of SOGI asylum claimants' reasons for flight (Chap. 5). A policy worker with a mainstream refugee agency in the UK, when asked about the specific needs and experiences of SOGI asylum claimants, said: 'maybe more people claiming on those grounds [have] experienced sexual violence and torture' (Eleanor, NGO worker).

Lesbian, bisexual and trans women claiming asylum and with refugee status in the UK told us of being raped, sometimes by family members:

> [T]he whole community is mocking me, talking about me, you know, and some girls were even saying what kind of, because, everybody expects that when you get to a certain age as a girl you get married to man. So they would always mock me, like, what kind of man is going to want a girl that has been, you know, damaged by her father. You know, and I was 13, for crying out loud (Stephina, UK).

A trans woman told us of being sexually abused by her brother-in-law and another woman had also been raped by a close family member. Two women had had children as a result of being sexually abused, children who were either still in the country of origin or with them in the UK.

A UK barrister, speaking of her clients who were claiming asylum on SOGI grounds, told us: 'There is a significant proportion of people who have experienced torture. I cannot put a percentage on it, but it is significant' (Annabelle, barrister and NGO chair, UK). She connected this with the mental health problems that many of these individuals experienced:

> In the many years of working in this field, I have met only a couple of LGBTQI claimants who did not report at least some degree of mental ill health normally associated with their experiences in their country of origin, even where those do not amount to physical abuse (long term fear, isolation, discrimination...).

In the UK, medical professionals in NGOs such as Freedom from Torture and the Helen Bamber Foundation provide asylum claimants and refugees who have experienced torture, with expert counselling and, on the instruction of the legal representative, also write medico-legal reports for individuals to inform the decision-making process. However, as the demand for medico-legal reports and specialist therapeutic support is significant, there can be a long wait for the reports and, if the claimant does not qualify for legal aid, they may be unaffordable or unavailable to claimants – particularly at the initial decision-making stage:

> Some lawyers will also be hesitant to arrange for these reports earlier than the appeal stage, because the Legal Aid Agency may refuse to grant funding on the basis that such move would be pre-emptive, that is, "why should we fund a report to prove your client's case, when there is no proof that the HO will refuse their claim?" (Mateo, solicitor and NGO worker, UK).

This contributes to unnecessary delays in the asylum process. Individuals who have experienced violence and sexual abuse in private, as is often the case in SOGI asylum claims, are unlikely to have documentary evidence to support their claim and then 'everything turns on their account which might be rejected for reasons of lack of coherence or consistency, which should be expected from a torture victim or a person suffering from poor mental health' (Annabelle, barrister and NGO chair, UK). Medico-legal reports will be particularly important in such cases, but as they are, usually only available at the appeal stage, it is likely that many strong claims for protection will initially be refused only to succeed on appeal when the critical medico-legal report has been provided. This extends the time decision-making takes from start to finish, unnecessarily increasing the stress and difficulty for claimants, as well as the cost to the state. Moreover, the definition of 'torture' used by some NGOs may not cover abuse at the hands of family members as often experienced by SOGI minorities (Freedom from Torture 2019).

There are also concerns that when they are commissioned, these reports are not recognised as authoritative in the way that they should be. Freedom from Torture is one organisation providing these services, and, as mentioned in Chap. 7, has highlighted strong concerns about the UK government's mishandling of medical evidence of torture. The organisation claims that the Home Office Asylum Policy Instruction on how expert medical evidence should be treated is being ignored, that clinical expertise is questioned by untrained caseworkers, and that the wrong standard of proof is applied (Freedom from Torture 2016).

The services of organisations such as Freedom from Torture are not specifically for SOGI minorities and the organisation does not monitor its clients on the basis of SOGI identity. Yet, another participant whose organisation provides medico-legal reports in cases of human rights abuse estimates that, of the organisation's clients, '[a]round 90% of females and more than 50% of males have been raped as part of what has happened to them, either during trafficking or in their home country' (Carl, doctor with an organisation providing medico-legal reports, UK). This is true regardless of SOGI. However, he also believes that a quarter of his and the organisation's clients are LGBTIQ+. While this is only one individual's estimate, it suggests that the problems that Freedom from Torture have identified in relation to decision-makers' misuse of medical evidence of torture have a strong significance for SOGI minorities seeking asylum, many of whom have experienced torture.

It is clear from our fieldwork that SOGI minorities need both expert therapeutic care as torture survivors and medico-legal experts to provide evidence in their cases. While the above findings from organisations providing medico-legal reports and support to torture victims comes from the UK, the experiences of torture, violence and sexual violence were more widespread and came from participants and their supporters in all three countries (Chap. 5). This suggests that specialist support for LGBTIQ+ survivors of torture is a vital need. Yet, we found little such support in Germany or Italy, and in the UK demand outstrips supply, with one psychotherapist estimating that 'even when we were taking one new client [referring to general provision] every fortnight, we would be turning away eight others' (Ashley, psychotherapist). A similarly dire situation can be observed in relation to mental health, as we will now consider.

9.2.4 Mental Health

Asylum claimants, particularly those who have experienced sexual violence and torture, have a heightened risk of mental health problems such as PTSD, severe depression, isolation, and feelings such as shame and helplessness (Hopkinson et al. 2017; Longacre et al. 2012; Reading and Rubin 2011). For members of SOGI minorities, it has been suggested that the relationship between early victimisation and negative mental health outcomes may be more pronounced (Hopkinson et al. 2017, p. 1650).

The combination of persecution by family or community in their country of origin with alienation from diaspora communities in the host country means that SOGI claimants are likely to experience isolation, both voluntary and self-imposed isolation, as well as PTSD, depression and other mental health problems (Alessi and Kahn 2017; Hopkinson et al. 2017; Micro Rainbow International 2013, pp. 27–28; Shidlo and Ahola 2013; Tabak and Levitan 2013; UNHCR 2013). Sexual violence can cause feelings of self-blame and self-hatred (Women's Refugee Commission 2019). This research supports our findings, where the most commonly recurring health needs in our study related to mental health. Mental and physical health problems relating to the persecution they had experienced or the process of claiming asylum were reported by 56% of the respondents in our claimants' survey. This is not surprising in the context of the experiences of some SOGI claimants: one anonymised medico-legal report we were given access to documented the physical evidence of torture experienced by a lesbian woman from an East African country. She had been raped at the age of 12, forced into marriage at 15, and she and her partner had had acid thrown at them alongside other attacks. The report documented evidence of PTSD, problems with 'intrusive memories and visual and tactile flashbacks to her adverse experiences, particularly the rape'. The report stated that '[s]he also displays evidence of depression and panic attacks, which are often found among survivors of torture and related abuses' (anonymised report from January 2019 provided by Carl, doctor with an organisation providing medico-legal reports, UK).

Such experiences of torture, violence and sexual abuse were connected to experiences of PTSD in the accounts we heard from asylum claimants and also from the

9.2 Physical and Mental Health

NGOs and professionals working with or supporting them. Lutfor (UK) explained how having PTSD jeopardised his study plans, preventing him from going to college on the student visa that was how he originally entered the UK. Ximena (UK) also told us that:

> I suffer about the post traumatic disorder, for all those things happening in my life. Sometime, when sometime I say when I remember all those things happening to me, I feel sad. Because I remember my friend, I would like they were here, but they pass away. They were killed just for being transgender woman. But I am trying to continue with my life.

Carl explained that '[p]atients [who have been tortured] often think they are going crazy. They need to be reassured that they are having a normal human reaction to an intolerable situation. That, for me, is what actually PTSD is'.

Many people described how they felt to us. For example, in Germany, Halim explained:

> And it's not really visible, and people think that now because I'm traumatised I'm going to be sitting home crying all the time. I'm trying to function, however it really affects my ability, or has affected for me my ability to function for a long time. And when I think back about it, of course the first year I was traumatised and it reflected on my energy, my concentration in a lot of ways. Yeah, but people don't really understand this.

In Italy, we were told that '[a] lot of us have temporary madness, which can be treated, caused by the Sahara Desert [their route to Italy], temporary madness. It's not easy to watch your friends dying around, and they expect you to be normal' (Nice Guy, focus group no. 1, northern Italy). And in the UK, someone who had come through the worst of her mental ordeal said: 'at the height of it, I wanted to take my brain and rip it out because it was a mental pain that you couldn't put your hand on, but it hurts like someone chopping you on the hand' (SWG, focus group no. 4, London, UK).

Shame and guilt also featured in our participants' stories. Ximena (UK) told us she was sexually abused by a teacher but did not tell her mother because she felt scared and ashamed. Shame is also the justification for the abuse she experienced. She told us of her father's violence towards her and her mother: 'and he told me "I don't want to have a son who will be a shame for me, for my last name. For me you are die, it is your fault, you are feminine child"'. He blamed Ximena's mother for raising a 'very feminine' son and asked Ximena to leave home when she was 14.

Most common were accounts of depression like Sandra's (Germany): 'I felt empty, defeated, lost, tired, very, very tired. I lost all the motivation and all the thinking that I had about life and what I wanted to achieve and everything'. Very often, people talked about their depression unprompted, for example when talking about being unable to work, which, according to one focus group participant makes you feel worthless 'and that messes with you mentally' (focus group no. 1, Hesse, Germany). Other people, like Christina, felt hopeless. They had suffered a great deal from depression since arriving in the UK. At one point, they said 'Iwas contemplating if I should go back home because they are going to send me home anyway and I might as well just do it and if I have to die, just die, I don't really care anymore, I was going through that whole depression'. We asked Christina if they had felt able to get support and they said:

> To be honest, I am always the one who gives advice. I never get advice. So it was, for me it was really hard to open up to people and say: "Oh look, I am struggling mentally, I need help".

This shows how difficult many people find it to be dependent, and to feel unable to control their own lives, a theme we analyse further in Chap. 10.

There were many accounts of the known symptoms of depression such as sleeplessness. Rosette (Germany) told us:

> Most of the time I don't even sleep. Most of the time I think that I'm old, I should at least be at my place enjoying my life. (crying) At my age people are just enjoying their life. Why can't I enjoy my life (whispering, very upset).

Survey respondents reported similar experiences, such as this lesbian woman from Uganda who was appealing against her refusal in Germany:

> I have developed a sickness mentally I think it's because of over thinking and I can no longer sleep. I have sleepless nights and am on drugs per now. If I don't take drugs I can't sleep (C44).

Sometimes, people were unable to sleep because of recurring flashbacks. Water, for example, was unable to find peace because 'if I am sleeping, I see the pictures of everything, you know' (focus group no. 4, northern Italy). Sometimes, sleeplessness was due to real and present fears. Marhoon, for instance, was scared that the male members of his family would come after him to Germany: '[I]n the dream, I see, OK my family has found me and they're coming here to kill me'. He had developed agoraphobia and had panic attacks when he went out in public.

We heard many accounts of suicidal thoughts and behaviours from lawyers, NGO workers and claimants themselves (for example Ali, UK; Amber, UK; Sandra, Germany). This was often linked to the asylum process and was sparked by a refusal of the claim (Lutfor, UK; Sadia, UK). People who had been detained also talked about how these experiences contributed to suicidal feelings:

> I remember when I was in detention like I felt like I am being targeted for no reason and like you know, my emotional state was so bad like and I wanted to like, you know, commit suicide and I said I wanted, I don't want to live anymore, I just want to like kill myself, and get away from it (Lubwa, focus group no. 1, Manchester, UK).

Avoiding public places and social engagement was another common symptom of depression for our participants, though often difficult to separate from practical reasons for isolation such as the lack of accessible SOGI-friendly spaces (Chap. 8). Several people described staying in their rooms and doing nothing: 'Because I barely talk, I don't talk to people, I was just all alone. I could just sit in the room, all day long not coming out' (Just Me, focus group no. 3, northern Italy). Other examples were given by Halim (Germany), Sandra (Germany), Selim (UK), Meggs (focus group no. 1, Manchester, UK), and Joyce (focus group no. 5, Nottingham, UK).

The conditions in which people lived aggravated their mental health issues. Halim was in a reception camp in Germany:

9.2 Physical and Mental Health

> I was having a very difficult time of my life and I couldn't close the door and say I'm on my own now, I didn't have a chance to do that. So it was very hard, the system and the people treating you, it felt like part of a herd of people, so it just didn't feel… it was very bad for my mental health I was very depressed at the time.

Two further phenomena are important to note here. The first is the impact of mental health and health factors on the asylum process. It is clear that the impact of suffering from PTSD or depression needs to be recognised by decision-makers. Research shows how trauma affects memory (Herlihy and Turner 2007). This was confirmed by our participants. While trying to secure documentation of mental health problems in advance of the asylum interview for people who are vulnerable, Chiara, an NGO worker in Italy, recognised that 'people can be in a confused state, they can be extremely, how can I say, inaccurate when you ask them questions about, say, particularly difficult moments in life, so it is possible that there are contradictions'. As previous chapters have shown, it is difficult for SOGI claimants to provide the evidence decision-makers require to be convinced they are 'genuine' – genuinely LGBTIQ+ and genuinely at risk of persecution (as discussed in Chap. 7). Being severely depressed or suffering from PTSD compounds the difficulty in presenting a convincing testimony:

> You know, my mind was not working and I was, my mind was like pushing me to stand there and watch that thing. Nothing else I remember. But when we went for our interview, when I told them "look, I am not mentally fine, I know when we came here [UK], what happened to us, I can tell you, but few things I really don't remember". But they did not believe me (Mary, UK).

Mary's partner Zaro, jointly claiming with her, confirmed her account. In another case that illustrates insufficient awareness of claimants' mental health issues, in one appeal hearing in the UK, the claimant's barrister told the judge of the claimant's longstanding depression and suicidal thoughts. The Home Office presenting officer acting for the Secretary of State subsequently said to the claimant: 'you said when [your representative] asked that you lived openly as gay man, in what ways?'. The claimant explained in his response that because of his depression he had found it difficult to relate to people, and go to gay bars and find a boyfriend – and he also could not afford to do this (First Tier Tribunal observation, London, November 2018). The lack of resources and mental health problems combined for this man in a way that made it harder to prove his claim in the ways that the UK asylum system expects. However, in this instance the appeal was successful and he received refugee status.

A government official in the UK also confirmed the impact of mental health in interviews and explained that if somebody has PTSD, then 'you have got to take that into account that they may not remember stuff' (Olivia, UK). Yet, as we saw in Chaps. 6 and 7, inconsistency is a frequent basis for refusal based on lack of credibility. We were told by one NGO worker:

> and then they [people whose claim is refused] will be told "your language was vague, you didn't specify your feelings". I think sometimes it is people's mental health that causes them not to be able to say much about their feelings, as well, you know, they are withdrawn (Debbie, NGO worker, UK).

In terms of treatment and support, the mental health of asylum claimants and refugees is recognised both as an area where specialist services and expertise are needed, and also as an area where needs are not being met and there is not enough evidence (Basedow and Doyle 2016; Mind 2009; Piwowarczyk et al. 2017; Slobodin and de Jong 2015). Other research suggests that SOGI asylum claimants are often likely to have experienced childhood persecution and are survivors of childhood trauma, meaning that particular forms of clinical treatment such as art and music therapy may be appropriate (Hopkinson et al. 2017, p. 1662).

The need for mental health support is recognised as being high among LGBTIQ+ populations and, similarly, there is a high demand for therapeutic work with people who have been tortured (Eleanor, NGO worker, UK). A further complication is that healthcare, even if it is available, is often not culturally appropriate. An NGO worker in Italy pointed out that the standardised [diagnostic] tests used by psychologists and psychiatrists are modelled on Italian or Western patients and cannot be used with foreign patients (Chiara, NGO worker, Italy). Compounding this, it was suggested that cultural factors sometimes make it harder for SOGI minority asylum claimants to ask for mental health support:

> I have done some work with BAME [Black, Asian and minority ethnic] communities across Greater Manchester and the biggest barrier was the stigma around mental health. So you have that cultural stigma, as well as being LGBT, so people find it really difficult to access services (Justina, NGO worker, UK).

However, some of the people we talked to had received counselling (Ibrahim A., UK; Meggs, UK), but far more common were references to being prescribed anti-depressant medication:

> My GP, bless him, at that time he was also very supportive, yes, and he give me a lot of advice and I am still on antidepressants, until today, so like that was a big, big part, because I went suicidal as well at that time (Selim, UK).

In the UK, in particular, people told us they were taking medication to combat depression. Lutfor was taking 'mirtazapine, zopiclone, paroxetine, or paroxetine something, and iron'. Ibrahim A. had been taking anti-depressants but stopped, because he did not like the changes they caused to his behaviour. Joyce and Selim gave us similar accounts of lives that consisted of staying in their rooms and taking their medication.

Non-medicinal support or talking therapies was not always provided through formal counselling. Melisa (NGO worker, UK) told us:

> We have a group called "Sister Sister", which is a support group for women only, LBT women, and we also have a choir, and sometimes we have theatre groups, we do some theatre work. We believe in tackling all trauma through, we take a holistic approach in tackling the trauma of LGBT asylum seekers and refugees.

Similarly, SGW (focus group no. 4, London, UK) also found it uplifting to join a support group: 'But the thing for me what worked was like I found [a local lesbian support group], so I used to go to Manchester every month to look forward to being in a surrounding'.

A less positive phenomenon that emerged in the research is that many people are re-traumatised – rather than supported – by the process of claiming asylum. This corresponds to research showing that LGBTIQ+ refugees are exposed to trauma not only prior to leaving their country of origin, but throughout the entire transit and reception process (Alessi et al. 2018). In Germany, Leon described this as almost inevitable: 'And then it is mutually dependent. If you already have a trauma and you are in a hopeless situation, the trauma will be amplified' (Leon, NGO worker, Germany). Similarly, a SOGI group volunteer in Italy told us:

> let's not open the Pandora's box on how the system makes people sick. Because the system makes people sick. (…) The system brings out the post-traumatic disorders, the fact of continually reliving the negative element, continuously telling how I was beaten, the non-recognition of what I claim to be. It has effects on asylum claimants. The continuous expectation, the need to be identified by an external subject with respect to what I am, creates a disturbance to people (Giulio, LGBTIQ+ group volunteer, Italy).

Chiara (NGO worker, Italy) also explained that the Italian reception system 'creates pathologies'. While people bring with them trauma from their country of origin, she felt that this then becomes chronic or more acute as a result of the reception system. Likewise, a doctor confirmed that '[t]he Home Office practice of disbelief on top of people's past experiences frequently causes re-traumatisation' (Carl, doctor with an organisation providing medico-legal reports, UK).

This suggests that there needs to be both more sensitivity within the asylum decision-making and reception system to trauma-related needs, and also greater specialist provision outside these systems for individuals, and provision that is tailored to their needs in terms of SOGI, country of origin, gender and other characteristics. As with health, there are SOGI-specific aspects to employment, the subject of the next Section.

9.3 Work

9.3.1 The Right to Work

The right to work and to freely choose one's work is recognised as fundamental to human existence.[3] Despite this, and despite the requirements of Article 15 of the Reception Directive mentioned above, all our three case study countries prevent – legally or in practice – asylum claimants from working for some or all of the period that they are waiting for a decision on their application. In Germany, claimants may not work for the first three months of their application (§61(2) Asylum Act Germany), and those from 'safe countries' placed in reception centres are unable to work for the entire period that their claim is being decided. After three months, they can apply for work but many will not speak German to the level needed for

---

[3] Article 23(1), UDHR; Article 6 ICESCR.

employment. In Italy, asylum claimants can start work within 60 days of making an asylum application, but in practice they face problems securing the residence permit needed to work. Moreover, Decree Law no. 113/2018, abolished the provision of vocational training for asylum claimants that existed under the former SPRAR system (ECRE, AIDA & ASGI 2019, p. 102). In the UK, asylum claimants are prohibited from working, although they can apply for permission to work if their claim is outstanding after a year. However, even then, they can only apply for jobs where workers are in short supply and these are narrowly defined (for example, consultant in neuro-physiology) (ECRE, AIDA & Refugee Council 2019, p. 72). There is one exception: people in immigration detention are able to work for a fixed rate of £1 per hour for 'routine activities' (Home Office 2019, p. 5), a policy seen as exploitative but that was unsuccessfully challenged in 2019.[4] In the UK, research has found that asylum claimants are susceptible to forced labour and that payment below the national minimum wage is normal for asylum claimants and refugees, with or without permission to work (Lewis et al. 2013).

Those with refugee status should have equal access to the labour market but, in reality, asylum claimants and people with refugee status experience similar barriers to finding a job in terms of language, negotiating the bureaucracy of the host country, employer prejudice, lack of recognised qualifications, and lack of what may be called social capital or networks – the kinds of connections that often enable citizens and established residents to find out about and secure jobs. More than one respondent pointed out the importance of language in finding work. For example, Moses (Italy) said 'you have to perfect the Italian language before they can probably employ you, and on the other hand, scouting for job here it is not really that easy'.

Location plays a role in employment prospects. No country under comparison had a comprehensive package of employment support for refugees. The UK's Refugee Integration and Employment Service (RIES) funding ended in 2011 (Hill 2011) and refugees' access to support in finding a job is determined largely by dispersal location during asylum, or by where they go after recognition if they are able to move. If people are able to find work, it is often at a much lower level of pay and status than their occupation in their country of origin. Alphaeus (Germany), working as a care provider for older people, had been an engineer, owning his own construction company. Sandra (Germany) also talked about building a new life, but one that is 'way far from being the same level' as she was used to (Chap. 5).

The inability to work is a huge cause of frustration for all asylum claimants, as was well documented through our fieldwork. In Germany, one participant said: 'Put me somewhere where I can even babysit a child, take care of an old person. You know? Clean somebody's house and get paid. It's still a job, you know?' They continued 'As a nail technician, I'm used to working long hours. I'm not used to being at home, looking at the ceiling every day' (focus group no. 1, Hesse, Germany).

---

[4] *Morita & Ors v The Secretary of State for the Home Department* (2019) EWHC 758 (Admin). Toufique Hossain, director of public law at the law firm Duncan Lewis, which brought the legal challenge on behalf of the five former detainees, said: 'Being paid £1 an hour for essential work is obscene' (Taylor, 2019).

9.3 Work

A claimant in Italy described the period when some people claiming asylum were housed in camps as a missed opportunity to provide people with training and education:

> when you leave the camp, you can be able to be useful to yourself. Not selling, you see some boys doing nonsense in the street, selling nonsense, some are doing, some girls are doing prostitution, why? Because they have to pay their house rent, they have to feed, they have to do all that things (Bella, Italy).

In the UK, a coalition has campaigned around the call for the government to 'lift the ban' on asylum claimants working.[5] There is both a financial imperative to people's wish to work and a psychological one: being denied a fulfilling occupation and the means to support oneself is demoralising, particularly over a long period. Silver put it very simply: 'I have to be autonomous. I have to pay for myself' (Silver, Italy).

A lack of work often continued after the grant of international protection. A report by the Refugee Council in the UK on the problems people experience in moving on with their lives on being granted status found that no participant managed to get a job within their 'move on' period of 28 days: 'participants voiced frustration at their experiences of searching for work and their interactions with staff at the Jobcentre and they felt were not giving them the support they needed' (Basedow and Doyle 2016, p. 20). However, both before and after a decision on their application, many individuals became involved in community organisations or other voluntary activities, as we consider in the next Section.

9.3.2 Voluntary Work and Community Involvement

Many of our participants chose to become involved in community engagement or voluntary work – either working with existing civil society organisations or helping to establish new ones. These unpaid contributions sometimes continued after the grant of international protection and provided the basis for or a stepping stone to paid employment. As this unpaid campaigning or support or advocacy work was often with LGBTIQ+ migrant groups, this was the basis for individuals from SOGI minorities moving into this area of work. This was the case with Jayne, in the UK, who experienced a lengthy legal battle for asylum, during which time she helped to establish a local branch of a larger African-led LGBTIQ+ asylum organisation. Jayne said:

> maybe those are the kinds of things that help me to keep sane... Trying to occupy myself. Yes, because you need to have a purpose in life and this whole system that is, what it does, you live a purposeless life, so it takes, I didn't come here educated, but I have met midwives, teachers, who are just now reduced to nothing, go to foodbank and come back and that is it. Even to get to volunteer, it is difficult because the documentation hinders doing a DBS [the government certification needed to work with vulnerable people in the UK] application, yes, so it is... it is difficult, a lot of people will lose it [mental health] along the way.

---

[5] https://www.refugee-action.org.uk/lift-the-ban/

Other people's experiences led them to pursue volunteering and undertake training to enable them to help people through the difficulties they had experienced, or as Lubwa explained, 'to give back to society' after people had supported him when he needed it (focus group no. 1, Manchester, UK). Joyce (UK) did a course on mental health and wellbeing so she could help people who had gone through the same problems as she had, having realised how common depression is.

Voluntary work was seen as a way to get experience, engage with people and fill the time while waiting for a decision. For example, Angel (Germany) said: 'So I want to start volunteering my time, like now that I can't work, volunteer my time, so that when I can work, I will have the experience'. However, there were no opportunities to do this in the rural area where she was accommodated (Chap. 8). In the UK, Lutfor told us about four different charities he had volunteered with, including the Red Cross, over more than two years while waiting for his claim to be decided.

At the same time, some participants felt exploited by the expectation they carry out unpaid work – one person even said they felt forced to take on voluntary work (Nice Guy, focus group no. 1, northern Italy). Furthermore, Wendy, an NGO worker in the UK, reported confusion on the part of officials as to whether asylum claimants barred from paid employment were also barred from volunteering – which they are not. Wendy had to have several 'robust conversations' with UKBA staff to inform them of people's rights to volunteer and claim expenses that do not constitute payment. Not surprisingly, the difficulties individuals experienced in joining the formal job market often led them to situations where they were exploited or at risk, as we go on to consider.

9.3.3 Sexual Exploitation and Sex Work

The UNHCR has recognised the 'specific protection risks that LGBTI refugees may experience in the country of asylum', including '[r]eliance on survival sex work, exposing individuals to various physical dangers and health risks, including sexual and physical violence, and sexually transmitted diseases' (UNHCR 2013, p. 4).

This was confirmed by our research. A number of people we talked to – both people claiming asylum and people working with them – gave us accounts of sexual or other forms of exploitation and suggested that this might be a problem of particular concern for SOGI claimants, especially transgender claimants. Bringing this point home, Ibrahim (Germany), a beneficiary of subsidiary protection entitled to work and was involved with an LGBTIQ+ organisation, said that, in 2015, he had been in contact with seven male-to-female transgender refugees, one of whom was in sex work in Berlin while the other six had returned to Turkey (the country through which they had travelled to reach Europe). He explained that, in Germany:

> [t]hey don't have any working opportunities. But when they were working in prostitution, they had an income, they had money, they were able to satisfy themselves, to go out and do things. But when they come here, you know, a woman needs a lot of expensive, like, make-up and all this stuff. And with this small amount of money and the lack of knowledge in the

language, and they are not allowed to work, they were in a lot of depression and so... imagine at some point, some people go "look how I was looking in Turkey. How I look here." Imagine. So that is why a lot of people went back (Ibrahim, Germany).

Jules, staff member at ILGA-Europe, pointed out that the costs of medical treatment were another reason why transgender claimants were more likely to resort to prostitution.

Unsurprisingly, accounts of sexual exploitation and sex work were more commonly given by NGO workers or lawyers, rather than by claimants themselves. An NGO worker in Germany talked about casual prostitution or 'sugar daddy' relationships involving local German White men (Noah, NGO social worker). In Italy, we were told by Giulia (LGBTIQ+ group volunteer, Italy) that this was 'the easiest way to make money' She went on:

[t]here are (countrymen) homosexuals who make the rounds in front of the reception centres, they load two and leave twenty euros. The boys tell me almost all of these things happen, then if they do it voluntarily and it's okay to take those €20, I will never judge them.

Some claimants did talk about this kind of exploitation. One of our participants said that after she broke up with her partner, she got involved in sex work to help her survive, describing it as 'one of the darkest time in my life, if I'm honest'.

Sometimes, as we saw in Chap. 5, sexual abuse or exploitation – sexual or other – was a factor in people's journey to and arrival in Europe. We heard of SOGI asylum claimants – usually women – who were trafficked to Europe and either claimed protection (initially) as victims of trafficking or escaped and claimed protection on a SOGI basis. One UK participant had been brought to the UK on the promise of work, but on arrival found that the 'job' was prostitution, which is when she ran away to claim asylum. Another, also in the UK, told a similar story:

I will cut it a bit short because it is a bit emotional (…) I came to this country very young, in my 20s and it was, I passed through a lot in Cameroon. I was forced to get married very young, age of 17/18 years, I had a lot of domestic violence… And then I came to England through someone who brought me into the country. After the man brought me here, I had a lot of, I mean was forced to prostitution which I mean, because I never wanted to go back to Cameroon…

There were also accounts of sexual abuse and even sexual violence at the hands of supporters or individuals claiming to be allies. Ibrahim was working as an activist to empower refugees to prevent this kind of abuse. However, this kind of exploitation is widely recognised. Jules (staff member at ILGA-Europe) also told us of people offering help 'under the guise of being volunteers or supporters' and exchanging sexual favours for money or medication.

These kinds of accounts of sexual exploitation were common and based on inequalities in power and assets of those concerned:

Yeah, that power, that power relation... yeah, yeah. So I had cases too. But thank God not many. So a few cases were reported to me, where in fact older, White, gay men have approached very young refugees waiting for an asylum decision and have offered support, such as offering their flat. But not only out of pure kindness, they also wanted something in return. So they quite explicitly have also put their terms on the table. These are the better ones. Because then there are also those that package it as a kind-hearted offer, but where then actually something more is required, but that is not openly framed as "trade". Such cases happened, but fortunately they were not so many, not so often. Well, that happens (Kadir, NGO worker, Germany).

In the UK, we were also told about people becoming sex workers or providing sex services, either formally or informally through transactional relationships in which sex was exchanged for accommodation or some kind of assistance with 'strings attached' (Gary, NGO worker; we also heard this from Eleanor, NGO worker, and Joseph, NGO volunteer). Moreover, exploitation did not necessarily end with the asylum decision, even if it was a positive one. Selim (UK) described how the lack of support on receiving asylum exposed him to sexual exploitation: 'I need to sleep with someone to be able to sleep on their couch. And that was never, never the case before'.

Meggs (focus group no. 1, Manchester, UK) had been doing her own research on vulnerability in preparation for a feminist conference she was helping to organise and was shocked to find out what young women were going through: 'In this country. I am not talking about back home. In this country. I have been destitute since last year March when my accommodation... I was kicked out of because my case was finished'. She compared her situation to other women claiming asylum:

> so some of the girls, because there is no accommodation, they will spend most of the times in Piccadilly going up and round with their bags full of Home Office files thinking that "after 8 o'clock where am I going to sleep? Which door can I knock on so I can sleep?" (...) any men who is going to approach them, they will have to take you because it is the survival of the fittest. (...) And it is now happening in this country, where we are expecting to be safe.

Not surprisingly, NGOs working with SOGI asylum claimants identify the risk of sexual abuse as an important one to address. In our survey we heard from one respondent that there was sexual abuse within and outside 'their own community' and that there had been cases of sexual favours demanded in exchange for giving witness evidence (S122, UK). It is not surprising if people with no income sometimes resort to such means of making money. However, not all exploitation we heard about was sexual as considered in the Section that follows.

9.3.4 Discrimination and Exploitation in Employment

Exploitation is not always sexual, we encountered situations where people were given work but underpaid or supported on an 'in kind basis' – in both situations, on the basis that people claiming asylum had no alternative but to accept these conditions. Here it is impossible to identify whether SOGI is a reason why these individuals were targeted in this way. What is easier to say with confidence is that their status as both asylum claimants or people who had yet to claim asylum, in combination with their SOGI minority status deprived them of alternatives and sources of support.

Zena thought she was coming to the UK to study, but instead was made to work as an unpaid nanny and domestic servant by a couple who took away her passport and would not let her leave the house alone (Zena, First Tier Tribunal Appeal, London, 2018 decision paper). But abuse is not always this blatant. Melisa, an NGO worker in the UK, said:

> in terms of women, we have seen a lot of domestic servitude, where LGBT women are looking after children, doing domestic chores, and just for a roof over their head. Sometimes they are given a little bit of money but sometimes they are not.

Melisa's organisation provided life coaching for SOGI female asylum claimants in this situation, helping them to move on, be proactive and find employability and educational support:

> because if she has been in domestic servitude for a long time, you sometimes forget yourself. Forget your ambitions, you forget the things that you are able to do. So what life coaching does, it brings that out, you know, they will talk to you about what you want to do, your ambitions, and you can actually make a journey path with your coach...

In the case of Lutfor (UK), mentioned in the previous chapter, he left his home country to escape persecution, but was unaware that he could claim asylum on that basis in the UK. He became destitute and was taken in by fellow nationals, who were unaware of his sexual orientation. He lived with them for two years, cleaning and cooking and only leaving the house to go to the shops, receiving food and accommodation in exchange. He felt fondly about his hosts:

> They were really nice people. I mean, they helped me [in] the situation when no one else did, I didn't get any kind of support from my family, but they did as much as they can. Sometimes they gave me their old clothes to wear... there is an open market in [location x], I go buy some groceries, come home, that was my life. Like every two or three days later I go for shopping, because there are too many people, like nine, including me in this house, four bedroomed house, nine guys, living here, so even too many vegetables, fish and meat, everything, and that is why I go out, otherwise I don't. I didn't go out of the house. That is all, that was my life.

Lutfor was detained when he eventually claimed asylum and taken to Harmondsworth, where his mobile phone was taken away from him. When he was released and returned to the house, the people in the house had packed up his possessions, having replaced him: 'they said we already got another one'.

Some of our participants also worked informally while waiting for a decision. For example, Prince Emrah (Germany), a belly dancer, worked sometimes on a paid and sometimes on an unpaid basis, including by dancing at Soli parties ('solidarity' fundraising events), such as a fundraiser for someone to pay for breast construction surgery. Payment for informal work is likely to be below the national minimum wage and irregular, especially in Italy, where many claimants and refugees are exploited in the agriculture sector working without a contract: 'they pay me *giornata*' – by the day (Franco, Italy).

Exploitation could be at the hands of European nationals, but sometimes also by people from the same diaspora community and sometimes based on prejudice:

The second difficulty is in the world of work because the world of work, obviously in some contexts, can still be homophobic, especially if in that world of work you come… unfortunately they are very exposed to the phenomenon of the ethnic *capolarato* [illegal migrant labour or gangmaster system based on ethnic or national ties]. So when a Bengali young man is inserted in a context of Bengali young men, who is hosted by a fellow countryman, who is inserted into the world of work by a compatriot, revealing his sexuality to them could be strongly negative, precisely because they are his social and labour integration (Silvana, judge, Italy).

For those in a position to seek formal employment, there were two stages of discrimination: when looking for work and once they were in post. For some job-seekers, SOGI was clearly a reason why they could not find work. Sylvia, in Germany (focus group no. 5, Bavaria), described what happened with one potential employer:

the would-be boss said "I want to give you a chance to try and see if you could fit this job". When I went to this lady and said "OK, I'm here, I would want to try", she requested my Facebook account. She had appreciated my working skills, but when the lady realised on Facebook that I'm a lesbian, she called me on the phone and asked "Are you really a lesbian?" I am not scared to say that I am a lesbian. Indeed, I confirmed to her that I am one. And she lost interest in employing me. So we still have challenges. There are people who still don't understand us here.

Discrimination might also be on the basis of migrant, refugee or minority ethnic status. To combat the discrimination or simply the bureaucratic problems facing someone with refugee status, Selim (UK) had developed a strategy to avoid being rejected at the outset and which he used to get a post as a flight attendant with British Airways: 'I learnt my lesson, I don't go ahead and tell my employer before I start working with them that I am a refugee, because that is a dead start, they will not accept me. I wait until I pass all the interviews…' When he was offered a job and asked for his passport, he offered his travel document instead, because the Home Office had retained his passport. British Airways were initially uncertain about his entitlement to work and, although he was eventually taken on, it took two months of waiting before they confirmed his job offer, showing the difficulties facing newly recognised refugees. Water (focus group no. 4, northern Italy) reported seeing their CV thrown away before their eyes: 'They just take it from you, and dump it. In your presence, they just tear it…'.

Similarly, once in work, LGBTIQ+ refugees were not always treated as equal to other citizens or residents, and would not necessarily know whether SOGI was a factor. Nelo, with refugee status in Italy, had been working as an interpreter for the police ('carabinieri') in Bologna and reported being paid only EUR4 per hour, however, for him it was a good experience because 'it was a way to express my… decency… and decency, the kind of person you are. Like, I don't have the interest of come here to spoil your country'.

We also heard about discrimination when employers and work colleagues discovered individuals' SOGI. Alphaeus (Germany) explained that:

I work and I'm working… my boss came to know that I'm gay and somehow the attitude changed with the co-workers, the colleagues at work. Yeah, people who used to laugh with me before they get to know that, because how they get to know that is when we had a CSD

[Christopher Street Day] march here, German for the Gay Pride. And I was like, I had to participate in that. And somehow I had to ask for permission from my boss, and then of course she has to ask "what are you going to do, what is it all about?" and all that stuff. So when I explained that it's a CSD, then she came to know that I am gay, and she maybe shared it with the colleagues at work, whereby some people felt it uncomfortable.

Sadia (UK), with refugee status, described how, after her employer – a fellow national – saw her taking part in a Pride event, he moved her from her job on the shop floor of a shoe shop to the stock room and reduced her hourly pay from GBP10 to GBP8.50, telling her: 'You are very bad girl, if you are like this [a lesbian]'.

As with many of the concerns identified in this chapter, such problems affect all asylum claimants and refugees, but have specific dimensions for those with SOGI-based claims. Most obviously, the number of grounds on which they experience discrimination may be difficult to discern and therefore address. But they may also lack access to community support and the kinds of diasporic social networks that often enable newly arrived people to find work. In the UK, members of SOGI minorities may benefit from the kind of support offered by one NGO that provides accommodation for SOGI asylum claimants and accompanies it with one-to-one 'moving on support' for a period of 6–12 months to help find employment. The organisation provides further employment support:

We also give support in business support to some LGBTI refugees who started small businesses, we have had quite a few successes. A lesbian from Nigeria, for example, started a cleaning business, and it grew, she started working on her own and now she employs other people (Melisa, NGO worker, UK).

Finally, when people did secure work, it could be a great source of personal satisfaction for members of SOGI minorities as with any other claimant: 'So I am happy with this, because I am independent, and I am proving that, no, I am equal to anybody else, I am a productive person, I am working, I am working hard to stay here' (Ibrahim, Germany).

There is, of course, a strong connection between employment on the one hand, and education and training – the subject of the following and final Section of this chapter.

9.4   Education and Training

This chapter concludes with a brief discussion of education: brief because we came across fewer SOGI-specific dimensions here than in other areas. Education was sometimes the first step in claiming protection for claimants, particularly in the UK, like Martin, who came on a student visa to study Mechanical Engineering but was forced to leave his country of origin because of civil unrest and who subsequently made a sur place (in-country) application (Chap. 5).

Here, it is important to distinguish children's schooling from higher or further education: children and young people claiming asylum, whether on an unaccompanied basis or with their families, are entitled to educational provision as a fundamental right recognised in all the countries covered by this project.[6] They will inevitably have specific needs and experiences in schooling based on their SOGI, however, our research mainly focused on adults seeking asylum. In this context, education was a concern in two ways: access to and provision of language classes in the host country, and access to further and higher education. While for the most part these did not emerge as areas where SOGI minorities had different experiences to other asylum claimants, there were some particularities relating to SOGI.

Gaining fluency in the language of the host country is a fundamental need for all people attempting to establish themselves in a new country (ECRE, AIDA & ASGI 2019, p. 85). Provision differs between Germany, Italy and the UK and within each of these countries, and it also changes depending on the policy of the government of the day. In Germany, the federal government provides language classes as part of the integration course that beneficiaries of international protection are usually obliged to attend on receipt of their residence permit and that is also provided to asylum claimants 'with good prospects of remaining in the country' (Federal Ministry of Labour and Social Affairs 2015). This last point has a particular bearing on SOGI claimants, as few of the countries where SOGI claimants come from correspond to a good 'staying perspective' ('Bleibeperspektive'), that is, an acceptance rate of 50% (Gisela, lawyer, Germany). In Italy, following the implementation of Decree Law no. 13/2017, language courses are no longer part of the reception package for asylum claimants (ECRE, AIDA & ASGI 2019, p. 85). In the UK, the cost and availability of ESOL provision (English for Speakers of Other Languages) for adult learners differs between England, Scotland, Wales and Northern Ireland, and also varies depending on how an individual came to the UK, with the government announcing a GBP ten million funding boost for English language tuition in 2016, but only for those arriving as part of the Syrian Vulnerable Persons Resettlement Scheme (Home Office 2017).

Our participants had the same problems as other people claiming asylum in learning the language of their new country: 'I'm just like a baby, learning language, learning... all A, B, C, D. It's difficult for me...' (Kennedy, Italy). Access to classes is often a problem and one that relates to location. In Germany, one NGO working with lesbian, bisexual and transgender women told us 'there are women who are, for example, in a small village in Donau-Ries-Kreis, there's no German course at all' (Sofia and Emma, NGO workers).

Where people were able to find language lessons, fears of hostility or discrimination by other students based on homophobia or transphobia were mentioned as a concern. One participant in Germany described a German language class where the teacher asked students why they had left their home country and, to avoid discussing his SOGI, he said: 'it's politics, it's a political matter' (William, Germany). A

---

[6] Article 28 of the UN Convention on the Rights of the Child.

German NGO worker explained that many trans women abandon or do not attend their German courses, because they feel uncomfortable (Kadir, NGO worker). Another participant in Germany told us about his friend who barely attended school because 'he was always called a faggot… and that's not motivating anyone to learn German' (Zouhair, Germany).

Turning to access to further or higher education, entitlements vary, partly based on whether an individual has refugee status or is still waiting for a determination, but the critical barrier for most people is financial. Each of the countries we are comparing has some scholarship or bursary schemes available to asylum claimants and/or refugees, but these are limited and not easy to access.[7] Given that the process of claiming asylum can last several years, schemes to enable asylum claimants to access higher education are valuable and need to be expanded. We found that continuing their education was important for many people. Several of our participants were forced to flee before completing their studies: 'I went to college for finishing my graduation in Bangladesh but I couldn't, I had to flee after the first year' (Lutfor, UK).

Not surprisingly, education was often connected to training and improving one's employment prospects. A number of our participants had a strong wish to resume their education with this as a factor:

> My plans, if I get the papers, I will go back for some study so that I can get some certificates, because I don't think that I can manage to go on university, but I will try for the certificates so that I can get something professional… (Edith, focus group no. 3, London UK).

Finally, as we explained in detail in Chap. 7, the level of education people had in their countries of origin and their grasp of European languages inevitably affected the ease with which they were able to familiarise themselves with the legal system and support structures in the host country and also, importantly, their ability to make a claim and access necessary support. This was less of a problem for our participants in the UK, partly because some of them came from Commonwealth countries or countries that had been colonised by the UK and where English was widely spoken.

To sum up, education featured as a small but very important element in much of our fieldwork, encompassing the role of SOGI in disrupting people's education in their home countries, the role of education for people who make SOGI-based asylum applications having entered the EU originally to study, and the potential fear or actual experience of discrimination from fellow-students or nationals in language classes as a factor undermining the development of new language skills.

Lack of access to language classes, training, employment and education was difficult in various ways, but with one common outcome for many: the sense of time being wasted while they waited for a decision, but being unable to move on with their lives in terms of acquiring an education, language or work skills, or earning money. If and when refugee status is granted, individuals have to rebuild their lives

---

[7] For example, Unibo for Refugees in Italy (http://viedifuga.org/unibo-for-refugees-rifugiati-universita-bologna/) or the Article 26 scholarships provided by the Helena Kennedy Foundation in the UK (http://article26.hkf.org.uk/)

from scratch, having been denied access to work and usually to education and training as well during the time that their claim is pending. SOGI claimants and refugees are likely to have few sources of support in rebuilding their lives, as they may have been less able to avail themselves of the usual refugee community organisation support.

9.5 Concluding Remarks

The areas of entitlement, need and service provision explored in this chapter again highlight the failure within reception provision to fully recognise the rights and needs of SOGI asylum claimants and refugees and the extent of discrimination and marginalisation they encounter.

The problems people experience in relation to education, work and health, in particular mental health, are not always easily identifiable as a direct result of being a member of a SOGI minority. When people experience depression or panic attacks, it is not usually possible to trace the cause back to their experiences of fleeing homophobia or transphobia, for example. Equally, when people are entitled to work but are not offered a job interview for a position for which they are clearly highly qualified, they may not know whether it is because of their SOGI, their ethnicity or their refugee status. If the latter, this may be due as much to confusion on the part of the employer about the identity document legally required to employ someone as it is to prejudice. What is clear from the testimonials we received is that belonging to a SOGI minority often contributes to people's experiences and, importantly from a policy and practice perspective, may mean that specific expertise and services are needed which are often not available at present.

There are implications in terms of a joined-up reception system that makes important connections between different areas of policy and service delivery: for example, recognition of the need for continuity of medical care for trans people claiming asylum to avoid repeated relocation with new doctors would require immigration officials to, first, systematically record applications with a gender identity basis and, second, liaise with providers of asylum reception and health services, with implications for confidentiality. These implications are revisited in our recommendations.

References

Action for Trans Health. (2015). *Trans people in immigration detention centres.* http://actionfor-transhealth.org.uk/2015/04/04/trans-people-in-immigration-detention-centres/

Alessi, E. J., & Kahn, S. (2017). A framework for clinical practice with sexual and gender minority asylum seekers. *Psychology of Sexual Orientation and Gender Diversity,* 4(4), 383–391. https://doi.org/10.1037/sgd0000244.

References 415

Alessi, E. J., Kahn, S., & Chatterji, S. (2016). 'The darkest times of my life': Recollections of child abuse among forced migrants persecuted because of their sexual orientation and gender identity. *Child Abuse & Neglect, 51,* 93–105. https://doi.org/10.1016/j.chiabu.2015.10.030.

Alessi, E. J., Kahn, S., Woolner, L., & Horn, R. V. D. (2018). Traumatic stress among sexual and gender minority refugees from the Middle East, North Africa, and Asia who fled to the European Union. *Journal of Traumatic Stress, 31*(6), 805–815. https://doi.org/10.1002/jts.22346.

Basedow, J., & Doyle, L. (2016). *England's forgotten refugees: Out of the fire and into the frying pan.* Refugee Council.

ECRE – European Council on Refugees and Exiles, AIDA – Asylum Information Database, & ASGI. (2019). *National Country Report: Italy, 2018 update.* ECRE – European Council on Refugees and Exiles. http://www.asylumineurope.org/sites/default/files/report-download/aida_it_2018update.pdf

ECRE – European Council on Refugees and Exiles, AIDA – Asylum Information Database, & Asyl und Migration. (2019). *National Country Report: Germany, 2018 update.* ECRE – European Council on Refugees and Exiles. https://www.asylumineurope.org/sites/default/files/report-download/aida_de_2018update.pdf

ECRE – European Council on Refugees and Exiles, AIDA – Asylum Information Database, & Refugee Council. (2019). *National Country Report: United Kingdom, 2018 update.* ECRE (European Council on Refugees and Exiles). https://www.asylumineurope.org/reports/country/united-kingdom

EHRC – Equality and Human Rights Commission. (2018). *Making sure people seeking and refused asylum can access healthcare: What needs to change?* EHRC – Equality and Human Rights Commission.

EHRC – Equality and Human Rights Commission. (2019). *The lived experiences of access to healthcare for people seeking and refused asylum.* https://www.equality-humanrights.com/en/publication-download/lived-experiences-access-healthcare-people-seeking-and-refused-asylum

European Commission. (2020). *European web site on integration.* https://ec.europa.eu/migrant-integration/resources/documents

Federal Ministry of Labour and Social Affairs. (2015). *Learning German.* https://www.bmas.de/EN/Our-Topics/Info-for-asylum-seekers/Learning-german.html%20accessed%208%20September%202019

Ferrera, M., Rhodes, M., & Rhodes, M. (2013). *Recasting European welfare states.* London: Routledge. https://doi.org/10.4324/9781315039916.

Freedom from Torture. (2019). *Making a referral to freedom from torture for therapy and practical help.* https://www.freedomfromtorture.org/sites/default/files/2019-04/Guidance_notes_to_make_a_referral_for_therapy_and_practical_help_at_Freedom_from_Torture_0.pdf

General Medical Council. (2020). *Trans healthcare.* General Medical Council. https://www.gmc-uk.org/ethical-guidance/ethical-hub/trans-healthcare

Herlihy, J., & Turner, S. W. (2007). Asylum claims and memory of trauma: Sharing our knowledge. *The British Journal of Psychiatry, 191*(1), 3–4. https://doi.org/10.1192/bjp.bp.106.034439.

Hill, A. (2011). Refugee services to take a heavy hit due to 62% funding cuts. *The Guardian.* https://www.theguardian.com/world/2011/feb/01/refugee-services-heavy-hit-cuts

Home Office. (2017). *Syrian vulnerable persons resettlement scheme (VPRS) guidance for local authorities and partners.* GOV.UK. https://assets.publishing.service.gov.uk/government/uploads/system/uploads/attachment_data/file/631369/170711_Syrian_Resettlement_Updated_Fact_Sheet_final.pdf

Home Office. (2019). *Detention services order 01/2013. Paid Activities.* Home Office. https://assets.publishing.service.gov.uk/government/uploads/system/uploads/attachment_data/file/814058/DSO_01_2013_Paid:Activities.pdf

Hopkinson, R. A., Keatley, E., Glaeser, E., Erickson-Schroth, L., Fattal, O., & Sullivan, M. N. (2017). Persecution experiences and mental health of LGBT asylum seekers. *Journal of Homosexuality, 64*(12), 1650–1666. https://doi.org/10.1080/00918369.2016.1253392.

Kennett, P., & Lendvai-Bainton, N. (2017). *Handbook of European social policy*. Cheltenham: Edward Elgar.

Lewis, H., Dwyer, P., Hodkinson, S., & Waite, L. (2013). *Precarious lives: Experiences of forced labour among refugees and asylum seekers in England*. http://lastradainternational.org/lsidocs/Precarious_lives_main_report.pdf

Longacre, M., Silver-Highfield, E., Lama, P., & Grodin, M. (2012). Complementary and alternative medicine in the treatment of refugees and survivors of torture: A review and proposal for action. *Torture: Quarterly Journal on Rehabilitation of Torture Victims and Prevention of Torture, 22*(1), 38–57.

Micro Rainbow International. (2013). *Poverty, Sexual Orientation and Refugees in the UK*. Micro Rainbow International.

Mind. (2009). *Improving mental health support for refugee communities – An advocacy approach*. https://www.mind.org.uk/media/192447/Refugee_Report_1.pdf

Ohonba, E. (2017). Critical primary-source literature review on the mental health factors of the LGBQ asylum claim. *Global Health Special Topics, Spring*. https://www.academia.edu/33279935/Critical_Primary-Source_Literature_Review_on_the_Mental_Health_factors_of_the_LGBQ_Asylum_Claim

Piwowarczyk, L., Fernandez, P., & Sharma, A. (2017). Seeking asylum: Challenges faced by the LGB community. *Journal of Immigrant and Minority Health, 19*(3), 723–732. https://doi.org/10.1007/s10903-016-0363-9.

Reading, R., & Rubin, L. R. (2011). Advocacy and empowerment: Group therapy for LGBT asylum seekers. *Traumatology, 17*(2), 86–98. https://doi.org/10.1177/1534765610395622.

Shidlo, A., & Ahola, J. (2013). Mental health challenges of LGBT forced migrants. *Forced Migration Review, 42*, 9–11.

Sigvardsdotter, E., Vaez, M., Rydholm Hedman, A.-M., & Saboonchi, F. (2016). Prevalence of torture and other warrelated traumatic events in forced migrants: A systematic review. *Torture: Quarterly Journal on Rehabilitation of Torture Victims and Prevention of Torture, 26*(2), 41–73.

Slobodin, O., & de Jong, J. T. V. M. (2015). Mental health interventions for traumatized asylum seekers and refugees: What do we know about their efficacy? *The International Journal of Social Psychiatry, 61*(1), 17–26. https://doi.org/10.1177/0020764014535752.

Tabak, S., & Levitan, R. (2013). LGBTI migrants in immigration detention. *Forced Migration Review, 42*, 47–49.

Taylor, D. (2019). Judge rules £1/hr wages for immigration detainees are lawful. *The Guardian*. https://www.theguardian.com/uk-news/2019/mar/27/judge-rules-1hr-wages-lawful-for-immigration-centre-detainees

TGEU – Transgender Europe. (2018). *Trans healthcare in asylum reception conditions*. TGEU – Transgender Europe. https://tgeu.org/trans-healthcare-in-asylum-reception-conditions/

UNHCR – UN High Commissioner for Refugees. (2013). *Resettlement assessment tool: Lesbian, gay, bisexual, Transgender and intersex refugees*. UNHCR – UN High Commissioner for Refugees. https://www.refworld.org/pdfid/5163f3ee4.pdf

UNHCR – UN High Commissioner for Refugees. (2020). *The Core International Human Rights Instruments and their monitoring bodies*. https://www.ohchr.org/EN/ProfessionalInterest/Pages/CoreInstruments.aspx

Women's Refugee Commission. (2019). *"More than one million pains": Sexual violence against men and boys on the Central Mediterranean route to Italy*. https://reliefweb.int/report/italy/more-one-million-pains-sexual-violence-against-men-and-boys-central-mediterranean-route

Open Access This chapter is licensed under the terms of the Creative Commons Attribution 4.0 International License (http://creativecommons.org/licenses/by/4.0/), which permits use, sharing, adaptation, distribution and reproduction in any medium or format, as long as you give appropriate credit to the original author(s) and the source, provide a link to the Creative Commons license and indicate if changes were made.

The images or other third party material in this chapter are included in the chapter's Creative Commons license, unless indicated otherwise in a credit line to the material. If material is not included in the chapter's Creative Commons license and your intended use is not permitted by statutory regulation or exceeds the permitted use, you will need to obtain permission directly from the copyright holder.

Part III
Forging a New Future for SOGI Asylum in Europe

Chapter 10
SOGI Asylum in Europe: Emerging Patterns

I don't like labelling people, judging people.

(Sandra, Germany)

I decided to leave my country because I did not have the same right to live as others. That's why I had to leave my country.

(Silver, Italy)

Just find organisations that help people in the situation, reach out, talk to people, make friends, you will feel a lot better. Don't just stay at home and be depressed like what I did.

(Christina, UK)

10.1 Introduction

This chapter brings together some of the recurring but not always visible phenomena relating to SOGI asylum that have remained below the surface in the previous chapters. We are keen not to conflate or homogenise what are often very different individual experiences in Germany, Italy and the UK. Rather, we identify themes and common factors that may take diverse forms but that, at the same time, shaped the experiences of our participants and are the basis for the targeted recommendations in our final chapter. We group these phenomena under four headings: identities, discrimination, place and agency. By doing so, this chapter draws together the recurring or more significant findings from the chapters that constitute Part II, and presents and analyses them using the theoretical approaches in Chap. 3 to show that what may appear to be discrete phenomena in fact derive from systemic failures to apply an intersectional, queer, feminist and human rights based understanding to SOGI asylum.

© The Author(s) 2021
C. Danisi et al., *Queering Asylum in Europe*, IMISCOE Research Series,
https://doi.org/10.1007/978-3-030-69441-8_10

10.2 Identities

Chapter 3 looked to feminism and queer theory to disrupt essentialist portrayals of marginalised individuals and groups, specifically women and SOGI minorities. This approach resonates with the experiences of SOGI asylum claimants addressed in Part II of this work. It is particularly helpful in understanding how stereotypes based on SOGI, but also on SOGI in relation to other characteristics – such as age, gender, religion, education – come together to create expectations of how a particular claimant should present themselves for their claim to be successful.

10.2.1 Homogenisation

SOGI asylum is very often based on extrapolating the needs and experiences of a minority – generally young gay men – to the wider and diverse group of individuals claiming asylum based on SOGI. Throughout our fieldwork, the acronym LGBT (or a variation of it such as LGBTIQ+ as we use) was used by decision-makers, lawyers, NGO staff and often claimants themselves. However, on further questioning, the claimants speaking or being discussed were generally members of a narrower group: 'One has to say that we have relatively few lesbians...' (Nina, legal advisor, Germany); 'We have no lesbian or transgender experience' (Giulia, LGBTIQ+ group volunteer, Italy); 'I have only had gay and lesbian [claimants], so I have never had transgender. Oh, we have had one, I have had one bi client...' (Deirdre, lawyer, UK).

Bisexual claimants were especially absent and we were not able to contact any claimant who identified as intersex or having intersex variations. The lack of research and awareness of bisexual individuals' experiences of claiming asylum has been identified in a North American and Australian context by Sean Rehaag (2009). It is likely that in Europe the same difficulty applies in reconciling bisexuality with the immutability generally looked for as contributing to credibility:

> I think there is still the reliance on stereotypes is another thing. And that for example particularly for the bi community then that erases them entirely. Because if you have a person who identifies as bisexual, then you will have responses along the lines of "oh, well, but if you like both the opposite sex and the same sex you can go back home and just be with someone of the opposite sex", that simple (Jules, staff member at ILGA-Europe).

Laurie Berg and Jenni Millbank (2013) have explained the harm done by miscategorising trans asylum claims as a subset of sexual orientation claims, resulting in trans invisibility and the inappropriate application of COI. Similar harm is caused by homogenising all SOGI claims based on stereotypes of gay men's experiences: the persecutory experiences of lesbian women, bisexual men and women, and trans people are obscured, and appropriate COI is neither sourced nor adequately used for these groups (Chaps. 6 and 7). In the UK, for example, women from countries where only male same-sex behaviour is criminalised may encounter problems.

Meggs (UK) told us how unexpected this was at her first appeal when she was told [Meggs' words]: 'Ok, even if you are gay in Zimbabwe, it is legal for women to be gay according to law, but it is illegal for male....' While women's experiences are often ignored, as in this example, they may also be heard but used to undermine a claim, as is typically the case where women have been married – often through a forced marriage – or had children:

> There is also that problem of... if you come from countries where young marriages or forced marriages are common, then you have issues like... I mean the recent very prominent case in, recent, long on-going case in the UK with Aderonke... where her claims of being a lesbian were doubted because she was once married and had kids, but that fails to recognise the local context of the country of origin that in many cases people don't have a choice (Jules, staff member at ILGA-Europe).

Women also told us about their pain at being separated from their children and how an important motive in securing refugee status was to then be able to bring their children to Europe to join them through family reunion (Meggs, UK; Stephina, UK): 'It was the most difficult thing for me to leave my daughter because I love her to death like, every fibre in me appreciates that I have got a child as brilliant as she is' (Stephina, UK).

10.2.2 Stereotypes

These experiences of the harsh impact of asylum rules are only one example of why the category of SOGI asylum needs to be disaggregated to recognise the different paths and needs of different individuals within this grouping. Following our theoretical frameworks (Chap. 3), here we consider it in relation to the complex layering of stereotypes, norms and expectations displayed by decision-makers and which affect their decision-making. An example of this is the case of Zena, UK, where the judge in her first appeal did not find her credible because:

> Although [Zena] has a slightly "mannish" appearance, I place no real weight on that, in determining whether she is reasonably likely to be a lesbian, if only because

(a) That slightly "mannish" appearance was substantially attributable to the manner in which her hair was cut and the fact that she wore no (or very little) "make up" and, to a degree, to her age (she is now 39 years old),
(b) The manner in which [Zena's] hair was cut and her appearance are (obviously) very much matters over which she has substantial control,
(c) [Zena] is not a large, muscular and/or well-built woman, but, on the contrary, is slightly built, so that her appearance is not striking, and
(d) since her claim to asylum is based on the contention that she is a lesbian, it would not be surprising if, whether or not she is, in reality, a lesbian, she would take steps to ensure that, at the hearing of her appeal, her appearance was consistent with her claim.

> Nor do I place any weight on [Zena's] evidence that, when she had been c. 14 or 15 years old, she had had a brief lesbian relationship with a school friend, [name], a relationship which, on the basis of what [Zena] stated, lasted only c. 3 weeks at or about the [month] holiday in 1996. Many young women (and young men) at that age are confused about their

sexuality. The fact (if fact it be) that at that age (or even slightly older) they involve themselves in homosexual activities with other young women (in the case of women) or young men (in the case of young men) says nothing of any consequence about whether 20 years or more later they are homosexuals (whether male or female) (First Tier Tribunal, London, 2018, decision paper).

Zena's case was first discussed in Chap. 7, but this passage is worth quoting in full because it brings together a number of different assumptions based on gender, age, sexuality and culture or country of origin. Zena's claim depended on her credibility as a lesbian, as so many claims do. The judge deconstructed her appearance and manner to argue that she could safely return because, whether or not she was a lesbian, she did not need to look like one: she was 'mannish' but at the same time had a small physique, so with a more feminine haircut could avoid persecution. This stereotype is (hetero)sexist but also culturally specific, based on Western portrayals of a typical lesbian appearance. As a matter of legal accuracy, there is no evidence that such stereotypes are prevalent in the East African country of origin in this case, meaning there is no evidence that this is relevant to how Zena would be perceived if she were returned. Similarly, the assumption that young people are 'confused' about their sexuality and flirt with homosexuality is another culturally-specific trope. Finally, Zena's age is used against her as a further reason why her 'mannish' appearance would not reveal her to be a lesbian; she would simply be seen as old. In addition, her age would mean that her single childless status would not attract attention:

If [Zena] were returned to Kenya, she would (plainly) not live with a husband or male "partner" and she would have no dependent children. But I am not satisfied that those facts would lean any person who did not know her, or her history, to conclude that she was, or might be, a lesbian. Widowhood and marital breakdown are by no means uncommon. Because [Zena] is now c. 39 years old, the fact that she has no dependent children is not reasonably likely to cause questions to be asked, or suspicions to arise (she is of an age at which formerly dependent children might themselves have grown up) (First Tier Tribunal, London, 2018, decision paper).

The implication here is that, in Kenya, for a young woman, having dependent children is evidence that one is not a lesbian, while for a woman in her thirties this is not the case. No evidence to support these assumptions is given in the decision paper. We have already heard that the Home Office may find it harder to believe older people are gay (Chap. 7). One plausible reason for this is that stereotypes for the LGBTIQ+ community in the UK rarely depict older people, so there are no templates for decision-makers to use when assessing the credibility of an older person.

Zena's case also highlights the particular susceptibility of SOGI claimants where a number of different stereotypes – not only based on SOGI – come together in a system so heavily dependent on 'credibility', which is, at the end of the day, an individual judgment. It also shows how gender and sexuality are intrinsically linked (Chap. 3). In fact, the extreme prejudice showed by this judge ultimately worked to Zena's advantage. This decision was appealed and the judge found to have materially erred and failed to apply the guidance in the Equal Treatment Bench Book.

10.2 Identities

However, a fair system should not allow decisions to be made on the basis of such biases in the first place.

Moreover, Zena's case was just one example of the humiliating and demeaning nature of the appeal process for some SOGI claimants and the way SOGI claims are managed, particularly when, on appeal, they reach the sometimes public arena of a courtroom (Sect. 6.4 of Chap. 6). It is difficult to think of another situation where an individual who has not been charged with a crime may find themselves in a courtroom with lawyers and government representatives debating across them whether they are indeed a lesbian, a process in which the claimant generally has little opportunity to speak for themselves.

Many less startlingly egregious examples than the case of Zena remain unchallenged. These relate to characteristics other than sexuality, for example religion, where we found assumptions about the relationship between religious and SOGI minority identities that, again, are culturally specific. As discussed in Chap. 7, and as one of our survey respondents explained: 'Applicants whose religions are generally intolerant of sexual minorities are expected to provide an intellectual explanation for their own faith. If they cannot do so their claims are then liable to be rejected as incredible' (S4, lawyer, UK).

Ibrahim A. (UK) explained how religion was addressed in his main Home Office interview:

> [the interviewer] asked if I am consider myself religious and I just answered her "what do you mean by religious?" Because there is not something called like, there is no blue print of religious. (…) it is differs from a person to another. And then she asked me a very specific questions: "are you praying five times a day?" I was like, "I used to, but not now." "Were you going to mosques regularly?" I told her, "well, I used to, but not now." Ok, at some point I felt like she was profiling me if I am an extremist (laughs) or something like that.

However, Ibrahim A.'s solicitor explained to him that was not the case. She told him:

> they thought that if you are truly gay, you will have this … LGBT, you will have this kind of … internal discussion between your sexual orientation and your religion and if you didn't have it, so you are not serious enough about what you are doing. So that was her questions I guess about… she asked me about practicing, prayers, she asked me about going to mosques, I don't remember if she asked me about fasting or not … then she asked me about how do, how do Islam look to the LGBT and gays, and I told her, "well, there are many opinions on that, it depends on the interpretation of the text itself".

What we encountered were assumptions about identity that influenced decision-makers and acted as a barrier, preventing SOGI claims from being heard as individual narratives without the imposition of culturally specific assumptions about how SOGI claimants behave depending on whether they are gay or lesbian, young or old, male or female, Muslim or Christian, etc. As Jules (staff member at ILGA-Europe) told us, in every country we can find:

> this Westernised perception of what it is to be homosexual. And that you have to behave in a certain way and you have to act in a certain way, and if you don't live up to these expectations, then you are viewed as not being credible.

Jules pointed out that this is harmful in two ways: it reinforces stereotypes and forces people to perform their SOGI. As Ibrahim (Germany) explained: 'I told them what they want to hear [in an asylum interview]. Because they want to hear violence, discrimination, your fears of going back, your prostitution'. This corresponds to the concerns in the literature on homonationalism (Chap. 3), and generates a cyclical process where claimants are encouraged to conform to the culturally-specific and heteronormative stereotypes that decision-makers impose upon them in order to maximise the chances of a successful claim.

10.2.3 Language and Culture

The requirement to conform to a particular narrative is more difficult for some claimants than others. Language and interpretation issues were explored in Chap. 6, but what might be described as cross-cultural differences are not always easy to pin down, particularly when they come up against the hard certainties of legal systems.

Rudi (UK), whose case was first touched on when we discussed the notion of PSG (Sect. 7.2.2 of Chap. 7) did not identify as transgender when he first came to the UK, but as a lesbian. His Upper Tribunal appeal was partly based on the fact that although he no longer identified as a lesbian, because of his birth-assigned gender, he would be perceived to be a lesbian in his country of origin – Kenya. The appeal succeeded because in this instance the Upper Tribunal judge was sensitive to the specificities of the case, and it was held that the judge in his First Tier Tribunal appeal had failed to take into account 'the evidence documenting the risks to transgender men or to women perceived to be masculine lesbians, and also failed to take into account crucial evidence, setting out the unique risks which faced a transgender man or a lesbian woman perceived to be masculine' (Upper Tribunal, London, 2018, decision paper, para. 8). However the case, in which attributions of SOGI – as well as the claimant's self-definition – changed over time, shows how difficult it is for asylum law to capture individual identity through permanent labels such as 'lesbian'. As Cristina (UNHCR officer, Italy) pointed out, 'very often it happens that trans people talk about sexual orientation rather than gender identity, or they define themselves as gay or as lesbians'. Most importantly, it shows why the question of whether claimants are 'truly' members of a SOGI minority should be recognised as redundant, not only because SOGI is fluid and complex, but also because identity, regardless of SOGI, is never definitively fixed. SOGI identities in the context of asylum, as in many other contexts, are negotiated in the context of the state, of the surrounding environments, and through personal relationships. Furthermore, identification may evolve in a process of intense 'subjectivation', in other words, transformation by one's own practices (Fassin and Salcedo 2015, p. 1124).

10.2 Identities

The relationship between identity and the language used to describe identity came up in several accounts. Roberto (decision-maker, Italy) explained that:

a young man who speaks Wolof, who was born and raised speaking Wolof, he does not have a term to self-identify that is not an insult. I continuously hear guys who can't get to an awareness of themselves, because they can't, there is no "coming out from the closet"... because there aren't even "closets".

Similarly, and as mentioned in Chap. 6, we heard from Celeste, a social worker in Italy, about a client's self-description:

It was not "I am" or "I was lesbian" but "I do lesbian", as if it were a practice ... there is no awareness of "I am this". I mean, I'm doing it, it's what I do... rather than what I am.

The differences in how SOGI identity are experienced across cultures and countries were also analysed by Ashley (psychotherapist, UK):

I know from gay Iranian friends, for example, but also clients that I have worked with, that the issue of trans and gay might be conflated because of one is more acceptable than the other, rather than the powerful attachment of identity choices and features that goes with some of the Western levels of identity.

As these reports illustrate, an asylum system that requires claimants to deploy the language and terminology for SOGI minorities used in European societies will unfairly fail to recognise the very real but different ways that they experience or are threatened with persecution. As Allan (lawyer, UK) described the situation:

You have got some languages and cultures where they don't have a concept of being gay. The concept of having sex with your own sex might exist, but the concept of being gay doesn't, so often you get this confusion about what that is. If it [is] not confusion, it is disbelief. You often get clients who say that they only realised they were gay when they came to the UK, even though they may have had a relationship in their country of origin or at least sexual encounters. Then there is this confusion. The Home Office will say, "You couldn't have realised you were gay when you came here because you were having sex in Pakistan." No, they didn't realise they were gay. It's not really a concept. That is in loads of countries. That is Pakistan, Bangladesh. Less so in the African countries, but also in the African countries. Cameroon, etc., it is not really a concept as much as we have it here. Here you have got identity politics. There it is not seen as an identity. There is a clash there.

This experience of sexuality as behaviours rather than claimed identities is in tension with the expectation by decision-makers that claimants describe a journey of self-discovery, or have gone through a process of awareness and self-acceptance (Jansen 2019, p. 168; Wessels 2016). Yet, as we saw in Chap. 7, not all participants can provide such an account of sexual self-discovery in the emotional or sentimental terms that decision-makers want to hear. Giulia (LGBTIQ+ group volunteer, Italy) described this in the context of questioning by the Commission:

So, they often ask him "when did you understand?", "do you remember how it was when you realised you were homosexual?" Because young men tend to tell when it was their first homosexual sexual experience. So always facts and not feelings. From this point of view, however, the Commission tries to investigate the path of discovery with the Western mentality.

On the receiving end of such expectations, Ibrahim A. (UK) told us about a particular line of questioning by his Home Office interviewer who found it difficult to comprehend that a relationship he had had with a classmate had been based entirely on sex:

> Somehow she didn't accept that. She asked me like, I stayed with him like two years, and she was like "how come two years you don't know what he is interested in?" And at this point actually when I get very, I have to say upset, I just told her, "I need to explain something, I just was meeting him for sex, and that is it. Outside this I was just his classmate".

As the success of SOGI claims appears increasingly to depend on articulating an internal and emotional journey to decision-makers, those who are not equipped with the language (and cultural) skills to do that are more likely to fail. In Chap. 7 we highlighted the prohibition on sexually explicit material in evidence as a positive development in European and domestic law and policy. There is no question that this is a welcome change, however, it corresponds to the privileging in its place of a particular kind of account of gay persecution based on the claimant's inner life and not their outer behaviour – and not everyone can provide this account.

In the above accounts, a common factor is the contrast between the reality of sexuality and gender identity as experienced by our participants and the desire on the part of officials to discover a claimant's 'true' identity – gay or dissembling – once and for all. Also apparent from the above accounts is the often demeaning way in which this process takes place, through interrogating people about their earliest and most personal experiences, which are often then discredited and devalued.

Several participants described cultural communication problems as having a particular bearing on SOGI claims, because of their inevitable focus on sexual activity:

> I remember the silly question that they asked me and it is still on my refusal is that, "when the police came in, what were you doing?" I said, "I was sleeping with my partner". [She] Said, "oh, you were sleeping with your partner", I said, "yes, I was sleeping with my partner, naked, you know". I couldn't say we were having sexual intercourse, I was still holding back on that thing that, you know, so on my refusal they said, "she said they were just sleeping. So, as girl child or they can just sleep as friends" (Meggs, UK).

Meggs went on to say: 'So, most of the times, the most important information you just withhold out of respect, out of cultural beliefs, out of the way you have been raised but not intentionally'. Gary confirmed this:

> I am not sure sometimes if the interviewer gives due weight to how difficult it is for people from some cultures to talk about sexuality. I mean, I don't just mean about being gay or lesbian, but about anything to do with sex really. And I think it is not in, like, African culture, you don't particularly talk about it in your families or anything. That is certainly true of Pakistan, I think, so I think sometimes people [claimants] say, you know, "I met somebody and he was a very nice person", and then people [decision-makers] say "well, that is not a sexual relationship" in their report. So, I think being a little bit more aware of the cultural reticence and, I mean, I am always saying to people I know it is really difficult, but you are just going to have to say what you mean (Gary, NGO worker, UK).

Many of the legal and NGO advisors we spoke to explained that they told their clients and members how important it is to be open about their experiences precisely because they understood how difficult this would be in two ways: first, the very natural reluctance to talk about subjects often seen as private, and more likely to be seen as such in many of the countries from which SOGI claimants come; second, the understandable fear that many people will have about sharing with officials the kind of information that they have tried to keep concealed for years.

As well as misunderstandings and misrecognition based on culture, there were also difficulties for people who, for whatever reason, simply rejected the kinds of identity labels that they needed to embrace for the purposes of claiming asylum. A focus group participant in Germany described herself as an 'immigrant', not a refugee:

> Watching the television and you see refugees, you see flies all over them, they're barefooted, they're dirty, they're malnourished and that's what we see in Jamaica as refugees. That's what we see on our TV screens when we hear about refugees, you know? I came to Germany well-dressed. When I see refugees on the TV, they just throw on something, they're in boats for days. I rode comfortably in a plane. You know? Lufthansa. Slept all night, and stuff like that (Sandy, focus group no. 1, Hesse, Germany).

Christina (UK) had gradually come to identify as non-binary, but was relaxed about identifiers: 'I don't have a problem with pronouns so I use male and female pronouns. I have also got a female person which is Christina. She / he, I am not fussed. I am ok with pronouns'. As we saw in Chap. 7, both Sandra and Christina would be well-advised to avoid such thoughtful questioning of identity categories, at least until their credibility is established in the eyes of decision-makers.

While this section has considered the complexities of identity and identifiers in SOGI-based asylum claims, the next section identifies the experiences of discrimination and prejudice that our participants had experienced in different contexts and at different times in their journeys to and in Europe.

10.3 Discrimination

Many of our participants shared with us overt experiences of discrimination and hostility. We look at these experiences first in terms of discrimination by the host community and then in terms of discrimination within the diaspora community, with the proviso, however, that 'host' and 'diaspora' are not discrete categories and that this may be increasingly true over time as individuals who were once asylum claimants settle and take on roles in policy and service provision within the 'host' community to support a later cohort of claimants.

10.3.1 Racism

Discrimination was often experienced in terms of racism as well as homophobia or transphobia. In a focus group in Germany, Jackie told us:

Well, yeah, it makes you think before exposing yourself, because you are cautioning yourself. I am Black and I am gay, so it's like you can't expose yourself. So racism is like, it's racism. But as for me, yeah, there is… I mean, you cannot be in a White man's land for even a year and you don't experience a little bit of racism. That won't happen. And maybe it is like on a train or something, you go and sit down, there are German people, White people, sitting in front of you. They will get up and change seats, you know? So it happens. But as long as no-one is hurting me physically, I just look at it and move on (focus group no. 2, Bavaria, Germany).

And Halim in Germany was worried about racist attacks and right-wing politics:

Now that I can read German and I read the news, I'm really scared sometimes. Recently there was this demo against AfD [Alternative für Deutschland, extreme right-wing party] and it was really nice to see all the people show up against it, but yeah, I don't know.

Angel's descriptions of some of her school-age daughter's experiences were also distressing: 'Oh God. She has been called a "Black bitch". She have been called [the N-word]. She have been called a monkey. She have been standing at the bus stop and a football was kicked on her purposely' (Angel, Germany). Her daughter was not the only child from an asylum or refugee background at the school; however, she was the only one who was Black.

Similarly, Stephen (Germany) had the unpleasant experience of realising that his presence was unwelcome and that he was viewed with suspicion:

Then another very bad experience was in winter, I was at a bus stop. Now, a lady came with a "Kinderwagen" [baby pram] [baby pram] and she had two kids. One was seated in the "Kinderwagen", and another one was playing. It was a bus stop. So when I moved towards the front to check the time, so I went towards her. The closer I moved that was when she was showing me, she was holding a handbag and pulling the "Kinderwagen" towards her and calling the kids. You know, kids always play and go to an extent, so I was like looking at the kid now. I realised there was something happening to the mum, and the mum was like calling the kid away. To me, I didn't take it like something that was serious, but then after two or three minutes I understood that my presence there was causing a discomfort to them. So what happened was, I had to leave the bus stop and move, like, some metres away. And immediately the bus came and they were the first people to enter inside. To tell you the truth, I didn't enter that bus.

In Italy, as well, Kamel had a bad experience at his third Pride event in Bologna, where two girls shouted 'go back to your home' and someone else shouted 'Viva Salvini' [leader of extreme right-wing party]. Also in Italy, Alain A. had become used to discrimination:

Living in Italy as a Black, you face many difficulties first. So many, many, many difficulties as a Black. I have never been discriminated as an LGBT but as a Black, yes. Normally you face discrimination every day as a Black even on the buses, so it is not even something I talk about again because it is just like a normal way of life, but I think with time things will change.

In the UK, Mary and Zaro had eggs thrown at the exterior of their accommodation and 'Fuck you' written on their door while their application was pending. There were several accounts of people moving away from asylum claimants on buses, trains and in public spaces (also mentioned in Chap. 8), including C49, a survey respondent in the UK, who wrote: 'Most of the time especially in the trains people rather stand than sit next to you'.

Some of our participants reported being targeted because they were Black, and some because they were Black and gay: 'You face two things at a go, you are Black and you are gay…' (Alphaeus, Germany); 'One old woman in the S-Bahn [suburban train], they say "Blacks are smelling" [laughter]' (Mayi, focus group no. 4, Bavaria, Germany). And again in Germany, Liz said 'I think us Blacks, the way they are treating us is very different from the way they treat the Asians' (Liz, focus group no. 5, Bavaria, Germany).

While racism was common in our participants' accounts, equally, they endured homophobic and transphobic abuse that was often not only distressing but also frightening as recounted in the next Section.

10.3.2 Homophobia, Transphobia and Cross-Cutting Discrimination

Alongside overt racism, SOGI minorities claiming asylum shared their experiences of different kinds of hostility and harassment. These occurred in public and social spaces and were not necessarily connected to status as an asylum claimant or refugee, as Amber's experiences highlight:

> [Location X] is kind of creepy actually. I was cornered several times when I went for a walk, like I was crossing a road and there was a car that came and then stopped me from crossing and then the driver gestured me to come inside his car. I was in a quiet neighbourhood, so that was a bit scary. Then you get people calling you names sometimes, when you walk in public. I was walking with one of my housemates and she identify as non-binary, and she does attract attention and I experience weird interactions from strangers with her. But, I think that can happen anywhere (Amber, UK).

Janelle (UK) had had at least two unpleasant homophobic and transphobic experiences:

> I was walking on the streets in Sheffield, and a guy was driving and he wanted to know what is my identity and he was like, "are you a boy or a girl?" So I just started walking faster. And I had this particular time I was going to the grocery store and there were like two Jamaican kids, and they were using like terms like batty man and like faggot and stuff…

We were also told of varying degrees of unfriendliness and exclusion from within LGBTIQ+ spaces in the host countries. Ibrahim, in Germany, said that, '[f]or example, we have this issue here in Cologne. A lot of gay people are not allowed to go to them [LGBTIQ+ venues] because they are brown-skinned'. in Italy, LGBTIQ+ group volunteer Giulio said: 'I have never had so much discomfort entering an LGBT night club as much as when I entered with a Black person. I mean, it seemed like it was bad, bad because I'm White dancing with a Black…'.

We also heard of discrimination within UK LGBTIQ+ communities:

There is still racial discrimination in some parts of the UK LGBTQ+ community. There is also still [a] drink/drug culture in parts of the LGBTQ+ community, including issues around chemsex etc, that would make it difficult for LGBTQ+ refugees to integrate into the LGBTQ+ community here (S83)

A number of accounts were of discrimination by other asylum claimants. This is not surprising, as thei main day-to-day contact for most SOGI claimants will be with other asylum claimants. In such cases, hostility and discrimination tended to be on the basis of SOGI. For example, Chloe, a worker with a refugee women's organisation, described how the women using the service had started a choir. Chloe said:

I run the choir and everybody loves the choir and it is a really big part of the drop-ins and we sing at various different events and it is really great, and we were singing at a Pride event, or we got invited to a Pride event, and… when we told the choir what it was, none of them wanted to do it. And that was just really shocking. And upsetting. Because I just had no idea, which was so naïve of me. And nobody turned up. And we couldn't explore it because they didn't want to talk about it.

In Chap. 8 we described some experiences of discrimination in shared accommodation. We heard accounts of hostility from flat or house mates from Trudy Ann and Alphaeus in Germany, Ken and Kennedy in Italy, Meggs and Lutfor in the UK, among others. A survey participant stated: 'My roommate told me face to face that he wished all gay people would be denied asylum and that he wished the worse for all of us, a statement that can never go off my mind' (C38, Germany). One NGO worker at an LGBTIQ+ organisation also told us that they sensed the 'gay village' [in Manchester] was quite racist: 'They don't really want them [asylum claimants] here' (Caroline, NGO worker, UK). According to one survey respondent:

In 2016 July, me and some gay friends of mine were denied entrance to one gay club in Munich because we were Blacks. They first claimed that three of us didn't have the membership card like the one issued at SUB [gay communication- and culturecentre Munich] (S36, Germany).

It is possible to generalise to some degree about types and sources of discrimination, as Nicola (LGBTIQ+ group volunteer, Italy) did: 'SOGI [minorities] are discriminated outside the cooperative [camp] because they are Black and within the cooperative [camp] because they are gay, among other refugees'. Diane, in Germany, expressed it differently: 'I also get transphobia here. In Iran, too, is transphobia, but here is transphobia with racism about it'. She had been turned away by a lesbian counsellor who told her 'You are not a woman'; she found that the White trans community also had no interest in trans refugees. Likewise, Kamel (Italy) told us: 'So, I'm a trans, but nobody thinks I'm trans; I am a refugee and of colour'. These comments highlight the peculiar situation of many SOGI claimants and refugees who experience abuse on the basis of different aspects of their identities which they, and their abusers, may not always be able to distinguish. While in some places and contexts asylum claimants' identity as part of a SOGI minority would be the target of hostility, at other times it would be their ethnicity, but there was also a perception of a specific dislike of migrants, perhaps even specifically of refugees. Failing to recognise these intersections leads to failures to recognise the totality of individuals' experiences, as highlighted in Chap. 3.

As soon as one looks at participants' accounts of experiencing discrimination and harassment, it is clear that they – like anyone else – cannot enter the mind of their harasser to identify the grounds on which they have been targeted. Is it because they are Black, gay, a woman, Muslim, a refugee, short, fat, young, some, all or none of these? In any case, it is beyond doubt that the experience of being member of a SOGI minority seeking asylum in Europe makes individuals more exposed to abuse in various ways. As Julian (focus group no. 5, Bavaria, Germany) said: 'And also when you're under the refugee status, and you add the word "lesbian", then you are Black... me, I'm being realistic [laughing]. It's like, you've killed yourself with three bullets at once. That's the fact'.

The experiences of discrimination that our participants recounted varied significantly depending on their location, showing how important a factor 'place' is, both within and outside the decision-making process.

10.4 Place

The previous chapters have highlighted notable variations in the three countries under comparison, including variations in the treatment of SOGI claims and in the wider social experiences of individuals claiming asylum on these grounds. In understanding why wide variations persist despite many regulations and measures designed to facilitate consistency, we look back to Chap. 3, where we used queer geographies to highlight how focusing on space can help us to understand SOGI asylum experiences – space understood from macro to micro level.

10.4.1 Receiving Country and Region

In understanding persistent variations in decision-making and non-legal experiences in the face of attempts to facilitate consistency, we look back to Chap. 3, where we used queer geographies to highlight how focusing on space can help us to understand SOGI asylum experiences – space understood from macro to micro level. Our fieldwork affirmed the value of thinking in this way, as we saw how both country of origin and host country determined people's experiences, with applications relating to particular countries treated with greater scepticism than others (Chap. 6). We have compared the policies, laws and practices that deal with SOGI asylum in each country (Chaps. 4, 5, 6, and 7) and in the sections above we show how country of origin combines with SOGI to create different trajectories for individuals. Nonetheless, where claimants settle or are settled within each country is equally important both to the outcome of their claim and to their broader experiences as we consider here.

Despite key asylum instruments being defined by the central authorities in all three of our case study countries, participants reported regional differences in decision-making and wider support that inevitably affect the likelihood of a claimant's claim succeeding. In Germany, one participant identified 'huge differences' between courts: 'I would say that with these, the cases that I'm negotiating about Chechens in Berlin, of which I win many here, I do not win in – I would not win all those in Frankfurt (Oder) and Potsdam' (Barbara, lawyer). Regional differences were also visible in relation to support outside the asylum decision-making process. Frank S. (legal advisor) explained that in Germany there is still much progress to be made across the country:

> Well, let's just say that basically I think Berlin is already halfway well positioned in terms of financial resources and counselling services, but of course [it] is a very big problem that other federal states are not equipped with a counselling infrastructure with special accommodation or housing offers or queer shelter ready or queer shared flats.

There were two specific concerns in Bavaria: one was the lack of state-supported sheltered accommodation for SOGI refugees and the other was the state government's reluctance to authorise work permits (Thomas, NGO volunteer, Germany). In contrast, asylum claimants in Saxony are likely to receive more comprehensive support, perhaps surprisingly, given the incidence of racist hate crime reported in this area (AFP 2019):

> Saxony, so if you are a queer refugee and come to Saxony, then everything is actually secured. (…) they are all sent to Dresden, queer refugees, there is a street in Dresden, since the 23 apartments have been rented for the accommodation of queer refugees. And that is all organised by the community through the CSD [LGBTIQ+] club Dresden (Knud, NGO worker).

In Italy, distinctions were made between the services and expertise available to SOGI claimants in Calabria and Emilia-Romagna (Titti, decision-maker), and Damiano, a lawyer, told us that '[t]hose who come to the centre [of Italy] are luckier, especially in Emilia Romagna, Tuscany, all in all in Liguria, in certain areas of Lombardy and Piedmont'.

In the UK, immigration (including asylum) is a reserved matter, meaning that policy is made centrally and not devolved to any of the UK's constituent nations. Yet, approaches to integration do vary within the four nations (Chap. 4). For example, Scotland's 'New Scots' strategy states explicitly: 'The key principle of the New Scots strategy is that refugees and asylum seekers should be supported to integrate into communities from day one of arrival, and not just once leave to remain has been granted' (Scottish Government 2018, p. 11). In this light, we heard that while the asylum policy structure and immigration rules are the same across the UK, there may be differences in how officials engage with external partners:

> So I have engaged in a number of forums where… we have Scottish asylum seekers forum that SRC [the Scottish Refugee Council] co-chair with myself, so we have that. We have the new Scots forum, new Scots integration forum, so I'm involved in I think probably every one of the strands of the new Scots integration forum. So, we are very visible and we are very willing to engage (Olivia, government official, UK).

There are no official statistics on LGBTIQ+ asylum claims (other than the UK's 'experimental' data) and consequently there are no published statistics for decisions on SOGI claims at a regional level. Nor are there figures available on the concentration or dispersal of SOGI claimants to different parts of Germany, Italy or the UK. It is therefore not possible to analyse differences in acceptances and refusals based on location within each country. Nonetheless, as highlighted here, interviews with NGO workers and volunteers and with lawyers in each country suggest significant differences do exist within each country.

It is easier to demonstrate the personal and social impact of location for individuals if we consider whether they moved or were moved to a city or large town, or to a small town or village. In none of our countries was SOGI a consideration in where people were sent or accommodated by the authorities (Chaps. 5 and 8). The impact of living in a rural or remote location was particularly striking in Germany, as discussed in Chap. 8. One participant told us: 'I feel like a fish out of water, I'm the only lesbian in [small locality] as far as I see it. When I hear about a lesbian group, it's either in Frankfurt, in Kassel, in Fritzlar, in somewhere' (Sandy, focus group no. 1, Hesse, Germany).

Marhen (Germany) was asked about gay life in Saaarbrucken and whether it was possible to integrate into the gay community. He said: 'No, here most of them speak only German. And the ones I met who spoke English, there is a socialising code that I couldn't crack'. At 37, age was a further barrier: 'And to find gay Germans my age who share similar interests... no. There is [NGO X], but then [NGO Y], all of them are in their twenties'.

In Italy, better services and support are available in cities such as Bologna (Anna, LGBTIQ+ group volunteer, Italy). Similarly, in Milan, for two men to walk hand-in-hand would be acceptable in a way that it would not be elsewhere (Livio, lawyer, Italy). In the UK, Ibrahim A. contrasted the environment at the university where he was studying with that of the nearest town:

> my experiences wasn't nice, because the campus is very international environment and it is kind of isolated from the city, it's on the borders of the town, the town or the city. And the town is conservative, White, people were still giving you the looks of like how you look like if you are different person. Sometime I was getting like the feeling like that we are not belong to here, we are not speaking English the same way I am speaking. I was getting this a lot from the bus drivers, in specific. If I am asking to go to specific station and I am not pronouncing it the right accent, that he is using too, he claim he doesn't understand me. It happened many times that other people on the bus, British, like tell him he said this station. And then he just understands (Ibrahim A., UK).

It is unsurprising that people we interviewed found it easier to 'settle', make friends, and become part of communities in cities and large towns than they did in rural locations and smaller conurbations, and that location was a significant factor in whether or not they reported feelings of isolation.

10.4.2 Isolation

The impacts of isolation and dispersal were a recurrent feature in our participants' accounts:

> I mean, you have cities where there is a big group that is organising support for LGBTI asylum seekers, that you know is also specifically looking at their stories, at the traumatisation, the traumas they might have, at the specific needs they might also have, that is integrating them into the community in the city, they are sometimes or often at least in Germany also supported by the state, but then you have places where if you are sent there, there is nothing. Yes and you are really like looking into the void (Terry, member of the European Parliament).

As well as the personal and emotional impact of living in a small town without established LGBTIQ+, migrant, or LGBTIQ+ migrant communities, there is a very practical implication for individuals in terms of their application. One survey respondent summed up the combination of problems experienced in this context:

> Recently I have come across many cases of LGBT+ people seeking asylum had been dispersed to areas which are not diverse and there is no LGBT+ community and that has had an enormous impact on their mental health and in proving their case and Home office want to know if they had been to any LGBT+ bars or clubs since coming to UK (S145, Community Development Worker, UK).

Such expectations from decision-makers were explored and found problematic in Chap. 7. Anna's account of how this affected the work of NGOs reiterated such concerns:

> [T]he most difficult problem that we are sincerely meeting to integrate, at the level of inclusion, is that these guys are scattered, lost in places that are not reachable by public transport. Obviously, they are not equipped with their own vehicles and they are badly connected with the cities where we generally do events, we organise events. So what happens? That we have a problem. Even if they can come, then they don't know how to get back (Anna, LGBTIQ+ group volunteer, Italy).

We were told about a young Syrian refugee who had been dispersed to Northern Ireland with his family, but who was not 'out' to his family. He was getting support from LGBTIQ+ organisations locally, but keeping that part of his life separate from his family relations (Lucas, NGO worker, UK). Given the absence of dedicated SOGI asylum support groups and networks outside of the main cities in Great Britain (England, Scotland and Wales), it is likely that claimants in other locations will find it expedient to compartmentalise their lives as this young man has done, seeking different kinds of support from different and unconnected networks and organisations. In this way, we can see that some individuals feel forced to fragment their identities, having very few spaces available to be open about their identity. This is more likely to be the case for individuals dispersed to areas where there is no LGBTIQ+ asylum support network, but it was a wider phenomenon, and we now address these experiences of isolation, whether physical or mental, externally or self-imposed.

10.4 Place

While for some people feelings of isolation corresponded to and were shaped be their remote location, others experienced a sense of separation and inability to be themselves in the world despite living in a city and in constant contact with others. Chloe, working for a women's refugee NGO in a large city in the UK, told us she thought there were women using their general services who were not open about their sexuality because of their need for support from the network. Justina (NGO worker, UK) told us something similar: 'And they might not be out, they might be seeking asylum, but are not out and they may never be because actually it is more important for them to have that network within the cultural and / or faith'.

There were also very practical reasons why claimants felt unable to be open about their SOGI: 'for me, because I've not been accepted, I don't want to tell all the world that I am a lesbian, [in case] tomorrow I am sent back to my country' (Juliet, Germany). Similarly, Halim, also in Germany, did not tell the people in his accommodation that he was gay:

> I kept a distance from people. I always ate on my own, there were always groups of people… Yeah, I didn't really, I just tried to maintain a distance because I was worried about what could happen. I was worried that people would start to ask me a lot of questions.

Ashley (psychotherapist, UK) told us of similar experiences of isolation that many people have because they live with people who – for religious or cultural reasons – would not offer practical support to a SOGI claimant:

> [these SOGI asylum claimants] find themselves in the new "closet" of not talking about their cases in the asylum accommodations that they have (…) with all the limitations that any asylum seeker has of access to life in the UK, it becomes even more problematic to access a life in the UK for someone LGBTQI with all the risks that goes on, with the costs that goes on with it as well. So it is incredibly isolating.

Alongside this, many of our participants were keen that their experiences be used to support others in their situation in combatting isolation. In this respect, Christina (UK) told us that:

> a lot of people go through what I am going through and they feel really alone, nobody to talk to, especially if you are going through asylum and you have, you are getting support, you feel alone, you don't have any friends, you can't really pick yourself up and say "you know what, I am going to go to a gay pub and sit and try to make some friends", because you barely get enough money to survive, much alone go and have a drink. Just find organisations that help people in the situation, reach out, talk to people, make friends, you will feel a lot better. Don't just stay at home and be depressed like what I did.

In contrast, one very positive spatial dimension for some SOGI claimants was the strong affection for and sense of identification that they developed with their new home area. This was particularly true in the UK. Daphne said she wanted to stay in Manchester 'forever' and Luc told us 'Glasgow is the best place to live'. Jayne, as well, said that 'I love it [Birmingham]. When I first came, it was a little town [I came from], it was so overwhelming I did not like it, but I have grown to like it and it is… a very friendly city' (Jayne, UK). Similarly, Amos (focus group no. 5, Nottingham, UK) said that:

Nottingham itself has been quite amazing, because I am even able to run in the morning without fearing and it is maybe dark at around 5, and I am running, jogging that there is no one who will harm me.

Similar accounts were shared in Germany and Italy. Odosa (Italy), for example, said: 'I like Italy, I like Italy seriously'. Halim (Germany) also said that:

I think Berlin as a city offers a lot of great opportunities. I'm a person that enjoys culture and there's a lot of cultural events, like film, Brazilian film festival for example. A lot of spaces... there's now much more spaces where queers and not only queers, people of colour are organising. It gives me a lot more spaces and options to move in and to feel comfortable and be myself.

While it is pleasing to be able to end this section on so positive a note, the important point to note about these feelings of attachment to place is that they tend to develop when claimants – whether pre- or post-determination of their claim – are able to develop an identity in their new home. This often corresponds to feeling a sense of agency, and that they are contributing to improving the lives of themselves and others in a similar situation.

10.5 Agency

The final section of this chapter identifies some of our participants' experiences relating to agency and lack of agency. By this we mean the ability to act autonomously and in a way that is self-determining (Friedman 2003, pp. 4–5).

10.5.1 Losing Agency

A very important factor contributing to individuals' feelings that they had no control over events in their lives was, of course, the length of time they often had to wait for a final decision on their claim, particularly those who needed to go through the appeal process. As explored in Chap. 6, Susanna, a social worker in Italy, told us that what she more often heard from the people with whom she worked and who were appealing against negative decisions was 'I can't take it anymore'. She gave the example of one person who had been due to have their appeal in December and it was delayed until July: 'and he told me over the phone "I can't wait any longer, I don't know what to do with my life"'. Claimants feel powerless and deprived of their agency during these long waiting periods.

For people in detention, mainly in the UK, the indeterminate length of their detention was often a specific problem in impeding their access to the sources of advice and information needed to strengthen their claims, but for all asylum claimants, waiting for often unknown and faceless officials to make decisions determining the course of their lives was made more stressful by the uncertainty about how long they would have to wait. In none of the countries studied were precise time-frames for making an initial decision applied and adhered to. For example, a parliamentary question in the UK elicited the fact that in December 2018 more than 12,000 claimants had been waiting for a decision for longer than the Home Office target of 6 months and in May 2019 it was reported that this target had been abandoned (Allison and Taylor 2019).

Prolonged waiting contributes to the dehumanising and sometimes cruel treatment people experience during the asylum process. In Chaps. 6 and 7, we heard of the long probing interviews people, some of whom had experienced rape, had to endure in attempting to establish credibility. We also heard how stressful they find the experience. Some participants had a sense that their life was slipping away from them: 'Yeah, I feel that at my age I've not achieved the things I wanted to achieve. I'm still living in a student area with some young people. I wish to have my own space and be happy' (Sandra, Germany).

The denial of the right to work in law or in practice – discussed in Chap. 9 – was a further frustration during this waiting period, preventing them from making the kinds of career and life plans that most citizens take for granted in the EU:

I don't want to be here in Germany and dependent on social [welfare] all the days of my life. No. I want to go out, I want to work, [have] my own money. I want to pay taxes, I'm getting older. I need a pension (Sandy focus group no. 1, Hesse, Germany).

These words were paralleled in a group discussion in the UK:

I need freedom… you can't, you feel like you are suffocating inside because you are held somewhere in a cage, you can't do anything, it is about freedom, they just let us free, should have let us live freely like everybody else and you can only feel, live that way if you are able to provide for ourselves. We want more education, the years are going by, so we just don't want to get, we feel stagnant, you know, we are just stuck there, can't move right or left (focus group no. 3, London, UK).

While all asylum claimants will suffer from the uncertainty of waiting and it is impossible to quantify this suffering, there will be particular difficulties for SOGI claimants who may not be or feel able to access the kinds of community support that other claimants can.

SOGI claimants we talked to had gone from being dynamic agents instigating change in their lives to being dependents of the asylum system. We asked Angel (Germany) what she did all day and she said: 'Nothing, I just lay here and smoke'. Shany (Germany) also explained that 'I used to be like "fleißig" [diligent], like somebody worked very hard, and I can do everything, and I don't like to have this name, this nickname of "victim", you know'.

Halim, also in Germany, reiterated similar feelings, saying he felt frustrated and had found his experiences 'really dehumanising (…) People talk about integration all the time as if it's just the duty of us. But how do we do it if we're never seen as equal or never seen as someone who can give back?' Halim was clear that he was not asking for favours but for protection that he was entitled to and that would enable him to start contributing to society again:

for a person like me, I had a lot of experiences before I moved here. I moved here with like (....) 30 years old, at this point I've travelled a lot. I was working, and I perceived this whole asylum thing as for me, claiming my right to asylum and safety. I don't see it as a gift, as somebody's giving something I don't deserve. So I feel that this makes my prospective things a bit different. Because I feel I am entitled to protection and being supported until I become a person who is giving back to society as I'm doing now.

Such awareness of their rights on the part of SOGI claimants was hard to hold onto in the face of often insurmountable obstacles imposed by the asylum system and society more generally. In the UK, for example, Ali found it difficult to gather the evidence he needed for his case without compromising his sense of independence:

it is difficult because I had to ask my friends including not close friends, and to me, in my nature I like to be independent. I don't like to be dependent on somebody else. I really am always independent so, if I want to do something, the last thing is to ask somebody else or make them involved in my struggles and problem particularly when it is so personal, the first thing would be is to try to do it by my own. But since I had no choice and totally intimidated and fearful of the possibility of being sent back home then I had to make my private and personal life to be an open book and having to open up and also live my past traumas every day throughout the process. Well, I have got close friends who I am happy to actually tell them anything, but still not everyone. I hate being, well, I had so many incidents when I was fallen a victim, though, I hate the word victim. Because me seen as a victim is, as to me it reflects the vulnerability and the weakness that I'm always trying to overcome and since we have no choice but to be strong and brave during the tough times, is not an option in order to survive.

The desire to retain a sense of individual agency and independence is unsurprising in the face of legal and regulatory systems in which all control lies with the decision-maker and is exercised inconsistently: while asylum claimants in all countries must comply with many deadlines (dates on which they need to sign in with the authorities, dates on which they must attend interviews, deadlines for appealing), decision-makers either have no targets for decision-making or breach them with impunity, as in the UK.

The experience of flight and claiming asylum is often portrayed in simple terms, with persecution replaced by security. Yet in contrast with our approach based on a HR reading of the Refugee Convention that was not how our participants necessarily perceived the asylum journey, which very often further damaged their agency. Sandy (focus group no. 1, Hesse, Germany) talked about why some asylum claimants return to their country of origin:

Safety was my issue, why I leave to come here. Not only safety for me, but safety for my child. But I was working, I was living in a city, I could socialise, I could communicate, I could go to the clubs if I wanted to go to the clubs, you know? I could go get ice cream if I want. So even though [now] I'm safe, I still feel in prison.

For Sandy, and others like him, the result of claiming asylum was a trade-off, with some gains and some losses.

10.5.2 Taking Control

Many of the people we spoke to were trying to achieve what they articulated as freedom – but were restricted as much within the host country as in their country of origin, including in concrete physical ways, for example by camp life in Italy, rural isolation in Germany, and detention in the UK. In contrast, several participants described ways in which their lives had become freer and they were able to express themselves. Marhoon, in Germany, talked about his changing experience of going to Pride and how he used to act as an agent for change:

> And this year I enjoyed it more. The first time, my first gay Pride ever was here in Saarbrucken in Germany and I was so nervous, although I didn't go in my traditional clothes I had a sign that said "Queer refugees". (...) this year, I went but this time I decided to go full traditional clothes, to show, not only here in Germany, but also my gay community in Oman, to show them that they're not alone, that I'm here marching on their behalf. Well, some of them, because for many of them I don't represent them. I did it, I was nervous again this year, but yeah, again I was fine, nobody harassed or anything.

Janelle (UK) also said that 'Yes, I am very open with my identity. I don't hide [it]. I used to hide [it] when I was back home, now I can just be free'. For Amis (focus group no. 2, Bavaria, Germany), freedom and agency were experienced in an ambiguous way. On the one hand:

> [T]he best thing is that I am protected and I am free to be who I am. I am out of the closet, I am gay and I am proud to be gay, because even if I walk on the street I tell everyone who I am. If I am with a boy, I kiss him. I feel like, calling him my "boyfriend", that's okay.

Yet, at the same time, Amis also acknowledged:

> I have that psychological torture. Like, I could say being traumatised, but it's a torture anyway. Because I am not that free anyway. I am free when I'm in Munich, in that area. But when I'm in my place, I am totally not free.

In general, for those participants who talked about ways in which their lives had improved, this was due to two elements. The first, as Amis' words show, was living in a country where they were able to be open about their SOGI, usually for the first time, despite the continuing mental trauma. The second was the feeling of strength and agency that people found through their own developing self-confidence and from engaging with others in a similar situation. Christina (UK) explained that:

> when I moved here, that's when I started learning about different things and I always liked dressing up, because I would do back home but secretly and then, now that I have got a wider spectrum to explore here, and a lot more avenues to get information from, that is how I start understanding that I am non-binary.

Rosette (Germany) also felt a sense of freedom:

> Nobody is going to take maybe a razor blade to cut me, so that the devil gets out. I will say whatever I want because now I feel that I have a paper which I can show that I'm a free person.

Stephina (UK) also highlighted the importance of the sense of freedom she developed while claiming asylum:

I knew I would be fighting my case, but at least I am outside, I have got that freedom to go places, meet people, hang out with people and because I am coming from a country where you can't say out loud that you are LGBT and being here, it was like I can breathe. I don't even have to explain myself. I can date whoever I want to date, go places where I want to go, if I go to a gay bar, whoever sees me I really don't care, because I didn't have to explain myself to them. So I think that freedom is what kept me going, even when I knew my case was still going, because you can see from 2014 I just got my stay now [2018], so it has been a journey but (laughs) yes.

These positive accounts may be connected to the confidence and enhanced agency that comes with being aware of rights and how to exercise them. One volunteer described this to us:

I see a radical change between the young people who arrive and contact the association and those who perhaps then leave because they find work somewhere else. The evolution of these people thanks to the group factor (…) is incredible in the awareness of oneself but also in one's self-confidence (Giulia, LGBTIQ+ group volunteer, Italy).

Meggs (focus group no. 1, Manchester, UK) confirmed this sense of increasing self-confidence that derives from greater rights awareness: 'I have always been that person who will sit back, but now I have learnt to stand up and fight not only for myself but for other people as well who come after us'. She also had a very clear idea of what she wanted to do with her life:

I want to work with people. I want to work with underprivileged people, and in due time I want to open an organisation back home for young women, because (…) where I grew up no telly in the village, no telly, no Wi-Fi, they know nothing what is happening around the world. So I want an organisation where they will know they are more important, they come first and education is the key, they should not be groomed to be somebody else's wives, they should have their own decisions and make their own decisions.

In Meggs' case, we can see the kinds of fluctuations in life that many claimants must experience: taking the difficult decision to seek a safer, freer life but then, paradoxically, losing all individual autonomy and often experiencing new forms of persecution in the country of supposed refuge. Finally – if international protection is granted – it may be possible to regain the sense of control of one's life and even be an agent of positive change for others. Alain A., in Italy, also shared a renewed sense of agency:

I would still choose Italy because it wasn't about choosing a place, it wasn't, it was about being where you are accepted, where you can live the life you want to live, without judgement, without persecution, so anywhere would have been good and thank God it is Italy. I didn't ever think of that. I didn't ever think of there will be a day when I will tell somebody like I am gay and the person accepts me and just smile and live with me no matter, I didn't ever think of that. (…) when I came to Italy, I got so much support and especially the support of acceptance, when people accept you for who you are, that is so big, it gives you, like, freedom to be able to express your mind and freedom to be able to sit with people and talk.

A number of the SOGI asylum claimants and refugees who made time to talk to us were either working to support others in their situation or planning to do so.

Jayne (UK), for example, told us that '[m]y moto now is I don't want to see anyone going through what I went through'. They did it to support others, but also recognised the benefits to themselves:

> I am involved with [group X], I am involved with, I also volunteer with the [group Y], through the weekend I was doing a peer mentoring programme with [group Z], I am involved with nationally director with [group W] ... Yes, so maybe those are the kind of things that help me to keep sane, to be fair (Jayne, UK).

In this section, we have attempted to highlight how much all our participants valued their independence and their desire to take back control of their lives. Of course this is not unique to SOGI asylum claimants, but a feeling likely to be common to all refugees. However, we have also illustrated some of the distinct ways in which the agency of SOGI claimants is both undermined and may – eventually – be enhanced in their European host country. Particularly striking was the increasing number of NGOs and community organisations set up and managed by SOGI asylum claimants, either during their wait for a decision, or upon finally receiving refugee status (where that was the case). These efforts may have started as a response to the prohibition on asylum claimants taking paid employment on the part of people committed to using this period of waiting in a constructive way. However, such endeavours often developed into permanent career pathways for people keen to improve the asylum process for others following in their footsteps.

10.6 Concluding Remarks

In this chapter, as in our whole work, one difficulty has been separating the experiences of SOGI minorities claiming asylum that relate specifically to their SOGI from those experiences that relate more generally to their identities as asylum claimants in Europe. This is unsurprising: as our focus on intersectionality and queer theories shows (Chap. 3), identities are fluid, with different characteristics mattering more or less at different points in life and in different contexts. That means that improving the experiences of SOGI asylum claimants will require addressing their experiences in a holistic way, recognising the impact of age, religion, gender, ethnicity and many other factors, as we consider in our next and final chapter.

Laying the basis for that, this chapter has been considered under four headings: identities, discrimination, place and agency. Our argument is that these, broadly speaking, are helpful ways to think about the obstacles for SOGI minorities claiming asylum in Europe – obstacles in terms of having a fairly assessed claim and obstacles in terms of wider integration and engagement in a new society. Addressing our participants' experiences through these four lenses highlights many potential areas for improvement based on validating identities, reducing discrimination, creating supportive spaces and enhancing agency. We do this in more concrete ways in the final chapter that follows.

References

AFP. (2019). Racist crime rises sharply in state of Saxony. *The Local*. https://www.thelocal.de/20190307/racist-crime-rises-sharply-in-saxony

Allison, E., & Taylor, D. (2019). Home Office abandons six-month target for asylum claim decisions. *The Guardian*. https://www.theguardian.com/uk-news/2019/may/07/home-office-abandons-six-month-target-for-asylum-claim-decisions

Berg, L., & Millbank, J. (2013). Developing a jurisprudence of transgender particular social group. In T. Spijkerboer (Ed.), *Fleeing homophobia* (pp. 121–153). Routledge. https://papers.ssrn.com/sol3/papers.cfm?abstract_id=2312887

Fassin, E., & Salcedo, M. C. (2015). Becoming gay? Immigration policies and the truth of sexual identity. *Archives of Sexual Behavior, 44*, 1117–1125. https://doi.org/10.1007/s10508-015-0551-z.

Friedman, M. (2003). *Autonomy, gender, politics*. Oxford/New York: Oxford University Press.

Jansen, S. (2019). *Pride or shame? Assessing LGBTI asylum applications in the Netherlands following the XYZ and ABC judgments*. COC Netherlands. https://www.coc.nl/wp-content/uploads/2019/01/Pride-or-Shame-LGBTI-asylum-in-the-Netherlands.pdf

Rehaag, S. (2009). Bisexuals need not apply: A comparative appraisal of refugee law and policy in Canada, the United States, and Australia. *The International Journal of Human Rights, 13*(2–3), 415–436.

Scottish Government. (2018). *New Scots: Refugee integration strategy 2018 to 2022*. https://www.gov.scot/publications/new-scots-refugee-integration-strategy-2018-2022/

Wessels, J. (2016). "Discretion", persecution and the act/identity dichotomy. *Vrije University Migration Law Series, 12*. https://rechten.vu.nl/en/Images/Wessels_Migration_Law_Series_No_12_jw_tcm248-760198.pdf

Open Access This chapter is licensed under the terms of the Creative Commons Attribution 4.0 International License (http://creativecommons.org/licenses/by/4.0/), which permits use, sharing, adaptation, distribution and reproduction in any medium or format, as long as you give appropriate credit to the original author(s) and the source, provide a link to the Creative Commons license and indicate if changes were made.

The images or other third party material in this chapter are included in the chapter's Creative Commons license, unless indicated otherwise in a credit line to the material. If material is not included in the chapter's Creative Commons license and your intended use is not permitted by statutory regulation or exceeds the permitted use, you will need to obtain permission directly from the copyright holder.

Chapter 11
Believing in Something Better: Our Recommendations

> *I have the impression that the topic is getting more and more important. And there is also a commitment to do it better in the future.*
>
> (Kadir, NGO worker, Germany)

> *It takes trained staff, who have the time, who rotate and who are prepared to do this job.*
>
> (Roberto, decision-maker, Italy)

> *But the only thing I would say to people is just like, keep on pushing. Keep on pushing.*
>
> (Patti, UK)

11.1 So What?

The previous chapters have offered an in-depth, empirically and theoretically informed analysis of a broad range of issues affecting SOGI asylum claimants and refugees in Europe, with a focus on Germany, Italy and the UK. This analysis has applied new insights to findings unearthed by previous research and shone light on issues that have so far been relatively neglected. But the question often posed to us as academics is 'so what?' To address this question, this chapter offers a range of recommendations addressed to decision-makers, policy-makers, governments, NGOs and service providers, aimed at improving the socio-legal framework that applies to SOGI asylum. These apply mainly at a domestic level, but also refer to the European level, where relevant, to offer proposals that recognise the intersections of national, European and international frameworks. As in the previous analysis, we are strongly guided by our participants' voices, complemented by broader scholarly debates and our analysis and views of these. Our data and analysis thereof also shed light on broader issues in the asylum system, and many of the recommendations set out here would benefit non-SOGI asylum claimants and refugees as well. We hope they will be of wider value in this way.

© The Author(s) 2021
C. Danisi et al., *Queering Asylum in Europe*, IMISCOE Research Series,
https://doi.org/10.1007/978-3-030-69441-8_11

The context for this chapter is the clear sense that '[t]he world no longer speaks of refugees as it did in my time [1980s]. The talk has grown hostile, even unhinged, and I have a hard time spotting, amid the angry hordes, the kind souls we knew' (Nayeri 2019, p. 12). And although '[i]t is changing and I would say that we have achieved an incredible amount, and yet... It's not all that good by far, so... basic things, things just do not necessarily get better' (Sabrina, NGO worker, Germany). There is much work still to be done to render the SOGI asylum system 'fit for purpose', both in terms of rendering the legal adjudication process more appropriate (Daniele, decision-maker, Italy) and to create a more supportive process of social integration (Titti, decision-maker, Italy).

The issues that need to be addressed are different in each domestic and even regional context, and any recommendations need to be tailored to a particular situation. Our recommendations address two broad problems. On the one hand, there are systematic and structural issues that require legal and policy reforms, including changes to asylum reception conditions and procedures. On the other hand, there is a widespread concern that these systems are arbitrary, and that decision-making in all countries is worryingly inconsistent: 'it is often remarked it is luck of the draw and that seems to be the, the biggest problem. It is so difficult to surmount because we are dealing with human beings' (Bilal, presenting officer, UK). Recommendations need to address both systemic issues and the 'lottery' functioning of the current SOGI asylum system.

Any set of recommendations also needs to reckon with the tensions that exist within any asylum system, for example, the difficulty in protecting the human rights of persecuted individuals within a hostile context where asylum is politicised for propaganda purposes and the state imperative of border control. Further tensions exist between promoting the welfare of claimants without invoking disempowering discourses of victimhood and vulnerability. Moreover, we should endeavour to undermine homonationalist discourses (Puar 2013). In this chapter, building on the approach set out in Chaps. 2 (Sect. 2.3) and 3, we make recommendations that attempt to reconcile such tensions so far as possible.

Our recommendations in this final chapter are divided into sections that approximately mirror the analysis in Chaps. 4, 5, 6, 7, 8, and 9. In Sect. 11.2, we discuss how to improve people's journeys to Europe and their reception in countries of arrival. In Sect. 11.3, we focus on how to enhance the RSD process, both in terms of procedures and substantive analysis. In Sect. 11.4, the focus shifts to the improvement of accommodation, housing and detention, and Sect. 11.5 is dedicated to recommendations concerning three main areas of life beyond the RSD process, namely in the fields of health, work and education. In Sect. 11.6, we put forward recommendations to ensure that the legal and social dimensions of SOGI asylum claimants and refugees' experiences are less disjointed and better aligned. Finally, in Sect. 11.7 we set out what we see as the underpinning values needed to guide a fair SOGI asylum system.

11.2 The Journey to Europe and Reception

As explored in Chap. 5, members of SOGI minorities seeking asylum in Europe often undergo horrifying experiences in their countries of origin forcing them to undergo long and risky journeys in the attempt to escape. European countries have a responsibility to reduce the risk of persecution in countries of origin through their external relations policies, including through EU structures and mechanisms:

> the European Union, in the past 10 years I think, has improved on working on LGBTI issues in third countries, but I think there is still a long way to go. So when we look at the situation of LGBTI people in many countries all over the world… it is still so deplorable, and I think that if we want to be credible… we really need to put a focus on this and say "no, these are really the minorities also that show you if there is an acceptance of human rights, if there is real democracy, if people are given the freedom to decide about their own lives." I would say that next to having an asylum system in place that meets the needs both of SOGI claimants as well as others… we also need to look at what can we actually do in the home countries to improve the situation (…) So, also really to do something about that, and to highlight that and to make this a priority of external, of the external action service. (Terry, member of the European Parliament)

The same point was made by refugee participants:

> So, if possible, European government can share this idea [of respect for SOGI minorities' rights] with African leaders to make their law, they can amend the law, they are the one who make the law, they can amend it, it is possible for them. So to amend the law, so that it is at least the country can be a little bit favourable to people, if not just favour them in a big way, just little bit. (Fido, focus group no. 4, northern Italy)

In line with the need to protect human rights and freedom while avoiding cultural essentialism (Chap. 3), such pressure through the EU's and domestic external relations policies needs to promote greater awareness of and respect for SOGI minorities' rights and needs, without exacerbating perceptions that human rights are a Western imposition serving economic interests and with little genuine wish to address the global inequalities that create (SOGI) asylum claims in the first place (Danisi 2017).

While the risk of persecution for members of SOGI minorities is the driver for flight from many countries, we also need to address the perilous journeys that these individuals undertake and the degrading conditions in which they are received on arrival in Europe:

> one must realise that a humanitarian catastrophe is already happening in Libya, but partly also from what happens to people in Greece, Hungary and Italy… This is really a humanitarian disaster that happens there. So that you do not then push more people into this, into this hell. (Sabrina, NGO worker, Germany)

To avoid these journeys, it is essential that humanitarian tools are introduced as a matter of urgency to allow asylum claimants – SOGI or otherwise – to reach Europe safely, in parallel to already more established mechanisms such as resettlement. This can be done through humanitarian admission programmes and, in particular, humanitarian visas that provide documentation to people in flight – a mechanism with a strong historical basis as well (Politzer and Hylton 2019). They could be operated through 'humanitarian corridors', similar to those facilitated by the Community of Sant'Egidio (Community of Sant'Egidio 2019). Some countries, like Germany,[1] already possess a legal basis for such initiatives, and these need to be used more systematically. Such humanitarian initiatives are, however, not yet regulated at a EU level and domestic authorities generally do not make such provision (Moreno-Lax 2019). This has prompted the European Parliament to support the creation of a Protected Entry Procedure (European Parliament 2018a, b), but binding measures are yet to be introduced.

In terms of reception, and in light of the context of general hostility to migrants in Europe, juxtaposed with persistent and in some cases increasing homophobia and transphobia and lack of information on SOGI asylum upon arrival (Chap. 5), it is essential to promote a more friendly and welcoming environment for SOGI asylum claimants and refugees. For these purposes, awareness efforts addressing potential and actual claimants and the wider public need to be intensified, through national and local dissemination of materials about the asylum system, and the rights of claimants. This should include information about SOGI asylum provided in different languages, graphic and easy-read formats, made available in places accessed by SOGI claimants – or by individuals entitled to claim asylum on a SOGI basis but who may not be aware of this fact. This might include airports and other transport hubs, medical facilities, schools and colleges, LGBTIQ+, refugee and migrant NGOs, and public spaces such as libraries (Fares, Germany; Knud, NGO worker, Germany; Juliane, public official, Germany).

Upon arrival and at the point of lodging an asylum claim, it is essential to offer claimants the opportunity – and indeed encourage them – to disclose any potential reason for needing protection, including their SOGI. One suggestion is to include a box about SOGI in a form alongside other optional questions (Kadir, NGO worker, Germany). Support in completing forms from trained staff and interpreters would be useful. However, there would need to be guidance for officials, to ensure there were no negative consequences for claimants who disclosed their SOGI only at a later stage in the asylum process, as many claimants will not feel sufficiently confident to mention their SOGI at this time. As we see in Italy (Chap. 6), such questions can be asked at the screening stage, without main interviewers or decision-makers penalising claimants who chose not to answer. Obtaining information on a voluntary basis in this way could facilitate the provision of more appropriate information and services throughout the remainder of the asylum process. More generally, forms should be designed to give as much flexibility to claimants to complete them based on their particular circumstances in terms of SOGI, as well as in all other aspects of their lives (ORAM 2016b). The identification of SOGI asylum claimants should lead to the automatic signposting of claimants to relevant groups,[2] in order to ensure

---

[1] §22 of the German Asylum Act regulates admission from abroad 'in accordance with international law or on urgent humanitarian grounds'.

[2] Regarding the training and funding required by these groups, see Sect. 11.6.

they receive more tailored and effective legal advice and social support (focus group no. 1, Hesse, Germany). This approach is reflective of a fairer sharing of responsibility amongst all asylum system actors, with asylum officers taking a more proactive approach to identifying SOGI claimants than is currently the case.

Whether SOGI asylum claimants should generally fall within a legal category of 'vulnerable' or not remains a contentious issue (Chap. 3). While this is not the case under the current EU legal framework, some local and regional practices and policies identify SOGI claimants as 'vulnerable' (Chap. 4). Some of the participants we interviewed were adamant that SOGI asylum claimants should be considered 'vulnerable' for purposes of the asylum process (Ibrahim, Germany; Matthias, social worker, Germany). Others were opposed to it because of the stigmatising effects of this kind of labelling and the risk of creating a hierarchy among asylum claimants, encouraging competition as to who is considered the 'most vulnerable' to obtain some 'advantage' in terms of support or provision (Noah, NGO social worker, Germany). Finally, the 'vulnerable' label can be seen as an easy remedy, but one that conflates vastly different kinds of disadvantage, discrimination and exclusion (Peroni and Timmer 2013, p. 1071). If the designation 'vulnerable' is retained in relation to asylum claimants, it should only be with the recognition that vulnerability is not an inherent characteristic but derives from circumstances and experiences and is – it is to be hoped – a temporary state (Peroni and Timmer 2013, pp. 1059–1061; Chap. 3).

The move to the notion of 'specific needs' in the current CEAS reform largely addresses the shortcomings of the notion of 'vulnerability' (Chap. 4), as it shifts the debate from 'labelling' someone as vulnerable (or more vulnerable than other claimants) to addressing the specific needs of each individual, in this way avoiding stigmatising whole categories of asylum claimants as somehow lacking in capacity or resourcefulness. Rather than creating hierarchies built upon generalisations, actors in the asylum system should strive to make individual assessments that address the needs of each claimant in a sensitive manner (Noah, NGO social worker, Germany), as already required by human rights law (Chap. 3).

To this extent, we favour including SOGI claimants amongst those likely to have specific needs, which may trigger adaptions to make the asylum system more responsive to SOGI needs. This would ensure SOGI claimants receive information and services tailored to their circumstances, such as details about the legal framework relating to SOGI in the host country, the availability of SOGI specific accommodation, confidentiality obligations, freedom to 'come out', etc. (Gisela, lawyer, Germany). This also has an impact on the RSD process, to which we now turn.

11.3 The Asylum Application Process

RSD processes have the pernicious ability 'to flatten out difference, demand simplicity over nuance, and compel the distillation of messy, complicated lives down to a manageable set of narrative fragments' (Macklin 2011, p. 137). SOGI asylum claims are generally anything but simple, and the legal process needs to recognise and deal with that in a respectful and targeted manner, compatible with the human rights, feminist and queer analytical underpinnings outlined in Chap. 3.

11.3.1 Institutional and Policy Framework

Asylum adjudication agencies should be immune from the 'politics of the day' in delivering human rights compliant decisions, and one way to achieve this may be moving towards independent or semi-independent UNHCR-like models. The inclusion of UNHCR representatives as members of the Italian territorial commissions increases the quality of decision-making, at least to the extent of ensuring that decisions adhere to relevant UNHCR guidelines. We thus espouse ECRE's recommendation that:

> caseworkers should work in an institutional environment that is adequately human rights and protection-oriented, regardless of any EU or national interest. The main objective for determining authorities should always be protection, namely to identify applicants who qualify for international protection. ECRE thus warns against the placement of determining authorities within Ministries which follow certain objectives at the expense of the asylum seekers' right to a fair and transparent asylum procedure. (AIDA and ECRE 2019, p. 57)

Although our decision-maker participants said that the rules of individual assessment were followed (Olivia, UK), there was a strong suspicion amongst many of our participants – both claimants and supporters – that public authorities operate some kind of quota system (Chap. 4). We also saw in our fieldwork that claims regarding some countries of origin are more rigorously inspected, viewed with scepticism and have a higher rate of refusal. Despite the lack of objective evidence that quotas exist, the perception on the part of some claimants that they do reflects the broadly hostile climate that exists towards migrants and refugees in Europe, and the not unreasonable belief that this leads to attempts by decision-makers to minimise the number of successful claims. Any sort of quotas or targets should be eliminated, as they are in contravention with international refugee law and our human rights analytical underpinnings (Chap. 3).

As we saw in Chap. 4, not all domestic asylum systems provide SOGI guidelines, which leaves decision-makers unsupported and claimants at the mercy of unreliable and inconsistent standards of decision-making. Even when SOGI guidelines exist, their application is often inadequate:

> The Home Office's own published policy is extremely well informed, I mean, it is a very good [policy], people would be quite amazed, and if anyone who is transgender had a claim, and the Home Office applied its own policy, they would very, very likely succeed. (Adrian, judge, UK)

All asylum adjudication authorities should introduce SOGI guidelines (where there are none) and ensure they are applied consistently (when there are guidelines but they are applied inconsistently, as in the UK), to ensure consistency within each jurisdiction (Giuseppe, lawyer, Italy).

11.3 The Asylum Application Process

Any transparent and accountable asylum system needs to keep and publish rigorous and up-to-date statistics on different types of asylum claims and their outcomes, including SOGI-based claims. Statistics should not only include the number of SOGI claims submitted, but also what grounds are used to refuse or accept them (Kadir, NGO worker, Germany). This would also provide an evidence basis for measuring the successes and shortcomings of SOGI asylum decision-making. Reasons put forward to avoid the production of such statistics – for example, costs, confidentiality, data privacy, etc. – remain unconvincing and can be easily addressed.

As much as policy and guidance, the successes and shortcomings of any determination process depend on who the decision-makers are. Our fieldwork and analysis prompt a number of recommendations in relation to decision-makers. In terms of the selection process, the qualifications required for UK Home Office officials were a concern:

> some of my colleagues are... have a legal background, so they have done a law degree and they have either done the bar or they have done the LPC [legal practice course] and they seem to have, again just observationally, they seem to have an advantage over new entrants that don't have any such background. (…) I thought it was better when we asked for a legal background, because it makes much more sense, obviously, and it [UK] is such a case law heavy jurisdiction, so, very peculiar choice [not to require a law degree], I think. (Bilal, presenting officer)

A legal qualification should not necessarily be a requirement to become a decision-maker, as good decision-makers may have different academic and professional qualifications (Vincenzo, LGBTIQ+ group volunteer, Italy; Filippo, senior judge, Italy). Yet, appropriate qualifications are necessary to ensure a high standard of decision-making. Participants were practically unanimous that, once selected, decision-makers at both the administrative and judicial level should receive a minimum level of training in SOGI asylum – including not only asylum law and policy, but also more general matters such as equality and unconscious bias – and undergo a period of shadowing before making decisions autonomously on asylum claims (Sect. 11.6). As analysed in Chap. 6, the duration of training at administrative level was also of concern. For example, the 5-week general training received by the case-workers at the UK Home Office, including one single day on SOGI matters, was believed to be insufficient by decision-makers themselves, even if complemented by 'shadowing' more experienced decision-makers and mentoring (David, official). A positive development in this respect is the new systematic training programme started in 2018 in Italy, in cooperation with the UNHCR.

The task of adjudicating asylum claims is an arduous and complex one, and, as a result, asylum agencies should ensure they have sufficient senior caseworkers to provide effective mentoring and oversight of new and junior caseworkers. Something similar to the 'bulletin of jurisprudence for the Cour Nationale du Droit d'Asile'[3] (Amanda, NGO worker, Brussels) could help decision-makers at both

---

[3] A regular summary of asylum case law developments to support the work of asylum practitioners and decision-makers: http://www.cnda.fr/Ressources-juridiques-et-geopolitiques/Actualite-jurisprudentielle/Bulletins-et-notes-juridiques-de-la-CNDA.

administrative and appeal levels to remain up-to-date with latest developments in specific asylum areas, including SOGI asylum. Governments should provide flexible working conditions, career breaks, and appropriate forms of staff support to help caseworkers avoid burn-out, recover from vicarious trauma and prevent desensitisation. As Helena, an EASO staff member, shared with us, counselling or support for decision-makers is not common, not even in the wealthiest administrations. We heard that those working in the asylum system for more than 2 years are highly likely to experience vicarious trauma or burn out. As Helena pointed out, it is almost impossible not to be affected by listening to stories of war, rape and torture, and the easiest response is to stop believing those stories. Deirdre, a lawyer in the UK, shared similar concerns about Home Office staff:

> I think they can become desensitised. I mean, that is what can happen. That's the risk, that you become so exposed to it, so exposed to it that you do to protect yourself and how you are feeling, you almost try and close the door and it is just words, it is just words.

It should go without saying that career progression in decision-making bodies should in no way be related to the number of rejections or grants of international protection that officers produce, as some of our participants suspect happens in some countries, even if unofficially (Thomas, NGO volunteer, Germany).

We heard different opinions about who is best placed to make SOGI asylum decisions, recognising the inevitable limitation of any individual decision-maker in light of the intersecting characteristics of each claimant:

> you can provide training but I think there is a limit to the amount that you can provide, because you cannot also expect each officer to be fully versed in LGBTI issues but in also issues to do with minors and to do with different races and religions and so on. (Jules, staff member at ILGA-Europe)

A corollary of this may be that caseworkers should specialise in one area, for example SOGI asylum, and all such claims should be allocated to those caseworkers; such specialised caseworkers might then form units specialising in and pooling expertise on SOGI claims (Frank S., legal advisor, Germany; Diana, Germany; Milad, Germany). This is already the case in some countries: for example, Sweden and Switzerland have SOGI specialist caseworkers, Belgium and France have specialised Gender and SOGI Units, and Germany covers SOGI under the umbrella of gender-specific units (AIDA and ECRE 2019, p. 11; European Migration Network 2016). This could also apply to the judiciary, with a survey respondent suggesting that 'LGBTQI people should be judged by judges who are experts in lgbtqi issues' (S152, NGO volunteer, Italy), however our focus is on better training for all judges.

Different types of cases may indeed require different skill-sets and even mind-sets: 'every now and again you might get an LGBT claim thrown in, in my diary, my scheduling, so if I haven't done any LGBT for a couple of months, then all of a sudden "right, Monday morning, I have got an LGBT interview", it is really difficult because you are trying to get back into that frame of mind' (Qasim, decision-maker,

11.3 The Asylum Application Process

UK). Nonetheless, specialisation is not a guarantee of quality, and has risks relating to saturation and the development of cynicism regarding certain narratives and types of issues (Evelyne and Anne, lawyers, Germany). Consequently, while there may be arguments in favour of specialisation – in relation to SOGI asylum – the priority should instead be on improving training, shadowing, mentoring and staff welfare measures. Specialised units could be framed broadly, for example encompassing gender-based violence and SOGI (as is the case in Germany), to ensure decision-makers have the necessary skills to deal with more complex but often interrelated and overlapping claims. However, as important as expertise on the part of decision-makers is the willingness to reach out and network with other 'experts':

> but in a large part also facilitating really good connections between them and organisations that are specialised in LGBTI issues (...) So, recognise that no single organisation and no single person can be an expert in everything, but that if you can network the organisations with their respective expertise, that they can then support each other in that way. (Jules, staff member at ILGA-Europe)

SOGI awareness and competences should, in any case, be mainstreamed across all public (as well as NGO and support) services, as any asylum claimant may be LGBTIQ+ and any LGBTIQ+ person may be an asylum claimant (Portman and Weyl 2013, p. 45).

As explored in Chap. 6, some participants have suggested that more decision-makers should be LGBTIQ+ themselves (William, Germany; Veronica, Germany; Alphaeus, Germany). A caseworker's SOGI is obviously no assurance of the quality or fairness of their decision-making, and during our fieldwork we heard of LGBTIQ+ decision-makers relying excessively (even inappropriately) on their personal experiences and beliefs to assess SOGI asylum claims. Whether or not some form of positive discrimination would be viable or useful, it is important to ensure decision-makers dealing with SOGI claims do not hold homophobic or transphobic views, as has been done in the USA (Sridharan 2008). Aside from any specific measures to ensure that decision-makers on SOGI asylum claims are aware of and sensitive to the needs of these groups of claimants, they should, of course be complying with equality and human rights law and guidance more broadly, relating to sexual orientation and gender identity, but also to 'race', gender, disability, age, and religion or belief. In the UK, employees in public bodies should go further than simply refraining from discrimination to positively promote equality of opportunity under the Equality Act 2010. And recruiting a diverse workforce is now recognised as good practice in most employment contexts, whether in the public, private or voluntary sector: the Home Office, the BAMF and the territorial commissions in Italy should be encouraging recruitment of SOGI minorities, just as they should be encouraging applications for decision-making posts from members of all under-represented groups in society.

Finally, country of origin knowledge is so critical to SOGI (and other) claims that asylum authorities should explore the possibility of allocating caseloads on the basis of staff members' country-specific understanding. This already happens to some extent in Germany and 'enables caseworkers to gain in-depth knowledge of the general situation prevailing in the countries of origin of applicants, which helps to ensure an accurate and appropriate assessment of the circumstances surrounding the application' (AIDA and ECRE 2019, p. 12). To combat possible desensitisation, this approach again needs to be complemented by high-quality training, shadowing, mentoring and staff welfare measures.

Once criteria are established to allocate cases to certain caseworkers – including a certain degree of specialisation, as described above – the screening interview should be used to identify the most appropriate interviewer for the main, substantive interview (Alphaeus, Germany), as already done, at least informally, in some territorial commissions in Italy. Guidance should prompt selected caseworkers (and also judges) to be honest in recognising their limited knowledge and skills (Titti, decision-maker, Italy). This may mean suspending interviews on occasions, or calling in a more experienced colleague, or postponing the interview until such a colleague is available, or scheduling a second interview to ask for further clarification and build on previous questions on the basis of knowledge the interviewer may have acquired subsequently. The same is true for appeal hearings.

Finally, on the matter of whether the interviewer and the decision-maker should be the same person or not, those participants who expressed an opinion about it favoured combining both roles in the same individual (Daniele, decision-maker). This solution facilitates the comprehensive use of all evidence gathered throughout the interview, including non-verbal cues and the claimant's demeanour, although it is important that these are not interpreted on the basis of cultural, hetero or cisnormative or any other kind of stereotype. This may help to avoid depersonalising the claim and objectifying the claimant. Combining the role of interviewer with that of decision-maker should also contribute to quicker, but no less rigorous, decision-making. A peer-review mechanism can help avoid any risk of loss of objectivity, especially in case the first decision proposed is negative (Jansen 2019, p. 124).

11.3.2 Procedural Rules

Asylum adjudication procedures are one of the key elements of SOGI claimants' overall experiences, and have therefore been a focus for recommendations (Hruschka 2019; Jansen and Spijkerboer 2011). Although the nature of the procedure – adversarial, inquisitorial or mixed – was used as one of the criteria to choose the country case studies (Chap. 2), our analysis did not reveal significant differences for SOGI claimants on account of that element in particular. Instead, a problem that very many of our participants raised was the length of time that the asylum process takes (Chap. 6). We heard of the terrible impact this has on claimants:

> at least to consider the amount of time they keep people in asylum, because now they are psychologically damaging people who would have made a positive impact on the economy

11.3 The Asylum Application Process

or something, but people now get out of this and end up just maybe being on benefits because they have forgotten themselves, they have lost themselves. (Jayne, UK)

Many of the participants in our research thus highlighted the need for 'quicker decision making' (S8, NGO worker, UK), a 'clearer process, less dragged out' (S74, NGO volunteer, UK), and believed that to 'make the process quicker definitely helps' (C50, UK). Speed should be complemented by greater consistency: 'And I think in general the system needs to have clear dates and outlines of... this waiting without knowing when [you will get a decision] is very difficult for people to deal with' (Halim, Germany).

Nonetheless, speed should not come at the price of lower standards in decision-making or fewer procedural safeguards, as it is often the case in accelerated procedures (Chap. 6). Shorter procedural deadlines may undermine the capacity of SOGI claimants to prepare adequately and present their case effectively:

> give them time to be prepared for the asylum or how to present their case, and don't use the fact of that we have to do it fast, fast, fast, to finish the procedure. Because some people don't know what to speak, don't know what to say. Maybe they faced violence, maybe they faced discrimination, but they don't know that they have to say it. (Ibrahim, Germany)

Ibrahim, along with several other participants, thus advised against placing SOGI claimants in fast-track or accelerated procedures (S119, NGO worker, Germany; Noah, NGO social worker, Germany). A quicker process must never be at the expense of a fair and individualised assessment.

An important aspect in this respect is the notion of 'safe country of origin', which is often the basis for fast-tracking an asylum claim (Chap. 6). Importantly, countries listed as 'safe' by domestic authorities are anything but safe for SOGI minorities:

> look at how many trans women have been killed in Turkey in the last five years (…). So, as long as we accept that as a reality, I think more and more people will say "then I have no choice but to leave this country". (Terry, member of the European Parliament)

Our recommendation is that the notion of 'safe country of origin' is inappropriate in general, but certainly for SOGI claims, as even countries with a generally good human rights record may be unsafe for SOGI minorities (Ferreira et al. 2018). Our participants were also of this opinion, arguing that asylum claims should rely purely on individual assessments, according to IRL and IHRL (Chap. 3).

Alongside the speed of the procedure, participants were generally adamant that the interview environment needs to be considerably improved: 'Making the process gentle is very important!' (C50, UK) The interviewing technique needs to be made less intimidating and decision-makers should adopt a kinder and more empathic style, as well as being more open to hearing the claimant (Evelyne and Anne, lawyers, Germany). As Mara, a lawyer in Italy, recommended, 'they [interviewers] should have adequate preparation to do the interview with serenity and try to understand who is in front of them'. She stressed the need for empathy to be established in the interview.

Following the example provided by Titti, a decision-maker in Italy, which was explored in Chap. 6, this may entail using more neutral locations, the decision-maker should introduce themselves, ask if the claimant has any questions before starting the interview, explain that the claimant should feel confident and secure in expressing their opinion and thoughts. It may help to start with some 'small talk', ensure claimants feel at ease by offering them breaks, a glass of water, etc., and perhaps even say something like 'you know, we're both here, [I know] it's not going to be easy, [but] try to give as much as you can' (Emily, decision-maker, UK). Participants also emphasised that '[w]e should be given enough time during the interview and with some time to relax' (C38, Germany). To ensure this empathetic environment, decision-makers should adopt the terms used by SOGI asylum claimants to describe themselves (unless the terms are pejorative) and refer to their circumstances in a manner consistent with the relevant COI, avoiding Eurocentric perceptions (Helena, EASO staff member). Creating an atmosphere conducive to open disclosure by the claimant also means ensuring interviews are carried out in a private setting, confidentiality is respected by the interviewer and also by any interpreter or third part present, and explaining this to claimants to make sure that they are confident that this is the case (Breen and Millo 2013, p. 56). This is an issue that particularly needs to be addressed in the context of the first, 'screening' interview (Livio, lawyer, Italy), often held in large and semi-public spaces.

Integral to building a trusting relationship is adopting a 'stage-by-stage approach' during the main interview, whereby each time period of the claimant's journey and each relevant issue is dealt with in turn and at an appropriate pace. This allows for adequate exploration of issues (Sofia and Emma, NGO workers, Germany), gives the opportunity to claimants to clarify any apparent contradictions, and renders the overall interview experience less stressful and traumatising for the claimant. SOGI asylum interviews should be based on neutral, open-ended questions that interviewers can adapt as they see fit, but which are the starting point for the interview.

Some participants also suggested that claimants should be able to ask for a different interviewer, not only on grounds of gender but also religious belief and ethnic or national origin, where the interviewer's identity is likely to inhibit the claimant in responding. Although respecting such preferences could be seen as discriminatory towards the interviewer and would in many contexts be considered unjustifiable (Chap. 6), we submit that the asylum system's core concern should be to deliver fair decision-making. If that requires – under certain limited circumstances and without breaching equality principles or law – the replacement of an interviewer to facilitate more open testimony, then asylum agencies should allow it (Ferreira et al. 2018).

Besides the interviewer, another key actor in the interview setting is the interpreter, whose role was a concern for many participants (Chap. 6). Such concerns related to the interpreter's gender, religious beliefs, ethnicity and, more importantly, their sensitivity towards SOGI matters. All these factors may have an impact on the quality of the interpretation and atmosphere of the interview, so great care needs to be taken in the choice of interpreter (Shany, Germany). Public authorities should also ensure interpreters have appropriate training (Sect. 11.6) and be open to replacing them when claimants do not feel confident speaking openly not only because of the interpreter's sex/gender but also religious belief or ethnic or national origin (Ferreira et al. 2018).

Another important participant in the process – sometimes striking for their absence – is the legal representative. Our participants' concerns about asylum legal representation are the basis for a number of important recommendations. In light of the issues discussed in this regard in Chap. 6, legal representation should be not only available, but also compulsory and supported through legal aid from the start of the process; in other words, not only at appeal, but also at administrative level (C3, Germany; S57, NGO volunteer, UK; S141, NGO worker, Germany; Noah, NGO social worker, Germany; Nazarena, lawyer, Italy; Hruschka 2019). By securing free legal representation even before the screening process, potential claimants will be able to understand the possible grounds on which they can claim asylum and how to prepare their initial claim (Sofia and Emma, NGO workers, Germany; Giuseppe, lawyer, Italy; Daniele, decision-maker, Italy; Right to Remain 2019). Moreover, if members of SOGI minorities receive legal support before they submit their claims, they are more likely to file well prepared and credible asylum claims, avoiding the likelihood of a refusal and the costs to all parties of going through an appeal (Held et al. 2018).

This approach extends to ensuring access to legal representatives and to NGOs offering legal advice for claimants living in detention and accommodation centres, as well as at hearings. In Germany and Italy, in particular, the presence of the legal representative in interviews was seen as important (Thomas, NGO volunteer, Germany; Nazarena, lawyer, Italy). Where no free legal representation is available at administrative level, then independent legal advice and information by NGOs should be guaranteed. Alternatively, reception staff and accommodation centres' staff should be trained to assist claimants in producing their personal statements, as happens in the Italian accommodation system, providing that the quality and independence of such support can be ensured (Chap. 8). In short, participants were adamant that the quality and availability of legal advice and representation must improve (S74, NGO volunteer, UK).

Although the claimant, interviewer and interpreter (or language mediator) are usually the only actors present at the interview, several participants argued for allowing supporters to be present, at least at the main interview. This helps reducing the power imbalances that characterise an asylum interview (Daniele, decision-maker, Italy; Giuseppe, lawyer, Italy). Where supporters are present at appeal hearings, the positive effect this has on claimants' confidence is palpable (Court observation, Hesse, 2018; Tribunal observation, northern Italy, 2018). A further way of empowering claimants, while also improving the credibility and transparency of asylum systems, would be to introduce and effectively establish an accessible and accountable complaints system (Noah, NGO social worker, Germany; Frank S., legal advisor, Germany; Barbara, lawyer, Germany), covering the roles of interviewers, decision-makers or interpreters. This should go hand-in-hand with strong quality assurance and control mechanisms (AIDA and ECRE 2019, p. 58).

In any asylum claim, the claimant's testimony and evidence should be considered alongside the available COI, as discussed in Chap. 6. In this regard our participants recommended that the quality of COI urgently needs to be improved, that there should be more SOGI-specific information available, and that similar COI should be available and used more widely throughout the EU. As pointed out by Roberto, a decision-maker in Italy, the poor quality of COI in some countries, as in Germany and Italy, seems to coexist with the danger, particularly in the UK, of using COI as 'mathematical models' leading to automatic conclusions regarding asylum claims. It is therefore necessary not only to improve the quality of COI, but also to use it in an appropriate and individualised manner. Even when SOGI-specific COI exists, its focus on persecution can be problematic when the country in question does not criminalise same-sex acts, does not enforce those laws, or has just recently repealed them. SOGI-specific COI needs to cover a range of aspects related to the legal and social experiences of SOGI minorities and go well beyond broad-brush generalisations about country conditions for them. To achieve this, and inspired by practices and proposals of some social and NGO workers in Italy (Valentina, social worker; Vincenzo, LGBTIQ+ group volunteer), NGOs in the countries of origin concerned might be invited to contribute to the production of COI, always recognising that the quality of any contributions would need to be assessed (McNeal 2019). Finally, in terms of rendering COI of greater European application, EASO has made a significant contribution, including in relation to SOGI-specific matters (EASO 2015), and we recommend that EASO further develops the provision of accurate SOGI-specific COI, and that decision-makers make better use of this material.

The Dublin system was another matter of concern and basis for recommendations from our participants. The pending reform of the Dublin Regulation will need to review the criteria in place for allocation of responsibility to a state for a given asylum claim, while addressing the specific needs of asylum claimants, including SOGI claimants, and ending the inhumane practice of transfers of people between EU countries. As analysed in Chap. 6, current Dublin rules throw claimants – very often SOGI claimants as well – into situations of stark uncertainty and although many claimants cannot be returned to the country of first entry in the EU for practical or legal reasons, they become involved in protracted legal and administrative processes while efforts at their social integration are inadequate (Louis, NGO volunteer, Germany; Susanna, social worker, Italy). We recommend that EU institutions collaborate in the context of the CEAS reform to achieve a more humane system, one that allocates responsibility for asylum adjudication to member states in light of criteria that are more in tune to SOGI claimants' needs and rights, such as family and other personal connections, cultural background, linguistic knowledge and protection of SOGI minorities.

At the appeal stage, and as with administrative-level interviews, improvements need to be made to the environment in which hearings take place. There needs to be greater consistency in the way that judges treat claimants: they should always be respectful, demonstrate cultural sensitivity, and use the pronouns preferred by the claimants. All judicial authorities should develop a code of conduct that encompasses rules on these matters, with a focus on equality, diversity and fairness, similar to the UK Equal Treatment Bench Book (Judicial College 2018). There must also be measures in place, such as induction and training, to ensure that all judges are familiar with and apply such codes.

A question of particular importance in the Italian context is the removal of the claimant's entitlement to be heard in person in case of appeal. This is no longer a statutory obligation, and only happens when the judge (or legal representative) asks to hear the claimant rather than simply relying on the recording of the claimant's interview with the territorial commissions (Chap. 6). Although this can have advantages such as not re-traumatising the claimant, it prevents the judge from requesting clarification and eliciting further information directly, and risks depersonalising the asylum claimant in the eyes of the judge. We recommend that judges ask to hear the claimant in person whenever possible, and particularly when they are inclined to reject the appeal.

The recommendations above would contribute to fairer asylum procedures that, in turn, may influence positively the asylum claim determination.

11.3.3 The Asylum Claim Determination

As we discussed in Chap. 7, asylum adjudicators need to engage with the range of international protection alternatives available within their legal system and the requirements for each one of these alternatives. The ultimate aim for SOGI – as for all – claimants is to obtain refugee status under the Refugee Convention, and reach a point of stability and security, where the full spectrum of their human rights is respected in the host country. To provide meaningful international protection, the narrow definition of a refugee under the Refugee Convention should be broadened by encompassing human rights law more consistently than is currently the case, in line with the approach outlined in Chap. 3. As such a development is unlikely in the current political context, here we concentrate on more realistic and pragmatic possibilities.

The first logical step in the substantive assessment of a SOGI asylum claim – determining the ground that is the basis for claiming asylum – generally consists in establishing the claimant's membership of a PSG (Chap. 7). Our first recommendation in this regard is for decision-makers to also consider grounds for claiming asylum besides membership of a PSG, such as political or religious belief. Recognition of the multiple and intersecting grounds for claiming protection would better recognise the many factors and identities that are the basis for persecution, in line with our feminist and queer theoretical underpinnings (Chap. 3), and as supported by a large body of literature on intersectional discrimination and beyond (Macklin 1995; Markard 2016; Solanke 2009; Verloo 2006). Some of our participants (Sofia and Emma, NGO workers, Germany) argued that establishing membership of a SOGI minority in case of countries of origin where persecution of SOGI minorities is widespread should suffice to grant international protection, without the need for evidence of individual persecution. While this may be desirable, establishing individual persecution is at the heart of IRL, and in that context, our recommendations focus more, not less, on the specific circumstances of the individual. However, we do recommend that establishing membership of a SOGI minority be done on two bases, as has been already recognised in case law at EU and national level: first, the recognition that 'objectively proving' a claimant's SOGI is an impossible task, no matter whether the focus is placed on the claimant's identity or behaviour, as identities are complex, fluid, and develop in culturally specific contexts (Chap. 3); second, actual membership of a PSG is secondary, as *perceived* membership is the relevant issue (Ferreira and Venturi 2018; UNHCR 2012, para. 41).[4]

The second logical step in the asylum claim assessment – assessing the risk of persecution – has also been the object of recommendations by our participants. The most important of these relates to the need to follow the law in adopting a more appropriate (lower) threshold for determining what constitutes persecution (Elias, lawyer, Germany; Chap. 7). Furthermore, the risk of persecution needs to be assessed using the human rights analytical underpinnings delineated in Chap. 3. Although it is a battle that appears to have been won in most legal systems, there is still a need to increase awareness of the role, importance and impact of persecution by private actors in the context of international protection (Gisela, lawyer, Germany), as well as of the need for adequate verification of the reasons why protection by country of origin's authorities is not available in these cases.

Whether or not the criminalisation of same-sex acts in the country of origin should suffice to make a finding of persecution was a concern for our participants. Such criminal laws – whether enforced or not – lead to stigmatisation, victimisation, blackmail and increased vulnerability to degrading treatment, sometimes including torture. The mere existence of criminal laws should therefore, according to several authors, be recognised as persecutory (Bejzyk 2017; Jansen and Spijkerboer 2011). The fact that Italian Supreme Court case law has also taken this approach gives SOGI asylum researchers and activists a weapon for campaigning to extend this approach (Danisi 2019; Jansen and Spijkerboer 2011).[5] We add our voice to theirs in recommending that criminalisation of same-sex acts should suffice to make a finding of risk of persecution for the purpose of granting international protection.

Similarly, it is indisputable that there remain traces of 'discretion reasoning' in asylum adjudication in Europe when determining the risk of persecution (Chap. 7). These traces need to be eliminated (Elias, lawyer, Germany; Beth, lawyer, UK), because decision-makers should 'not tell people to change who they are so that [they can] live' (C59, UK). To achieve this, greater abidance by CJEU jurisprudence prohibiting 'discretion reasoning' – namely the decision in *X, Y and Z* – is recommended (Louis, NGO volunteer, Germany). Still in the context of assessing the risk of persecution, we also recommend that decision-makers develop a more acute understanding that there are no internal relocation alternatives in most cases of SOGI asylum claims (Sofia and Emma, NGO workers, Germany).

Our recommendations relating to the standard and burden of proof are largely prompted by our participants' direct experiences. First, decision-makers must keep

---

[4] Case C-473/16, *F v Bevándorlási és Állampolgársági Hivatal*, Judgment of the Court of Justice of the EU, 25 January 2018, ECLI:EU:C:2018:36, paras. 31–32; Italian Supreme Court, decision no. 2875, 6 February 2018.

[5] Decision no. 15981, 20 September 2012; judgment no. 11176, 27 February 2019.

11.3 The Asylum Application Process

uppermost in their minds that the applicable standard of proof is only to a 'reasonable degree' and take far more seriously than at present the principle of the benefit of the doubt (Chap. 7). As one participant said, there needs to be '[p]roper adherence to the low standard of proof (refusals are made too often without real reason)' (S114, lawyer, UK). The burden of proof is to be shared between the claimant and asylum authorities, as clearly stated by the UNHCR (1998, para. 6, 2011, para. 196) and recognised by high judicial instances.[6] In this respect, ECRE rightly points out that 'it is crucial that determining authorities have sufficient financial resources at their disposal to conduct a thorough and rigorous assessment of the application, especially where it includes gathering information and evidence by their own means' (AIDA and ECRE 2019, p. 26). There are, however, proposals for going further than this and using the reversal of the burden of proof in asylum law, as happens in discrimination law (Network of Legal Experts in the Non-Discrimination Field 2015). One of our participants (who asked to remain anonymous) argued that we should reverse the burden of proof and that it should be for the authorities to prove that a claimant should not be granted international protection once claimants put forward what – at least at first – seems to be an overall believable claim.[7] This is a bold, but interesting avenue of reform, which has the potential to rebalance the power dynamics in the asylum process. Whether or not it is explored further, adjudication authorities need to adopt a more proactive approach in collecting information that may confirm claimants' claims (as the Italian judiciary has defended – Sect. 7.4, Chap. 7), and not dispute minor facts and small points of evidence submitted in order to dismiss a claim, as so often happens at present.

As for forms of evidence, here there is much scope for improvement. One of the gravest concerns is decision-makers' expectation to have evidence – even if only in the form of personal testimony – pertaining to very personal and private aspects of claimants' lives. Although decision-makers should by now be aware that no evidence of a sexual nature should be elicited or accepted, we saw in Chap. 7 (Sect. 7.4.2) that in all three country case studies lines of questioning may be excessively sexualised. Our participants were adamant that decision-makers need '[t]o stop asking private sex questions to asylum seekers who are LGBT just to prove that they're LGBT people' (C53, UK) and that 'during the interview asking people questions to do with their bedroom should stop because most of these are so embarrassing not only to us but also to the interviewers' (C38, Germany), something reiterated by several other participants (C59, UK; S121, lawyer, UK; Christina, UK). While sexually explicit evidence is rarely solicited or accepted, the dismissive attitude of authorities in relation to other evidence provided then puts indirect pressure on claimants to provide details of an intimate nature (ICIBI 2014, p. 29). More generally, the type of evidence expected and how it is elicited need to be more culturally

---

[6] Italian Supreme Court, decisions no. 9946, 19 April 2017; no. 26921, 28 September 2017.

[7] In technical terms, this is termed establishing a *prima facie* case, in other words, creating the appearance of a case.

462   11 Believing in Something Better: Our Recommendations

and socially sensitive, requiring a greater level of sophistication and tailoring by decision-makers:

> So it is one thing I would emphasise, BAMF should look at that, the evidence that it asks for people, normally it is hard to get. Or people were not in the position of getting it. You are running for your life, you're in big trauma, you're in fear and now you're taking a selfie or you're recording voices?!. (William, Germany)

> I've been dealing with 16/17 year olds who can't read or write, you have a greater perception of how to interview them if you know the context. I mean, a person who can't read the clock, you'll know that you'll have to ask him if it was day or night, "was it before or after Ramadan?"... and not "what month was it". (Roberto, decision-maker, Italy)

In order to respect claimants' sense of personhood and autonomy, self-identification should be the default position (Hinger 2010, p. 405) and starting point for any asylum determination process. The burden of proof should then be on the authorities to find evidence negating the claimed SOGI, and any such evidence would need to be carefully analysed. More generally, lines of questioning should avoid implicitly assuming the claimant's lack of credibility:

> if you feel that you are under a lot of pressure, if you feel that this is an interrogation, and not so much an open discourse or something like that, probably the stress level is absolutely high and then maybe also wrong findings are much more likely. So I think it is actually in the interests of both sides that there is a process and a procedure put in place that gives the space to tell the stories, and then to grant asylum on the basis of that. (Terry, member of the European Parliament)

An open line of questioning is essential to develop the trusting relationships that lead to good decision-making:

> And then to open up about something that makes you even more vulnerable, that just takes time and it takes trust and so if you have... officials and/or interpreters who really understand it and actually are able to express it and convey it and develop this trust with people, I think that is honestly the only real way, [it] is through conversation, because each individual is individual. (Jules, staff member at ILGA-Europe)

Credibility assessment, being the crux of the matter in most asylum claims (Chap. 7), deserves careful consideration. First and foremost, the '[c]ulture of disbelief must go' (C58, UK). Determination systems need to change so that decision-makers do not adopt as default position that asylum claimants are lying, a point that was made repeatedly during our fieldwork – and in all three countries (Kadir, NGO worker, Germany; Maria Grazia, decision-maker, Italy; S74, NGO volunteer, UK). Credibility assessment also needs to be conducted in a culturally sensitive manner and responsive to individual circumstances, rather than based on stereotypes related to SOGI (or any other characteristics). This affects how interviews are carried out and decisions reached: besides not basing the credibility assessment of claimants on stereotypes, authorities need to 'give more context to the applicant's history' (S106, lawyer, Italy). We reject the CJEU's assertion that 'questions based on stereotyped notions may be a useful element'.[8] On the contrary, stereotypes should have no bearing on the assessment of a claimant's membership of a SOGI minority; any stereotypes will necessarily rely on Western understandings of SOGI, and also be racialised, gendered and class-based (Chap. 3). Accepting stereotypes is in inherent conflict with the individualised approach that is the basis of refugee law, and should be abandoned as a component of decision-making (ICIBI 2014, pp. 26–27).

Decision-makers also need to move away from the range of prejudices explored in Chap. 7, such as the belief that proving SOGI depends on having a partner: 'I wish the decision makers would change their mentality of expecting that every LGBTQI person should have a partner before going to the interview. For someone who went through a traumatising situation it's not that easy' (C37, Germany). It should also be irrelevant how a claimant 'performs' their SOGI, for instance how they dress or socialise (Helena, EASO staff member), and little weight should be placed on 'late disclosures' as such, in line with the CJEU decision in *A, B and C* (Ferreira et al. 2018). In short, credibility assessment needs to be carried out more carefully, negative assessments of credibility need to be better justified by making appropriate use of COI (Nazarena, lawyer, Italy) and more trust needs to be placed on evidence – particularly the personal testimony – submitted by claimants (Amanda, NGO worker, Brussels).

If a decision to grant international protection is made, then it should most commonly be refugee status, as subsidiary protection and humanitarian protection are in most circumstances not legally appropriate for SOGI claimants. Furthermore, legal statuses should entail residence permits of longer duration than currently exists in most states,[9] so that beneficiaries of international protection have enough time to recover from the ordeals many of them have gone through and can start to integrate in the host country (Bebars, Germany). Freedom of movement within the host country, as well as within the EU, should be facilitated (Marlen, legal advisor, Germany). If international protection is denied, it is unacceptable that 'people [are] removed before they can properly explore avenues to stay' (S57, NGO volunteer, UK). Removal is also frequently connected to detention and accommodation, to which we now turn.

---

[8] Joined Cases C-199/12, C-200/12 and C-201/12, *X, Y and Z v Minister voor Immigratie, Integratie en Asiel*, 7 November 2013, ECLI:EU:C:2013:720, para. 62.

[9] EU Member States issue residence permits to beneficiaries of refugee status for a period of 3 years (ten countries), 4 years (one country), 5 years (eight countries), 10 years (two countries) and permanent duration (six countries) (ECRE 2016, p. 10). We recommend residence permits be of permanent duration, and at any rate of the longest duration possible, but never shorter than 5 years.

11.4 Detention and Accommodation

Accommodation and detention issues explored in Chap. 8 were the focus of much concern by our participants.

The question of whether or not there should be SOGI-specific accommodation became an increasingly live issue during our fieldwork. The majority of our participants recommended the provision of accommodation exclusively shared by SOGI claimants, across Germany (Veronica; Thomas, NGO volunteer; Frank S., legal advisor; Milad; focus group no. 1, Hesse), Italy (Kennedy; Odosa; Antonella, LGBTIQ+ volunteer) and in the UK (Melisa, NGO worker). This would ensure 'that people can support each other and [do] not have to be "in the closet" in their own homes for fear of discrimination' (S74, NGO volunteer, UK). We share this recommendation to the extent that we believe that SOGI-specific accommodation should be made available, but also believe that such accommodation facilities need to be discreet, of small scale, and only used upon confirmation that the claimants in question prefer it to general asylum or refugee accommodation, to ensure the safety and self-determination of claimants. Good experiences have been reported by refugees in Nairobi (Kenya) who have chosen to live in separate LGBTIQ+ accommodation with their costs covered (Breen and Millo 2013, p. 55).

In line with our human rights, feminist and queer analytical lenses, we would thus put the emphasis on safety, on the one hand, and on autonomy and freedom (Chap. 10), on the other, rather than endorsing assumptions about what is best for claimants. To ensure safety, we recommend a system of certification of accommodation facilities as 'LGBTIQ+ friendly', as already in place in Sweden (European Migration Network 2016), although one might well argue that *all* accommodation should be SOGI-friendly, welcoming and safe. This would require, amongst other things, mandatory training for staff and regular monitoring. Accommodation should be tailored to meet claimants' needs, and claimants should have as much choice as possible about the area where they live and the type of housing they live in. To avoid putting claimants in situations of social isolation and hostility, access to appropriate information, support groups and social activities needs to be ensured (Ibrahim, Germany; Louis, NGO volunteer, Germany; Kadir, NGO worker, Germany; Jonathan, LGBTIQ+ group volunteer, Italy; Gary, NGO worker, UK): 'People should not be given accommodation far away from the places where there are facilities for LGBT people such as advice centres, places of worship' (S86, NGO volunteer, UK). There are particular concerns for trans claimants, making trans-specific accommodation upon request a priority (Kamel, Italy; Celeste, social worker, Italy).

We have some recommendations that are common to SOGI-specific and general accommodation facilities. First, 'camp-style' accommodation should be discontinued where it still exists, and 'regular', less conspicuous accommodation should be provided to facilitate social integration for both claimants and refugees (Halim, Germany; Tina, Germany; Chiara, NGO worker, Italy). Second, consideration should be given to individual and group dynamics in accommodation design, to reduce instances of the kinds of harassment, bullying and violence that our

11.4 Detention and Accommodation

participants have experienced (Chap. 8). There may be tensions between SOGI claimants and their co-nationals: 'There should be greater attention to the problems that can be created within the reception centres between LGBTQI+ people and compatriots' (S106, lawyer, Italy). Third, when issues and conflicts do arise in the accommodation allocated, it is important that these be addressed in a way that respects minorities, equality and diversity (Kennedy, Italy). If wished, transfer to more appropriate accommodation should be facilitated, especially to larger cities to avoid social isolation (S119, NGO worker, Germany; Fares, Germany). Fourth, privacy should be respected (Dev and Fred, Italy), including in shared toilet and bathroom areas. Fifth, accommodation facilities and housing more generally – when not managed by public entities – should not be contracted out to organisations that reflect excessively conservative or religious values (Celeste, social worker, Italy) or who recruit staff from extremist (racist or homophobic) organisations (Komaromi 2016), where there is a risk that SOGI claimants will feel coerced to stay 'in the closet'. Accommodation providers, whether public bodies or private contractors, need to be compliant with LGBTIQ+, gender, 'race' and other domestic equality law and good practice. This needs to be monitored and publicised to ensure that claimants have confidence in their accommodation-providers. Sixth, and relating to the previous point, information dissemination and awareness raising in accommodation facilities is crucial. This concerns asylum in general, but also SOGI in particular:

> It is also important that in accommodations, there are various flyers or something like that, [to make it clear that] there are LGBT people, this is quite normal, maybe that is not normal for you but still you need to get used to that, they [SOGI claimants] want to have some support here, you shall behave yourself as it is stated in the law, and for other people in the accommodation say that it is also quite OK. (Julia, Germany)

As further explored in Sect. 11.6, accommodation facilities should support training and events led by LGBTIQ+ organisations to raise awareness of SOGI equality and rights (Giulia, LGBTIQ+ group volunteer, Italy).

Detention is a matter that, although affecting the UK in particular, merits general attention. If we had to choose a single recommendation here, it would undoubtedly be that 'no asylum seeker should be detained' (S83, religious minister, UK) and to 'end immigration detention for all' (S74, NGO volunteer, UK). Detention may be particularly traumatic for SOGI asylum claimants as we saw in Chap. 8, and we were told on several occasions that there should be 'no detention of LGBTQI+ asylum seekers' (S57, NGO volunteer, UK). Unsurprisingly, therefore, our recommendation is that there should be no detention of SOGI claimants. This is supported by a presumption that detention is an injustice to any individual who has not been charged with or found guilty of a crime, and that includes all asylum claimants, although our focus here is on SOGI claimants.

Finally, provision of accommodation should not cease as soon as, or soon after, international protection is granted to SOGI claimants. Rather, it is essential that SOGI claimants – as asylum claimants more generally – retain access to publicly-funded accommodation for a period sufficiently long to allow them to find alternative accommodation, while searching for work, accessing education or making other suitable arrangements for their particular circumstances.

These recommendations should go a long way to improving SOGI claimants' accommodation experiences. Yet, outside the place where they live, they also meet considerable challenges, including in the fields of health, work and education.

11.5 Life 'Beyond Papers'

Asylum claimants and refugees often live in precarious conditions, with insufficient resources and close to destitution: 'not being able to work, having to survive on very little money – this all forces people into poverty' (S110, NGO volunteer, UK). As we discussed in Chaps. 4 and 9, the social integration of asylum claimants and refugees in general, and those who claimed international protection on SOGI grounds in particular, is under-planned and under-resourced. Countries should move towards an individualised and tailored approach to social integration, to ensure each claimant and refugee is welcomed and quickly recognised as an appreciated member of the host society. Here we make relevant recommendations particularly relating to health, work and education.

Access to health services should be universal, and not restricted to emergency provision. Privacy and specific training stand out as the priorities in this field. To ensure effective access to such services, however, the costs of interpretation and travel need to be publicly provided (whether through health insurance schemes or otherwise). Two particular areas of healthcare must be more responsive to SOGI asylum claimants' needs. First, mental health (Halim, Germany; Ashley, psychotherapist, UK), where there is a need for '[b]etter access to psychological therapies – many [SOGI claimants] are traumatised' (S74, NGO volunteer, UK). Second, hormonal treatment for trans claimants and refugees, including continuity of medical care, confidential treatment of data and respect for claimants' choices to a greater extent (Kamel, Italy).

Access to the labour market has also been highlighted as essential by our fieldwork participants:

> I don't know any refugee who doesn't wish to work (…) social benefits and asylum support are pretty good at the beginning, but people realise very quickly that everything that people would really like to afford is not affordable with that money and people must simply work. (Thomas, NGO volunteer, Germany)

Rules on access to the labour market should be interpreted according to the aim of the EU Reception Directive, rather than in a narrowly restrictive way. In other words, any job should in principle be accessible to asylum claimants after 6 months of filing an asylum claim. Reception centres and accommodation facilities should play a role here: 'the accommodation centre should always provide a training programme in order to enable them [claimants and refugees] to find a job when they go out of the camp' (S4, lawyer, UK). Broader public policies in the field of employment should facilitate these efforts, including through the creation of part-time jobs and paid training schemes such as the German one (Chap. 9), to allow claimants and refugees to gradually integrate into the labour market and provide them with an independent income. Such efforts would help SOGI claimants and refugees to avoid exploitation, including through working illegally (Just Me, focus group no. 3, northern Italy).

Finally, access to education for SOGI claimants and refugees needs improvement. While education has less of an overt SOGI dimension than the other aspects of service provision and public policy discussed, it is included here because it contributes to the employment potential, social integration and general wellbeing of SOGI (and all) claimants and refugees, in particular their mental health (C50, UK). Participants highlighted the need for better access to language courses, especially where claimants are unlikely to speak the host country language, as was common in Italy and Germany (S8, NGO worker, UK; Diana, Germany; Susanna, social worker, Italy). The right to education of SOGI claimants needs to be respected in a non-discriminatory manner, including on grounds of their 'refugeeness' and the intersection of their various characteristics.

These kinds of educational integration measures should include easier recognition of academic and vocational qualifications from countries of origin, in line with the Qualification Directive (Article 28). This would enable claimants to further their education in the host country and also facilitate integration in the labour market.

A great deal of social care and what we may call 'cultural interpretation' is required to support the social integration of SOGI asylum claimants and refugees in the areas explored above and others. Where appropriate, such social care and cultural interpreting work can be carried out by people of the same country of origin or ethnicity as the asylum claimant or refugee in question, as that may facilitate understanding and rapport (Angel, Germany). These and other aspects transversal to both social integration and the legal adjudication process are now discussed.

11.6 Building Capacity and Enhancing Competences

While legal adjudication and social integration processes are, for the most part, considered separately for analytical purposes, they sometimes pose similar challenges for SOGI claimants and refugees and coordinated action may be needed to address those challenges. As highlighted by our participants, social care needs to go hand-in-hand with the legal process and start simultaneously (Noah, NGO social worker, Germany). Previous chapters in this work have shown that SOGI has a significant bearing on the experiences of claimants and refugees at a legal and social level, suggesting that specific expertise, services and measures are required to address the shortcomings identified at both levels. Here we make recommendations to build the capacity and enhance the competences of different categories of actors encountered by SOGI claimants and refugees, first focusing on training.

Once recruited and trained, good staff need to be retained. Burnout, short-term contracts, low salaries, insufficient funding and promotions make careers in the asylum system short-lived and this has a negative impact on the quality of decision-making and services provided (Sabrina, NGO worker, Germany; Cristina, UNHCR officer, Italy). High turnover of staff also makes it difficult to make the best use of the training that individuals receive, and the skills and experience they develop. Support for those working in the asylum system is essential, to prevent vicarious trauma, burnout and desensitisation, but this generally does not exist (Evelyne and Anne, lawyers, Germany). Employee self-care needs to be adequately resourced, as a corollary of the duty of care that the state has towards its civil servants, just as any employer or service-provider does. It is in the interests of employees and employers but also the basis for sensitive case-work and service provision in the asylum field.

This applies not only to public servants, but also to NGOs and support groups, a point raised by several of our participants and which generated a number of recommendations. Participants saw a need for 'more support groups within the community' (S57, NGO volunteer, UK) and with better access to accommodation centres to support residents who wished it (focus group no. 1, Hesse, Germany). Support groups and small LGBTIQ+, asylum and migrant organisations need better resources to provide this kind of individual support, as well as use their experience in lobbying, campaigning and policy work. We were also told that 'more awareness raising [is] needed in LGBT communities about how they can support LGBT asylum seekers – why people are fleeing persecution, and just how traumatising and unjust the system is' (S110, NGO volunteer, UK), to address the discriminatory attitudes that subsist within the LGBTIQ+ community (Chap. 10). As with any area of support and service provision, strong protection and safeguarding policies need to be in place in NGOs and support groups that work with SOGI asylum claimants and refugees, to prevent abuse by support workers and volunteers and improve 'awareness and empowerment for refugees regarding sexual violence' (Ibrahim, Germany).

Measures to empower SOGI asylum claimants and refugees themselves are crucial. For this to be possible, there needs to be 'better investment in community development projects for LGBT asylum seekers and refugees – to enable them to effectively self organise, provide an effective social support network and to campaign' (S5, NGO worker, UK). SOGI beneficiaries of international protection:

> should also be supported to give back to the community. They have a lot of experiences and… yeah… people should be accessing some sort of spaces to organise for their communities. And there are definitely natural leaders and people who show up and can start projects and start initiatives or spaces. So there will be empowerment and also helping the new ones to integrate or to make their way. (Halim, Germany)

Across all areas of what we might call the SOGI asylum system – decision making, appeals, accommodation, and other public services – there was a consensus amongst our participants about the need for more and better SOGI asylum training, as already pointed out by the UNHCR (2012, para. 60(iv)). This applies to officials and public employees working in asylum, but also to those acting on behalf of the state (where services have been contracted out, most obviously in accommodation and reception services) and those offering legal advice and representation to SOGI claimants. SOGI asylum training materials should cover all aspects of an asylum journey, including terminology, procedural safeguards, interviewing technique, substantive status determination, housing, work, health and education, and incorporate the recommendations outlined in this chapter. Training should include how to adopt a caring and sensitive approach (Mariya, NGO worker, Germany), including acquiring skills in empathy, as well as competences in equality and human rights law and policy, and an understanding of confidentiality requirements (Cristina, UNHCR officer, Italy). Furthermore, it should include how to avoid micro-aggressions and minimise power dynamics and imbalances (Kadir, NGO worker, Germany), where to signpost claimants who have particular needs, tools to combat homonormativity (Vincenzo, LGBTIQ+ group volunteer, Italy) and content covering SOGI matters in the most common countries of origin (Nazarena, lawyer, Italy). Importantly, training should address how to avoid re-traumatising claimants:

> programmes to train the staff to be more sensitive, not to laugh when these people come through who have been traumatised. I didn't have to go through war to leave my country but I was traumatised in a different way. So you laughing when I mention my country doesn't help me. I might look poised and confident but I'm struggling, I'm panicking, I developed agoraphobia now since I came to Germany. I get panic attacks every now and then in public spaces. (…) It's training with how to deal with traumatised people. (Marhoon, Germany)

Training needs to be adapted to different categories of decision-maker or service-provider. Several organisations have produced good quality SOGI asylum training materials (Gyulai et al. 2013, 2015; IOM and UNHCR 2019; ORAM 2015; Rumbach 2013), but besides the need to ensure these materials are regularly updated and culturally appropriate, there is undoubtedly room to improve their dissemination and impact.

However, adequate training and training materials are unlikely to be a complete solution, as decision-makers and other SOGI asylum system actors may become 'training-resistant' (Barbara, lawyer, Germany). Training needs to take such factors into consideration, it needs to be in-depth and it should be revised and repeated on a regular basis (Breen and Millo 2013, p. 55; Rumbach 2013, p. 42). In the case of Italy, this needs to include all territorial commission members (Maria Grazia, decision-maker, Italy; Chiara, NGO worker, Italy). Owing to the large number of people working or in some way involved in asylum systems in Europe, there may be call for a cascade approach to training; in other words, states should ensure that key officials at a domestic level receive the necessary training, and these officials should then disseminate it to their colleagues. With time, an across-the-board requirement should be introduced that all employees and officials acting on behalf of the state who are responsible for decision-making and/or in direct contact with claimants need to have received training, including a SOGI-specific component, based on UNHCR and EASO guidance.

Having regard to the trends emerged in Chap. 6, different kinds of training are needed for the many different actors that a SOGI asylum claimant will encounter during the asylum process. Staff meeting new arrivals in reception and accommodation centres, or responsible for administering initial or screening interviews, will need to be well-trained in how to create a safe and relaxed space for people who find themselves in an unfamiliar environment. Asylum adjudicators were also singled out as needing training: 'They do not have to do diversity training, they do not have to do awareness training, they do not have cultural competence training, nothing, none of this' (Barbara, lawyer, Germany). As a particular example, Marlen, a legal advisor in Germany, said that 'it may not be normal in your [decision-maker's] own life reality that lesbian women have children, but there are other realities in life, and you should probably have already learned that if you go into this [asylum system]'. Equally, in the UK, we heard:

> there should be training within the HO [Home Office] on understanding sexuality and gender identity issues. There are often very stereotypical and westernized ideas regarding how someone realizes they [are] LGBTQI and also stereotypical ideas of how they should then live their life. (S126, NGO worker)

Judges hearing SOGI appeals were often recognised as having the required legal expertise, but not the necessary life experience or human skills to deal with these cases (Elias, lawyer, Germany), making 'more training on unconscious bias for all courts' a requirement (S57, NGO volunteer, UK) and, more generally:

> The people who conduct hearings need to be well trained in LGBTIQ lifestyles. And not only lesbian, gay and bisexuality, but maybe – but not maybe, but certainly – pansexuality, asexuality and gender outside the binary gender system and not ask questions about it, but simply accept how people define themselves. (Mariya, NGO worker, Germany)

Similarly, training for asylum adjudicators needs to raise 'awareness of LGBTQI+ issues, the difficulties faced by individuals from different cultural backgrounds and encourag[e] questioning of heteronormative assumptions' (S147, barrister, UK), in line with our queer theoretical underpinnings (Chap. 3). Decision-makers themselves acknowledged the need for greater training, particularly in relation to interrogation techniques, and went so far as suggesting individual coaching by psychologists on how to conduct hearings and interviews (Emilia, judge, Germany; Filippo, senior judge, Italy). Judges may require training in asylum law in general, as very often they are general administrative or family law judges, for example, with no particular knowledge in the field of asylum or even migration (Emilia, judge, Germany). As Filippo, senior judge in Italy, said, 'preparation means being self-taught'. A more systematic, comprehensive and sophisticated approach to the training of judges is necessary.

Those offering legal advice and representation to SOGI claimants should also benefit from training to be able to deliver their services with the necessary quality: 'legal professionals should [be trained to] have specific competences in knowing how to identify LGBTQI+ people and how to support users in preparation for the Commission with greater professionalism' (S106, lawyer, Italy).

Ensuring better trained interpreters and translators (where relevant) was also identified as a priority (S119, NGO worker, Germany; Zouhair, Germany). Considering the importance of the interpreter's role (Chap. 6), 'it has to be made sure that… also for the interpreters there is this specific form of training and an awareness around the situation of people who flee on the grounds of sexual orientation and gender identity' (Terry, member of the European Parliament). This includes ensuring interpreters are appropriately trained in terms of cultural competences and confidentiality.

NGOs working in this area also have training needs. We were told of the need for 'equalities awareness within the LGBTI scene to improve migrant integration' and that 'LGBTI groups should receive immigration training' (S8, NGO worker, UK). Conversely, 'immigration support organisations and immigration solicitors should receive training to increase their LGBTI sensitivity' (S8, NGO worker, UK). SOGI claimants and refugees themselves might benefit from some training, such as 'general sensitisation workshops, where not only LGBT themes are treated, but also other forms of discrimination, such as sexism, ableism and, yes, racism', as well as some knowledge about asylum law and policy (Louis, NGO volunteer, Germany). As part of any training, organisations should develop and implement codes of conduct to ensure SOGI asylum claimants are treated respectfully and adequately (ORAM 2016a).

The quality of training, and the skills and experience of training providers is critical. SOGI asylum claimants and refugees are the main source of expertise here, and should be involved in training decision-makers and service providers to a far greater extent than they currently are, if at all. Other potential trainers include, for example, UNHCR officers, therapists and psychologists, SOGI support groups, NGO and academic researchers (Anne, lawyer, Germany; Barbara, lawyer, Germany; Cristina, UNHCR officer, Italy; Mara, lawyer, Italy; Qasim, decision-maker, UK). NGOs and support groups should give each other training and support, especially when new groups are being set up who may benefit from the experience of more established activists (Giulia, LGBTIQ+ group volunteer, Italy). Good quality training can be complemented by establishing telephone advice lines for everyday queries by lawyers, decision-makers and claimants (Barbara, lawyer, Germany), as well as networks of asylum supporters such as the SOGIESC network hosted by ILGA-Europe.[10]

Frequency of training is another concern. Training courses need to be regularly reviewed and updated, particularly where there is a high staff turnover, with refresher training addressing knowledge and skills in particular areas (Vincenzo, LGBTIQ+ group volunteer, Italy; Cristina, UNHCR officer, Italy), in a form of continuous professional development programme. Both initial and refresher training should be compulsory (Jonathan, LGBTIQ+ group volunteer, Italy). This area of need was highlighted by public officials themselves:

> We did do [have follow-up training on SOGI asylum], several years ago, but surprisingly and actually disappointingly we haven't had any follow-up on that and that is no doubt going to be, should be one of your recommendations, if I could be so bold to mention that, because we haven't had it for years. (…) And it would be very helpful because these are extremely sensitive and extremely complicated areas. (Bilal, presenting officer, UK)

---

[10] https://www.ilga-europe.org/sogiesc-asylum.

Given the importance of training in the context of SOGI (and other forms of) asylum, this should be an area of public provision and not dependent on volunteer initiatives (Giulia, LGBTIQ+ group volunteer, Italy). Training is not only important to SOGI claimants and refugees, but also benefits decision-makers and service providers. Better awareness of SOGI and SOGI asylum will help them feel more confident about their work, in how they conduct themselves and in the quality of their decisions (Anne, lawyer, Germany; Kadir, NGO worker, Germany).

Crucially, training should encourage all actors in the asylum system, particularly decision-makers, to adopt an intersectional approach in their work, in line with our theoretical approach (Chap. 3):

> [it] is absolutely important to look at the person as a whole, and to see this individual and to look at the different aspects of why they were forced to flee the country, what kind of discriminations they were facing, what kind of persecution they were facing, what kind of difficulties they had in their lives in general, and then on the basis of this to make a decision. (…) there can be multiple discriminations that come together, because of your sexual orientation, gender identity but also because of other aspects that actually force you to leave the country and then look for asylum somewhere else. So I think it is very important to have this more holistic image in order to take a decision in the end. (Terry, member of the European Parliament)

We look forward to a time when Europe's asylum systems look at asylum claimants through such an intersectional, holistic lens.

11.7   Something to Look Forward To

At this final stage of these volumes, readers may feel that they have accompanied SOGI asylum claimants on a long and terrible journey – albeit one that is unimaginable to most of us. It is true that SOGI asylum claimants and refugees face ordeals that no one should undergo, but there is also scope for hope. This hope – and determination in the face of negative experiences – is patent in our participants' testimonies and recommendations. We met an absolute and inspiring determination in many of our participants to protect the rights of SOGI minorities and a resistance to efforts to 'homogenise society' (Kadir, NGO worker, Germany). We also heard of individuals' passionate commitment to improving asylum for those who followed them, so that their bad experiences became the basis for making improvements to help other people in a similar situation.

For this to happen, we need more material and human resources across the whole asylum system, from the initial reception stage through to social integration. A better-resourced system, would not only bring immediate benefits in protecting claimants' human rights (Chap. 3), but would also benefit host societies both socially and economically.

Change also needs to occur in asylum law and policy, as highlighted throughout these volumes and specifically in the recommendations above. Not only are shortcomings in the SOGI asylum system visible, but there is also a striking contrast

11.7 Something to Look Forward To

between the law and policy that applies to 'domestic' SOGI minorities and those that apply to SOGI asylum claimants. Such differential treatment is unwarranted and unacceptable from an equality and human rights perspective. On a positive note, 'there is kind of like a stubbornness in certain countries for the better' (Amanda, NGO worker, Brussels), for example on criminalisation of same-sex acts where currently only Italy recognises this as persecution in itself. On a more gloomy note, the scope for countries to be different 'for the better' may disappear if the current CEAS reform transforms the Qualification and Procedures Directives into Regulations, as EU regulations offer far less flexibility to EU member states in implementing EU standards. By limiting EU member states' scope to set higher standards, this harmonisation effort entails a serious risk of lowering, rather than raising current standards (Ferreira et al. 2018, pp. 6–7; Peers 2017). The Brexit process may also have a negative impact on the asylum system for SOGI claimants in the UK and lead to fewer options for SOGI claimants elsewhere: 'I think Brexit will make everything worse for migrants, for equality supporters, for refugees and asylum seekers. I think the question now is how to ride the current' (S112, NGO volunteer, UK).

To counteract these risks at European level, we may look to the UN Global Compact for Safe, Orderly and Regular Migration (UN 2018) and the UN Global Compact on Refugees (UNHCR 2018). The Migration Compact will be monitored, unlike the Refugee Convention, but neither Compact includes any actionable commitments in relation to SOGI minorities or the causes of migration at global level (Apap 2019). Despite making no explicit reference to SOGI (Chap. 5), these instruments contain some promise for SOGI minorities owing to their multiple references to 'gender', 'equality' and 'empowerment'. However, lacking any enforcement mechanism, they are unlikely to bring about any radical change in the current situation of SOGI – or any other – refugees. A far more promising approach in our view is to put the Refugee Convention and human rights treaties – and the values that underpin them – at the heart of Europe's asylum systems, and read them jointly as the basis for raising standards of protection.

Yet, no injection of funding or change in statutes or policies will, in themselves, solve all the problems we have highlighted. A more fundamental and colossal shift in the social and political mind-set is required. We need to stop using asylum claimants and refugees as pawns in political debates:

> refugees should not be misused as an election campaign theme. Because I honestly think that it's an absurdity, people are always talking about [refugees] and they just do not speak for themselves. (…) And that's such a nonsense. I mean, that's in the Basic Law [constitution], what – what are we even discussing?! Alas, for me it's just right-wing populist abuse of people who have come here in need and that is an absurdity. (Louis, NGO volunteer, Germany)

The only way to achieve a better mind-set at an institutional and systemic level is to start with the individual and a humane concern for their experiences. We heard that 'if you are not an LGBT person, you may not know how to put yourself [in their shoes]… that is, you need great empathy to put yourself in the shoes of a minority if you don't belong to it' (Anna, LGBTIQ+ group volunteer, Italy). So besides greater investment, improvements at a legal and policy level, and radical changes to the social and political mind-set, we need a great deal more empathy at an individual level and on the part of every single actor in the system. More empathy by all actors involved can impact positively on policy-making, decision-making and social practices, leading to a kinder asylum system.

It may seem simplistic to conclude with allusions to empathy and kindness, but in the words of Aldous Huxley, '[i]t's a bit embarrassing to have been concerned with the human problem all one's life and find at the end that one has no more to offer by way of advice than "try to be a little kinder"' (quoted in Smith 1964). This does not mean any less a determination to improving the lives of SOGI asylum claimants and refugees. Indeed, in the words of Maya Angelou, 'we may encounter many defeats, but we must not be defeated' (Angelou 2009). We trust these volumes will make some contribution to the fight for a better world for SOGI claimants and refugees.

References

AIDA – Asylum Information Database, & ECRE – European Council on Refugees and Exiles. (2019). *Asylum authorities: An overview of internal structures and available resources.* ECRE – European Council on Refugees and Exiles. https://www.asylumineurope.org/sites/default/files/shadow-reports/aida_asylum_authorities.pdf

Angelou, M. (2009). *An interview with Maya Angelou.* Psychology Today. http://www.psychologytoday.com/blog/the-guest-room/200902/interview-maya-angelou

Apap, J. (2019). *The concept of 'climate refugee': Towards a possible definition.* EPRS – European Parliamentary Research Service. http://www.europarl.europa.eu/RegData/etudes/BRIE/2018/621893/EPRS_BRI(2018)621893_EN.pdf

Bejzyk, M. (2017). Criminalization on the basis of sexual orientation and gender identity: Reframing the dominant human rights discourse to include freedom from torture and inhuman and degrading treatment. *Canadian Journal of Women and the Law, 29*(2), 375–400.

Breen, D., & Millo, Y. (2013). Protection in the city: Some good practice in Nairobi. *Forced Migration Review, 42,* 54–56.

Community of Sant'Egidio. (2019). *Humanitarian corridors.* https://www.santegidio.org/pageID/30112/langID/en/Humanitarian-Corridors.html

Danisi, C. (2017). Promoting human rights through the EU external action: An empty 'vessel' for sexual minorities? *European Foreign Affairs Review, 22*(3), 341–356.

Danisi, C. (2019). Crossing borders between international refugee law and international human rights law in the European context: Can human rights enhance protection against persecution based on sexual orientation (and beyond)? *Netherlands Quarterly of Human Rights, 37*(4), 359.

EASO – European Asylum Support Office. (2015). *Researching the situation of lesbian, gay, and bisexual persons (LGB) in countries of origin.* EASO – European Asylum Support Office. https://www.easo.europa.eu/sites/default/files/public/Researching-the-situation-of-LGB-in-countries-of-origin-FINAL-080515.pdf

ECRE – European Council on Refugees and Exiles. (2016). *Asylum on the clock? Duration and review of international protection status in Europe.* ECRE – European Council on Refugees and Exiles. https://www.ecre.org/wp-content/uploads/2016/07/AIDA-Briefing-Asylum-on-the-Clock-duration-and-review-of-international-protection-status-in-Europe_-June-2016.pdf

European Migration Network. (2016). *Ad Hoc query on NL AHQ on national asylum policies regarding LGBT-asylum seekers.* https://ec.europa.eu/home-affairs/sites/homeaffairs/files/what-we-do/networks/european_migration_network/reports/docs/ad-hoc-queries/ad-

References

hoc-queries-2016.1061_-_nl_ahq_on_national_asylum_policies_regarding_lgbt-asylum_ seekers.pdf

European Parliament. (2018a). *Humanitarian visas*. Publications Office of the EU. https://op.europa.eu/en/publication-detail/-/publication/a3b57ef6-d66d-11e8-9424-01aa75ed71a1/language-en/format-PDF

European Parliament. (2018b). *Humanitarian visas to avoid deaths and improve management of refugee flows*. https://www.europarl.europa.eu/news/en/press-room/20181205IPR20933/humanitarian-visas-to-avoid-deaths-and-improve-management-of-refugee-flows

Ferreira, N., & Venturi, D. (2018). Testing the untestable: The CJEU's decision in Case C-473/16, F v Bevándorlási és Állampolgársági Hivatal. *European Database of Asylum Law*. https://www.asylumlawdatabase.eu/en/journal/testing-untestable-cjeu%E2%80%99s-decision-case-c-47316-f-v-bev%C3%A1ndorl%C3%A1si-%C3%A9s-%C3%A1llampolg%C3%A1rs%C3%A1gi-hivatal

Ferreira, N., Danisi, C., Dustin, M., & Held, N. (2018). *The reform of the Common European Asylum System: Fifteen recommendations from a sexual orientation and gender identity perspective*. SOGICA/University of Sussex.

Gyulai, G., Kagan, M., Herlihy, J., Turner, S., Hárdi, L., & Udvarhelyi, É. T. (2013). *Credibility assessment in asylum procedures—A multidisciplinary training manual—Volume 1*. Hungarian Helsinki Committee. https://www.refworld.org/docid/5253bd9a4.html.

Gyulai, G., Singer, D., Chelvan, S., & Given-Wilson, Z. (2015). *Credibility assessment in asylum procedures—A multidisciplinary training manual, Volume 2*. Hungarian Helsinki Committee. https://helsinki.hu/wp-content/uploads/CREDO-training-manual-2nd-volume-online-final.pdf.

Held, N., Rainbow Refugees Cologne-Support Group e.V., Aidshilfe Düsseldorf e.V., You're Welcome – Mashallah Düsseldorf, Kölner Flüchtlingsrat, Projekt Geflüchtete Queere Jugendliche, & Fachstelle Queere Jugend NRW/Schwules Netzwerk NRW e.V. (2018). *Projektbericht: Erfahrungen mit der Anhörung von LSBTIQ* Geflüchteten*. https://schwules-netzwerk.de/wp-content/uploads/2018/10/Projektbericht-zur-Anh%C3%B6rung-von-LSBTIQ-Gefl%C3%BCchteten.pdf

Hinger, S. (2010). Finding the fundamental: Shaping identity in gender and sexual orientation based asylum claims. *Columbia Journal of Gender and Law, 19*(2), 367–408.

Hruschka, C. (2019). How to design fair and efficient asylum procedures in populist times? *ECRE – European Council on Refugees and Exiles and Refugee Council*. https://www.ecre.org/op-ed-how-to-design-fair-and-efficient-asylum-procedures-in-populist-times/

ICIBI – Independent Chief Inspector of Borders and Immigration. (2014). *An investigation into the Home Office's handling of asylum claims made on the grounds of sexual orientation March-June 2014*. GOV.UK. https://assets.publishing.service.gov.uk/government/uploads/system/uploads/attachment_data/file/547330/Investigation-into-the-Handling-of-Asylum-Claims_Oct_2014.pdf

IOM – International Organization for Migration, & UNHCR – UN High Commissioner for Refugees. (2019). *LGBTI Training Package*. https://lgbti.iom.int/lgbti-training-package

Jansen, S. (2019). *Pride or shame? Assessing LGBTI asylum applications in the Netherlands following the XYZ and ABC judgments*. COC Netherlands. https://www.coc.nl/wp-content/uploads/2019/01/Pride-or-Shame-LGBTI-asylum-in-the-Netherlands.pdf

Jansen, S., & Spijkerboer, T. (2011). *Fleeing homophobia: Asylum claims related to sexual orientation and gender identity in Europe*. Vrije Universiteit Amsterdam. https://www.refworld.org/docid/4ebba7852.html

Judicial College. (2018). *Equal Treatment Bench Book*. https://www.judiciary.uk/publications/new-edition-of-the-equal-treatment-bench-book-launched/

Komaromi, P. (2016). Germany: Neo-Nazis and the market in asylum reception. *Race & Class, 58*(2), 79–86.

Macklin, A. (1995). Refugee women and the imperative of categories. *Human Rights Quarterly, 17*(2), 213–277.

Macklin, A. (2011). Refugee roulette in the Canadian casino. In J. Ramji-Nogales, A. Schoenholtz, & P. G. Schrag (Eds.), *Refugee roulette: Disparities in asylum adjudication and proposals for reform* (pp. 135–163). New York University Press. https://nyupress.org/9780814741061/refugee-roulette.

Markard, N. (2016). Persecution for reasons of membership of a particular social group: Intersectionality avant la lettre? *Sociologia del Diritto*, 45–63. https://doi.org/10.3280/SD2016-002004

McNeal, K. E. (2019). Confessions of an ambivalent country expert: Queer refugeeism in the UK and the political economy of (im)mobility in and out of Trinidad and Tobago. *Anthropological Theory*, 19(1), 191–215. https://doi.org/10.1177/1463499618812600.

Moreno-Lax, V. (2019). *Model instrument for an emergency evacuation visa*. International Bar Association. https://www.academia.edu/40441161/Model_Instrument_for_an_Emergency_Evacuation_Visa_International_Bar_Association_2019

Nayeri, D. (2019). *The ungrateful refugee (Main edition)*. Canongate Books.

Network of Legal Experts in the Non-Discrimination Field. (2015). *Reversing the burden of proof: Practical dilemmas at the European and national level*. Publications Office of the European Union. https://publications.europa.eu/en/publication-detail/-/publication/a763ee82-b93c-4df9-ab8c-626a660c9da8/language-en

ORAM – Organization for Refuge, Asylum and Migration. (2015). *Sexual and gender minorities: What refugee professionals need to know and do. A sampling of presentation slides*. http://oramrefugee.org/wp-content/uploads/2016/05/Sample-Training-Slides-English.pdf

ORAM – Organization for Refuge, Asylum and Migration. (2016a). *Enhancing protection of sexual & gender minority beneficiaries and staff in organizational codes of conduct: Model code & analyses*. ORAM – Organization for Refuge, Asylum & Migration. http://oramrefugee.org/wp-content/uploads/2016/10/Code-of-Conduct.pdf

ORAM – Organization for Refuge, Asylum and Migration. (2016b). *Incorporating sexual and gender minorities into refugee and asylum intake and registration systems*. ORAM – Organization for Refuge, Asylum and Migration. http://oramrefugee.org/wp-content/uploads/2016/05/Registeration-Forms-Memo-English-1.pdf

Peers, S. (2017). *The new EU law on refugees takes shape: More harmonisation but less protection?* http://eulawanalysis.blogspot.com/2017/07/the-new-eu-law-on-refugees-takes-shape.html

Peroni, L., & Timmer, A. (2013). Vulnerable groups: The promise of an emerging concept in European human rights convention law. *International Journal of Constitutional Law*, 11(4), 1056–1085. https://doi.org/10.1093/icon/mot042.

Politzer, M., & Hylton, A. (2019). Caught between borders. *Longreads*. https://longreads.com/2019/06/11/caught-between-borders/

Portman, S., & Weyl, D. (2013). LGBT refugee resettlement in the US: Emerging best practices. *Forced Migration Review*, 42, 44–49.

Puar, J. K. (2007). *Terrorist assemblages: Homonationalism in queer times*. Durham: Duke University Press. https://doi.org/10.1215/9780822390442.

Puar, J. (2013). Rethinking homonationalism. *International Journal of Middle East Studies*, 45(2), 336–339. https://doi.org/10.1017/S002074381300007X.

Right to Remain. (2019). *The right to remain toolkit*. Right to Remain. https://righttoremain.org.uk/toolkit/

Rumbach, J. (2013). Towards inclusive resettlement for LGBTI refugees. *Forced Migration Review*, 42, 40–43.

Smith, H. (1964). Aldous Huxley—A tribute. *The Psychedelic Review*, I (3 – Aldous Huxley Memorial Issue), 264–265.

Solanke, I. (2009). Putting race and gender together: A new approach to intersectionality. *The Modern Law Review*, 72(5), 723–749. https://doi.org/10.1111/j.1468-2230.2009.00765.x.

Sridharan, S. (2008). *The difficulties of U.S. asylum claims based on sexual orientation*. Migration Policy Institute. https://www.migrationpolicy.org/article/difficulties-us-asylum-claims-based-sexual-orientation

References

UN. (2018). *Global compact for safe, orderly and regular migration.* https://refugeesmigrants.un.org/migration-compact

UNHCR – UN High Commissioner for Refugees. (2012). *Guidelines on international protection no. 9: Claims to refugee status based on sexual orientation and/or gender identity within the context of Article 1A(2) of the 1951 convention and/or its 1967 protocol relating to the status of refugees (HCR/GIP/12/09).* UNHCR – UN High Commissioner for Refugees. http://www.unhcr.org/509136ca9.pdf

UNHCR – UN High Commissioner for Refugees. (2018). *Global compact on refugees.* https://refugeesmigrants.un.org/refugees-compact

UNHCR – UN High Commissioner for Refugees. (1998). *Note on burden and standard of proof in refugee claims.* UNHCR – UN High Commissioner for Refugees. https://www.refworld.org/docid/3ae6b3338.html

UNHCR – UN High Commissioner for Refugees. (2011). *Handbook on procedures and criteria for determining refugee status under the 1951 Convention and the 1967 Protocol relating to the status of refugees.* UNHCR – UN High Commissioner for Refugees. https://www.unhcr.org/publications/legal/5ddfcdc47/handbook-procedures-criteria-determining-refugee-status-under-1951-convention.html

Verloo, M. (2006). Multiple inequalities, intersectionality and the European Union. *European Journal of Women's Studies, 13*(3), 211–228. https://doi.org/10.1177/1350506806065753.

Open Access This chapter is licensed under the terms of the Creative Commons Attribution 4.0 International License (http://creativecommons.org/licenses/by/4.0/), which permits use, sharing, adaptation, distribution and reproduction in any medium or format, as long as you give appropriate credit to the original author(s) and the source, provide a link to the Creative Commons license and indicate if changes were made.

The images or other third party material in this chapter are included in the chapter's Creative Commons license, unless indicated otherwise in a credit line to the material. If material is not included in the chapter's Creative Commons license and your intended use is not permitted by statutory regulation or exceeds the permitted use, you will need to obtain permission directly from the copyright holder.

Index

A

Accelerated, 182, 185, 247–249, 455

Accommodations, 12, 16, 41, 82, 83, 118, 123–125, 161, 169–171, 173, 175, 183, 186, 190, 192, 193, 199, 202, 206, 213, 250, 251, 324, 331–384, 391, 408, 409, 411, 430, 434, 437, 446, 449, 457, 463–466, 468, 469

Activism, 12, 13, 44, 65, 141, 144, 193, 210, 262, 263, 304

Adoption, 102, 140, 186, 191, 227–234, 271

Adversarial, 24, 454

Advice, 32, 38, 46, 105, 149, 173, 186–188, 192, 196–199, 208, 252, 349, 358, 382, 393, 400, 402, 438, 449, 457, 464, 469–471, 474

Age, 26, 29, 31, 38, 69, 70, 100, 107, 121, 125, 148, 163, 265, 282, 298, 302, 310, 318, 320, 321, 332, 396, 398, 400, 407, 422–424, 435, 439, 443, 453

Agencies, 16, 43–45, 73–75, 84, 107, 153, 163, 189, 198, 274, 299, 324, 396, 397, 421, 438–444, 450, 451, 456

AnkER centres, 163, 180, 186, 247, 339

Anti-essentialism, 70–73

Appeal Rights Exhausted (ARE), 183, 366

Appeals, 16, 29–31, 34, 35, 46, 108, 115, 121, 128, 179–183, 190–194, 196–201, 216, 217, 219, 222–232, 235, 236, 239, 240, 242, 247–250, 261, 266, 269, 271, 274, 275, 278, 280, 281, 290, 295–297, 299, 303, 305, 306, 308, 310, 313–315, 319–322, 336, 339, 342, 364, 367, 397, 401, 409, 423, 425, 426, 438, 452, 454, 457–459, 468, 470

Arrivals, 10, 12, 16, 27, 34, 98, 128, 140, 141, 155, 158, 160–176, 179–181, 184, 186, 229, 246, 251, 269, 313, 323, 332, 335, 336, 366, 377, 383, 407, 434, 446–448, 469

Asexual, 14, 29

Asylum Accommodation and Support Services Contracts (AASC), 337

B

Bias, 56, 83, 107, 179, 185, 200, 202, 203, 205, 209, 210, 219–221, 227, 230, 232, 233, 252, 309, 451, 470

Biphobic, 103

Bisexuals, 6, 7, 10, 27, 29, 31, 69, 79, 84, 117, 238, 266, 267, 274, 280, 294, 315, 318, 323, 351, 368, 396, 412, 422

Borders, 3, 4, 13, 62, 80, 98, 107, 108, 110, 111, 121, 151, 152, 155, 156, 159, 161, 169, 173, 175, 180, 182, 249, 251, 297, 435, 446

Bundesamt für Migration und Flüchtlinge; Federal Office for Migration and Refugees (BAMF), 40, 41, 100, 106, 114, 116, 117, 120, 121, 128, 161, 180, 186, 205, 209, 210, 213, 222, 223, 227, 228, 235, 241, 242, 245, 262, 264, 265, 267, 272–274, 281–284, 291, 292, 295, 298, 301, 302, 313, 333, 453, 462

Bundesministerium des Innern, für Bau und Heimat; Federal Ministry of the Interior, Building and Community (BMI), 6, 114, 116, 117, 209, 213, 235, 241, 333, 335

© The Author(s) 2021

C. Danisi et al., *Queering Asylum in Europe*, IMISCOE Research Series, https://doi.org/10.1007/978-3-030-69441-8

480 Index

Bundestag (German Federal Parliament), 98, 123, 334
Burden of proof, 249, 260, 285–289, 322, 460–462

C

Capacity, 14, 34, 80, 231, 239, 319, 322, 333, 336, 339, 374, 449, 455, 467–472
Caseworkers, 16, 115, 120, 162, 179, 207–213, 215, 217, 219–222, 230, 232, 243, 249, 263, 279, 286, 287, 290, 297, 397, 450–454
Charter of Fundamental Rights (CFR), 52, 54, 62, 175, 390
Children, 28, 74, 102, 115–117, 125, 143, 146, 150, 183, 190, 194, 205, 214, 233, 238, 267, 292, 298, 303–305, 316, 321, 334, 346, 349, 352, 356, 361, 367, 368, 390, 396, 399, 404, 409, 412, 423, 424, 428, 430, 440, 470
Classes, 13, 26, 69, 72, 75, 79, 82, 83, 218, 302, 311, 319, 320, 369, 383, 412, 413
Commercial and Operational Managers Procuring Asylum Support Services (COMPASS), 337, 359
Common European Asylum System (CEAS), 8, 9, 12, 24, 97, 99, 104, 105, 114, 116, 117, 125, 127, 128, 184, 201, 236, 244, 247, 253, 449, 458, 473
Communities, 5, 7, 11–13, 26, 53, 72, 73, 78, 121, 123, 124, 126, 129, 142, 144, 147–150, 163, 166, 169, 175, 186, 187, 198, 199, 219, 232, 236, 242, 243, 249, 262, 266, 272, 279, 306, 307, 311, 312, 320, 337, 350, 363, 364, 366, 367, 369, 370, 372, 376, 383, 390, 396, 398, 402, 405–406, 408, 409, 411, 414, 422, 424, 429, 431, 432, 434–436, 439, 441, 443, 448, 468
Comparative, 5, 7, 13, 23, 24, 28, 101
Competences, 197, 225, 226, 241, 243, 324, 453, 467–472
Council of Europe (CoE), 4, 23, 99, 149
Countries of origin, 4, 5, 12, 26, 27, 30, 31, 36, 44, 55, 59, 64, 65, 75, 81, 82, 100, 104, 105, 115, 120, 122, 124, 126, 139–176, 180, 182–184, 189, 194, 198, 202, 210, 211, 219, 220, 223, 228, 229, 234–240, 247–249, 262, 265, 266, 269, 270, 272–277, 279–281, 283–285, 287, 288, 292, 293, 295, 298, 299, 301, 311, 312, 314, 316–318, 344, 348, 349, 351, 357, 367, 371, 372, 376, 382, 393, 395,
396, 398, 403, 404, 411, 413, 423, 424, 426, 427, 433, 440, 441, 447, 450, 453–455, 458–460, 467, 469
Country of Origin Information (COI), 11, 16, 108, 185, 203, 210, 216, 220, 227, 228, 230, 234–240, 252, 285, 422, 456–458, 463
Country Policy Information Notes (CPIN), 115, 237–239
Couples, 28, 57, 102, 109, 126, 152, 168, 174, 191, 194, 233, 244, 251, 279, 294, 351–352, 357, 359, 366, 380, 396, 409, 452
Court of Justice of the European Union (CJEU), 11, 55, 56, 60, 102, 110, 112, 115, 128, 151, 213, 224, 236, 252, 263–265, 267, 269, 273, 277, 281, 291, 295–298, 460, 462, 463
Credibility, 5, 10–12, 16, 83, 84, 122, 160, 166, 191, 198, 202, 208, 209, 216, 223–225, 227–231, 240, 244, 245, 249, 260, 266, 267, 272, 275, 277, 279, 285, 287, 288, 290, 293–295, 298, 300–323, 396, 401, 422, 424, 429, 439, 457, 462, 463
Criminalisation, 5, 16, 112, 114, 148, 238, 260, 270, 273–276, 280, 290, 322, 460, 473
Cultures, 16, 26, 27, 67, 68, 71–75, 80, 84, 98, 107, 108, 145, 147, 150, 173, 213, 215, 219, 221, 260, 265, 273, 286, 287, 303, 304, 307, 311–316, 319, 322, 324, 347, 383, 424, 426–429, 432, 438

D

Decision-maker, 24, 106, 107, 115, 122, 144, 165, 166, 181, 183, 185, 190, 202, 204–218, 220, 221, 236, 239, 240, 242–244, 252, 270, 271, 276, 282, 285–288, 291, 293–297, 301, 302, 309–311, 313, 317, 319, 336, 342, 427, 434, 440, 446, 450–452, 454–458, 462, 469–471
Departures, 61, 139–176, 295
Destitution, 16, 333, 366–368, 466
Detentions, 16, 42, 44, 105, 117–119, 157, 159, 161, 170–173, 206, 248, 333, 337, 345, 377–382, 392, 393, 400, 404, 438, 441, 446, 457, 463–466
Disabilities, 63, 79, 117, 318, 321, 332, 352, 383, 453
Disbelief, 16, 108, 160, 232, 260, 265, 286, 303, 312–316, 322, 403, 427, 462

Index

Discretion, 11, 105, 115, 125, 151, 213, 224, 238, 243, 260, 273, 274, 276–283, 303, 322, 460

Discriminations, 4, 10, 16, 45, 56–58, 63–65, 69, 84, 101–103, 108, 118, 123, 140, 142, 145, 150, 202, 203, 236, 238, 240, 270, 271, 273, 274, 279, 284, 288, 292, 312, 323, 332, 333, 337, 344–359, 364–366, 369, 372, 373, 376, 379, 382, 383, 389, 396, 408–414, 421, 426, 429–433, 443, 444, 449, 453, 455, 459, 461, 464, 471, 472

Doctrinal, 24, 122

Documentary, 25, 39–40, 378, 397

Dublin, 29, 110, 128, 185, 222, 247, 249–252, 458

E

EASY, 14, 36, 146, 151, 159, 170, 173, 185, 199, 207, 294, 297, 332, 333, 336, 345, 347–349, 356, 370, 376, 393, 399, 404, 413, 426, 449, 456, 463

Education, 16, 30, 31, 38, 63, 103, 107, 123, 168, 169, 202, 211, 218, 319, 320, 324, 376, 383, 384, 389–414, 422, 439, 442, 446, 466, 467, 469

Employment, 63, 101, 102, 105, 123, 142, 210, 236, 243, 324, 390, 403–406, 408–411, 413, 443, 453, 467

Equality Act 2010, 102, 378, 453

Ethical, 33, 34, 42–47, 243

Ethics, 43, 241

Ethnicities, 11, 26, 69, 100, 220, 263, 307, 319, 320, 365, 369, 414, 432, 443, 456, 467

European Asylum Support Office (EASO), 9, 112, 125, 163, 167, 201, 204, 209, 226, 234–236, 273, 286, 288, 290, 303, 452, 456, 458, 463, 469

European Commission, 6, 98, 118, 128, 288–290, 390

European Convention on Human Rights (ECHR), 52, 97, 102, 105, 109, 110, 120, 126, 142, 149, 167, 196, 222, 249, 371, 378, 390, 395

European Court of Human Rights (ECtHR), 11, 56, 62, 163, 173, 236, 240, 252, 280, 332

European Parliament, 4, 7, 109, 116, 127–129, 140, 162, 174, 175, 270, 287, 332, 436, 447, 448, 455, 462, 471, 472

European Union (EU), 4, 6, 8, 9, 11, 12, 23–25, 52, 60, 97–102, 104–106, 109–111, 114, 116, 118, 120, 125, 127, 128, 140, 151, 159, 161, 163, 167, 170, 174, 175, 180, 184, 193, 201, 203–205, 220, 234, 249–252, 259, 263, 266, 272, 278, 279, 285, 322, 332, 335, 379, 395, 413, 439, 447–450, 458, 460, 463, 466, 473

European Union Fundamental Rights Agency (FRA), 10, 24, 101

Evidence, 5, 11, 24, 46, 58, 67, 118, 128, 148, 166, 183, 186–188, 191, 194, 195, 197–200, 203, 224, 226–229, 231–234, 236, 238–240, 248, 249, 251, 260, 270, 274, 279, 282, 286–300, 303, 305, 306, 309, 312, 313, 322, 323, 353, 379, 395, 397, 398, 401, 402, 408, 423, 424, 426, 428, 440, 450, 451, 454, 457, 459, 461–463

Exploitation, 72, 73, 120, 155, 156, 342, 366, 367, 390, 406–411, 467

F

Families, 7, 10, 11, 13, 26, 28, 53, 56, 57, 64, 102, 121, 124–126, 141–143, 146–149, 151, 152, 154, 157, 159, 167, 172–174, 187, 198, 209, 218, 226, 229, 238, 250, 272, 280, 300, 317–320, 322, 331, 334, 339, 341, 352, 357, 361, 363, 366, 367, 369, 371, 374, 396–398, 400, 409, 412, 423, 428, 436, 458, 470

Family reunification, 64, 123, 125, 126, 151, 183, 250

Fears, 8, 13, 26, 33, 55, 57–59, 65, 72, 103, 114, 127, 141, 144, 150, 154, 158–160, 162, 164, 165, 171, 174, 175, 188, 198, 206, 213, 214, 229, 231, 234, 238, 240, 245, 251, 261, 269, 270, 273, 276, 277, 279, 284, 285, 292, 299, 319, 322, 345, 359, 367, 380, 395, 396, 400, 412, 413, 426, 429, 462, 464

Federal Administrative Court, 9, 112, 113, 180, 264, 273, 288

Female Genital Mutilation (FGM), 68, 71, 72, 116

Feminism, 52, 64–68, 70, 74, 79, 84, 85, 422

Feminists, 7, 9, 13, 15, 23, 51–85, 104, 129, 194, 279, 305, 318, 408, 421, 450, 459, 464

Focus groups, 7, 25, 27, 28, 31–36, 43, 45–47, 150, 153, 158, 160, 162, 166–172, 175, 184, 186–188, 190, 192, 194–196, 199, 206, 212, 214–216, 219, 223, 233, 241, 244, 253, 284, 292, 294–296, 298, 299,

482 Index

Focus groups (*cont.*)
  304, 309, 311, 314–316, 320–322, 341,
    342, 345, 348–353, 355, 357, 361, 363,
    364, 366, 368–371, 374–379, 381, 395,
    396, 399, 400, 402, 404, 406, 408, 410,
    413, 429–431, 433, 435, 437, 439–442,
    447, 449, 464, 467, 468
Freedom of Information (FOI), 25, 40–42, 378

G

Gay, 6, 7, 9, 10, 13–15, 29, 31, 34, 45, 66, 68,
    76, 78, 80–82, 84, 85, 112, 113, 117,
    129, 144–150, 156, 158–160, 165–167,
    169, 172, 173, 188–190, 198, 199, 202,
    203, 206, 207, 209, 211, 213, 215, 216,
    218, 221, 225, 228, 230, 232–234, 236,
    239, 244, 245, 247, 250, 251, 261, 262,
    265, 266, 268, 269, 271, 272, 274, 275,
    277, 279, 280, 282–284, 289–297,
    302–308, 310–312, 314–316, 319–323,
    345–351, 354, 358, 359, 364, 365,
    368–372, 374, 376, 377, 401, 407, 410,
    411, 422–428, 430–433, 435, 437, 441,
    442, 470
Gender, 4, 10, 13–15, 24, 29, 31, 37, 45, 63,
    65–69, 71–84, 100–103, 114, 121, 122,
    128, 129, 189, 206, 207, 209, 215, 217,
    221, 268, 282, 284, 303–305, 318, 320,
    321, 332, 338, 352, 357–359, 365, 369,
    376, 393, 394, 403, 422, 424, 426, 443,
    452, 453, 456, 465, 470, 473
Gender identities, 3–17, 25–27, 29, 31, 32, 37,
    51, 55, 60, 75, 77, 78, 102, 114, 115,
    117, 121, 127, 128, 140, 153, 173, 207,
    209, 233, 234, 238, 261, 262, 265–268,
    270, 271, 283, 290, 297, 301–303, 318,
    332, 333, 336, 338, 357, 365, 374, 379,
    414, 426, 428, 453, 470–472
Gender Identity Clinic (GIC), 394
General Practitioner (GP), 196, 391, 394, 402
Geneva Convention, 8, 312
Germany, 6, 7, 13, 23–29, 31, 33–36, 38, 40,
    41, 45–47, 73, 97–106, 111–114, 116,
    117, 119–123, 125, 128, 140–146,
    148–150, 152–165, 167–172, 175, 176,
    180, 181, 183, 184, 186–194, 196, 198,
    199, 201, 203–206, 208–211, 213, 214,
    218–223, 225–228, 233, 235–237, 241,
    243–245, 247, 248, 250–253, 259–261,
    264, 265, 267–274, 280–282, 284,
    288–292, 294–302, 304–306, 309,
    311–317, 319–323, 331–333, 335,
    339–342, 344–347, 350–359, 361,

    363–365, 367, 368, 370, 372–378, 382,
    383, 391, 393, 395, 396, 398–400, 403,
    404, 406–413, 421, 422, 426, 429–441,
    445–449, 451–473
Giudici onorari, honorary judges (GOT),
    229, 230
Governments, 6, 27, 40, 41, 45, 47, 66,
    98–103, 106, 107, 110, 111, 117–119,
    123–126, 129, 143, 145, 147, 148, 154,
    180, 196, 207–209, 211, 212, 218, 235,
    239, 246, 248, 249, 274, 281, 284, 297,
    319, 331, 334–338, 344, 346, 362,
    371–373, 381, 392, 395, 397, 401, 405,
    412, 425, 434, 445, 447, 452
Grounds, 5, 7, 9–12, 42, 45, 46, 52, 53, 55, 60,
    62, 64, 78, 82, 102, 104, 112–114, 121,
    125, 126, 141, 142, 144, 152, 153, 155,
    162, 163, 165, 166, 168, 173, 174, 180,
    186, 190, 195, 198, 203–205, 207, 209,
    211, 213, 220, 223, 229, 234, 236, 247,
    248, 250, 251, 253, 260–269, 272–275,
    277, 278, 282, 284, 299, 301, 304, 315,
    320, 322, 323, 332, 336, 342, 353, 357,
    364, 374, 396, 411, 433, 451, 456, 457,
    459, 466, 467, 470
Grundgesetz, German Basic Law (GG), 105

H

Harassment, 4, 16, 78, 103, 118, 273, 337,
    341, 345, 346, 348, 356, 359, 362, 367,
    379, 431, 433, 464
Harmonisation, 8, 111, 161, 213, 285, 473
Health, 16, 43, 69, 123, 158, 163, 169, 189,
    251, 306, 312, 324, 336, 341, 357, 358,
    381, 383, 389–414, 446, 466, 469
Healthcare, 16, 63, 150, 390–394, 402, 466
Hearings, 25, 28, 34, 35, 160, 180, 183,
    185–195, 197, 199, 200, 204, 219,
    224–234, 238, 239, 241, 242, 245, 246,
    250, 269, 290, 297, 299, 305, 306, 313,
    320, 322, 323, 359, 365, 380, 401, 423,
    454, 455, 457, 458, 470
Heteronormative, 6, 78, 80, 85, 103, 125, 151,
    171, 250, 252, 267, 303, 308, 345,
    351–353, 361, 426, 470
Heteronormativity, 80, 85
Heterosexuality, 77, 266
Homelessness, 16, 333, 366–368
Home Office, 6, 42, 44, 65, 100, 101, 107,
    108, 111, 115, 117–121, 126, 128, 129,
    173, 182, 183, 191, 193, 196–198, 207,
    208, 211, 218, 219, 221, 222, 225, 227,
    230–233, 235–239, 246, 248, 263, 267,

271, 275, 277–279, 284, 286, 288, 290,
294, 297, 299, 302, 303, 305–308, 310,
311, 313–315, 318–320, 337, 338, 343,
350, 359, 368, 371, 380, 381, 397, 401,
403, 404, 408, 410, 412, 424, 425, 427,
436, 439, 450–453, 470
Homogenisation, 234, 238, 422–423
Homonationalism, 71, 80, 426
Homonationalist, 80, 81, 382, 446
Homonormative, 6
Homonormativity, 57, 80, 82, 316, 377, 469
Homophobia, 54, 66, 72, 81, 99, 103, 108,
111, 140, 144, 145, 147, 148, 150, 152,
159, 165, 203, 216, 233, 243, 250, 272,
275, 336, 349, 355, 356, 359, 365, 382,
383, 412, 414, 429, 431–433, 448
Homophobic, 73, 75, 80, 81, 103, 129, 148,
219, 225, 245, 246, 271, 274, 276, 283,
288, 311, 332, 345, 359, 365, 367,
374–376, 379, 382, 410, 431, 453, 465
Homosexuals, 10, 15, 77, 78, 80, 113, 144,
146–148, 165, 166, 175, 213, 220, 226,
229, 238, 267, 271, 274, 275, 277, 280,
290, 294–297, 301, 306, 309, 313, 320,
323, 338, 358, 407, 424, 425, 427
House of Commons, 99, 102–103, 107, 119,
124, 152, 211, 249, 303, 337, 343,
344, 379
House of Lords, 72, 113, 265, 378
Housing, 16, 45, 117, 123, 124, 193, 331–384,
434, 446, 464, 465, 469
Humanitarian protection, 35, 105, 119, 120,
122, 164, 285, 317, 318, 463
Human rights, 4, 7, 10, 13–15, 23, 32, 44,
51–85, 99, 101, 104, 109–111, 118,
127, 129, 139, 150, 151, 159, 176, 189,
207, 238, 239, 249, 253, 259, 262, 269,
270, 278, 279, 282, 284, 317, 332, 390,
397, 421, 446, 447, 449, 450, 453, 455,
459, 460, 464, 469, 472, 473
Human Rights Council (HRC), 4, 56, 332

I
Identities, 5, 6, 11–16, 24, 38, 43, 45, 54–56,
67, 68, 70, 71, 73–82, 84, 101, 118,
141, 143, 145, 150, 188, 195, 202,
211, 229, 262, 263, 265–269, 276,
277, 281, 289, 293, 294, 296, 306,
311, 315, 319, 321, 323, 347, 348,
351, 354, 355, 363, 371, 373, 376,
377, 383, 397, 414, 421–429, 431,
432, 436, 438, 441, 443, 444, 456,
459, 460

Independent Chief Inspector of Borders and
Immigration (ICIBI), 6, 11, 74, 99, 108,
115, 119, 121, 231, 238, 246, 268, 297,
303, 311, 338, 349, 461, 463
Information, 6, 16, 26, 28, 32, 33, 36, 40–44,
108, 116, 119, 126, 145, 147, 153, 157,
160–168, 173, 175, 185–189, 198, 200,
202, 203, 210, 211, 216, 218, 227, 230,
233–240, 268, 274–276, 283, 288–290,
292, 293, 299, 300, 305, 310, 314, 324,
363, 428, 429, 438, 441, 448, 449, 457,
459, 461, 464, 465
Inquisitorial, 24, 216, 219, 231, 287, 454
Integration, 5, 12, 13, 62–64, 104, 106, 110,
123–125, 142, 172, 219, 229, 299, 334,
336, 363, 365, 404, 410, 412, 434, 439,
444, 446, 458, 464, 466, 467, 471, 472
Interdisciplinary, 7, 23, 24, 51
Internal relocation alternatives, 11, 260, 273,
283–285, 317, 322, 460
International Covenant on Civil and Political
Rights (ICCPR), 10, 142
International Covenant on Economic, Social
and Cultural Rights (ICESCR), 403
International Human Rights Law (IHRL),
52–55, 57–62, 64, 97, 141, 142, 151,
180, 220, 259, 390, 455
International Organization for Migration
(IOM), 4, 139, 161, 469
International Refugee Law (IRL), 52–55,
57–61, 64–67, 111, 141, 180, 220, 286,
450, 455, 459
Interpretations, 51, 53, 57–62, 84, 112, 185,
228, 240–247, 252, 323, 425, 426, 456,
466, 467
Interpreters, 16, 35, 59, 176, 179, 190, 198,
206, 213, 228, 229, 240–247, 320, 336,
345, 357, 378, 410, 448, 456, 457, 462,
470, 471
Intersectional, 7, 14, 23, 25, 32, 64, 68–70, 75,
76, 78–81, 83, 104, 129, 141, 154, 176,
191, 194, 206, 218, 260, 263, 270, 302,
317–321, 332, 351–356, 365, 367, 376,
382, 421, 459, 472
Intersectionality, 6, 13, 15, 23, 25, 44, 63,
68–71, 73, 76, 79, 120, 364, 389, 443
Intersex, 6, 7, 10, 14, 27, 44, 117–119, 268,
356–359, 364, 422
Interviews, 7, 16, 25, 27–33, 35, 36, 43,
45–47, 63, 106, 116, 162, 167, 171,
173, 175, 179–181, 183, 185–193,
196–198, 201, 204–222, 224, 227, 232,
234, 239, 241–247, 253, 263, 290–292,
295–300, 304, 305, 309, 310, 313–315,

Interviews (*cont.*)
322, 331, 333, 336, 340, 347, 350, 353, 364, 369, 378, 379, 383, 401, 410, 414, 425, 426, 435, 439, 440, 452, 454–459, 461–463, 469, 470

Islamophobia, 71, 81, 365

Isolation, 12, 16, 46, 123, 156, 171, 172, 334, 335, 363–365, 368, 371, 383, 396, 398, 400, 435–438, 441, 464, 465

Italy, 7, 13, 14, 23–29, 31, 33–36, 38, 40–42, 45, 46, 73, 97–106, 110, 111, 113, 114, 117–123, 125, 129, 140–144, 146, 147, 150, 152, 153, 155–163, 165–175, 181–196, 198–204, 206–210, 212–216, 218–223, 225, 226, 228–230, 233, 235–237, 239–246, 249–253, 259, 262, 263, 266–273, 276, 282, 285–288, 290–299, 301, 302, 304–306, 309, 311–314, 316, 317, 319–322, 331–333, 335–337, 342–344, 347–352, 357, 359, 365–367, 370–378, 382, 383, 391, 393, 396, 398–407, 409, 410, 412, 413, 421, 422, 426, 427, 430–432, 434–436, 438, 441, 442, 445–448, 450–458, 462–473

J

Journeys, 12, 16, 129, 140, 153, 155–160, 174, 175, 179, 201, 229, 233, 287, 295, 309, 310, 319, 359, 368, 382, 407, 409, 427–429, 440, 442, 446–449, 456, 469, 472

Judges, 5, 6, 16, 35, 107, 110–113, 121, 122, 127, 150, 160, 168, 179–181, 191, 193–202, 204, 206, 210, 216, 217, 223–237, 239–246, 250, 253, 260, 261, 263, 266, 267, 269–271, 275, 276, 279, 281, 283–289, 292–294, 296–300, 304–306, 309, 310, 313, 314, 316–319, 322, 323, 347, 368, 375, 379, 381, 401, 407, 410, 423, 424, 426, 450–452, 454, 458, 459, 470

Judicial, 7, 15, 27, 30, 102, 103, 108, 118, 160, 179, 183, 185–194, 200, 222–234, 236, 238, 239, 241, 253, 276, 280, 281, 303, 305, 317, 321, 323, 451, 458, 461

L

Languages, 15, 16, 32, 34, 36, 43, 103, 123, 163, 164, 168, 175, 181, 214, 225, 226, 235, 241–244, 246, 291, 336, 338, 369,

376, 392–394, 401, 404, 407, 412, 413, 426–429, 448, 457, 467

Lawyers, 27, 29, 33, 35, 66, 81, 110, 111, 113–115, 121, 122, 126, 128, 147, 162, 163, 165, 173, 175, 186, 187, 190–206, 208, 209, 211, 213, 214, 216, 219, 220, 222–230, 233–237, 239–243, 245, 246, 248, 250, 251, 265, 267, 270, 271, 273–276, 278, 280, 281, 283, 284, 286, 289, 295–297, 299, 301, 305, 307, 308, 310–312, 315, 317, 319, 320, 322, 323, 331, 336, 337, 345, 351, 361, 364, 365, 374, 379, 380, 397, 400, 407, 412, 422, 425, 427, 434, 435, 449, 450, 452, 453, 455–457, 460–463, 465, 466, 468–472

Legal representation, 16, 179, 192–201, 364, 457

Lesbians, 6, 7, 10, 13, 15, 27, 29, 31, 34, 45, 69, 73, 74, 76, 78, 80, 82, 84, 85, 117, 121, 146–150, 164, 165, 170, 187, 189, 190, 195, 199, 200, 203, 206, 214, 220, 221, 225, 233, 234, 238, 246, 249, 261, 269, 271, 274, 275, 280, 283, 284, 289, 290, 294, 295, 302, 305, 307, 308, 315, 316, 318, 319, 323, 347, 351, 353–356, 358, 364, 365, 368, 369, 371, 379, 380, 396, 398, 400, 402, 410–412, 422–428, 432, 433, 435, 437, 470

LGBTIQ+ accommodation, 334, 346, 358, 372, 373, 375–377, 382, 383, 464

M

Main interviews, 165, 168, 181, 185–193, 204–222, 228–230, 232, 246, 378, 456, 457

Mental health, 11, 16, 43, 183, 196, 250, 251, 291, 332, 333, 344, 346, 347, 355, 356, 363, 370, 371, 374, 380, 381, 390–403, 405, 406, 414, 436, 466, 467

Men who have sex with men (MSM), 167, 268

Methods, 15, 24–28, 30, 32–43, 199, 240, 301

Misogyny, 85, 128

Multiculturalism, 67, 68, 70

N

Non-binary, 103, 351, 356–359, 429, 431, 441

Non-governmental organisation (NGO), 6, 25, 27, 33, 35, 39, 43, 45, 46, 99, 108, 109, 111, 112, 114, 116, 121, 127, 129, 163, 180, 183, 184, 186–193, 196, 197, 199, 201, 203, 205, 209, 210, 212, 218–223,

Index

225, 227, 231, 233, 235, 236, 239, 242,
  245–248, 250, 252, 261, 262, 265,
  267–269, 271–274, 279–284, 289–295,
  298–300, 302, 304, 305, 307, 309, 311,
  312, 314–316, 319, 320, 322, 323, 333,
  334, 340, 344–346, 349–351, 356–358,
  361, 362, 365–376, 379, 380, 382, 393,
  396, 397, 400–403, 406–409, 411–413,
  422, 428, 432, 434–437, 446–449,
  451–453, 455–460, 462–473

O

Observations, 7, 17, 25, 28, 34–35, 115, 160,
  190, 193, 194, 200, 203, 219, 223,
  227–229, 231–233, 238, 242, 243, 245,
  269, 272, 275, 276, 279–281, 293, 294,
  296, 299, 301, 304–306, 311, 313, 319,
  340, 401, 457

P

Pansexual, 14, 29
Particular Social Group (PSG), 8, 9, 11, 16,
  55, 66–68, 113, 114, 144, 260–269,
  277, 285, 303, 304, 322, 323, 426,
  459, 460
Performative, 77
Persecution, 4–7, 9, 11, 12, 14, 16, 52, 55,
  57–59, 61, 64–67, 72, 73, 78, 79, 105,
  112, 114, 115, 117, 140, 141, 144, 150,
  154, 165, 168, 174, 180, 200, 203, 205,
  207, 213, 219, 220, 224, 228, 229, 232,
  234, 236, 238, 240, 245, 247–249, 251,
  260–264, 266, 268–287, 292, 295, 296,
  298–300, 303, 317, 320, 322, 323, 348,
  395, 398, 401, 402, 409, 424, 427, 428,
  440, 442, 447, 458–460, 468, 472, 473
Personhood, 14, 54–57, 61, 63, 84, 141, 462
Policy-makers, 25, 27, 29, 33, 43, 127
Political opinion, 8, 113, 261, 262
Polyamorous, 14
Post-traumatic stress disorder (PTSD), 10, 11,
  43, 294, 295, 310, 398, 399, 401
Powers, 4, 24, 45, 46, 53, 70, 99, 111, 114,
  127, 169, 190, 232, 241, 243, 252,
  289, 305, 324, 341, 407, 457,
  461, 469
Procedures, 6–9, 16, 24, 35, 60, 62, 64, 78,
  106, 109, 114, 116, 117, 141, 161–163,
  167, 169, 176, 179–253, 259, 286, 288,
  289, 331, 335, 339, 374, 393, 446, 448,
  450, 454, 455, 459, 462

Procedures Directives, 9, 97, 116, 163, 180,
  194, 205, 206, 213, 222, 240, 249, 473
Proof, 11, 115, 125, 240, 248, 260, 285–290,
  293, 307, 314, 322, 380, 397, 461
Psychotherapists, 140, 198, 279, 294, 295,
  380, 393, 398, 427, 437, 466
Public international law, 259

Q

Qualification Directives, 9, 97, 104, 110, 113,
  114, 116, 263, 264, 266, 268, 269, 272,
  283, 285, 467
Queers, 4, 6, 7, 9, 13–15, 23, 29, 37, 51–85,
  104, 129, 169, 171, 195, 221, 265, 267,
  271, 279, 293, 305, 323, 344, 355, 363,
  364, 421, 422, 433, 434, 438, 441, 443,
  450, 459, 464, 470

R

Races, 8, 13, 32, 45, 69, 70, 73, 75, 79–83,
  110, 113, 125, 261, 262, 315, 332, 365,
  369, 383, 452, 453, 465
Racism, 69, 70, 73, 79, 81, 85, 99, 108, 159,
  320, 342, 355, 356, 358, 359, 365, 371,
  372, 382, 383, 429–432, 471
Rapes, 116, 117, 150, 238, 249, 250, 292, 295,
  308, 318, 335, 344, 350, 353, 390, 396,
  398, 439, 452
Reception Directives, 9, 97, 110, 115, 117,
  170, 173, 332, 335, 377, 390, 403, 466
Receptions, 8, 9, 16, 41, 62, 63, 99, 105, 109,
  116, 118, 140, 156, 159, 161, 162,
  166–173, 175, 185–190, 193–196, 202,
  223, 242, 243, 246, 247, 251, 295, 299,
  312, 331–337, 339–343, 345–349, 352,
  354, 356, 359, 363, 365, 370, 373–377,
  382, 390, 391, 400, 403, 407, 412, 414,
  446–449, 457, 465, 466, 469, 472
Refugee Convention, 8, 51–54, 57–64, 67, 84,
  97, 104, 105, 109, 113, 114, 122, 180,
  207, 211, 213, 227, 240, 252, 253,
  260–269, 272, 322, 390, 440, 459, 473
Refugeeness, 32, 45, 75, 76, 83, 84, 332, 467
Refugee status, 9, 11, 31, 55, 60, 63, 66, 100,
  104–106, 113, 119, 120, 122–124, 126,
  144, 162, 164, 174, 183, 195, 197, 200,
  219, 220, 234, 250, 260–272, 275, 279,
  281, 285, 286, 292, 293, 317, 318,
  368–370, 384, 393, 396, 401, 404,
  410, 411, 413, 414, 423, 433, 443,
  459, 463

486 Index

Refugee Status Determination (RSD), 12, 51, 109, 111, 119–126, 173, 185, 197, 259, 260, 266, 303, 317–321, 336, 374, 446, 449

Religions, 8, 10, 13, 26, 30, 32, 67, 69, 79–81, 83, 100, 113, 143, 147, 149, 191, 215, 218, 221, 261, 262, 306, 307, 318, 320, 323, 332, 341, 352, 369, 375, 383, 422, 425, 443, 452, 453

Residence Obligation, 334, 335, 368

Resources, 7, 46, 73, 111, 112, 124, 127, 144, 166, 191, 192, 207, 220, 243, 253, 286, 300, 312, 322, 324, 383, 401, 434, 461, 466, 468, 472

Rural, 236, 333, 334, 341, 346, 355, 359–366, 383, 391, 406, 435, 441

S

Screening, 116, 162, 165–169, 175, 179, 192, 207, 214, 246, 262, 290, 448, 454, 456, 457, 469

Sexism, 69, 70, 73, 81, 359, 471

Sexual characteristics, 14, 261

Sexualities, 4, 13, 24, 25, 32, 37, 45, 69, 71, 75–84, 112, 143, 149, 153, 164, 166, 173, 195, 198, 200, 211, 218, 225, 234, 238, 264, 265, 267, 275, 277–279, 281, 284, 290, 292, 294, 297, 305–311, 314, 318, 319, 323, 344, 345, 348–353, 363, 365, 367, 380, 383, 410, 424, 425, 427, 428, 437, 470

Sexual orientations, 3–17, 26, 29, 31, 34, 37, 51, 52, 54, 55, 60, 65, 75, 78, 102, 112–115, 117, 118, 121, 127–129, 140, 146–149, 152, 153, 155, 163, 165, 191, 206, 207, 209, 210, 215, 220, 232, 233, 235, 238, 248, 261–268, 270, 271, 275, 278, 282, 283, 289, 293, 294, 296, 297, 301–303, 305, 307, 310, 313, 315, 318, 331–333, 336, 338, 345, 346, 348, 349, 371, 380, 409, 422, 425, 426, 453, 471, 472

Sex work, 367, 389, 390, 406–408

Shared accommodation, 344–359, 372, 373, 432

Social integration, *see* Integration

Socio-legal, 7, 13, 17, 24, 25, 46, 64, 83, 445

Spaces, 13, 14, 16, 28, 33, 46, 75, 76, 81–84, 142, 144, 155, 169–172, 188, 203, 304, 312, 339, 344, 351, 353, 355, 357, 358, 374, 375, 377, 383, 400, 430, 431, 433, 436, 438, 439, 444, 448, 456, 462, 468–470

SPRAR, 335, 336, 342, 348, 370, 374, 383, 391, 404

Stereotypes, 56, 63, 72–75, 78, 83, 142, 189, 202, 209, 210, 219, 272, 301–307, 319, 321, 382, 422–426, 454, 462, 463

Stereotyping, 11, 62, 190, 207, 297, 302–307

Subsidiary protection, 104–106, 119, 120, 122, 125, 126, 285, 317, 406, 463

Supports, 5, 10–12, 26, 27, 33, 35, 38, 40, 43–46, 55, 56, 63, 70, 75, 108, 116, 123, 124, 127, 140, 147, 148, 150, 152, 157, 159, 161, 162, 166, 168, 169, 171–174, 186–194, 196, 198–204, 206, 212, 214, 228, 229, 231, 233, 235, 237, 240, 242, 250, 251, 264, 265, 267, 268, 279, 288, 290, 292, 299, 305, 311, 318, 332, 336–338, 341, 345, 346, 350, 354, 357, 358, 361, 362, 364–366, 370–372, 376, 379–381, 383, 390, 391, 393, 394, 396–398, 400, 402, 404, 405, 407–409, 411, 413, 414, 424, 429, 434–437, 439, 442, 443, 448, 449, 452, 453, 457, 464–468, 470, 471

Supreme Court, 9, 110, 223, 224, 237, 269, 276, 277, 279, 288, 290, 302, 460

Sur place, 27, 174, 251, 411

Surveys, 7, 11, 25, 35–39, 44, 108, 121, 161, 163, 183, 192, 205, 225, 236, 240, 241, 249, 295, 304, 310, 311, 317, 318, 320, 331, 345, 346, 349, 367, 371, 372, 374, 377, 378, 396, 398, 400, 408, 425, 430, 432, 436, 452

T

Territorial commissions, 106, 107, 113, 114, 122, 181, 190, 201, 206–208, 210, 211, 214–216, 219, 220, 224, 228, 237, 240, 242, 243, 249, 266, 271, 292–295, 298, 310, 314, 317, 321, 336, 450, 453, 454, 459, 469

Tortures, 10, 16, 43, 62, 116, 117, 126, 148, 198, 205, 222, 295, 335, 344, 362, 381, 389, 390, 392, 395–398, 441, 452, 460

Trainings, 12, 16, 40, 43, 114, 123, 173, 179, 183, 185, 189, 192, 201–205, 209–213, 221, 226, 227, 229, 232, 236, 241–243, 252, 269, 297, 339, 346, 361, 362, 390, 404–406, 411–414, 451–454, 456, 458, 464–472

Transgenders, 10, 27, 69, 84, 102, 103, 117, 118, 148, 150, 159, 169, 173, 189, 202, 206, 210, 217, 220, 221, 227, 235, 237, 238, 251, 267, 268, 311, 321, 373, 379,

Index 487

390, 392, 393, 399, 406, 407, 412, 422, 426, 450
Transnational, 14, 80
Transphobia, 54, 81, 99, 103, 128, 140, 144, 150, 152, 159, 203, 216, 233, 243, 336, 346, 359, 365, 372, 382, 383, 412, 414, 429, 431–433, 448
Transphobic, 66, 75, 99, 103, 122, 129, 245, 276, 332, 357, 359, 382, 431, 453
Trauma, 11, 43, 116, 118, 140, 204, 226, 233, 234, 241, 286, 287, 291, 292, 295, 332, 381, 395, 396, 401–403, 441, 452, 462, 468
Travels, 5, 61, 139–176, 229, 236, 237, 251, 335, 369, 380, 410, 466

U
United Kingdom, 252, 271
United Kingdom Border Agency (UKBA), 107, 211, 406
United Kingdom Visas and Immigration (UKVI), 107, 118, 120, 161
United Nations (UN), 4, 8, 10, 11, 14, 56, 65, 99, 109, 110, 117, 139–141, 159, 235, 332, 334, 378, 473
United Nations High Commissioner for Refugees (UNHCR), 4, 11, 14, 24, 41, 58, 60, 98, 101, 104, 106, 107, 110, 111, 114, 115, 123, 124, 152, 155, 159, 169, 174, 190, 197, 201, 203, 204, 206–208, 210, 211, 213–215, 224, 226, 228, 235, 236, 240, 246, 252, 253, 260, 261, 263, 265, 266, 268, 271–273, 276, 278, 282, 283, 285–288, 293, 300, 322, 382, 383, 390, 392, 398, 406, 426, 450, 451, 460, 461, 468, 469, 471, 473
Universal Declaration of Human Rights (UDHR), 53, 60
Urban, 333, 334, 356, 359–366, 383

V
Vienna Convention on the Law of the Treaties (VCLT), 58, 60, 61
Violence, 4, 10, 16, 43, 58, 67, 68, 70, 72–74, 101, 116–118, 120, 122, 125, 139, 140, 145, 149, 152, 156, 157, 160, 165, 169, 220, 223, 225, 238, 244, 249–251,

270–272, 275, 286, 299, 316, 318, 335, 339, 345–348, 355–357, 359, 365, 367, 373, 375, 378–380, 389, 390, 392, 395–399, 406, 407, 426, 453, 455, 464, 468
Visas, 61, 64, 107, 125, 127, 129, 141, 151–155, 157, 174, 175, 251, 316, 399, 411, 447
Voluntary, 186, 187, 190, 201, 202, 212, 226, 227, 242, 244, 281, 382, 390, 398, 405–406, 448, 453
Volunteers, 35, 45, 108, 109, 111, 122, 144, 152, 153, 161–163, 166, 167, 174, 183, 184, 186–194, 196, 197, 199, 201–204, 210, 214, 216, 219–221, 224, 225, 233, 235, 237, 242–245, 247, 248, 262, 269, 271–273, 279, 282–284, 291, 293, 294, 298, 299, 304–307, 309, 311, 314, 319, 320, 322, 323, 336, 337, 346, 347, 349–351, 357, 364, 365, 369–376, 396, 403, 405–408, 422, 427, 431, 432, 434–436, 442, 443, 451, 452, 455, 457, 458, 460, 462–466, 468–473
Vulnerabilities, 6, 10, 41, 44, 63, 112, 115–119, 139, 155, 181, 190, 247, 295, 318, 334, 356, 361, 375, 377, 379, 408, 440, 446, 449, 460
Vulnerable, 26, 44, 63, 74, 101, 115–119, 123, 124, 140, 152, 155, 161, 170, 175, 201, 205, 206, 209, 219, 220, 286, 333–336, 338, 342–344, 346, 348, 353, 356, 365–367, 373, 375, 378–381, 390, 401, 405, 412, 449, 462

W
Works, 5, 7, 11, 16, 35, 38, 45, 52, 53, 58, 68, 69, 73–77, 79, 84, 104, 108, 109, 111, 123, 127, 129, 140, 143, 153, 159, 164, 175, 183, 186–192, 196, 198–200, 202, 203, 216, 225–227, 231, 237, 240, 247, 263, 267, 283, 287, 289, 290, 318, 333–335, 338, 361, 364, 370, 375, 379, 381, 382, 384, 389–414, 422, 434, 436, 439, 442, 443, 446, 450, 466–469, 472

X
Xenophobia, 99, 128, 365